pwc

Manual of accounting
Narrative reporting – 2016

UK Accounting Consulting Services
PricewaterhouseCoopers LLP, Chartered Accountants

Published by

Bloomsbury Professional

Bloomsbury Professional, an imprint of Bloomsbury Publishing Plc, Maxwelton House, 41–43 Boltro Road, Haywards Heath, West Sussex, RH16 1BJ

ISBN 9781784515300

British Library Cataloguing-in-Publication Data.
A catalogue record for this book is available from the British Library.

Printed in Great Britain.
Typeset by YHT Ltd, 4 Hercies Road, Hillingdon, Middlesex UB10 9NA

Authors

PricewaterhouseCoopers' Manual of accounting – Narrative reporting is written by the PricewaterhouseCoopers LLP's UK Accounting Consulting Services team.

Writing team led by
Peter Hogarth
Iain Selfridge

Authors, contributors and reviewers
Elaine Forrest
Margaret Heneghan
Patrick Leach
John Patterson

Preface

PwC's Manual of accounting – Narrative reporting is a practical guide to the legal and other regulatory requirements that impact quoted companies, often referred to as the 'front half' of the financial statements.

The Manual of accounting – Narrative reporting should be read in conjunction with the Manual of accounting – IFRS for the UK 2015, volumes 1 and 2 and the accompanying Manual of accounting – IFRS 2015 Supplement. These books deal with the back half of the financial statements and provide guidance to UK companies on the practical application of International Financial Reporting Standards and amendments to IFRSs issued by the International Accounting Standards Board.

There have been a number of significant developments with regard to narrative reporting in 2015 and this book has been updated to reflect these changes. The guidance included in this Manual applies to quoted companies. Equivalent guidance for other companies is included on our web site, inform.pwc.com.

The Manual of accounting series of publications include practical advice based on our work in PwC's UK Accounting Consulting Services team in advising the firm's clients, partners and staff.

We hope that finance directors, accountants, legal practitioners, company administrators, financial advisers and auditors will find this manual useful.

Peter Hogarth, Iain Selfridge
PricewaterhouseCoopers LLP
London
November 2015

Contents

Abbreviations and terms used

AAPA	Association of Authorised Public Accountants
ABI	Association of British Insurers
AC	Appeal Cases, law reports
ACG	Audit Committees guidance
Accounts	financial statements
ADR	American depositary receipts
AESOP	all employee share ownership plan
the 1985 Act	the Companies Act 1985 (as amended by the Companies Act 1989)
the 1989 Act	the Companies Act 1989
the 2006 Act	the Companies Act 2006
ACCA	Association of Chartered Certified Accountants
ACT	advance corporation tax
AFS	available-for-sale
AG	Application Guidance
AGM	Annual General Meeting
AIC	Association of Investment Companies
AIM	Alternative Investment Market
AIMR	Alternative Investment Market Rules
AITC	Association of Investment Trust Companies
All ER	All England Law Reports
AMPS	auction market preferred shares
APB	Auditing Practices Board
APC	Auditing Practices Committee
App	Application note of a Financial Reporting Standard
App	Appendix
ARC	Accounting Regulatory Committee
ARSs	auction rate securities
ASB	Accounting Standards Board
ASC	Accounting Standards Committee
AVC	additional voluntary contribution
BBA	British Bankers' Association
BC	Basis for Conclusions (to an accounting standard)
BCLC	Butterworths Company Law Cases
BERR	Department for Business, Enterprise and Regulatory Reform (formerly the DTI and now BIS)
BEV	business enterprise value
BIS	Department for Business, Innovation and Skills (formerly BERR before that DTI)
BNA 1985	Business Names Act 1985
BOFI	banks and other financial industry entities
BVCA	British Venture Capital Association
C	currency unit
CA85	the Companies Act 1985
CA06	the Companies Act 2006
CCA	current cost accounting
CCAB	Consultative Committee of Accountancy Bodies Limited
CC	The Combined Code – Principles of good governance and code of best practice
CC(CP)	Companies Consolidation (Consequential Provisions) Act 1985
CEO	chief executive officer
CESR	Committee of European Securities Regulators
CGAA	Co-ordinating Group on Audit and Accounting Issues
CGU	cash-generating unit
Ch	Chancery Division, law reports
Chp	Chapter
chapter (1)	'PricewaterhouseCoopers' Manual of accounting' – chapter (1)
CIF	cost, insurance, freight
CIMA	Chartered Institute of Management Accountants
CIPFA	Chartered Institute of Public Finance and Accountancy

CISCO	The City Group for Smaller Companies
Cmnd	Command Paper
CBO	collateralised bond obligation
CDO	collateralised debt obligation
CLO	collateralised loan obligation
CMO	collateralised mortgage obligation
CODM	chief operating decision maker
COSO	Committee of Sponsoring Organisations of the Treadway Commission
CPP	current purchasing power
CR	Report of the committee on The Financial Aspects of Corporate Governance (the 'Cadbury Report')
CSR	corporate social responsibility
CTD	cumulative translation difference
CUV	continuing use value
DCF	discounted cash flow
DG XV	Directorate General XV
the 7th Directive	EC 7th Directive on Company Law
DP	discussion paper
DRC	depreciated replacement cost
DTI	Department of Trade and Industry
DTR	Disclosure rules and transparency rules
EASDAQ	European Association of Securities Dealers Automated Quotation
EBIT	earnings before interest and tax
EBITDA	earnings before interest, tax, depreciation and amortisation
EC	European Community
ECU	European currency unit
ED	exposure draft
EEA	European Economic Area
EEE	electrical and electronic equipment
EFRAG	European Financial Reporting Advisory Group
EGM	extraordinary general meeting
EITF	Emerging Issues Task Force (US)
EPS	earnings per share
ESOP	employee share ownership plan
ESOT	employee share ownership trust
EU	European Union
EU 2005 Regulation	Regulation (EC) No 1606/2002 on the application of International Accounting Standards
EUV	existing use value
FASB	Financial Accounting Standards Board (US)
FEE	The European Federation of Accountants
FIFO	first-in, first-out
financial statements	Accounts
FLA	Finance and Leasing Association
FM	facilities management
FOB	free on board
FPI	foreign private investors (US-listed)
FRAG	Financial Reporting and Auditing Group of the ICAEW
Framework	Framework for the preparation and presentation of financial statements
FRED	Financial Reporting Exposure Draft
FRA	forward rate agreement
FRC	Financial Reporting Council
FRN	floating rate note
FRRP	Financial Reporting Review Panel
FRS	Financial Reporting Standard
FRSSE	Financial Reporting Standard for Smaller Entities
FSA	Financial Services Authority
FTSE	The Financial Times Stock Exchange
FVLCS	fair value less costs to sell
FVTPL	at fair value through profit or loss
GAAP	generally accepted accounting principles (and practices)
GAAS	generally accepted auditing standards
GB	Great Britain

GCFR	Going Concern and Financial Reporting - published by the joint working group of the Hundred Group of finance directors, ICAEW and ICAS
GRI guidelines	Global Reporting Initiative guidelines
HEFCE	Higher Education Funding Council for England
HMSO	Her Majesty's Stationery Office
HP	hire purchase
HMRC	HM Revenue & Customs
HR	human resources
IAASB	International Auditing and Assurance Standards Board
IAS	International Accounting Standard (see also IFRS)
IASB	International Accounting Standards Board
IASC	International Accounting Standards Committee
IBF	Irish Bankers' Federation
IBNR	incurred but not reported
ICAEW	Institute of Chartered Accountants in England and Wales
ICAI	Institute of Chartered Accountants in Ireland
ICAS	Institute of Chartered Accountants of Scotland
ICFR	Internal Control and Financial Reporting - published by the joint working group of the Hundred Group of finance directors, ICAEW and ICAS
ICR	Industrial Cases Reports
ICSA	Institute of Chartered Secretaries and Administrators
ICTA	Income and Corporation Taxes Act 1988
IFAC	International Federation of Accountants
IFRIC	International Financial Reporting Interpretations Committee
IFRS	International Financial Reporting Standard (see also IAS)
IG	Implementation Guidance (to an accounting standard)
IGU	income-generating unit
IIMR	Institute of Investment Management and Research (see SIP)
IIR	internal rate of return
IIRC	International Integrated Reporting Committee
IoD	Institute of Directors
IOSCO	International Organisation of Securities Commissions
IPO	initial public offering
IPR&D	in-process research and development
IR	Statement on interim reporting issued by ASB
ISA	International Standard on Auditing
ISA (UK & Ire)	International Standard on Auditing (UK and Ireland)
ISDA	International Swap Dealers Association
ISP	internet service provider
IVSC	International Valuation Standards Committee
JWG	Joint Working Group
LIBID	London inter-bank bid rate
LIBOR	London inter-bank offered rate
LIFFE	the London International Financial Futures and Options Exchange
LIFO	last-in, first-out
LR	UK Listing Authority's Listing Rules
LTIP	long-term incentive plan
MAC	material adverse change clause
MBO	management buy-out
MD&A	management's discussion and analysis
MEEM	multi-period excess earnings method
MR	Master of the Rolls
NASDAQ	National Association of Securities Dealers Automated Quotations
NAPF	National Association of Pension Funds
NCI	non-controlling interest
NCU	national currency unit
NIC	national insurance contributions
OECD	Organisation for Economic Co-operation and Development
OEICs	open-ended investment companies

Abbreviations and terms used

OFT	Office of Fair Trading
OFR	operating and financial review
OIAC	Oil Industry Accounting Committee
OTC	over-the-counter market
PA	preliminary announcement
para(s)	paragraph(s) of Schedules to the Companies Acts, or IFRSs or IASs or FRSs, or SSAPs, or FREDs, or EDs, or DPs, or text
PCAOB	Public Company Accounting Oversight Board (US)
PE	price-earnings
PHEI	previously held equity interest
PFI	Private Finance Initiative
PLUSR	Plus Rules for Issuers (for PLUS-quoted entities)
PPE	property, plant and equipment
PPERA	Political Parties, Elections and Referendums Act 2000
PPF	Pension Protection Fund
PRAG	Pensions Research Accountants Group
PS	Practice Statements
QC	Queen's Counsel
QCA	Quoted Companies Alliance
QUEST	qualifying employee share ownership trust
R&D	research and development
RCN	replacement cost new
RCNLD	replacement cost new less depreciation
RDG	regional development grant
Reg	regulation of a statutory instrument (for example, SI 1995/2092 Reg 5 = regulation 5 of The Companies (Summary Financial Statements) Regulations 1995)
RFR	relief-from-royalty
RICS	Royal Institution of Chartered Surveyors
ROI	return on investment
RS	Reporting Standard
SAC	the Standards Advisory Council
SAC	subjective acceleration clause
SAS	Statement of Auditing Standards
SC	Session Cases
Sch	Schedule to the Companies Act 1985 (eg CA85 4A Sch 85 = Schedule 4A, paragraph 85)
SDC	Standards Development Committee
SEC	Securities and Exchange Commission (US)
Sec(s)	Section(s) of the 1985 Act/Sections(s) of the 2006 Act
SEE	social, environmental and ethical
SERPS	State earnings related pension scheme
SFAC	Statement of Financial Accounting Concepts issued in the US
SFAS	Statement of Financial Accounting Standards issued in the US
SI	Statutory Instrument
SIC	Standing Interpretation Committee of the IASC (see IFRIC)
SIP	Society of Investment Professionals (formerly IIMR)
SIPs	share incentive plans
SMEs	small and medium-sized entities
SOI	Statement of Intent
SoP	Statement of principles
SORIE	statement of recognised income and expense
SORP	Statement of Recommended Practice
SPE	special purpose entity
SPV	special purpose vehicle
SSAP	Statement of Standard Accounting Practice
Stock Exchange (or LSE)	the London Stock Exchange
STRGL	statement of total recognised gains and losses
TR	Technical Release of the ICAEW
TSR	total shareholder return
TUPE	Transfer of Undertakings (Protection of Employment) Regulations
UITF	Urgent Issues Task Force

UK	United Kingdom
UKCGC	UK Corporate Governance Code
US	United States of America
VAT	value added tax
VIU	value in use
VIE	variable interest entity
WACC	weighted average cost of capital
WARA	weighted average return analysis
WEEE	Waste electrical and electronic equipment
WLR	Weekly Law Reports
xBRL	extensible business reporting language

Chapter 1

Introduction

1 i

Introduction

Corporate reporting today

1.1 Recent years have seen major changes in financial reporting worldwide. The biggest single change has been the process of global harmonisation around international financial reporting standards (IFRS), including their adoption for the consolidated financial statements of listed companies in the UK and the rest of the EU. But an important further trend has been the increasing importance and role of what is often called the 'front half' of the annual report, including management's commentary on business performance and future prospects, governance reports and directors' remuneration reports. This second trend is the subject of this book.

1.2 It is widely recognised that pure accounting numbers, however good the accounting policies and however extensive the notes disclosure, are only part of the story. To be really useful to investors and other users, they need to be supplemented by additional information – often in narrative form – that seeks to give a sense of context, an explanation of what is going on and a sense of what might happen in the future. This, taken in aggregate, can be described as 'corporate reporting', as opposed to financial reporting.

The politics of corporate reporting

1.3 The emphasis on a broader notion of corporate reporting is to some extent a social and political trend. There has been much debate about whether companies should have as their objectives a narrow focus on the shareholders or a wider focus on a range of stakeholders in the societies in which they operate.

1.4 Some aspects of the front half might also owe more to politics than to financial reporting. Politics, in a broad sense, is certainly taking corporate reporting into more fields, increasingly covering environmental and social reporting of various kinds, some of which are requirements of the Companies Act 2006 (the Act).

1.5 Politics, rather than accounting, arguably lies behind the UK's extensive disclosure requirements for directors' remuneration in quoted companies. Alongside these requirements, to give shareholders more scope to influence outcomes in advance, the government introduced legislation back in 2013 to give shareholders a binding vote on pay policy. And, to complete the circle, the 2014 version of the UK Corporate Governance Code now includes a provision for companies to explain to shareholders what actions they will take to understand the reasons behind any 'significant' votes against general meeting resolutions, such as those approving the remuneration report.

Engagement, accountability and stewardship

1.6 The detailed disclosure requirements for executive remuneration are intended to provide greater transparency about the link between pay and performance, so that shareholders have better quality information to enable them to hold companies to account. But the concepts of engagement, accountability and stewardship apply to more than remuneration.

1.7 A well-managed company has a clear vision of its ambitions, of how it will achieve its goals, measure its progress along the way and remunerate its people. By reflecting effective internal management in transparent external reporting, a company can give confidence to stakeholders that its management has the business on the right track, and that it is exercising effective stewardship over investors' funds. This concept underpins many of the recent changes in UK corporate governance and reporting requirements.

1.8 The strategic report, replacing the 'business review' previously required in the directors' report, is intended to provide a more forward-looking emphasis to the front half of the annual report. Again, this is intended to improve transparency and shareholder engagement with the development of the business. In its 'Guidance on the strategic report', the Financial Reporting Council sets out characteristics that should be reflected, not just in the strategic report but in the whole annual report, so that the annual report is fair, balanced and understandable, concise and focused on matters that are material to shareholders.

1.9 Shareholders themselves are being encouraged to play a more active and positive role in engaging with companies. The UK was a pioneer in introducing a Stewardship Code to guide the activities of institutional investors. The investment industry continues to take steps to play an enhanced role in the governance and reporting framework, against the background of possible additional regulation at the European level.

International practice

1.10 Narrative reporting is developing worldwide, with a consistent focus on the role of non-financial disclosures. The International Integrated Reporting Committee (IIRC) comprises a global cross-section of people from the corporate, investment, accounting, securities, regulatory, academic and standard-setting sectors as well as civil society. It promotes corporate reporting that demonstrates the linkages between a company's strategy, governance and financial performance, the social, environmental and economic context within which it operates and the range of impacts it has. The IIRC published its Framework for Integrated Reporting in December 2013 and continues to work with a number of major international companies through its pilot programme.

1.11 Outside integrated reporting, the European Union has mandated additional non-financial disclosures for UK companies with effect from 2017, including disclosures around anti-bribery and corruption measures.

1.12 There are further international comparisons that can be made. For example, both Australia and Canada have similar guidance and principles to those underpinning the strategic report. The US SEC requires a Management Discussion and Analysis (MD&A) which, while differing in detail, is also largely based on the same objectives and principles.

Corporate governance

1.13 The UK has a well-established corporate governance framework that continues to serve as a model other territories look to when developing their own arrangements.

1.14 At the centre of the framework is the UK Corporate Governance Code ('the Code') – which companies report against on a 'comply or explain' basis, whereby if a company has not complied with the Code's provisions during the year it provides an explanation of its position to shareholders in the annual report. The Code applies to all premium listed companies, including overseas companies.

1.15 Despite the widely recognised quality of the framework, the financial crisis in 2008 highlighted a number of perceived failings in the governance of UK listed companies that the Financial Reporting Council ('FRC') has been addressing in its periodic reviews of the Code. An increased focus on the role of the chairman, externally facilitated board effectiveness reviews and annual re-election of directors for FTSE 350 companies have been just some of the measures taken since then.

1.16 Also, continuing the theme of increased transparency in reporting, directors are now required to make a formal statement that they consider that the annual report and accounts, taken as a whole, is 'fair, balanced and understandable' and provides the information necessary for shareholders to assess a company's performance, business model and strategy. In practice, this has driven a widespread reassessment of the quality of companies' reporting processes.

1.17 Significantly, the Code now includes a number of formal statements like the fair, balanced and understandable confirmation. There is a real emphasis on having the directors involved in driving the right behaviours and culture within the business, and positive formal statements are seen as a means of achieving this. The 2014 version of the Code is particularly notable for its introduction of new statements on risk and on the prospects for businesses – the 'viability statement'. Following the financial crisis, the Sharman Inquiry looked again at the framework around going concern assessment and reporting and, in implementing the Sharman recommendations, the FRC has focused on embedding the management of risks to solvency and liquidity in the day-to-day activities of companies and boards.

1.18 The 2014 Code and the viability statement once again push the UK into the vanguard of governance and reporting, as so many of its initiatives have in recent years. It may therefore come as a relief to some that the FRC in its 'Strategy for 2016/19' has indicated that its priority now, once the European Union's Audit Regulation and Directive have been implemented in 2016, is *"to help companies embed the requirements that have already been introduced to ensure that the intended benefits are secured"*.

The approach in this Manual

1.19 Considerations relating to the front half apply to all UK companies, at least to some extent. Even the smallest company has to prepare a directors' report. Other requirements come into play once a company achieves a certain size, becomes listed or pays its directors above a certain amount. For these various reports, we give our views on what the requirements or recommendations mean and on what is good disclosure in the areas in which there are no rules or guidance. As part of that approach, this Manual contains many examples and extracts from financial reports. Chapters 2 to 5 of this Manual address the requirements for quoted companies. The requirements for unquoted companies are addressed in chapters 6 and 7, which are available online at inform.pwc.com.

1.20 This Manual can be viewed as a supplement to three other works: the 'Manual of accounting – UK GAAP', which gives guidance to the many UK companies that still follow UK GAAP; the 'Manual of accounting – IFRS for the UK', which applies to those UK listed groups that have to follow IFRS and other entities that have opted to apply IFRS; and the 'Manual of accounting – Other statutory requirements', which is available to subscribers online at inform.pwc.com. A further PwC publication 'Manual of accounting – New UK GAAP' explains the new UK accounting rules that will apply to the majority of UK companies from 2015.

Chapter 2

Directors' report and strategic report – quoted companies

Directors' report and strategic report – quoted companies

Introduction

2.1 The directors' report and strategic report are mandatory components of a company's annual financial statements and reports for members. This chapter deals with the directors' report and strategic report requirements for quoted companies. The requirements for unquoted companies are set out in chapter 6, which is available online on inform.pwc.com. Good practice guidance on the preparation of the strategic report is provided in chapter 3.

2.2 The duty (for all companies) to prepare a directors' report is contained in section 415 of the Companies Act 2006 ('the Act'). Section 416 of the Act sets out some disclosure requirements, but most of the requirements are included in supporting legislation: Schedule 5 to SI 2008/409, 'The Small Companies and Groups (Accounts and Directors' Report) Regulations 2008', for companies or groups falling within the definition of 'small' (see chapter 31 of the Manual of accounting – UK GAAP); and Schedule 7 to SI 2008/410, 'The Large and Medium-sized Companies and Groups (Accounts and Reports) Regulations 2008' for all other companies.

2.3 Section 414A of the Act requires companies (except those entitled to the small companies exemption) to prepare a strategic report. [CA06 Secs 414A, 414B]. Section 414C sets out its required contents. The level of disclosure varies according to the size and status of the company.

[The next paragraph is 2.5.]

2.5 The annual report and financial statements are important to listed companies in communicating with their shareholders. So the annual report is used to provide shareholders with information about all aspects of the company's activities, the environment in which it operates and its objectives. Some information might be presented outside the statutory directors' report or strategic report, for example, in the chairman's statement. Companies structure the 'front half' of their annual reports (that is, the elements of the annual report that come before the financial statements) in a variety of ways. Directors have a safe harbour from civil liability for statements or omissions in the directors' report, strategic report and directors' remuneration report; so companies might classify the whole of the front half within those reports (see para 2.137). Increasingly, most of the directors' report disclosure requirements are not included in a separate directors' report. Instead most disclosures are given in, for example, the strategic report or the corporate social responsibility report, with the remaining disclosures given in an 'other statutory information' section. (See para 2.13).

2.6 Directors have a responsibility to prepare the reports, even if none of the directors at the time when the report is produced were directors during the period covered by the report. They cannot avoid this responsibility simply because they were not responsible for all or some of the activities that are being reported on.

Companies reporting under IFRS

2.7 The directors' report and strategic report disclosure requirements apply to both IFRS and UK GAAP reporters.

Consolidated financial statements

2.8 Where an entity is a parent company and the directors prepare consolidated financial statements, the directors' report and the strategic report are consolidated reports covering the company and its subsidiary undertakings included in the consolidation. [CA06 Sec 415(2)].

2.9 Where appropriate, the consolidated report should give greater emphasis to matters that are significant to the company and its subsidiary undertakings included in the consolidation, taken as a whole. [CA06 Sec 415(3)].

Quoted company

2.10 A 'listed company' is not the same as a 'quoted company'. Rules applying to listed companies are set out in the FCA Handbook, which includes both the Listing Rules (LR) and the Disclosure Rules and Transparency Rules (DTR). Rules applying to quoted companies are set out in the Act. A company may be both 'listed' and 'quoted'; if it is, it has to comply with both sets of rules. A 'listed company' is defined in the FCA Handbook as one that has any class of its securities listed, but there are some disclosure exemptions for such companies (see para 2.12). A 'quoted company' is defined as a company whose equity share capital:

- has been included in the official list in accordance with the provisions of Part VI of the Financial Services and Markets Act 2000;

- is officially listed in an EEA State; or

- is admitted to dealing on either the New York Stock Exchange or the exchange known as NASDAQ.

[CA06 Sec 385].

2.11 The application of the definitions to different categories of company is set out in the table below.

Status of company's securities	FCA Handbook: 'listed company'	Companies Act 2006: 'quoted company'
Equity shares listed in the UK official list	✓	✓
Debt securities (but not equity shares) listed in the UK official list	✓	×
Equity shares listed in another EEA state or admitted to dealing on New York Stock Exchange or NASDAQ, but not on UK official list	×	✓
Equity shares traded on AIM	×	×

2.12 The contents of the directors' report and strategic report vary according to the status of the company. Although a company that has debt securities (but not equity shares) listed in the UK official list is a 'listed company', the Listing Rules disclosure requirements of chapter 9 of the Handbook do not apply to such a company. These requirements apply only to companies with a premium listing of equity shares. [LR 9.1R]. Similarly, such a company is exempt from some requirements of the Disclosure and Transparency Rules: the exemptions include DTR 4.1 ('Annual financial report'), DTR 4.2 ('Half-yearly financial reports') and DTR 4.3 ('Interim management statements'). As discussed in chapter 4, a company that does not have shares admitted to trading on a multilateral trading facility is exempt from most of the DTR 7 requirements and need only prepare a limited corporate governance statement. The Listing Rules and DTR disclosure requirements referred to in this chapter apply only to companies that have listed equity share capital, because other companies are exempt from those requirements.

Placement of information in the annual report

2.13 Although the law specifies required components for the 'front half' (directors' report, strategic report and directors' remuneration report), companies have considerable flexibility in how the required disclosures are placed within the annual report. The purpose of the annual report is to communicate with shareholders, and the annual report should be structured so that key messages are given prominence. The most material information should be presented 'up front', with supporting detail given elsewhere in the annual report. This might mean, for example, that some legally required information is included as an appendix to the annual report, but incorporated into the directors' report by cross-reference.

2.14 In particular, the FRC's 'Guidance on the Strategic Report' recognises that a strategic report disclosure requirement is sometimes best addressed outside the strategic report. For example, a company might wish to avoid duplication or to include certain disclosures with other related information. This is acceptable, provided that the strategic report includes a cross-reference to the required disclosure. Where such cross-referencing is used, the cross-reference should clearly refer (by page numbers, paragraph numbers or headings) to the specific section in the annual report. The FRC's guidance is discussed in chapter 3.

2.15 Some flexibility in the placement of directors' report disclosures is provided specifically in law. A company is permitted to present a directors' report disclosure requirement in the strategic report, provided it states that it has done so and makes clear in respect of which disclosure requirement. [SI 2008/410 7 Sch 1A]. Increasingly, most of the directors' report disclosure requirements are not included in a separate directors' report but elsewhere in the front half. The remaining disclosures are often given in an 'other disclosures' section.

2.15.1 The Listing Rules require a listed company to make specified disclosures in its annual report. LR 9.8.4C requires the disclosures under LR 9.8.4R to be provided in a single identifiable section, unless the annual report includes a cross-reference table indicating where that information is set out. Given the variety in the disclosure subjects required by LR 9.8.4R, a cross-reference table will be the most appropriate approach in most cases. LR 9.8.4R sets out disclosure requirements on the following subjects:

- Interest capitalised during the period (see chapter 16 of the Manual of accounting – IFRS for the UK).
- Publication of unaudited information.
- Directors' long-term incentive schemes as required by LR 9.4.3R (see chapter 5).
- Emoluments waived by directors (see chapter 5).
- Allotments of equity securities made by the company (or any major unlisted subsidiary) (see chapter 23 of the Manual of accounting – IFRS for the UK).
- Where the company is a subsidiary, participation by its parent in any share placing during the period.
- Contracts of significance (see para 2.82 onwards and para 2.127 onwards).
- Contracts for provision of services by a controlling shareholder (see para 2.127 onwards).
- Dividend waivers (see chapter 4 of the Manual of accounting – IFRS for the UK).
- Compliance with independence provisions where there is a controlling shareholder (see para 2.127 onwards).

[LR 9.8.4R].

2.15.2 Table 2.1.A is an example of a cross-reference table.

Table 2.1.A – Cross reference to information required by FCA Listing Rules

GlaxoSmithKline plc – Annual report – 31 December 2014

Corporate governance (extract)

Directors' Report

For the purposes of the UK Companies Act 2006, the Directors' Report of GlaxoSmithKline plc for the year ended 31 December 2014 comprises pages 71 to 95 of the Corporate Governance Report, the Directors' Responsibility Statements on pages 130 and 211 and pages 232 to 248 of Investor Information. As it is entitled to do by the Companies Act 2006, the Board has chosen to set out in the Strategic report those matters required to be disclosed in the Directors' Report which it considers to be of strategic importance to the company, as follows:

- risk management objectives and policies (pages 16, 17 and 70)
- likely future developments of the company (throughout the Strategic report)
- research and development activities (pages 24 to 34)
- inclusion and diversity (pages 44 to 45)
- provision of information to, and consultation with, employees (pages 44 to 45)
- carbon emissions (pages 46 to 47)

In addition, the disclosures relating to the appointment or replacement of Directors and Directors' Powers at year end as required by the UK Corporate Governance Code are disclosed on page 246. The information in the following table is also incorporated into the Directors' Report:

	Location of details in 2014 Annual Report
Interest capitalised	Financial statements, Notes 17 and 19
Publication of unaudited financial information	Group financial review, page 60
Details of any long-term incentive schemes	Remuneration report
Waiver of emoluments by a Director	Not applicable
Waiver of future emoluments by a Director	Not applicable
Non pre-emptive issues of equity for cash	Not applicable
Non pre-emptive issues of equity for cash by any unlisted major subsidiary undertaking	Not applicable
Parent company participation in a placing by a listed subsidiary	Not applicable
Contracts of significance	Shareholder information
Provision of services by a controlling shareholder	Not applicable
Shareholder waiver of dividends	Financial statements, Notes 15 and 42
Shareholder waiver of future dividends	Financial statements, Notes 15 and 42
Agreements with controlling shareholders	Not applicable

Contents of the strategic report

2.16 The purpose of the strategic report is to inform the company's members and help them to assess how the directors have performed their duty to promote the company's success. [CA06 Sec 414C(2)].

2.17 In promoting the company's success, directors should, in particular, have regard to the following:

- The likely consequences of any decision in the long-term.

- The interests of the company's employees.

- The need to foster the company's business relationships with suppliers, customers and others.

- The impact of the company's operations on the community and the environment.

- The desirability for the company maintaining a reputation for high standards of business conduct.

- The need to act fairly as between the company's members.

[CA06 Sec 172].

2.17.1 The Department for Business, Innovation and Skills (BIS) has confirmed that, whilst directors should have regard to the above matters when running the company, those matters would only be reported in the strategic report where it is necessary for an understanding of the position, performance and development of the company's business.

2.18 The strategic report must be 'balanced and comprehensive'. [CA06 Sec 414C(3)]. Also, the UK Corporate Governance Code requires a listed company's annual report to be 'fair, balanced and understandable'. [UK CGC C.1.1]. A balanced review is one that reports both good and bad news. Balanced reporting is discussed further in chapters 3 and 4.

2.19 The FRC's guidance on good practice in preparing a strategic report is discussed in chapter 3.

2.20 The legal requirements vary according to the type of company: a small company does not have to prepare a strategic report; all other companies should do so; but the reporting requirements vary depending on the company's size and status.

2.21 The legal requirements applying to different types of company are set out in the table below. A quoted company is required to disclose all of the matters listed below.

Type of company	Disclosure requirement
Medium-sized company	■ The strategic report must contain, at a minimum: 　■ A fair review of the company's business. 　■ A description of the principal risks and uncertainties facing the company. ■ The review should be consistent with the business' size and complexity and provide a balanced and comprehensive analysis of: 　■ The development and performance of the company's business during the financial year. 　■ The company's position at the end of the year. ■ The review should also include, to the extent necessary for an understanding of the company's business, analysis using *financial* key performance indicators (KPIs). ■ The review must contain, where appropriate, references to and additional explanation of amounts included in the financial statements. [CA06 Sec 414C(2)(3)(4)(6)(12)]. ■ In addition, any matters that are directors' report disclosure requirements but are considered to be of strategic importance should be included (see para 2.15). [CA06 Sec 414C(11)].
Large unquoted company	All of the above plus, where appropriate, analysis using other *non-financial* KPIs, including information on environmental and employee matters. [CA06 Sec 414C(4)(b)].
Quoted company (see para 2.10)	All of the above plus: ■ The main trends and factors likely to affect the future development, performance and position of the company's business.[1] ■ A description of the company's strategy (see para 2.24). ■ A description of the company's business model (see para 2.24). [CA06 Sec 414C(7)(a)(8)(a)(b)]. ■ A breakdown as at the end of the financial year: 　■ The number of persons of each sex who were company directors (see para 2.38). 　■ The number of persons of each sex who were company senior managers (excluding directors) (see para 2.38). 　■ The number of persons of each sex who were company employees (see para 2.38). 　[CA06 Sec 414C(8)(c)]. ■ Information about: [1,2] 　■ environmental matters (including the impact of the company's business on the environment) (see para 2.35 onwards); 　■ the company's employees (see para 2.35 onwards); 　■ social, community and human rights issues (see para 2.35 onwards); and 　■ including information about any of the company's policies in relation to those matters and the effectiveness of those policies. [CA06 Sec 414C(7)]. [1] These disclosures are required *"to the extent necessary for an understanding of the development, performance or position of the company's business"*. [2] If the review does not contain information on any of these items on the grounds that it is not material, it must state that fact, identifying which of this information is omitted. [CA06 Sec 417(5)].

2.22 The meaning of 'quoted company' is discussed in paragraph 2.10.

2.23 Where an entity is a parent company and prepares consolidated financial statements, the strategic report should be a consolidated report covering the company and its subsidiary undertakings included in the consolidation. [CA06 Secs 414C(13), 415(2)]. There is no requirement for the parent company to prepare a separate report for the company alone.

Strategy, business model and a fair review

2.24 Quoted companies are required to include in the strategic report:

■ A description of the company's strategy.

- A description of the company's business model.

[CA06 Sec 414C(8)(a)(b)].

2.25 The terms 'strategy' and 'business model' are not defined in the legislation but are defined in the FRC's 'Guidance on the Strategic Report'. A strategy is *"a plan or approach which is intended to help the entity achieve an objective"*. A company's business model is *"how the entity generates or preserves value over the longer term"*. [FRC Guidance App 1]. The business model is sometimes expressed as, for example, 'how we make money', 'how we create value' or 'what we do'. Clearly, a company's objectives, strategy and business model are related and, when taken together, the disclosures should explain what an entity does and why it does it. A quoted company's strategic report, in providing a fair review of the company's business, should describe its progress in achieving its objectives, set out its performance on achieving those objectives (measured against its KPIs), and set out the principal risks and uncertainties that could affect its ability to achieve its objectives in the future.

2.26 The UK Corporate Governance Code recommends that a listed company's annual report should include an explanation of the basis on which the company generates or preserves value over the longer term (the business model) and the strategy for delivering the company's objectives. [UK CGC C.1.2].

2.27 Chapter 3 provides more guidance on how to meet these requirements.

Principal risks and uncertainties

2.28 As noted in paragraph 2.21, the strategic report should include disclosure of the principal risks and uncertainties facing the company. [CA06 Sec 414C(2)(b)]. The FRRP has expressed concern at the quality of reporting of principal risks and uncertainties in the business review. (The requirement for a business review was replaced by a requirement for a strategic report but the requirement to disclose principal risks and uncertainties is the same.) In Practice Note 130, the FRRP states that, in reviewing the business review of certain companies, it has commented on a number of occasions on the issues it has encountered in assessing whether directors' reports comply with this requirement of the Act. In particular, the Panel has challenged a number of companies where:

- the directors' report does not clearly identify which risks and uncertainties the directors believe to be the principal ones facing the business;

- a long list of principal risks and uncertainties is given and the list raises a question as to whether all the risks and uncertainties on the list are actually principal ones;

- the description given of a risk or uncertainty is in generic terms and it is not clear how that risk or uncertainty applies to the company's circumstances;

- the disclosure is of a risk framework rather than of the risks or uncertainties themselves;

- the principal risks and uncertainties disclosed are not consistent with other information given in the report and accounts; and

- the directors' report does not state how the company manages its principal risks and uncertainties. As the purpose of the business review is to inform members of the company and to help them assess how the directors have performed their duty to promote the success of the company, the FRRP believes that a board should state how the company manages its principal risks and uncertainties.

2.29 The FRRP encourages boards of directors to consider their disclosure of the principal risks and uncertainties facing their businesses by considering the following questions:

- Do the disclosures state clearly which are the principal risks and uncertainties facing the business?

- Are those risks and uncertainties described as principal; that is the main risks and uncertainties that currently face the business? For example, have the risks and uncertainties listed as principal been the subject of recent discussions at board or audit committee meetings? Are there risks which have been the subject of such discussions that should be considered as principal?

- Is the description of each principal risk and uncertainty sufficient for shareholders to understand the nature of that risk or uncertainty and how it might affect the company?

- Are the principal risks and uncertainties described in a manner consistent with the way in which they are discussed within the company?

- Are the principal risks and uncertainties shown consistent with the rest of the report and accounts? Are there risks and uncertainties on the list which are not referred to elsewhere or are there significant risks and uncertainties discussed elsewhere which do not appear on the list?

- Is there a description, in the directors' report, or elsewhere in the report and accounts and explicitly cross-referenced from the directors' report, of how the company manages each of the principal risks and uncertainties?

2.30 In addition, the FRC report, 'An update for directors of listed companies: Responding to increased country and currency risk in financial reports', draws attention to issues that directors should consider when providing a balanced and understandable assessment of a company's position and prospects in the context of increased country and currency risk. The issues directors could consider include, where relevant:

- The company's exposure to country risk, direct or to the extent practical indirect, through financial instruments, through foreign operations and through exposure to trading counterparties (customers and suppliers).

- The impact of austerity measures being adopted in a number of countries on the company's forecasts, impairment testing, going concern considerations, etc.

- Possible consequences of currency events that are not factored into forecasts but may impact reported exposures and the sensitivity testing of impairment or going concern considerations.

- A post balance sheet date event requiring enhanced disclosures to adequately inform investors and other users.

2.31 Disclosure of principal risks and uncertainties is discussed further in chapter 3. The UK Corporate Governance Code includes disclosure requirements on the principal risks facing the company; these are discussed in chapter 4.

Key performance indicators

2.32 Key performance indicators (KPIs) are defined as *"factors by reference to which the development, performance or position of the business of the company can be measured effectively"*. [CA06 Sec 414C(5)]. The FRC's 'Guidance on the Strategic Report' provides a more detailed definition, describing KPIs as *"quantitative measures used by directors to assess progress against objectives or strategy, track principal risks, or otherwise monitor the development, performance or position of the business"*.

2.33 The Act does not prescribe specific KPIs that entities should disclose. Entities use a variety of different KPIs, and the relevance of a particular KPI varies from industry to industry and even from one entity to another within an industry. Also, methods of calculating particular KPIs may vary from one entity to another. So, directors need to determine which KPIs are necessary for an understanding of the business.

2.33.1 A KPI might be an alternative performance measure ('APM') as defined by the European Securities and Markets Authority ('ESMA'). In June 2015, ESMA issued guidelines on APMs, which will apply to information published by issuers of securities listed on a regulated market on or after 3 July 2016. The guidelines define an APM as *"a financial measure of historical or future performance, financial position, or cash flows, other than a financial measure defined or specified in the applicable financial reporting framework"*.

2.33.2 The guidelines apply to APMs disclosed in regulated information, such as:

- The 'front half' of annual reports and interim financial reports.

- Management reports prepared under the Transparency Directive.

- Disclosures made under article 17 of the Market Abuse Regulation (for example, ad-hoc disclosures including financial earnings).

- Prospectuses issued under the Prospectus Directive.

2.33.3 The guidelines do not apply to APMs disclosed in financial statements, including half-year financial statements. But the IASB's project on disclosure principles will address many of the same issues. As part of that project, amendments to IAS 1 set out rules for presenting additional line items, totals and sub-totals that are consistent with the ESMA guidelines. See chapter 4 of the Manual of accounting – IFRS for the UK.

2.33.4 The guidelines state that issuers should disclose the definition of each APM in a clear and readable way, including its components, the basis of calculation and any material hypotheses or assumptions used. They should also indicate whether the APM or any of its components relate to past or expected future performance.

2.33.5 The guidelines further require that:

■ APMs should be given meaningful labels reflecting their content and basis of calculation. To avoid misleading users, the guidelines caution that entities should not:

    ■ use overly-optimistic or positive labels, such as 'guaranteed profit' or 'protected returns';

    ■ use labels, titles or descriptions that are the same as, or confusingly similar to, measures defined in GAAP; or

    ■ mis-label items as non-recurring, infrequent or unusual where they affected past periods and will likely affect future periods (such as impairment losses or restructuring costs).

■ A reconciliation of the APM to the most directly reconcilable line item, sub-total or total in the financial statements should be presented. Where an amount cannot be extracted directly from the financial statements, the entity should disclose how it is calculated.

■ The use of APMs should be explained, to enable users to understand their relevance and reliability and, in particular, why an APM provides useful information on its financial position, cash flows or financial performance, together with the purposes for which management uses the specific APM within the business.

■ APMs should not be given more prominence, emphasis or authority than, nor distract from, measures directly stemming from financial statements.

■ APMs should be defined and calculated consistently over time.

■ In exceptional cases, where changes are made, an explanation of the change and the rationale for it (that is, why it provides reliable and more relevant information) should be disclosed. APM comparatives should be restated.

■ Where a previously reported APM is no longer reported, the entity should explain why it considers that that APM no longer provides relevant information.

[ESMA Guidelines on Alterative Performance Measures]

2.34 Further guidance on KPIs, including example disclosures, is provided in chapter 3.

Environmental, employee, social, community and human rights matters

2.35 Quoted companies should disclose information about the following in their strategic report:

■ environmental matters (including the impact of the company's business on the environment);

■ the company's employees; and

■ social, community and human rights issues,

including information about any policies of the company in relation to those matters and the effectiveness of those policies. [CA06 Sec 414C(7)(b)].

2.36 The disclosures are required *"to the extent necessary for an understanding of the development, performance or position of the company's business"*. If the strategic report does not contain information about environmental, employee, social, community or human rights issues, it must state that fact. In our view, the strategic report should include only information that is relevant to an understanding of the company's business model, development, performance and position. Environmental, employee, social, community and human rights matters that are not relevant to that understanding are, in our view, more suitably reported through channels other than the annual report; these might include, for example, disclosure on the company's website.

2.37 Further guidance on making disclosures in these areas is included in chapter 3.

Gender

2.38 Quoted companies are required to disclose the number of persons of each sex who were directors, senior managers (excluding directors) or employees. [CA06 Sec 414C(9)]. Unlike the disclosure requirements in respect of environmental, social and human rights issues, the breakdown of each category by gender is included in the strategic report, regardless of whether such disclosure is relevant to an understanding of the development, performance or position of the company's business.

2.39 A 'senior manager' is defined, for the purposes of this disclosure, as a person who has responsibility for planning, directing or controlling the activities of the company, or a strategically significant part of the company, and is an employee of the company. [CA06 Sec 414C(9)].

2.40 In a group strategic report, 'directors' means the parent company's directors. A subsidiary's director is a 'senior manager', even if the subsidiary is not a strategically significant part of the group. [CA06 Sec 414C(10)]. The FRC's 'Guidance on the Strategic Report' suggests that, where a group has a strategically insignificant subsidiary, an enhanced analysis of the statutory 'senior manager' category (into 'senior managers that are in strategically significant positions' and 'other senior managers') might be a useful addition to the required disclosures.

2.41 For IAS 24 purposes, a 'senior manager' of the parent company will also be 'key management personnel' of the group, but a director of a subsidiary might not. Where a subsidiary is an insignificant part of the group, its management would not be key management personnel under IAS 24, but would be senior managers for the purposes of the strategic report.

2.41.1 Table 2.1 is an example of disclosure of the gender of directors, senior managers and employees. In this example, 'TCLC' is the 'Thomas Cook Leadership Council', which is the group's top 140 leaders who meet every quarter to communicate, inspire, share progress and ownership.

Table 2.1 – Gender

Thomas Cook Group plc – Annual report and accounts – 30 September 2014

Strategic report (extract)
Our people (extract)

The table below shows the split at different levels within the organisation as at 30 September 2014.

	Male	Female	Total	% Male	% Female
PLC Board	5	4	9	56%	44%
Executive Committee	5	2	7	71%	29%
Senior Management (TCLC and Subsidiaries)	275	75	350	79%	21%
TCLC	134	47	181	74%	26%
Subsidiaries	141	28	169	83%	17%
Whole company	8,028	18,507	26,535	30%	70%

Seriously prejudicial

2.42 A limited exemption has been provided such that the strategic report does not have to include *"information about impending developments or matters in the course of negotiation if the disclosure would, in the opinion of the directors, be seriously prejudicial to the interests of the company"*. [CA06 Sec 414C(14)].

Contents of the directors' report

Likely future developments

2.43 The directors' report should contain an indication of the likely future developments in the company's business. [SI 2008/410 7 Sch 7(b)]. Also, the strategic report should contain an indication of the main trends and factors likely to affect the future development, performance and position of the company's business. [CA06 Sec 414C(7)(a)]. So it would be sensible for the directors' report disclosure requirement on 'likely future developments' to be met within the strategic report. Directors usually meet this requirement by describing matters that might have a significant impact on the company's future earnings and profitability. For example, disclosure of the development of new products or services, business expansion or rationalisation plans, capital expenditure plans and proposed disposals and acquisitions is fairly common.

2.44 Where a directors' report disclosure requirement is included instead in the strategic report, the directors' report should state that fact and state the specific disclosure requirement that is met in the strategic report. [SI 2008/410 7 Sch 1A].

Post balance sheet events

2.45 The directors' report is required to include particulars of any important events affecting the company that have occurred since the end of the financial year. [SI 2008/410 7 Sch 7(1)(a)]. This requirement gives rise to two potential inconsistencies between the law and FRS 21 and IAS 10:

■ FRS 21 and IAS 10 distinguish between 'adjusting events' and 'non-adjusting events'. Events that require adjustments to the amounts reported ('adjusting events') do not require separate disclosure in the financial statements; but 'non-adjusting events' are disclosed. The law does not make such a distinction, and requires disclosure of important post balance sheet events, whether adjusting or non-adjusting.

■ The law requires material events after the balance sheet date to be disclosed in the directors' report, whereas FRS 21 and IAS 10 require disclosure of non-adjusting events in the notes to the financial statements. A post balance sheet event might require disclosure in both the directors' report and the notes to the financial statements. Companies normally disclose the information only in one place – usually the notes – so as to avoid duplication. A cross-reference should be given in the directors' report to the precise location of the information.

The accounting standards are considered further in the Manual of accounting – UK GAAP and the Manual of accounting – IFRS for the UK.

Research and development activities

2.46 An indication of the activities (if any) of the reporting entity in the field of research and development should be provided in the directors' report. [SI 2008/410 7 Sch 7(1)(c)].

2.47 As the law does not indicate how much detail needs to be given, the extent of disclosure varies considerably between companies. Some companies, particularly those in the pharmaceutical sector, give significant details about their research and development activities. In other cases, a broad-based note that considers the commercial aspects of the research and development activities and their impact on the activities of the company or group might be sufficient. An illustration of this disclosure is shown in Table 2.1.1.

Table 2.1.1 – Research and development

Laird PLC – Annual report – 31 December 2013

Directors' report (extract)

Research and development

Investing in research and development programmes delivers product innovation and manufacturing improvements within Laird. Expenditure in 2013 on research and development amounted to £47.6m (2012, £37.4m), of which £11.6m has been capitalised (2012, £8.5m). Laird continues to develop its technology capabilities, with research and development expenditure during the year running at 8.9% of sales (2012, 6.9%). This is in line with our strategic objective to increase R&D expenditure in the year and focus on innovation.

2.48 The requirement to give an indication of the research and development activities of the company and its subsidiaries does not mean that the accounting policy for research and development should be disclosed in the directors' report. It should, instead, supplement the accounting policy and the other disclosure requirements of accounting standards.

Greenhouse gas ('GHG') emissions

2.49   Quoted companies are required to disclose in the directors' report the annual quantity of emissions, in tonnes of carbon dioxide equivalent, from activities for which the company is responsible, including the combustion of fuel and the operation of any facility (direct scope 1 emissions). [SI 2008/410 7 Sch 15(1)(2)]. Emissions arising from the purchase of electricity, heat, steam or cooling by the company for its own use (indirect scope 2 emissions) should also be disclosed. [SI 2008/410 7 Sch 15(3)]. The methodologies used to calculate the information are also disclosed. [SI 2008/410 7 Sch 16]. Guidance on how to meet the reporting requirements can be found in the Department for Environment, Food & Rural Affairs June 2013 'Environmental Reporting Guidelines' ('DEFRA guidelines').

2.50   'Emissions' means emissions into the atmosphere of a 'greenhouse gas', as defined in section 92 of the Climate Change Act 2008. 'Tonne of carbon dioxide equivalent' is as defined in section 93(2) of that Act. [SI 2008/410 7 Sch 20].

2.51   For GHG reporting purposes, companies need to set the boundaries of the organisation. The DEFRA guidelines advise that, if a company has a simple organisational structure and owns 100% of the assets that it operates, this is relatively straightforward: the company would report on the impacts from everything that it owns and operates. But, for example, where the company has subsidiaries in which there is a non-controlling interest, other approaches are possible. A company's boundaries can be based on financial control, operational control or equity share. Financial control is likely to be the approach taken by most companies. A company has financial control over an operation if it has the ability to direct the financial and operating policies of the operation with a view to gaining economic benefits from its activities; this would mean that a group directors' report would include details of the emissions of all of its subsidiaries, including those that are not wholly owned.

2.52   Where it is not practical for a company to obtain some or all of the above information, it should state which information has not been disclosed and why. [SI 2008/410 7 Sch 15(4)].

2.53   The directors' report is also required to state at least one ratio that expresses the company's annual emissions in relation to a quantifiable factor associated with the company's activities. [SI 2008/410 7 Sch 17]. In the example in Table 2.2, the company expresses its emissions per litre of product packaged.

2.54   Comparative information is required, except in the first year that the information is disclosed. [SI 2008/ 410 7 Sch 18].

2.55   If the information is presented for an annual period that is different from that of the directors' report, the company is required to state that fact. [SI 2008/410 7 Sch 19].

2.56   Table 2.2 is an example of greenhouse gas emissions disclosure.

Table 2.2 – Greenhouse gas emissions

Diageo plc – Annual report – 30 June 2014

SUSTAINABILITY & RESPONSIBILITY REVIEW: ENVIRONMENT (extract)

ENVIRONMENT

PERFORMANCE AGAINST 2015 TARGETS

Reduce carbon emissions equivalent by 50%

5% (VS 2013)   **30%** (VS 2007)

Eliminate waste to landfill

23% (VS 2013)   **83%** (VS 2007)

Reduce average packaging weight by 10%*

0.8% (VS 2013)   **6%** (VS 2009)

Increase average recycled content across all packaging to 42%

1% (VS 2013)   **37%** (VS 2009)

Make all packaging 100% recyclable/reusable

0.01% (VS 2013)   **98.6%** (VS 2009)

* A 2009 baseline was established for packaging targets versus the 2007 baseline for other environmental metrics.

Alongside water stewardship, our environmental programme focuses on reducing greenhouse gases and waste sent to landfill as well as improving the sustainability of our packaging.

Carbon emissions

We use the World Resources Institute/World Business Council for Sustainable Development Greenhouse Gas Protocol as a basis for reporting our emissions, and we include all facilities over which we have operational control for the full fiscal year.

This year Diageo's net carbon emissions (CO_2e) were reduced by 5% in absolute terms or 35,000 tonnes, compared to the prior year. We achieved this reduction despite production volume going up in the most energy intensive area of our business, malt and grain whisky distilling. Cumulatively we have reduced absolute net tonnes of CO_2e by 30% since 2007.

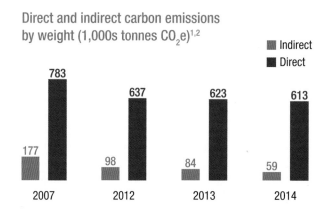

Direct and indirect carbon emissions by weight (1,000s tonnes CO_2e)[1,2]

1. CO_2e figures are calculated using the kWh/CO_2e conversion factor provided by energy suppliers, the relevant factors to the country of operation or the International Energy Agency, as applicable.
2. 2007 baseline data, and data for each of the six years in the period ended 30 June 2013, have been restated in accordance with the WRI/WBCSD Greenhouse Gas Reporting Protocol and Diageo's environmental reporting methodologies.

These results represent the sum of many small improvements, increases in green energy sourcing and the application of new technology combined with larger capital projects such as a £4 million investment in a combined heat and power plant at the Red Stripe brewery in Jamaica, which will reduce the site's carbon emissions by 4,000 tonnes per year.

Diageo's gross carbon emissions for this year are 865,000Δ tonnes, with an intensity ratio of 255 grams per litre packaged. Our targets for absolute reduction of carbon emissions, set in 2007, are based on net emissions. This is the first year we are reporting both net and gross emissions.

This year, approximately 59% of electricity at our supply sites came from low-carbon sources such as wind, hydro and nuclear (2013 – 52%). In the United Kingdom, 99% of our electricity came from low-carbon sources. This year marked our second year in the CDP (formerly the Carbon Disclosure Project) Supply Chain programme, a platform for engaging key suppliers on carbon emissions. Of the 146 suppliers we engaged, 83% responded to the CDP questionnaire.

This has provided important insights into the carbon impacts of our supply chain, and we will use the information to explore opportunities to reduce them.

Carbon emissions by weight by region
(1,000 tonnes CO$_2$ e) [1, 2]

	2007	2012	2013	2014
North America	218	67	51	56
Western Europe	364	318	333	337
Africa, Eastern Europe and Turkey	294	295	275	232
Latin America and Caribbean	32	23	19	19
Asia Pacific	29	15	13	13
Corporate	23	17	16	14
Diageo (total)	960	735	707	674Δ

1. CO2e figures are calculated using the kWh/CO2e conversion factor provided by energy suppliers, the relevant factors to the country of operation or the International Energy Agency, as applicable.
2. 2007 baseline data, and data for each of the six years in the period ended 30 June 2013, have been restated in accordance with the WRI/WBCSD Greenhouse Gas Reporting Protocol and Diageo's environmental reporting methodologies.
   Δ Within KPMG's limited assurance scope. Please see page 140 for further details.

Extract page 140

External limited assurance of selected Sustainability & Responsibility performance data

We engaged KPMG LLP to undertake a limited assurance engagement, reporting to Diageo plc only, over selected Sustainability & Responsibility (S&R) performance data marked with the symbol Δ within the Strategic Report section of this report. KPMG LLP used the International Standard on Assurance Engagements (ISAE) 3410: 'Assurance Engagements on Greenhouse Gas Statements' to assure the selected Greenhouse Gas performance data and ISAE 3000: 'Assurance Engagements Other Than Audits or Reviews of Historical Financial Information' to assure the other selected performance data, which includes data for water use, wastewater discharge (BOD) under direct control and waste to landfill, all marked with the symbol Δ.

KPMG LLP have issued an unqualified opinion over the selected S&R performance data and their full assurance opinion is available in the Responsibility section of our website at www.diageo.com.

The level of assurance provided for a limited assurance engagement is substantially lower than a reasonable assurance engagement. In order to reach their opinion, KPMG LLP performed a range of procedures which included interviews with management, examination of reporting systems and documentation, as well as selected data testing at various sites as well as at Head Office. A summary of the work they performed is included in their assurance opinion.

Non-financial performance information, greenhouse gas quantification in particular, is subject to more inherent limitations than financial information. It is important to read the selected S&R performance data contained within this report in the context of KPMG LLP's full limited assurance opinion and our reporting methodologies. Our reporting methodologies are included in the S&R Performance Addendum to the Annual Report, available at www.diageo.com.

Extract from the S&R Performance Addendum to the Annual Report

Greenhouse gas emissions – referred to as carbon dioxide equivalent (CO2e)

CO2e emissions data has been prepared in accordance with the WRI/WBCSD Protocol and IPCC (Intergovernmental Panel on Climate Change) methodology. A summary of the key elements of this standard and their application to Diageo' s business is outlined below.

Scopes

- **Scope 1 emissions** (i.e. direct CO2e emissions) from on-site energy consumption of fuel sources, such as gas, fuel oil, diesel, as well as fugitive and agricultural emissions are reported for all sites where we have operational control. Company-owned transport used for offsite purposes is determined as immaterial to overall company impacts. On-site non-production de minimis quantities less than 0.5% to a maximum of 50 CO2e tonnes are also excluded.
- **Scope 2 emissions** (i.e. indirect CO2e emissions) from purchased electricity and heat are also reported for these sites.
- **Scope 3 emissions** (i.e. indirect CO2e emissions) are from upstream and downstream supply chain activity (e.g. suppliers, distribution and logistics). Diageo is committed to understanding and reducing CO2e emissions along the key parts of the value chain, including scope 3 indirect emissions. CO2e emissions associated with the distribution and logistics component of the supply chain were quantified for the fiscal year 2013 and reported separately during this financial year.

Carbon dioxide emissions from the fermentation process are not included within our reported environmental data as these emissions are from a biological short cycle carbon source and are outside scopes 1, 2, and 3.

In accordance with the most recent WRI protocols, CO2e emissions are reported in terms of net emissions (i.e. 'market based', applying emission factors specified in contractual instruments for low CO2e, renewable electricity sourcing), and also of gross emissions, (or 'location based', applying grid average emission factors). Diageo's CO2e reduction targets and reporting protocols since 2007 have been based on net emissions; following changes in UK legislation, we have reported gross emissions for the first time this financial year, and added this to Diageo's reporting protocols. Emission factors are based on CO_2e where available; CO_2 only factors (e.g. International Energy Agency), which exclude other greenhouse gases, are not thought to have a material impact on total CO_2e.

Calculation methodology

CO_2e emissions data is externally reported in metric tonnes and is the measure used to compare emissions from the six main greenhouse gases (carbon dioxide; methane; nitrous oxide; hydrofluorocarbons; perfluorocarbons; sulphur hexafluoride) based on their global warming potential (GWP). The CO_2e emissions data has been calculated on the basis of measured energy and fuel use, multiplied by the relevant CO_2e conversion factors. Fuel and energy use are based on direct measurement verified through purchase invoices for the vast majority of our sites ($> 99\%$). In certain limited instances ($< 1\%$), where invoices are not available, it has been necessary to estimate energy and fuel use.

Employee information

2.57 All companies are required to include in the directors' report information regarding the company's policy in respect of the employment of disabled persons. Companies are also required to include information regarding employee involvement. These requirements apply only to the directors' report of a reporting entity that employs, on average, more than 250 employees in the UK each week during the financial year. [SI 2008/ 410 7 Sch 10(1), 11(1)]. Since the strategic report is also required to include information about employees, companies might choose to include the directors' report employee disclosures in the strategic report, with a specific cross-reference from the directors' report.

2.58 The directors' report should contain a statement that describes the company's policy during the year in respect of the following:

- Giving full and fair consideration (having regard to the persons' particular aptitudes and abilities) to applications for employment that disabled persons (as defined in the Disability Discrimination Act 1995) make to the company. The definition of 'disabled person' in the 1995 Act is a person who has a physical or mental impairment that has a substantial and long-term adverse effect on their ability to carry out normal day-to-day activities. [Disability Discrimination Act 1995 Sec 1].

- Continuing the employment of, and arranging appropriate training for, any of the company's employees who have become disabled during the period in which the company employed them.

- Otherwise providing for the training, the career development and the promotion of those disabled persons whom the company employs.

[SI 2008/410 7 Sch 10].

2.58.1 An illustration of the disclosures is given in Table 2.3.

Table 2.3 – Employee information

Marks & Spencer Group plc – Annual report and financial statements – 28 March 2015

Directors' Report: Governance (extract)

Employee involvement

We remain committed to employee involvement throughout the business. Employees are kept well informed of the performance and strategy of the Group through personal briefings, regular meetings, email and broadcasts by the Chief Executive and members of the Board at key points in the year to all head office and distribution centre employees and store management. Additionally, many of our store colleagues can join the briefings by telephone to hear directly from the business. These types of communication are supplemented by our employee publications including 'Your M&S' magazine, Plan A updates and DVD presentations. More than 3,500 employees are elected onto Business Involvement Groups ('BIGs') across every store, distribution centre and head office location to represent their colleagues in two-way communication and consultation with the Company. They have continued to play a key role in a wide variety of business changes.

The 20th meeting of the European Works Council ('EWC') (established in 1995) will take place in September 2015. This Council provides an additional forum for informing, consulting and involving employee representatives from the countries in the European Community. The EWC includes representatives from France, The Netherlands, Czech Republic, Slovakia, Greece, Bulgaria, Slovenia, Romania, Croatia, Hungary, Lithuania, Latvia, Estonia, Poland, the Republic of Ireland and the UK. The EWC has the opportunity to be addressed by the Chief Executive and other senior members of the Company on issues that affect the European business. This includes the Directors of International and Multi-channel and the Director of Plan A, who all have an impact across the European Community.

Directors and senior management regularly attend the national Business Involvement Group (BIG) meetings. They visit stores and discuss with employees matters of current interest and concern to both employees and the business through meetings with local BIG representatives, specific listening groups and informal discussions. The business has continued to engage with employees and drive involvement through a scheme called The BIG Idea. On a quarterly basis the business poses a question to gather ideas and initiatives on a number of areas including how we can better serve our customers. Several thousand ideas are put forward each time and the winning employee receives an award and the chance to see how this is implemented by the Company.

Share schemes are a long-established and successful part of our total reward package, encouraging and supporting employee share ownership. In particular, around 24,000 employees currently participate in Sharesave, the Company's all employee Save As you Earn Scheme. Full details of all schemes are given on pages 70 to 71.

We have a well established interactive wellbeing website designed exclusively for M&S employees. It gives any employee the opportunity to access a wealth of information, help and support. We cover all areas of wellbeing, from healthy eating and exercise to help in overcoming issues such as stress, financial challenges, achieving a positive work-life balance and problems with sleeping. Using this service, employees can access our personal support teams, such as counselling, as well as take part in a calendar of wellbeing events and initiatives.

Employees are able to interact with one another, post information about clubs and groups in their area and can gain access to information about corporate projects, which link to their personal health, via our employee social media platform, Yammer.

We maintain contact with retired staff through communications from the Company and the Pension Trust. Member-nominated trustees have been elected to the Pension Trust board, including employees and pensioners. We continue to produce a regular Pensions Update newsletter for members of our final salary pension scheme and have a fully interactive website for members of the defined contribution M&S Pension Savings Plan.

Equal opportunities

The Group is committed to an active equal opportunities policy from recruitment and selection, through training and development, performance reviews and promotion to retirement. It is our policy to promote an environment free from discrimination, harassment and victimisation, where everyone will receive equal treatment regardless of gender, colour, ethnic or national origin, disability, age, marital status, sexual orientation or religion. All decisions relating to employment practices will be objective, free from bias and based solely upon work criteria and individual merit. The Company is responsive to the needs of its employees, customers and the community at large. We are an organisation which uses everyone's talents and abilities and where diversity is valued. We were one of the first major companies to remove the default retirement age in 2001 and have continued to see an increase in employees wanting to work past the state retirement age. Our oldest employee is 88 years old and joined the business at age 80. In April 2015 the Company once again featured in The Times Top 50 Employers for Women, highlighting how equal opportunities are available for all at M&S.

Employees with disabilities

It is our policy that people with disabilities should have full and fair consideration for all vacancies. During the year, we continued to demonstrate our commitment to interviewing those people with disabilities who fulfil the minimum criteria, and endeavouring to retain employees in the workforce if they become disabled during employment. We will actively retrain and adjust their environment where possible to allow them to maximise their potential. We continue to work with external organisations to provide workplace opportunities through our innovative Marks & Start scheme and by working closely with JobCentre Plus. The Marks & Start scheme was introduced into our distribution centre at Castle Donington in 2012/13, where we work with Remploy to support people with disabilities and health conditions into work.

2.59 The directors' report should describe the action that the company has taken during the financial year to introduce, maintain or develop arrangements aimed at:

■ Providing employees systematically with information on matters of concern to them as employees.

■ Consulting employees or their representatives on a regular basis, so that the company can take the views of employees into account in making decisions that are likely to affect their interests.

■ Encouraging the involvement of employees in the company's performance through (for example) an employees' share scheme.

■ Achieving a common awareness on the part of all employees of the financial and the economic factors that affect the company's performance.

[SI 2008/410 7 Sch 11].

Disclosure of overseas branches

2.60 Companies are required to give an indication of the existence of branches that they operate outside the UK. [SI 2008/410 7 Sch 7(1)(d)]. For this purpose, a branch is defined to mean only branches within the EU (see further the Manual of accounting – UK GAAP). [CA06 Sec 1046(3)]. So, branches operated in the US, for example, would not require disclosure. Disclosure is required only of the company's branches, and not those of its subsidiaries. This means that the directors' report of a parent company need only refer to the existence of branches that it operates outside the UK and not to those that are operated outside the UK by its subsidiaries. Branches operated by its subsidiaries would be disclosed in the subsidiaries' directors' reports.

Dividends

2.61   The directors' report is required to disclose the amount (if any) that the directors recommend should be paid as a dividend. [CA06 Sec 416(3)]. Where the directors do not propose a dividend, it is customary to state that fact. An example of the relevant disclosure is given in Table 2.4.

Table 2.4 – Dividend payment

Imperial Tobacco Group PLC – Annual Report – 30 September 2013
Directors' Governance Report (extract)

FINANCIAL RESULTS AND DIVIDENDS

We include a review of our operational and financial performance, current position and future developments in our Strategic Report: Strategy, Risks, Performance and Governance sections.

The profit attributable to equity holders of the Company for the financial year was £937 million, as shown in our consolidated income statement on page 87. Note 3 to the Financial Statements gives an analysis of revenue and profit from operations (page 98).

An analysis of net assets is provided in the Consolidated Balance Sheet on page 89 and the related Notes to the Financial Statements.

In our Interim Management Statement made on 30 January 2013 we stated that we expected around 55 per cent of adjusted operating profits to be delivered in the second half of our financial year. On the basis of our actual results to 30 September 2013, 55 per cent of adjusted operating profits were delivered in the second half.

The Directors have declared and proposed dividends as follows:

£ million	2013	2012
Ordinary Shares		
Interim paid, 35.1p per share (2012: 31.7p)	**341**	314
Proposed final, 81.2p per share (2012: 73.9p)	**783**	729
Total ordinary dividends, 116.4p per share (2012: 105.6p)	**1,124**	1,043

The final dividend, if approved, will be paid on 17 February 2014 to our shareholders on the Register of Members at the close of business on 17 January 2014. The associated ex dividend date will be 15 January 2014. We paid an interim dividend on 16 August 2013 to shareholders on the Register of Members at the close of business on 19 July 2013.

2.62   In addition to giving the required information about the recommended dividend, SSE plc, shown in Table 2.5, provides information about the growth in dividends and future targets.

Table 2.5 – Dividend growth and targets

SSE plc – Annual Report – 31 March 2013

Financial overview (extract)

Dividend per share and adjusted earnings per share* (extract)

Increasing the dividend for 2012/13

SSE's first financial responsibility to its shareholders is to remunerate their investment through the payment of dividends. The Board is recommending a final dividend of 59.0p per share to which a Scrip alternative is offered, compared with 56.1p in the previous year, an increase of 5.2%. This will make a full-year dividend of 84.2p per share, which is:

- an increase of 6.8% compared with 2011/12;

- a real terms increase of 2%, based on the average annual rate of RPI inflation in the UK between April 2012 and March 2013, which meets the target set for the year;

- the fourteenth successive above-inflation dividend increase since the first full-year dividend paid by SSE, in 1998/99;

- just over 2.4 times the full-year dividend paid by SSE in 2002/03; and

- covered 1.4 times by SSE's adjusted earnings per share*.

SSE is now one of just five companies to have delivered better-than-inflation dividend growth every year since 1999, while remaining part of the FTSE 100 for at least 50% of that time, and ranks third amongst that group in terms of compound annual growth rate over that time.

Targeting above-RPI inflation dividend increases in 2013/14 and beyond
The stated goal of SSE's strategy is to deliver sustained real growth in the dividend and, as set out in its Annual Report 2012 and in its six-month financial report in November 2012, its target from 2013/14 onwards is to deliver annual dividend increases which are greater than RPI inflation while maintaining dividend cover over the medium term within a range around 1.5 times.

Inside this year's report (extract)
The Directors' Report is set out on pages 1 to 102.

---

*Unless otherwise stated, in line with SSE's approach since September 2005, this financial report describes adjusted operating profit before exceptional items, remeasurements arising from IAS 39, and after the removal of taxation and interest on profits from jointly controlled entities and associates, unless otherwise stated. In addition, it describes adjusted profit before tax before exceptional items, remeasurements arising from IAS 39 and after the removal of taxation on profits from jointly-controlled entities and associates. It also describes adjusted profit after tax and earnings per share before exceptional items, remeasurements arising from IAS 39 and deferred tax.

2.63   Listed companies should disclose particulars of any arrangements under which any shareholder has waived or agreed to waive any dividends. This requirement applies to waivers of future dividends, as well as to waivers of dividends payable during the past financial year. The Listing Rules state that waivers of dividends of less than 1% of the total value of any dividend may be disregarded, provided that some payment has been made on each share of the relevant class during the year. [LR 9.8.5].

Purchase of own shares and sales of treasury shares

Legal requirements

2.64   Where the company has an interest in its own shares, the directors' report is required to include specified information. The directors' report must contain the details set out in paragraph 2.65 where any of the following circumstances occur:

Acquisition of shares by the company

■   A company purchases its own shares (including treasury shares) or otherwise acquires them by forfeiture, or by surrender in lieu of forfeiture, or by way of a gift, or in a reduction of capital duly made, or by order of the court. [SI 2008/410 7 Sch 8(a); CA06 Sec 659(1)(2)].

Acquisition of shares in a public company by another person

■   A nominee of a public company acquires shares in the company from a third party without the company providing any financial assistance directly or indirectly, and the company has a beneficial interest in those shares. [SI 2008/410 7 Sch 8(b); CA06 Sec 662(1)(d)].

■   Any person acquires shares in a public company with the financial assistance of the company, and the company has a beneficial interest in those shares. [SI 2008/410 7 Sch 8(b); CA06 Sec 662(1)(e), 671].

Lien or charge on own shares held by the company

■   A company takes a lien or a charge (either express or implied) on its own shares for any amount that is payable in respect of those shares. [SI 2008/410 7 Sch 8(c); CA06 Sec 670(2)].

■   A company that has re-registered under section 1040 of the Act, holds a lien or a charge (either express or implied) on its own shares, and that lien or charge existed immediately before the company applied to be re-registered as a public company. [SI 2008/410 7 Sch 8(c); CA06 Sec 670(4)].

2.65   Where any of the above circumstances has occurred, the directors' report must state the following details:

In respect of shares purchased

■   The number and the nominal value of the shares that have been purchased in the financial year and the percentage of the called-up share capital which shares of that description represent.

■   The aggregate amount of consideration paid and the reasons for their purchase.

An example is given in Table 2.6 below.

In respect of shares acquired other than by purchase or charged

■   The number and the nominal value of any shares that have been otherwise acquired (whether by the company or by its nominee or any other person) or charged at any time during the financial year.

■   The maximum number and the nominal value of shares which, having been so acquired or charged (whether or not during the year), are held at any time during the financial year.

- The number and the nominal value of such shares that were disposed of by the company (or any other person holding them on behalf of the company) during the year, or that were cancelled by the company during the year.

- For each of the above, the percentage of the called-up share capital which shares of that description represent.

- The amount of any charge.

In addition to the above, there should be disclosed the amount or the value of any consideration for any shares that either the company or the other person disposed of during the financial year that the company or the other person acquired for money or money's worth.

[SI 2008/410 7 Sch 9].

Table 2.6 – Repurchase of own shares

AstraZeneca PLC – Annual Report and Accounts – 31 December 2012

Directors' report (extract)

Corporate Governance Report (extract)

Other matters (extract)

Distributions to shareholders and dividends for 2012

Our distribution policy comprises both a regular cash dividend and a share repurchase component, further details of which are set out in the Financial Review on page 94 and Notes 20 and 21 to the Financial Statements on page 173.

The Company's dividends for 2012 of $2.80 (178.6 pence, SEK 18.34) per Ordinary Share amount to, in aggregate, a total dividend payment to shareholders of $3,665 million. Two of our employee share trusts, AstraZeneca Share Trust Limited and AstraZeneca Quest Limited, waived their right to a dividend on the Ordinary Shares that they hold and instead received a nominal dividend.

A shareholders' resolution was passed at the 2012 AGM authorising the Company to purchase its own shares. Pursuant to this resolution, the Company repurchased (and subsequently cancelled) 57.8 million Ordinary Shares with a nominal value of $0.25 each, at an aggregate cost of $2,635 million, representing 4.6% of the closing total issued share capital of the Company. The Company suspended its share repurchase programme on 1 October as a prudent step to maintain flexibility while the Board and the newly-appointed CEO completed the Company's annual strategy update.

During our share repurchase programmes that operated between 1999 and September 2012, a total of 615.2 million Ordinary Shares were repurchased, and subsequently cancelled, at an average price of 2777 pence per share for a consideration, including expenses, of $29,352 million.

Listing Rules requirements

2.66 A listed company must give the following additional information concerning purchases or proposed purchases of the company's own shares and sales of treasury shares:

- Details of any authority given by the shareholders in general meeting for the company to purchase its own shares that is still valid at the year end.

- In relation to purchases other than through the market or by tender to all shareholders, the names of the sellers of the shares that have been purchased, or are to be purchased, by the company during the year.

- If the company has purchased any of its own shares since the year end, or has either been granted an option or entered into a contract to purchase its own shares since the year end, the equivalent information to that required under SI 2008/410 (as detailed in para 2.65).

- In relation to sales of treasury shares made other than through the market, or in connection with an employees' share scheme, or other than pursuant to an opportunity available to all shareholders on the same terms, the names of the purchasers of such shares sold, or proposed to be sold, during the year.

[LR 9.8.6R(4)].

[The next paragraph is 2.68.]

Financial instruments

2.68 Companies are required to provide the following disclosures in the directors' report:

- The company's financial risk management objectives and policies, including the policy for hedging each major type of forecasted transaction for which hedge accounting is used.

- The company's exposure to price risk, credit risk, liquidity risk and cash flow risk.

The disclosure is not required where such information is not material for the assessment of the entity's assets, liabilities, financial position and profit or loss. [SI 2008/410 7 Sch 6(1)].

2.69 These requirements are consistent with IFRS 7 and FRS 29. Those accounting standards require an entity to provide disclosures *"that enable users to evaluate: (a) the significance of financial instruments for the entity's financial position and performance; and (b) the nature and extent of risks arising from financial instruments to which the entity is exposed during the period and at the reporting date, and how the entity manages those risks"*. [FRS 29 para 1; IFRS 7 para 1]. Extensive quantitative and qualitative disclosures of each type of risk arising from financial instruments (credit risk, market risk and liquidity risk) are required. [FRS 29 paras 31-42; IFRS 7 paras 31-42]. (See the Manual of accounting – IFRS for the UK.)

2.70 Both IFRS 7 and FRS 29 require the disclosures to be given in the notes to the financial statements. For companies that comply with either IFRS 7 or FRS 29, to avoid the need for duplication, a specific cross-reference to the relevant note can be included in the directors' report.

Control and share structures

2.71 These are general requirements designed to bring greater transparency to the market, and they apply to companies whether or not they are involved in a takeover. The disclosure requirements apply to companies with voting securities that were admitted to trading on a regulated market at the end of the year. [SI 2008/410 7 Sch 13(1)].

2.72 The specific disclosure requirements must be provided, either in the directors' report or (by virtue of DTR 7.2.9R) in a document accompanying the annual report, provided that there is a specific cross-reference to the disclosures from the directors' report. The disclosure requirements include the following, which are to be given by reference to the end of the financial year:

- The structure of the company's capital, including the rights and obligations attached to the shares.

- Any restrictions on the transfer of securities.

- Any restriction on voting rights.

- Where a person has a significant direct or indirect holding, the identity of the person, the size of the holding and the nature of the holding (see further para 2.76 onwards).

- Where any person holds shares with specific rights regarding control of the company:
    - the identity of the person; and
    - the nature of those rights.

- Where the company has an employee share scheme, but shares relating to that scheme have rights regarding the control of the company that are not directly exercisable by the employees, how those rights are exercisable.

- Agreements between holders of securities known to the company that might result in restrictions on the transfer of securities or voting rights.

- Any rules that the company has about the appointment of directors, powers of directors or amendments to the company's articles of association.

- Significant agreements that the company is a party to that will be affected by a change in control of the company, together with the effects of such agreements (see further para 2.75 onwards).

- Any agreements with employees (including directors) of the company providing for compensation for loss of office or employment on the takeover of the company.

- Any necessary explanatory material on the matters listed above.

[SI 2008/410 7 Sch 13, 14].

2.73 Failure to include either the information concerning control and share structures or the explanatory material in the annual report will attract criminal sanctions. [CA06 Secs 415(4)(5), 419(3)(4)].

2.74 Listed companies are also required to disclose major interests in their shares (see para 2.76).

Agreements affected by a change of control

2.75 The extent to which agreements that a company has entered into will be affected by a change of control will vary, as will the nature of those contracts. Examples of agreements that may be affected (other than those specifically mentioned by the Act) are:

- Bank loan/facility agreements.
- Convertible and listed debt.
- Sale/supply agreements.
- Leases.
- Joint venture agreements.

An example showing both disclosure of agreements that would be affected by a change of control and a restriction of voting rights (that is also affected by a change of control) is given in Table 2.7.

Table 2.7 – Disclosure of agreements affected by change of control

Xstrata plc – Annual Report – 31 December 2012

Directors' report (extract)

Significant contractual arrangements (extract)

The Companies Act 2006 requires disclosure of the following significant agreements that contain provisions entitling the counterparties to exercise termination or other rights in the event of a change of control of the Company:

Relationship Agreement

The Company is party to the Relationship Agreement with Glencore International AG (Glencore) dated 20 March 2002. The Agreement regulates the continuing relationship between the parties. In particular it ensures that (a) the Company is capable of carrying on its business independently of Glencore as a controlling shareholder (as such term is defined in the Agreement); (b) transactions and relationships between Glencore (or any of its subsidiaries or affiliates) and the Company are at an arm's length and on normal commercial terms; (c) Glencore shall be entitled to nominate up to three directors or (if lower or higher) such number of directors equal to one less than the number of directors who are independent directors; and, (d) directors of the Company nominated by Glencore shall not be permitted to vote on any Board resolution, unless otherwise agreed by the independent directors, to approve any aspect of the Company's involvement in or enforcement of any arrangements, agreements or transactions with Glencore or any of its subsidiaries or affiliates. The Agreement provides that, save to the extent required by law, the parties agree that they shall exercise their powers so that the Company is managed in accordance with the principles of good governance set out in the Corporate Governance Code and that the provisions of the Code of Best Practice set out in the Corporate Governance Code are complied with by the Company. It is expressed that the Agreement terminates in the event that Glencore ceases to be a controlling shareholder of the Company following a sale or disposal of shares in the Company or if the Company ceases to be listed on the Official List and traded on the London Stock Exchange.

US$500 million notes due 2037

On 30 November 2007, Xstrata Finance (Canada) Limited issued $500 million 6.90% notes due 2037, guaranteed by the Company, Xstrata (Schweiz) AG and Xstrata Finance (Dubai) Limited. The terms of these notes require Xstrata Finance (Canada) Limited to make an offer to each noteholder to repurchase all or any part of such holder's notes at a repurchase price in cash equal to 101% of the aggregate principal amount of the notes so repurchased plus any accrued and unpaid interest on the principal amount of the notes repurchased to the date of repurchase, if both of the following occur:

i.   a change of control (as defined in the terms and conditions of the notes) of Xstrata; and

ii. the notes are rated below investment grade by each of Moody's and Standard & Poor's on any date from 30 days prior to the date of the public notice of an arrangement that could result in a change of control (as defined in the terms and conditions of the notes) until the end of the 60-day period following public notice of the occurrence of a change of control.

€600 million notes due 2015

On 23 May 2008, Xstrata Canada Financial Corporation issued €600 million 6.25% guaranteed notes due 2015 and £500 million 7.375% guaranteed notes due 2020 (the 2008 MTN Notes). The 2008 MTN Notes are guaranteed by each of Xstrata plc, Xstrata (Schweiz) AG, Xstrata Finance (Dubai) Limited and Xstrata Finance (Canada) Limited and were issued pursuant to the $6.0 billion Euro Medium Term Note Programme. Pursuant to the terms and conditions of the 2008 MTN Notes, if:

i.   a change of control occurs (as defined in the terms and conditions of the 2008 MTN Notes); and

---

ii. the 2008 MTN Notes carry, on the relevant announcement date of the change of control:

    a. an investment grade credit rating is either downgraded to a non-investment grade credit rating or is withdrawn; or

    b. a non-investment grade credit rating is downgraded by one or more notches or is withdrawn; or

    c. no credit rating and a negative rating event (as defined in the terms and conditions of the 2008 MTN Notes) occurs, each holder has the option to require Xstrata Canada Financial Corp. to redeem such 2008 MTN Notes in cash at the principal amount plus interest accrued to (but excluding) the date of redemption.

US$6.0 billion syndicated facility

On 24 October 2011, Xstrata (Schweiz) AG and the Company entered into a $6.0 billion multicurrency revolving syndicated loan facility agreement with the banks and financial institutions named therein as lenders (the Syndicated Facilities Agreement) and Barclays Capital acting as facility agent. Upon a change of control, no borrower may make a further utilisation unless otherwise agreed. The majority lenders, as defined in the agreement, can also require that the Syndicated Facilities Agreement is immediately terminated and declared that all outstanding loans become immediately payable. Alternatively, if the majority lenders do not require cancellation, but a specific lender does on the basis of internal policy, that particular lender can require that its commitments are cancelled and all amounts outstanding in respect of that lender's commitments shall become immediately payable.

US$3.0 billion multi-tranche notes

On 3 November 2011, Xstrata Finance (Canada) Limited issued $800 million 2.85% notes due 2014, $700 million 3.6% notes due 2017, $1.0 billion 4.95% notes due 2021 and $500 million 6.0% notes due 2041. The notes are guaranteed by the Company. The terms of the notes contain change of control provisions, in substance, identical to those set out in the referenced US$500 million notes due 2037 above.

US$4.5 billion multi-tranche notes

On 18 October 2012, Xstrata Finance (Canada) Limited issued $1.25 billion 1.8% notes due 2015, $1.75 billion 2.45% notes due 2017, $1.0 billion 4.0% notes due 2022 and $500 million 5.3% notes due 2042. The notes are guaranteed by the Company. The terms of the notes contain change of control provisions, in substance, identical to those set out in the referenced US$500 million notes due 2037 above.

€2.25 billion multi-tranche notes

On 15 November 2012, Xstrata Finance (Dubai) Limited issued €1.25 billion 1.5% guaranteed notes due 2016 and €1.0 billion 2.375% guaranteed notes due 2018 (the 2012 MTN Notes). The 2012 MTN Notes are guaranteed by each of Xstrata plc, Xstrata (Schweiz) AG, Xstrata Canada Financial Corporation and Xstrata Finance (Canada) Limited and were issued pursuant to the $8.0 billion Euro Medium Term Note Programme. Pursuant to the terms and conditions of the 2012 MTN Notes, if:

i. a change of control occurs (as defined in the terms and conditions of the 2012 MTN Notes); and

ii. the 2012 MTN Notes carry, on the relevant announcement date of the change of control:

    a. an investment grade credit rating is either downgraded to a non-investment grade credit rating or is withdrawn; or

    b. a non-investment grade credit rating is downgraded by one or more notches or is withdrawn; or

    c. no credit rating and a negative rating event (as defined in the terms and conditions of the 2012 MTN Notes) occurs, each holder has the option to require Xstrata Canada Financial Corp. to redeem such 2012 MTN Notes in cash at the principal amount plus interest accrued to (but excluding) the date of redemption.

Xstrata plc Long Term Incentive Plan

The rules of our employee share plans set out the consequences of any change of control of the Company on employees' rights under the plans. Generally such rights will vest on a change of control and participants will become entitled to acquire shares or, in some cases, to the payment of a cash sum of equivalent value.

Major interest in company's shares

2.76 A statement should be given of particulars of the nature and extent of the interests of any person, in any holding of 3% or more of the nominal value of any class of capital carrying rights to vote in all circumstances at general meetings of the company. The statement must be made at a date not more than one month prior to the date of notice of the annual general meeting. [LR 9.8.6R(2)]. The 3% threshold is higher for some entities; for example, market makers only disclose interests of 10% or more. [DTR 5.1.3R].

2.77 The particulars to be disclosed include the names of the persons and the amount of their interests. This information should be that which has been disclosed to the company in accordance with DTR 5. If there is no such interest, that fact should also be stated. [LR 9.8.6R(2)]. It is customary to give this information in the directors' report. An example is given in Table 2.8. The Act's requirement to disclose significant shareholdings (described in para 2.72) requires such holdings to be disclosed as at the end of the financial year, whereas the Listing Rules require disclosures as at not more than one month prior to the date of the notice of the AGM. The Act also requires the nature of the interest (direct or indirect) to be disclosed.

Table 2.8 – Major interest in company's shares

Marks and Spencer Group plc – Annual report and financial statements – 28 March 2015
Directors' report – Governance (extract)
Other disclosures (extract)
Interests in voting rights

Information provided to the Company pursuant to the Financial Conduct Authority's (FCA) Disclosure and Transparency Rules (DTRs) is published on a Regulatory Information Service and on the Company's website. As at 28 March 2015, the following information has been received, in accordance with DTR5, from holders of notifiable interests in the Company's issued share capital.

The information provided below was correct at the date of notification; however, the date received may not have been within the current financial year. It should be noted that these holdings are likely to have changed since the Company was notified. However, notification of any change is not required until the next notifiable threshold is crossed.

	Ordinary shares	% of capital	Nature of holding
Blackrock, Inc	81,834,738	5	Indirect (4.97%) & CFD (0.04%)
The Capital Group Companies, Inc	66,681,922	4.049	Indirect interest
The Wellcome Trust	47,464,282	3.01	Direct interest

Notifications were also received from William Adderley and Majedie Asset Management Limited during the year to disclose that they no longer held a notifiable interest.

2.78 In order to ensure that the share register is up to date, the Act gives listed companies the right to write to any person who it believes is (or has been during the previous three years) interested in the company's shares and ask them to confirm that fact, or to state the person to whom the interest was transferred. [CA06 Sec 793]. Further, the DTR require holders of more than 3% (or a higher threshold in some circumstances – see para 2.76) of a company's qualifying financial instruments to notify the company if that holding increases above or falls below any integer percentage holding equal to or higher than 3%.

Directors

Details of directors

2.79 Disclosure is required of the names of the persons who were directors of the company at any time during the financial year. [CA06 Sec 416(1)(a)]. This can be achieved either by listing the names of the directors in the report or by referring to the page where this information may be found. When cross-referring to a list elsewhere in the annual report, the list of directors is often at the balance sheet date or at the date the report and accounts were approved. Where there have been changes in directors during the year (or since the year end if the list is at the date the report and accounts were approved), it is necessary to provide details. Identification of directors and their roles is also required by the DTR (see para 2.95).

2.80 Although not required by law, it is customary to include the following information:

- The dates of appointments or resignations of directors occurring during the financial year.

- Changes in the directors since the end of the financial year.

- Retirement of directors at the AGM and whether they offer themselves for election.

Directors' interests in contracts

2.81 Under the Act, disclosure of directors' interests in contracts is not required in the directors' report. Disclosure is required in the financial statements of transactions and arrangements in which the director of a company has, directly or indirectly, a material interest (for example, contracts between a director and a company for the sale of non-cash assets). [SI 2008/410 1 Sch 72].

2.82 In addition, the Listing Rules require disclosure of particulars of any contract of significance (including substantial property transactions) subsisting during the period under review, to which the company, or one of its subsidiary undertakings, is a party and in which a director of the company is, or was, materially interested. [LR 9.8.4R(10)(a)]. (For the placement requirements for this disclosure, see para 2.15.1.) The disclosure does not have to be provided in the directors' report, but is often given there. In this context, a 'contract of significance' is one which represents in amount or value (or annual amount or value) a sum equal to 1% or more, calculated on a group basis where relevant, of:

- for a capital transaction or for a transaction of which the principal purpose is the granting of credit, the aggregate of the group's share capital and reserves; or

- for other transactions, the group's total purchases, sales, payments or receipts, as appropriate.

[LR App 1.1].

Disclosure of qualifying third party and pension scheme indemnity provisions

2.83   Where a qualifying third party indemnity provision and/or a qualifying pension scheme indemnity provision (made by the company or otherwise) was in force for the benefit of one or more directors at any time during the financial year, or at the time when the report is approved, a statement should be made in the directors' report to confirm this fact. [CA06 Sec 236(2)(3)]. An example of disclosure is provided in Table 2.9.

Table 2.9 – Disclosure of directors' indemnities

Mitchells & Butlers plc – Report and accounts – 27 September 2014

Directors' report (extract)

Directors' indemnity

As permitted by the Articles of Association, each of the Directors has the benefit of an indemnity, which is a qualifying third-party indemnity as defined by Section 234 of the Companies Act 2006. The indemnity was in force throughout the tenure of each Director during the last financial year, and is currently in force. The Company also purchased and maintained throughout the financial year Directors' and Officers' liability insurance in respect of itself and its Directors. No indemnity is provided for the Company's auditor.

2.84   A statement is also required in the directors' report where a qualifying indemnity provision has been made during the year, or at the time when the report is approved, by the company for the benefit of one or more directors of an associated company. [CA06 Sec 236(4)(5)]. An associated company is defined in section 256 of the Act. A holding company is associated with all of its subsidiaries, and a subsidiary is associated with its holding company and all of the other subsidiaries of its holding company.

2.85   A qualifying third party indemnity provision is one where the provision does not provide indemnity for any liability incurred by the director in respect of each of the following:

- An amount due to the company or any associated company.

- A fine imposed by criminal proceedings.

- A penalty payable to a regulatory authority in respect of non-compliance with any requirement of a regulatory nature.

- An amount payable:

    - in defending criminal proceedings in which the director is convicted;

    - in defending civil proceedings brought by the company (or an associated company) in which judgment is given against the director; or

    - in connection with any application in which the court refused to grant the director relief.

[CA06 Sec 234(2)(3)].

2.86   The Act defines a qualifying pension scheme indemnity provision as a provision indemnifying a director of a company that is a trustee of an occupational pension scheme against liability incurred in connection with the company's activities as a trustee of the scheme, provided the provision does not provide indemnity against any liability of the director:

- to pay a fine imposed by criminal proceedings;

- to pay a sum to a regulatory authority due to a penalty in respect of non-compliance with any regulatory requirement; or

- incurred by the director in defending criminal proceedings in which he is convicted.

[CA06 Sec 235(2)(3)].

Directors' responsibility statements

2.87   The UK Corporate Governance Code recommends that directors of listed companies make a statement of their responsibilities. [UK CGC C.1.1]. In addition, the Disclosure and Transparency Rules of the FCA require listed companies to make specified disclosures about directors' responsibilities (see further para 2.93 onwards).

2.88   ISA (UK&I) 700 (revised June 2013), 'The independent auditor's report on financial statements', refers to the responsibilities of those charged with governance (which, in a UK context, is the company's directors) and states that:

> *"The auditor's report should include a statement that those charged with governance are responsible for the preparation of the financial statements and a statement that the responsibility of the auditor is to audit and express an opinion on the financial statements in accordance with applicable legal requirements and International Standards on Auditing (UK and Ireland)."*
> [ISA (UK&I) 700 (revised) para 15].

2.89   The UK Corporate Governance Code includes a recommendation that the directors should state that they consider that the annual report and accounts, taken as a whole, is fair, balanced and understandable and provides the information necessary for shareholders to assess the company's performance, business model and strategy. [UK CGC C.1.1]. The Code also recommends that, where requested by the board, the audit committee should provide advice on this. The Code does not specify where the directors' statement is to be included, but in practice it is likely to be added to the existing directors' responsibilities statement, either as an addition to the formal acknowledgements of responsibility that the directors make under DTR 4.1.12 (see para 2.93) or within the body of the responsibilities statement required by the UK Corporate Governance Code.

2.90   The example financial statements for GAAP UK Plc, and IFRS GAAP Plc (see our separate publication, 'UK illustrative financial statements') each contain example wording for directors' responsibility statements.

2.91   In more complicated situations (for example, where the company is listed in a market outside the UK where different requirements might apply), the directors might need to take legal advice on what to include in the directors' responsibilities statement.

2.92   Quoted companies publish their financial reports on their websites. [CA06 Sec 430]. The directors are responsible for the maintenance and integrity of financial information contained on the company's website, and the directors' responsibility statement should state that fact. Table 2.10 below shows an example from published financial statements that reflects such responsibility. If this responsibility is included in the directors' responsibilities statement, it does not have to be included in the audit report.

2.93   For listed companies, the Disclosure and Transparency Rules require the annual financial report to include a responsibility statement. [DTR 4.1.5R]. The DTR require that the persons responsible within the listed company (that is, the directors) state that, to the best of their knowledge:

- The financial statements, prepared in accordance with the applicable set of accounting standards, give a true and fair view of the assets, liabilities, financial position and profit or loss of the listed company and the undertakings included in the consolidation taken as a whole.

- The management report includes a fair review of the development and performance of the business and the position of the company and the undertakings included in the consolidation taken as a whole, together with a description of the principal risks and uncertainties that they face (the same wording as is used in the strategic report requirements in Section 414C of the Act).

[DTR 4.1.12R].

2.94   The directors have a responsibility to provide financial statements, prepared in accordance with applicable accounting standards, that give a true and fair view. [CA06 Sec 393]. They are also responsible for preparing a strategic report (see further para 2.16 onwards). The DTR simply require the directors to make positive statements regarding their responsibilities.

2.95   The name and function of each person making a responsibility statement under the DTR must be clearly indicated in the responsibility statement. [DTR 4.1.12R]. If the responsibility statement is provided collectively by the board (and, for example, signed by the company secretary or a director on its behalf), all directors are, in substance, making the responsibility statement. It is usual for the directors' names and job titles to be listed elsewhere in the annual report; hence, to avoid duplication, a specific cross-reference from the directors' report would fulfil the DTR requirements.

2.96 Table 2.10 is an example of a directors' responsibility statement prepared before the business review requirement was replaced by the requirement for a strategic report and the recommendation regarding a 'fair, balanced and understandable' statement.

Table 2.10 – Directors' responsibilities

Dixons Retail plc – Annual Report and Accounts – 30 April 2013

Directors' Responsibilities

The directors are responsible for preparing the Annual Report and Accounts in accordance with applicable law and regulations. English company law requires the directors to prepare financial statements for each financial year and under that law, the directors have prepared the Group and the Company financial statements in accordance with International Financial Reporting Standards (IFRS) as adopted by the European Union.

The financial statements are required by law to give a true and fair view of the state of affairs of the Group and the Company and of the profit or loss of the Group for the period. In preparing the financial statements, the directors are also required to:

- Properly select and apply accounting policies;

- Present information, including accounting policies, in a manner that provides relevant, reliable, comparable and understandable information; and

- Provide additional disclosures when compliance with the specific requirements of IFRS is insufficient to enable users to understand the impact of particular transactions, other events and conditions on the financial position and financial performance.

In preparing both the Group and the Company financial statements, suitable accounting policies have been used and applied consistently, and reasonable and prudent judgements and estimates have been made. Applicable accounting standards have been followed. The financial statements have been prepared on the going concern basis as disclosed in the Statutory Information section of the Directors' Report and Business Review.

The directors are responsible for maintaining adequate accounting records and sufficient internal controls to safeguard the assets of the Company and to take reasonable steps for the prevention and detection of fraud or any other irregularities and for the preparation of a directors' report and directors' remuneration report which comply with the requirements of the Companies Act 2006 and, as regards the Group financial statements, Article 4 of the IAS Regulation. The directors are responsible for the maintenance and integrity of the corporate and financial information included on the Company's website. Legislation in the UK governing the preparation and dissemination of financial statements may differ from legislation in other jurisdictions.

Each of the directors confirm that to the best of their knowledge:

- The Group and Company financial statements give a true and fair view of the assets, liabilities, financial position and profit / (loss) of the Group and Company, respectively; and

- The business and financial review contained in this Annual Report and Accounts includes a fair review of the development and performance of the business and the position of the Group and Company together with a description of the principal risks and uncertainties they face.

By Order of the Board
Sebastian James   **Humphrey Singer**
Group Chief Executive   Group Finance Director
20 June 2013   20 June 2013

Compliance with UK Corporate Governance Code

2.97 The Listing Rules require companies to give a two-part narrative statement, to explain how they have applied the UK Corporate Governance Code's main principles and to confirm that they have complied throughout the year with its provisions – or to provide an explanation where they have not complied.

2.98 The Disclosure and Transparency Rules require the corporate governance statement to be included in the directors' report. [DTR 7.2.1R]. Many companies prepare a separate corporate governance statement. Where this is the case, a cross-reference should be provided in the directors' report to the specific location of the corporate governance statement elsewhere in the annual report. [DTR 7.2.9R].

2.99 DTR 7.2.10R states that the directors' report must include a description of the main features of the group's internal control and risk management systems in relation to the process for preparing consolidated accounts. The UK Corporate Governance Code requires that the annual report includes disclosures on the principal risks facing the company, including those that would threaten its business model, future performance, solvency or liquidity.

2.100   See chapter 4 for further discussion of corporate governance matters, including the principles and provisions of the UK Corporate Governance Code and the disclosures required by the DTR in the corporate governance statement.

Political donations

Summary of the provisions for disclosure and control

2.101   The directors' report should include information about political donations and expenditure in the UK/EU and outside the EU. [SI 2008/410 7 Sch 3, 4]. Prior shareholder authorisation is required in respect of political donations and expenditure in the UK and in other EU Member States.

Definitions

2.102   The legislation relates to political expenditure and to political donations made by companies to:

- Political parties (both those registered in the UK and those acting in connection with any election to public office in any other EU Member State).

- Political organisations other than political parties, which are any organisation:

    - Carrying on, or proposing to carry on, activities capable of being reasonably regarded as intended to affect public support for any political party (as defined in the first bullet point in this paragraph) or for independent candidates at elections to public office held in an EU Member State other than the UK.

    - Carrying on, or proposing to carry on, activities capable of being reasonably regarded as intended to influence voters in national or regional referendums held under the law of any EU Member State.

- Independent election candidates at any election to public office in the UK or another EU Member State.

[CA06 Sec 363].

2.103   The definition of a 'political donation' is wide. It includes:

- Any gift of money or other property.

- Any sponsorship provided to cover expenses relating to any party conference, meeting or event, the preparation, publication or dissemination of any party publication or any party political study or research (or to ensure that such expenses are not incurred).

- Any fee or subscription paid for membership of or affiliation to a political party or organisation.

- Any money spent in paying expenses incurred directly or indirectly by a political party, organisation or election candidate.

- Any money lent to a political party, organisation or election candidate otherwise than on a commercial basis.

- The provision (other than on a commercial basis) of property, services or facilities (including the services of any person).

The definition includes donations to any officer, member, trustee or agent of a political party, in his/her capacity as such. Also, it includes any donation made through a third party. [CA06 Sec 364].

2.104   A 'political donation' is defined by reference to Sections 50 to 52 of the Political Parties, Elections and Referendums Act 2000 (disregarding amendments made by the Electoral Administration Act 2006, which remove from the definition of 'donation' loans made otherwise than on commercial terms). [CA06 Sec 364].

2.105   Political expenditure means any expenditure incurred by a company in respect of:

■   the preparation, publication or dissemination of advertising, promotional or publicity material of any kind that is capable of being reasonably regarded as intended to affect public support for a political party or other political organisation, or an independent election candidate; or

■   any of the company's activities of the kind referred to in the definition of 'political organisation' (second bullet point of para 2.102).

[CA06 Sec 365].

Prohibition on political donations and expenditure

2.106   A company is prohibited from making any political donation to a political party, political organisation or independent election candidate, or incurring any political expenditure, unless the donation or EU political expenditure has been authorised by the company using an 'approval resolution' (see para 2.108). [CA06 Sec 366(1)].

2.107   This resolution must be passed before the donation or political expenditure is made or incurred or, if earlier, any relevant contract entered into. See also the special rules for subsidiaries in paragraph 2.110. Shareholder approval is not required of donations or expenditure for purposes that are not connected with party politics in any EU Member State, but these still require disclosure.

2.108   An approval resolution is a resolution passed by the company that:

■   Authorises the company to make donations not exceeding a specified total or incur political expenditure (including EU political expenditure) not exceeding a specified total for a period of not more than four years beginning with the date on which the resolution is passed.

■   Is expressed in general terms (accordingly, it must not purport to authorise particular donations or expenditure).

[CA06 Secs 367, 368].

Exemptions for donations

2.109   There are five exemptions from the requirement for prior shareholder authorisation:

■   Donations to trade unions (including those in countries other than the UK). The exemption covers donations such as the provision of company rooms for trade union meetings, the use of company vehicles by trade union officials, and paid time off for trade union officials to act in that capacity. However, a donation to a trade union's political fund is not covered by the exemption. [CA06 Sec 374].

■   Subscriptions paid to EU trade associations for membership (including trade associations that carry out their activities outside the EU). [CA06 Sec 375].

■   Donations to all-party parliamentary groups. [CA06 Sec 376].

■   Political expenditure that is exempt by virtue of an order by the Secretary of State. [CA06 Sec 377].

■   Small political donations: authorisation is not required unless the aggregate amount of the political donation and previous political donations by the company in the 12 months ending on the date of the donation exceeds £5,000. Donations by other group companies (including subsidiaries) must be taken into account in calculating whether the £5,000 threshold has been exceeded. [CA06 Sec 378].

[CA06 Secs 374-378].

Subsidiaries incorporated in the UK

2.110   If the company is a subsidiary of another company (its holding company), an approval resolution might need to be passed by the holding company's shareholders as well as or instead of those of the company. This is relevant where the company is not a wholly owned subsidiary of a UK-registered company. In addition to the resolution of the company, a resolution must be passed by its 'relevant holding company'. The relevant holding company is the ultimate holding company or, where such a company is not a UK-registered company, the holding company highest up the chain that is a UK-registered company. [CA06 Sec 366].

2.111 A wholly owned subsidiary of a UK-registered company is not required to pass a resolution approving political donations or expenditure, although its relevant holding company is required to do so. [CA06 Sec 366(3)].

> **Example 1 – Subsidiary of intermediate parent**
>
> X plc wishes to make a political donation. It is an 80% subsidiary of Y plc, which is a subsidiary of Z plc. Approval resolutions must be passed by X plc (the company) and Z plc (the ultimate holding company).

> **Example 2 – Ultimate parent incorporated outside the UK**
>
> The facts are the same as in example 1, except that entity Z is incorporated outside the UK. Approval resolutions must be passed by X plc and Y plc (the highest UK-registered holding company of X plc).

> **Example 3 – Wholly owned subsidiary**
>
> The facts are the same as in example 2, except that X plc is a 100% subsidiary of Y plc. An approval resolution must be passed by Y plc, but need not be passed by X plc.

Directors' liability

2.112 There are no criminal sanctions in relation to making unauthorised political donations or incurring unauthorised political expenditure. Civil remedies are available to a company in the event of a breach of the prohibitions, and they can be pursued in the normal manner by the company.

2.113 If the company makes an unauthorised payment, the directors (and, unless they took all available steps to prevent the political donation being made or the political expenditure being incurred, the directors of the relevant holding company) are liable to reimburse the company for the amount of the political donation or political expenditure and damages for any loss that it suffers, together with interest until the amount is repaid to the company. [CA06 Sec 369].

2.114 Action can be taken against the directors for reimbursement by not less than 50 members, or by members holding not less than 5% of the issued share capital. In addition, in any such action, the members are entitled to require the company to provide all relevant information. If the company refuses to do so, the court can make an order directing the company or its officers or employees to provide the information. [CA06 Secs 370(3), 373(1)].

Disclosure of political donations and expenditure

2.115 There are separate disclosure regimes for:

- Political donations and expenditure within the UK/EU area.

- Contributions to political parties in the rest of the world.

Company with no subsidiaries – not wholly owned by a UK parent

2.116 If a company has made any donation to a political party, other political organisation or independent election candidate, or has incurred any political expenditure, and the aggregate of those exceeds £2,000 in a financial year, it must disclose the following particulars in the directors' report for the year:

- For political donations, the name of each political party, political organisation or independent election candidate and the amount given to each in the financial year.

- The total amount of political expenditure incurred in the financial year.

[SI 2008/410 7 Sch 3(2)].

2.117 All contributions made by the company to non-EU political parties also require disclosure (although there is no requirement to name the parties). There is no threshold for these disclosures. So, if the company has in the financial year made any contribution to a non-EU political party, the directors' report for the year must contain:

- a statement of the amount contributed; and

- if it has made more than one contribution in the year, a statement of the total contributions.

[SI 2008/410 7 Sch 4(1)].

Company with subsidiary – not wholly owned by a UK parent

2.118 If the amount of the combined political donations and the political expenditure of the company and its subsidiaries exceeds £2,000, the directors' report for the year must disclose the particulars mentioned in paragraph 2.117 in relation to the company and each subsidiary by whom any such political donation or political expenditure has been made or incurred. [SI 2008/410 7 Sch 3(3)].

2.119 Where the company has subsidiaries that have made any contributions to a non-EU political party in the financial year, the following applies. The directors' report of the company is not required to disclose the amount of the company's own contributions, but should instead contain a statement of the total amount of the contributions made by the company and its subsidiaries in the year. There is no threshold for these disclosures. [SI 2008/410 7 Sch 4(2)].

Company that is a wholly owned subsidiary of a UK parent

2.120 A wholly owned subsidiary of a company incorporated in the UK does not have to disclose its donations, expenditure or contributions in its own directors' report, but these must be disclosed by its holding company (as mentioned above).

2.121 An example of disclosure of political donations is given in Table 2.11.

Table 2.11 – Political donations

Rolls-Royce Holdings plc – Report and Accounts – 31 December 2014

Other statutory information (extract)

Political donations

The Group's policy is not to make political donations and therefore did not donate any money to any political party during the year.

However, it is possible that certain activities undertaken by the Group may unintentionally fall within the broad scope of the provisions contained in the Companies Act 2006 (the Act). The resolution to be proposed at the AGM is to ensure that the Group does not commit any technical breach of the Act.

During the year, expenses incurred by Rolls-Royce North America Inc. in providing administrative support for the Rolls-Royce North America Political Action Committee (RRNAPAC) was US$52,690 (2013: US$69,430). PACs are a common feature of the US political system and are governed by the Federal Election Campaign Act.

The PAC is independent of the Group and independent of any political party. The PAC funds are contributed voluntarily by employees and the Company cannot affect how they are applied, although under US Law, the business expenses are paid by the Company. Such contributions do not require authorisation by shareholders under the Companies Act 2006 and therefore do not count towards the limits for political donations and expenditure for which shareholder approval will be sought at this year's AGM to renew the authority given at the 2014 AGM.

Statement on disclosure of information to the auditors

2.122 The directors' report must contain a statement to confirm, for all directors in office at the time when the report is approved, the following:

- So far as each director is aware, there is no relevant audit information of which the company's auditors are unaware. Relevant information is defined as *"information needed by the company's auditor in connection with preparing his report"*.

- Each director has taken all the steps that he ought to have taken in his duty as a director in order to make himself aware of any relevant audit information and to establish that the company's auditor is aware of that information.

Steps that a director ought to have taken would include making enquiries of other directors and the auditor, and any other steps required by the director's duty to exercise due care, skill and diligence.

[CA06 Sec 418(1)–(4)].

2.123 Table 2.12 gives an example of disclosure.

Table 2.12 – Statement on disclosure to auditors

Diageo plc – Report and accounts – 30 June 2014

DIRECTORS' REPORT (extract)

Disclosure of information to the auditor

The Directors who held office at the date of approval of this Directors' report confirm that, so far as they are each aware, there is no relevant audit information of which the company's auditor is unaware; and each director has taken all reasonable steps to ascertain any relevant audit information and to ensure that the company's auditor is aware of that information.

2.124 In determining the extent of each director's duty, the following considerations are relevant:

- The knowledge, skill and experience that may reasonably be expected of a person carrying out the functions of the company director.

- The knowledge, skill and experience that the director actually has.

[CA06 Sec 174].

2.125 The penalty for 'knowingly or recklessly' making a false statement in this regard, and failing to take reasonable steps to prevent the directors' report being approved, could be imprisonment or a fine, or both, for each director indicted. [CA06 Sec 418(5)(6)].

Re-appointment of auditors

2.126 It is customary, but not a statutory requirement, to state at the end of the directors' report that a resolution will be put to the general meeting, regarding the appointment or re-appointment of the auditors.

Controlling shareholder

2.127 LR 9.8.4R requires disclosures in respect of contracts and independence agreements with a controlling shareholder. For the requirements on the placement of these disclosures, see paragraph 2.15.1.

2.127.1 A 'controlling shareholder' is defined in the Listing Rules as any person who exercises or controls, on their own or together with any person with whom they are acting in concert, 30% or more of the votes able to be cast on all or substantially all matters at general meetings of the company. For the purposes of calculating voting rights, some voting rights are disregarded; these fall into the following categories (but the disregard is subject to conditions which are not described here):

- Voting rights exercised as bare trustee, investment manager, collective investment undertaking or long-term insurer.

- Voting rights held in relation to the business of underwriting the sale or issue of securities, placing securities (where committed to acquiring unplaced securities), and acquiring securities pursuant to an agreement to procure third party purchases of securities.

[LR 6.1.2A].

Contracts with a controlling shareholder

2.128 The annual report should include particulars of any contract of significance between the company (or one of its subsidiary undertakings) and a controlling shareholder subsisting during the year. [LR 9.8.4R(10)(b)]. For this purpose, a 'contract of significance' is one which is determined in accordance with the rules set out in paragraph 2.82. An example is given in Table 2.13 below. In the example, the company cross-refers from the directors' report to the notes to the financial statements, where extensive disclosure of contracts with the controlling shareholder is provided.

2.129 In addition, the annual report should disclose details of any contract with a controlling shareholder (as defined above) to provide services to the company or to one of its subsidiaries (see Table 2.13). This information is not required if the shareholder is providing services that it normally provides as part of its principal business and it is not a contract of significance that is required to be disclosed. [LR 9.8.4R(11)].

Table 2.13 – Contract with a controlling shareholder

Xstrata plc – Annual Report – 31 December 2012

Directors' report (extract)
Significant contractual arrangements (extract)

Glencore International AG is Xstrata's major shareholder and, at the date of this document, holds 33.65% of Xstrata's issued share capital. A Relationship Agreement regulates the relationship between Xstrata and Glencore to ensure all commercial arrangements are transacted on an arm's-length basis. Glencore is the sole distributor of Xstrata's nickel, cobalt and ferronickel production, has sales agreements with Xstrata Copper for some of its copper concentrate and copper cathode and is the marketing agent for much of Xstrata Alloys' ferrochrome and vanadium. Glencore has a market advisory role with Xstrata Coal. Full details of related party contractual arrangements are provided in note 35 of the financial statements.

Independence of a controlling shareholder

2.129.1   The annual report should include disclosures about the independence agreements with controlling shareholders.

2.129.2   Where a listed company has a controlling shareholder, it is required to have in place at all times a written and legally binding agreement which is intended to ensure that the controlling shareholder complies with the independence provisions set out in LR 6.1.4D. The annual report should include a board statement that:

- The company has entered into such an agreement as required or, if not, the FCA has been notified of the company's non-compliance, together with a brief description of the background and reasons for non-compliance, to enable the shareholders to evaluate its impact.

- The company has complied with the agreement's independence provisions during the period.

- As far as the company is aware, the controlling shareholder (or any of its associates) has complied with the agreement's independence provisions during the period.

- As far as the company is aware, where a signing controlling shareholder has undertaken to procure the compliance of a non-signing controlling shareholder, the signing controlling shareholder has complied with its procurement obligation during the period.

- Where an agreement's independence provision or procurement obligation has not been complied with during the period, the FCA has been so notified, together with a brief description of the background and reasons for non-compliance, to enable the shareholders to evaluate its impact.

[LR 9.8.4R(14)].

2.129.2.1   Table 2.14 is an example of such a statement.

Table 2.14 – Relationship agreement with controlling shareholder

Exova Group plc – Annual report – 31 December 2014

Corporate governance (extract)
Letter from the Chairman (extract)

In conjunction with the IPO, the Company and TABASCO B.V. (formerly Exova Group B.V.), the Company's principal shareholder and the holding company which is owned by CD&R Fund VII L.P., entered into a Relationship Agreement to ensure that the Company and its subsidiaries are capable of carrying on business independently of TABASCO B.V. and its associates and that transactions with them are at arm's length and on normal commercial terms.

Directors' report (extract)

Relationship Agreement

On 10 April 2014, the Company and TABASCO B.V., the holding company which is wholly owned by CD&R Fund VII L.P. and the Company's principal shareholder (holding 54% of the issued share capital as at 31 December 2014), entered into a Relationship Agreement, regulating the ongoing relationship between the Company and CD&R. The principal purpose of the Relationship Agreement is to ensure that the Company and its subsidiaries are capable of carrying on their business independently of TABASCO B.V. and its Associates (as defined in the Listing Rules), that transactions and relationships with TABASCO B.V. or any of its Associates (including any transactions and relationships with any member of the Group) are at arm's length and on normal commercial terms, and that the reputation and commercial interests of the Company are maintained. The Relationship Agreement with TABASCO B.V. will continue for so long as (i) the Company's shares are listed on the premium listing segment of the Official List and traded on the London Stock Exchange's main market for listed securities; and (ii) TABASCO B.V. together with its Associates hold, in aggregate, 10% or more of the issued share capital of the Company. Under the Relationship Agreement, TABASCO B.V. is able to appoint two Non-Executive Directors to the Board for so long as it and its Associates hold, in aggregate

---

25% or more of the issued share capital of the Company and one Non-Executive Director to the Board if they hold, in aggregate 10% or more, but less than 25% of the issued share capital of the Company. The first such appointee is Christian Rochat. A second appointment will not be made while Fred Kindle remains a Director. During the period from 10 April 2014 to 31 December 2014 the Company complied and, so far as the Company is aware, TABASCO B.V. and its Associates complied with the independence provisions and procurement obligations included in the Relationship Agreement.

2.129.3 Where an independent director declines to support the statement that the company has entered into such an agreement and is compliant with its provisions (and, as far as it is aware, the controlling shareholder is also compliant), that fact should be included in the board's statement. [LR 9.8.4A].

Change of name

2.130 A company can change its name either during the financial year or after the year end. Although there are no specific disclosure requirements set out in law, it is convention and best practice that an explanation of the change of name is given in the directors' report, whether the change of name occurred before or after the year end. The financial statements and reports should be in the new name, followed by the words 'formerly (old name)'. The name should also be stated this way on the front of the financial statements (and at the top of each page, if the company's name is stated there).

Special business

2.131 Holders of listed equity shares who are sent a notice of a meeting that is to occur on the same day as an AGM, which includes business that is considered not to be routine business of an AGM, must be provided with an explanation in the directors' report of such business, unless an explanatory circular accompanies the notice. [LR 13.8.8R(1)].

Approval and signing of directors' report and strategic report

2.132 The board of directors must formally approve the directors' report and the strategic report, and the reports must be signed on behalf of the board by a director or the secretary of the company. [CA06 Secs 414D(1), 419(1)].

2.133 Every copy of the directors' report and the strategic report that is laid before the company in general meeting, or that is otherwise circulated, published or issued, must state the name of the person who signed it on behalf of the board. [CA06 Sec 433(1)–(3)]. A copy of the directors' report and strategic report that are to be delivered to the Registrar of Companies must also be signed on behalf of the board by a director or the secretary of the company. [CA06 Sec 447].

Liability for contravention

2.134 Every person who was a director of the company at the end of the period within which the company's financial statements must be laid before the company in general meeting and delivered to the Registrar of Companies may be guilty of an offence if the directors' report or strategic report fails to comply with the Act's requirements. This offence is punishable by a fine. [CA06 Secs 414A(5), 414D(2)(3), 415(4)(5), 419(3)(4)].

2.135 It is a defence in such a situation for a director to prove that he took all reasonable steps to ensure that the directors' report and strategic report complied with all of the Act's requirements. [CA06 Secs 414A(5), 414D(2), 415(4), 419(3)].

2.136 Also, where the company does not comply with the requirements for the approval and signing of the directors' report and strategic report (as set out in paras 2.132 and 2.133), the company and every officer of it who is in default will be guilty of an offence and liable to a fine. [CA06 Secs 419(4), 433(5)].

Directors' liability: safe harbour

2.137 The Act contains a statutory liability regime for directors in respect of narrative reporting. [CA06 Sec 463]. This effectively incorporates a 'safe harbour' for information in the directors' report, strategic report and directors' remuneration report. A director is not subject to any liability to a person other than the company resulting from reliance, by that person or another, on information in such a report. A director is liable to compensate the company for any loss suffered by it as a result of any untrue or misleading statement in such a report, or the omission from such a report of anything required to be included in it. But the director is liable only if he knew the statement to be untrue or misleading, or was reckless as to whether it was untrue or misleading, or he knew the omission to be dishonest concealment of a material fact. An explicit statement is not required in the annual report for the 'safe harbour' protection to be invoked.

2.138 The 'safe harbour' applies to the reports described above. BIS has indicated that it extends to information cross-referenced from those reports to other parts of the annual report. So 'safe harbour' will cover, for example, separate voluntary narrative reporting outside those reports, provided that cross-referencing from them to the other parts of the annual report is explicitly provided. But the 'safe harbour' does not extend to information placed outside the annual report, even if the annual report contains a cross-reference to it.

2.138.1 BIS has expressed concern that, contrary to the intention of the legislation, the overly cautious might place inappropriately large volumes of information, over and above that required to meet a specific legal requirement, in the reports covered by the 'safe harbour' provision. BIS has stated that, should this manifest itself in such a way that it detracts from clear and concise reporting, it might revisit the operation of the 'safe harbour' provision in the future.

Position of the auditor

2.139 The auditors are required to state in their report whether, in their opinion, *"the information given in the strategic report and directors' report for the financial year for which the accounts are prepared is consistent with those accounts"*. [CA06 Sec 496]. Auditors' responsibilities, in respect of the requirement for an entity applying the UK Corporate Governance Code that the annual report as a whole is 'fair, balanced and understandable', are considered in chapter 4.

2.140 Auditors have a statutory responsibility to review the directors' report for consistency with the financial statements. This approach is supported by the Auditing Practices Board's ISA (UK&I) 720B, 'The auditor's statutory reporting responsibility in relation to directors' reports (2009)', and by APB Bulletin 2010/02, 'Compendium of Illustrative Auditor's Reports on United Kingdom Private Sector Financial Statements for periods ending on or after 15 December 2010 (Revised)'.

2.141 Auditors also have a statutory responsibility to review the strategic report for consistency with the financial statements. ISA (UK&I) 720B deals specifically with the auditor's statutory reporting responsibility in relation to directors' reports, and it requires the auditor to read the information in the directors' report and assess whether it is consistent with the financial statements. At the time of writing, ISA (UK&I) 720B has not been updated to include the strategic report. But the Financial Reporting Council's Bulletin 4, 'Recent Developments in Company Law, The Listing Rules and Auditing Standards that affect United Kingdom Auditor's Reports (Revised)', explains that, when reporting on the strategic report, the auditor applies the requirements and other explanatory material in ISA (UK&I) 720B to the extent that they are applicable to the strategic report.

2.141.1 Section A of ISA (UK&I) 720 (Revised October 2012) deals with the auditor's responsibility for other information in documents containing audited financial statements, so it covers both the strategic report and the directors' report. This responsibility includes reading the other information to identify any information that is apparently materially incorrect, based on, or materially inconsistent with, the knowledge acquired by the auditor in the course of performing the audit.

2.142 The auditor should seek to resolve any inconsistencies identified between the information in the 'front half' (including the directors' report and the strategic report) and the financial statements. If a material inconsistency between them is not resolved, details should be provided in the audit report. In addition, a qualified or adverse opinion would be necessary where an amendment that is necessary to the financial statements has not been made.

2.143 ISA (UK&I) 720B confirms that the information given in the directors' report includes information that is included by way of a cross-reference to other information presented separately from the directors' report. [ISA (UK&I) 720B para 3].

Enforcement

2.144   The Financial Reporting Council's Conduct Committee is responsible for ensuring that both public and large private companies comply with relevant reporting requirements, including the directors' report and strategic report. For this purpose, the Conduct Committee maintains a Financial Reporting Review Panel (FRRP), which considers cases of alleged non-compliance on behalf of the Conduct Committee. The Secretary of State (through Companies House) is responsible for enforcement in respect of other companies. [Companies (Audit, Investigation and Community Enterprise) Act 2004 Sec 14].

2.145   Under the enforcement regime in respect of defective accounts, a company can be required to revise its directors' report or strategic report if they do not comply with the Act's requirements. In cases of non-compliance, the Conduct Committee has the power, if necessary, to go to court to compel a company to revise its reports. Practice Notes issued by the FRRP include Practice Note 130 (discussed in para 2.28 onwards).

Chapter 3

Strategic report

Chapter 3

Strategic report

Introduction and legal framework

3.1   This chapter deals with the voluntary and good practice corporate reporting that is often set out in the front section ('front half') of an entity's annual report. This narrative reporting has been known by many names, including 'operating and financial review', 'business review' and 'management's discussion and analysis'. The Companies Act 2006 (Strategic Report and Directors' Report) Regulations 2013 require all entities (other than small entities) to prepare a strategic report.

3.2   Section 414C of the Companies Act 2006 ('the Act') requires a strategic report to contain:

■   A fair, balanced and comprehensive review of the development and performance of the company's business during the financial year, and its position at the end of the year. Large companies should include both financial and non-financial key performance indicators (KPIs) in their review; medium-sized companies do not need to include non-financial KPIs.

■   A description of the principal risks and uncertainties facing the company.

3.3   Quoted companies should also disclose a description of their strategy and business model, and information concerning the environment, employees, social issues and gender diversity. The legal requirements for a strategic report are further described in chapter 2.

3.4   To assist directors in preparing a strategic report, the FRC has released non-mandatory guidance. This guidance aims not only to encourage preparers to consider how the strategic report fits within the annual report as a whole, but also to enhance the quality of narrative reporting more generally.

[The next paragraph is 3.6.]

3.6   This chapter considers best practice in narrative reporting as it might be applied by a quoted company preparing a strategic report. It draws on the FRC's guidance, which is written with quoted companies in mind. As a description of best practice, the chapter might be relevant to unquoted companies. However, many unquoted companies might find the levels of disclosure described in this chapter excessive, in view of the Act's requirement for much of the information in a strategic report to be given 'to the extent necessary for an understanding of the development, performance or position of the company's business' and the specific references to 'quoted companies' in some of the requirements. Reference should be made instead to chapter 6 (available online), which sets out the requirements applicable to unquoted companies.

3.7   The following PwC publications provide additional guidance to companies on preparing a strategic report:

Title of publication	Description
Practical guide to corporate reporting – Narrative reporting changes 2013 – Implementing the strategic report	This guide provides a practical overview of reporting in line with the new regulatory requirements of the strategic report. It also offers a clear insight into the spirit of the regulations and into new directors' report requirements.
Implementing integrated reporting	This practical guide containing advice and steps to follow, is for anyone looking to implement a more holistic business management system or integrated reporting.
Guide to forward-looking information – Don't fear the future: communicating with confidence	This guide provides practical guidance on how the reporting of forward-looking information can be achieved, together with examples from progressive companies, both in the UK and elsewhere, that are already forward-looking in their narrative reporting.
Guide to key performance indicators – Communicating the measures that matter	This practical publication has been developed to highlight the increasing demand for reporting of key performance indicators (KPIs). It addresses many of the questions posed by these demands; and a collection of examples, drawn from the UK and elsewhere, demonstrates good reporting of KPIs.
Report Leadership: Tomorrow's reporting today	This brochure provides a framework, strategic thinking and practical ideas for improving the content of annual reports, including the narrative section.
Integrated reporting: What does your reporting say about you?	This paper sets out the information that can help to present a cohesive and persuasive picture of a business, including the way it is managed and governed.
12 Reporting Tips	These tips give simple actions and examples of best practice to make company reporting more accessible and to ensure effective communication.

All of these publications are available at www.pwc.com/corporatereporting, where further examples of good narrative reporting can be found. The publications are located in the 'Guides and good practice' section. Many examples of narrative reporting are available at inform.pwc.com.

Good practice reporting

3.8 Accompanying narrative reporting – that explains the entity's performance, cash flows and financial position in the context of its objectives, strategies and future prospects – can be very helpful to users of financial statements. Financial statements are mainly backward-looking, reflecting what has already happened. Although they give important information, particularly in judging the quality of management's stewardship, they do not fully explain why the entity performed as it did or what is likely to happen next.

3.9 The global financial crisis has raised questions about the adequacy of corporate reporting in its broadest sense. Investors want to know what the entity does and how it has performed; but they also want to know whether that performance is sustainable, given the risks and market conditions that face the entity. Our ongoing research programme has shown that investors often have insufficient contextual and non-financial information to enable them to model future cash flows. Good narrative reporting is intended to fill the gap between the information provided by financial statements and the information sought by investors.

3.10 In recent years, narrative reporting has been viewed as increasingly important, providing an opportunity to present integrated and comprehensive information about an entity to the capital markets and other user groups. The strategic report gives management an opportunity to present a complete picture of the entity to the outside world. Management needs to consider whether its external communications describe fairly and comprehensively the entity's value (however measured) and its ability to increase that value. Investors need to know how the entity and its management are organised, and the actions they will take, to ensure that value-creation actually happens.

3.11   The corporate reporting agenda is broadening. In 'Tomorrow's corporate reporting' (the May 2011 report of a collaborative research study undertaken by the Chartered Institute of Management Accountants, the UK firm of PwC and the London-based think-tank Tomorrow's Company), Prof Mervyn E. King states:

> *"The world has accepted that people, planet and profit are inextricably intertwined, and nowhere was this better illustrated that in July last year in London, when the International Integrated Reporting Committee was formed. The disparate bodies sitting around the table, such as A4S, GRI, the FASB of America, IASB, IFAC, IOSCO, WWF, Big Four etc., established within one hour an identity of purpose, namely that financial reporting was not sufficient to make an informed assessment about the sustainability of a business in the new economy. It was accepted that the annual report had to be an integrated one, that is one where there is a holistic representation of the financial and non-financial performance of the company. In short how the financial impacted on the non-financial and vice-versa."*

Integrated reporting – an overview

3.12   Effective reporting presents information about an entity in a logical and connected way. Where this information is presented externally, it answers the questions that investors want answered and excludes information that is irrelevant. The type of information and the method of presentation will vary between entities, depending on the nature and organisation of the business. For example, businesses comprising various segments should explain the objectives, strategy, performance and risks for each segment.

3.13   Effective reporting integrates the information presented by linking the various pieces of information together, so that the user gains an understanding of the entity as a whole. There are various ways in which this integration can be achieved. An integrated approach connects not just the various elements of the narrative reporting, but also the information in the financial statements with the 'front half'. So, for example, the explanation of performance in the strategic report should be linked to the performance statements in the financial statements.

3.14   Integrated reporting should seek to answer the following questions (by segment, where appropriate):

- What is the nature of the entity's business? In which industries does the entity operate? (See para 3.100 onwards.)

- What are the entity's objectives? What are the entity's strategies for achieving its objectives? (See para 3.71 onwards.)

- What is the entity's business model? How does the entity create value? (See para 3.86 onwards.)

- What are the resources and relationships that are essential to the achievement of those objectives? (See para 3.91 onwards.)

- How does the entity measure the extent to which it has achieved its objectives? (See para 3.125 onwards.)

- How has the entity performed in the current year compared with the objectives that it set in previous periods? (See para 3.82 onwards.)

- Is that performance sustainable? What are the risks that will affect the sustainability of the performance? To what extent is the performance based on recurring transactions or 'one-off' events? (See para 3.108 onwards.)

- What are the entity's future prospects? What will the entity do to ensure that it meets its objectives? What constraints exist that might hamper the entity's plans? (See para 3.73 onwards.)

3.15   The model in the diagram below highlights the scope of the information set that, in our view, entities need to have at their disposal if they are to be on top of the dynamics of a modern business. For entities to build trust with their stakeholders, they must communicate clear and focused management thought processes to the outside world. These communications are at the heart of strategic reporting.

Strategic report

Integrated reporting model

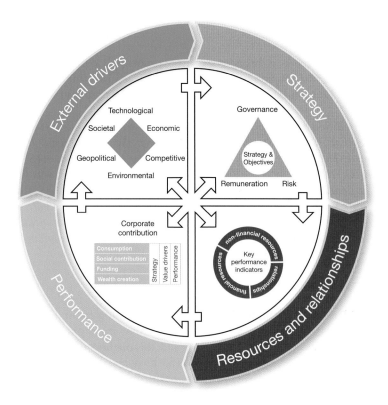

External drivers
■ Management's capability to understand and explain external market drivers is fundamental to effective decision-making and reporting.
■ The credit crunch and subsequent economic downturn have highlighted the need for entities to understand, monitor, manage and explain emerging risks and opportunities.
■ Processes must capture macro, competitive, regulatory and political factors shaping the market place, as well as changing societal expectations.
■ An understanding of sustainability 'mega trends', and their impact on the business model, will shed light on risks and opportunities.

Strategy
■ A clear strategy is fundamental to business success, and so it should underpin reporting.
■ Effective strategies are developed in the context of market drivers and are aligned with the core competencies of the resources and relationships of the business.
■ Strategic priorities should be clearly aligned with remuneration policies and the risks assumed.
■ An understanding of the culture/values and governance practices is increasingly important to determine how a strategy is embedded into the entity and the entity's attitude towards risk in pursuing strategic success.

Resources and relationships
■ Greater collaboration between businesses within the value chain means that an understanding of the scope of the business model is key.
■ Access to natural capital in a resource-constrained world will have profound implications for how business is carried out. The relative importance of resources (financial, human and natural capital) and relationships (such as customers, employees and suppliers) will flex, depending on changing market dynamics and strategies.

- Information on the relative strength of resources and relationships (and how they are being managed, developed and protected) is critical.

- This information should go beyond qualitative statements to a clear set of KPIs.

Performance

- The outputs of corporate activity need to be added to the other three categories in the integrated information set, in order to complete the picture.

- Financial performance is currently the dominant output, and it will remain critical, but we expect other outputs to play an increasingly significant role.

- Society's changing expectations will demand a more balanced assessment of corporate contribution. Resource consumption, wealth creation and wealth distribution, for example, can provide real insight into long-term sustainability of a business.

3.16 The suggested model provides a logical structure for thinking about the information needs of a business, as well as the critical links and interdependencies that exist between the various information sets – external, strategic, business and performance. The model is grounded in over 15 years of PwC research and work with investors and entities.

3.17 The model's insight and value become apparent when each category is considered in the context of another, rather than in isolation. The model succeeds when governance interfaces with remuneration and risk; when strategy is designed to exploit a changing market environment; and when strategic priorities align with key performance indicators (KPIs). It is this joined-up thinking that is so critical and that lies at the heart of the model.

3.18 Increasingly, a number of key dynamics influence strategy and the way in which businesses operate. These factors also change the information that management needs in order to make effective decisions, as well as the external reporting needed to meet the expectations of both society and shareholders. These dynamics include:

- *Macro trends*: Emerging issues – such as climate change, resource scarcity and demographics – all mean that the business environment is becoming more challenging and more intrusive. This results in a changed 'licence to operate' for business; that is, one driven more by the balance between consumption and contribution, fairness, trust and integrity.

- *Technological advancements*: The reporting environment is becoming more 'demand-pull' than 'supply-push'. This has clear benefits for entities that can collate a clear, consistent and integrated information set, and that use this consistently when tailoring their communications for different audiences.

3.18.1 In response to these and other dynamics, we expect businesses to be more collaborative in the development of business solutions. In this more integrated world, the ability to build and maintain key business relationships will be critical to long-term success, and insightful intelligence will become a 'must-have' capability.

3.19 The four core categories in our model are common to all industries and entities, but their relative importance (and the information that sits beneath each category) will need to flex, depending on how these dynamics impact industries and influence corporate strategies and business/operating models.

3.20 The model is consistent with the strategic report framework (see Table 3.15).

3.21 The International Integrated Reporting Council (IIRC) have developed their own voluntary IR framework to provide guidance to entities on the practicalities of producing an integrated report. The guidance has a range of guiding principles and content elements that govern the overall content of an integrated report, and explain the fundamental concepts that underpin them. The framework is consistent with Strategic report regulations.

3.22 Central to all discussions of integrated reporting is the emphasis placed on integrated thinking – internal processes and performance data to guide and support the external disclosures made.

FRC guidance on the strategic report

Scope and definitions

3.23 The FRC's guidance on the strategic report (referred to in this chapter as 'SR guidance') has been written with quoted companies in mind, but applies to any entity that prepares a strategic report. [SR guidance para 2.3].

3.24 The term 'quoted company' is defined in the Companies Act 2006 as a company whose equity share capital:

■ has been included in the official list in accordance with the provisions of Part VI of the Financial Services and Markets Act 2000;

■ is officially listed in an EEA State; or

■ is admitted to dealing on either the New York Stock Exchange or the exchange known as NASDAQ.

[CA06 Sec 385].

3.25 This means, for instance, that entities traded on AIM (and other public entities that are not 'quoted', as defined in the Act) are not required to produce a strategic report; nor are large private entities. However, many such entities can voluntarily prepare one.

Approach adopted by the FRC

3.26 The FRC guidance sets out a number of principles that directors should follow in preparing a strategic report, as well as the key content elements of a disclosure framework that directors should address.

Objective

3.27 The purpose of a strategic report is to enable the entity's shareholders to assess how the directors have performed their duty to promote the success of the entity for their collective benefit. [CA06 Sec 414C(1)].

3.27.1 The strategic report has three principal content-related objectives, which are to provide:

■ insight into the entity's business model and its main strategy and objectives;

■ a description of the principal risks that the entity faces and how they might affect its future prospects; and

■ an analysis of the entity's past performance.

[SR guidance para 4.6].

3.27.2 These objectives are consistent with the overarching legal requirements set out in paragraph 3.2 above.

3.28 To gain an appreciation of the overall position of the business, users need to be able to navigate the strategic report. Indeed, the FRC guidance states that the strategic report should provide signposting to show the location of supporting detail. Helpful navigation ensures that readers can find the information they need. A clear table of contents and an index, use of colour-coded sections or tabs, and clarity in headings and sub-headings will all help to achieve this. Entities can also repeat information, or provide cross-referencing to other areas of the report, to provide context, and they can use box-outs to highlight key issues or figures. In Table 3.1, ICAP plc uses a ten-point overview of its business at the front of its annual report; its business is specialised, and these explanations and clear diagrams assist the reader's understanding. Some of the ten points are shown here.

Table 3.1 – Navigation of the annual report

ICAP plc – Annual report – 31 March 2010

ICAP in ten (extract)

Welcome to ICAP in 10

ICAP is the world's premier voice and electronic interdealer broker and provider of post trade risk and information services.

In this section we provide a ten-point overview of ICAP, what we do and how we have performed.

Strategic report

Electronic and voice broking

An interdealer broker draws together willingness to buy and sell in wholesale markets. ICAP uses voice broking or electronic networks to bring these buyers and sellers together, facilitating price discovery and receiving a commission when a transaction is entered into. In many of the markets where ICAP operates, voice brokers help to create liquidity and facilitate the price discovery process. This is particularly important in non-standardised, bespoke markets where the number of parties willing to enter certain transactions may be limited. In more standardised markets with higher and more frequent participation, such as spot FX and government bonds, ICAP operates electronic broking platforms. ICAP's combined solution offers access to markets across all asset classes and levels of liquidity.

ICAP

- Voice broking
- Electronic broking
- Post trade risk

Post trade risk

ICAP also provides a range of post trade risk services to help its customers reduce operational and systemic risk in their markets. This increases their capacity, reduces their costs and creates new trading opportunities, which in turn benefits ICAP. As regulatory and market demand for such products and services increases, ICAP expects this business to grow.

Customer A
Customer A is interested in selling certain securities and contracts to dealer 1

Dealer 1
Dealer 1 places a sell order with ICAP

Dealer 2
The dealer who buys the securities will in turn sell them on to a customer

Customer B
Customer B buys the securities from dealer 2

04

ICAP in ten

3

What we do

ICAP is the world's premier voice and electronic interdealer broker and provider of post trade risk and information services. The Group is active in the wholesale markets in interest rates, credit, commodities, FX, emerging markets and equity derivatives.

Read more on page 24

ICAP in ten

5

Our strategic goals

 Read more
on page 19

ICAP's strategic goals are clear. We want to be:

→ the leading global intermediary;

→ the leading post trade risk provider; and

→ the main infrastructure provider to the world's wholesale financial markets.

We aim to have at least 35% of overall interdealer market revenues and to generate operating profit evenly distributed between voice broking, electronic broking and post trade risk and information.

There are three components to our strategy:

→ the expansion of our leading voice broking business;

→ the growth of our global electronic broking business both through increasing volumes of existing products and by developing new markets; and

→ the development of our post trade risk and information businesses to provide innovative services that enable our customers to reduce their costs and risks and to increase their efficiency, return on capital and capacity to process trades.

6
How we measure our progress

7
How we have performed

9
How we are rewarded

8
Managing risk

3.28.1 Some entitles have adopted the approach of having a quick reference section at the front of their reporting, in order to highlight the key themes of the report, to draw out key messages and to improve navigation. In table 3.1.1, Meggitt has structured its section around the key questions the report looks to answer for the reader.

Table 3.1.1 – Quick reference guide

Meggitt plc – Annual report 31 December 2014

Quick reference

What is Meggitt?	How did we perform in 2014?
○02	○04 ○31

What is our strategy and business model?	What are our markets and what drives them?
○06 ○08	○10

How do we manage risk?	What are our key performance indicators?
○24	○27

How do we perform as corporate citizens?	Who runs Meggitt and how do we reward them?
○38	○44 ○55

3.28.2 Entities have the option to produce the strategic report as a stand-alone document. If they choose to do this, management should consider what additional information to include, that might not be part of the annual report version, because shareholders might be making decisions on it alone.

3.28.3 It would be hard to argue against the need to include information on corporate governance and remuneration, and we would strongly advocate the inclusion of GAAP financial information.

3.28.4 ARM Holdings have produced a stand-alone strategic report and a separate governance and financials report – taken together, they form the annual report. The contents of both reports can be seen in Table 3.1.2. The strategic report includes financial and governance information, as well as a summary remuneration report.

Table 3.1.2

WELCOME TO OUR STRATEGIC REPORT

ARM's Annual Report is in two parts. The Strategic Report contains information about the Group, how we make money and how we run the business. It includes our strategy, business model, markets and key performance indicators, as well as our approach to governance, sustainability and risk management, and a summary of our financial management.

A copy of the Governance and Financial Report can be downloaded from www.arm.com/reporting2013.

The Governance and Financial Report contains the details about how we run the business and remunerate management, and how we organise ourselves financially.

Online you can find more information about our end markets, including case studies about how our technology is used in our customers' products. A more detailed Corporate Responsibility report is also available online.

STRATEGIC REPORT

Our Vision

GOVERNANCE AND FINANCIAL REPORT

Governance

ONLINE REPORTING

Front cover

Most major population centres are covered by 3G or 4G networks, and there were more than two billion smartphones and tablets connecting to the internet in 2013. With some mobile computers now costing as little as $35, many more people can afford to buy a smart device. An entry-level mobile computer may have up to four ARM®-based chips.

Downloads

More information about ARM and our end market opportunities are available on our web site.

Reports available online:

- Strategic Report
- Governance and Financial Report
- Corporate Responsibility report

www.arm.com/reporting2013

Principles

3.29 The FRC's guidance on the strategic report adopts a principles-based approach. The following seven communication principles are established, to provide guidance on the qualitative characteristics of the disclosures in a strategic report:

1. The strategic report should be fair, balanced and understandable. (See para 3.30 onwards.)

2. The strategic report should be comprehensive but concise. (See para 3.37 onwards.)

3. Where appropriate, information in the strategic report should have a forward-looking orientation. (See para 3.45 onwards.)

4. The strategic report should provide information that is entity-specific. (See para 3.53 onwards.)

5. The strategic report should highlightand explain linkages between pieces of information presented within the strategic report and in the annual report more broadly. (See para 3.58 onwards.)

6. The structure and presentation of the strategic report should be reviewed annually to ensure that it continues to meet its objectives in an efficient and effective manner. (See para 3.64 onwards.)

7. The content of the strategic report should be reviewed annually to ensure that it continues to be relevant in the current period. (See para 3.65.1 onwards.)

Principle 1 – Fair, balanced and understandable

3.30 This principle states that *"The strategic report should be fair, balanced and understandable"*. [SR guidance para 6.2]. The strategic report should address the positive and negative aspects of the development, performance, position and future prospects of the entity without bias. The directors should ensure that shareholders are not misled as a result of the presentation of, or emphasis given to, information in the strategic report, or by the omission of material information from it. [SR guidance para 6.3].

3.30.1 The compound term 'fair, balanced and understandable' comes from provision C.1.1 of the UK Corporate Governance Code, which requires the directors to make a statement that *"they consider the annual report and accounts, taken as a whole, is fair, balanced and understandable and provides the information necessary for shareholders to assess the company's position and performance, business model and strategy"*. See chapter 4 for guidance on the meaning of the term and how the directors can choose to support this statement.

3.30.2 The Code requires the annual report, taken as a whole, to be fair, balanced and understandable. This same principle should apply to the strategic report, particularly where it is issued separately from the annual report, so that shareholders are not potentially misled.

3.31 It is unrealistic to highlight only the positives when, for example, the entity's profitability has declined. Worse still, doing so could give the impression that management has not focused on a strategic plan for improving performance. Investors want to know which parts of the business have experienced difficulties, and they want to know what management's plans are for improving the position. The strategic report should discuss current year performance against target, highlighting good and bad performance. The principle of providing balanced and neutral analysis should also be observed when providing forward-looking information. Investors need to know the challenges that management sees as likely to affect future performance. For an example of a chairman's statement that balances positive and negative aspects of the business, see Table 3.2. The chairman's statement is not explicitly required in the strategic report but, in practice, entities generally choose to retain it.

Table 3.2 – Positive and negative aspects of the business

Xchanging plc – Annual report and accounts – 31 December 2010

We expect 2011 to be a year of transition for the company.

2010 was a difficult year, characterised by performance issues with parts of the Cambridge business and a weak economic background in our principal markets.

In 2010, revenue increased by 4%. Underlying operating profit was £67.3 million (FY 2009: £63.9 million), helped by contract settlements and consultancy income totalling £11.8 million (FY 2009 £8.0 million). In addition, exceptional items totalling £112.5 million have been recorded, including an impairment provision against goodwill arising from the Cambridge acquisition. The operating cash flow of the year was similar to 2009 and the net cash balance of £24.8 million at the year end was slightly higher than at the end of 2009 (£22.1 million).

Cambridge
Cambridge was purchased at the beginning of 2009 and the results to date, particularly in the American workers' compensation and ITO businesses, have been very disappointing. The business in India is performing well. The results from the Australian and the other Asian businesses have been mixed but do provide a platform for the future. The acquisition has been costly in terms of profitability, cash flow and management distraction. A plan is underway to resolve the major issues as quickly as possible.

Board changes
In October, Richard Houghton stood down from the Board and his role as Chief Financial Officer (CFO), and Ken Lever was appointed his successor.

On 9 February, we announced that David Andrews had decided to step down from the Board and his role as Chief Executive Officer (CEO) with immediate effect. As David was the founder and successful creator of Xchanging as a business, I am delighted he has agreed to take on a new role as Senior Adviser to me, to support Xchanging's business development initiatives.

We have begun the search for David's successor as CEO. Whilst this is ongoing, Ken Lever will be acting CEO in addition to his responsibilities as CFO, and I will support him as Executive Chairman.

Our people
It is in difficult circumstances that we recognise the strength and resolve of our people, our most valuable resource. The last few weeks have been challenging but I am confident that our employees have the determination to meet these challenges and to put Xchanging back on the path to becoming the global business processor of choice.

Our customers
Xchanging's strength is based on unrelenting attention to customer service. We have been reassured by the continued support of all of our customers and partners during 2010 and look forward to building on these relationships in 2011.

Liquidity
The Group's liquidity and cash position remain sound and cash generation will be a primary focus in the coming year.

Dividend
Shareholders will be disappointed by our decision not to declare a dividend in respect of 2010. However, we want to conserve our cash resources in the business for the changes we are effecting in 2011 and to fund the growth opportunities we see. We will review this again at the end of the year.

Action plan
We have developed a four-part action plan to overhaul our entire business, seeking value creation through regenerated profitable revenue growth and cash flow improvement. Where value is best created through disposal, we will pursue this option. The first part of our plan, a fundamental value assessment of our entire business, is complete, and we have already started taking specific action. We will report on progress at the half year. There will be costs associated with any such restructuring but we believe this will put the company in a better position to resume growth in 2012.

Outlook
We expect 2011 to be a year of transition for the company. We will continue to drive the successful and profitable parts of our business, focusing our sales efforts on our existing customer base and some potential new ones. I believe that the initiatives now underway will enable us to start rebuilding shareholder confidence and value.

Nigel Rich CBE
Executive Chairman

1 March 2011

3.32 The strategic report should be written in plain language. The excessive use of jargon or industry-specific terms should be avoided where possible. Where the use of such a term is necessary, it should be clearly defined and used consistently. [SR guidance para 6.4].

3.33 The use of a glossary should be considered, to explain any unavoidable terminology and to ensure clear understanding of other key terms. Table 3.3 is an extract from Land Securities plc's glossary, which defines key calculations as well as key terms.

Table 3.3 – Glossary

Land Securities plc – Annual Report and accounts – 31 March 2013

GLOSSARY

Adjusted earnings per share (EPS)
Earnings per share based on revenue profit after related tax.

Adjusted net asset value (NAV) per share
NAV per share adjusted to remove the effect of the de-recognition of the 2004 bond exchange and cumulative fair value movements on interest-rate swaps and similar instruments.

Adjusted net debt
Net debt excluding cumulative fair value movements on interest-rate swaps, the adjustment arising from the de-recognition of the bond exchange and amounts payable under finance leases. It generally includes the net debt of subsidiaries and joint ventures on a proportionate basis.

Average unexpired lease term
The weighted average of the unexpired term of all leases other than short-term lettings such as car parks and advertising hoardings, temporary lettings of less than one year, residential leases and long ground leases.

Book value
The amount at which assets and liabilities are reported in the financial statements.

BREEAM
Building Research Establishment's Environmental Assessment Method.

Combined portfolio
The combined portfolio comprises the investment properties of the Group's subsidiaries, on a proportionately consolidated basis when not wholly owned, together with our share of investment properties held in our joint ventures. Unless stated otherwise, references are to the combined portfolio when the investment property business is discussed.

Completed developments
Completed developments consist of those properties previously included in the development programme, which have been transferred from the development programme since 1 April 2011.

Development pipeline
The development programme together with proposed developments.

Development programme
The development programme consists of committed developments (Board approved) projects with the building contract let), authorised developments (Board approved), project under construction and developments which have reached practical completion within the last two years but are not yet 95% let.

Joint venture
An entity in which the Group holds an interest and is jointly controlled by the Group and one or more partners under a contractual arrangement. Decisions on financial and operating policies essential to the operation, performance and financial position of the venture require each partner's consent.

Lease incentives
Any incentive offered to occupiers to enter into a lease. Typically the incentive will be an initial rent-free period, or a cash contribution to fit-out or similar costs. For accounting purposes the value of the incentive is spread over the non-cancellable life of the lease.

LIBOR
The London Interbank Offered Rate, the interest rate charged by one bank to another for lending money, often used as a reference rate in bank facilities.

Like-for-like portfolio
The like-for-like portfolio includes all properties which have been in the portfolio since 1 April 2011, but excluding those which are acquired, sold or included in the development pipeline at any time since that date.

Like-for-like managed properties
Properties in the like-for-like portfolio other than those in our joint ventures which we do not manage operationally.

Loan-to-value (LTV)
Group LTV is the ratio of adjusted net debt, including subsidiaries and joint ventures, to the sum of the market value of investment properties and the book value of trading properties of the Group, its subsidiaries and joint ventures, all on a proportionate basis, expressed as a percentage. For the Security Group, LTV is the ratio of net debt lent to me Security Group divided by the value of secured assets.

Market value
Market value is determined by the Group's external valuers, in accordance with the RICS Valuation Standards, as an opinion of the estimated amount for which a property should exchange on the date of valuation between a willing buyer and a willing seller in an arm's-length transaction after proper marketing.

Mark-to-market adjustment
An accounting adjustment to change the book value of an asset or liability to its market value.

Net asset value (NAV) per share
Equity attributable to owners of the Parent divided by the number of ordinary shares in issue at the period end.

and capital gains from the property rental business are exempt from tax but the REIT is required to distribute at least 90% of those profits to shareholders. Corporation tax is payable on non-qualifying activities in the normal way.

Rental value change
Increase or decrease in the current rental value, as determined by the Group's external valuers, over the reporting period on a like-for-like basis.

Rental income
Rental income is as reported in the income statement, on an accruals basis, and adjusted for the spreading of lease incentives over the term certain of the lease in accordance with SIC 15. It is stated gross, prior to the deduction of ground rents and without deduction for operational outgoings on car park and commercialisation activities.

Retail warehouse park
A scheme of three or more retail warehouse units aggregating over 5,000m^2 with shared parking.

Return on average capital employed
Group profit before interest, plus joint venture profit before interest, divided by the average capital employed (defined as shareholders' funds plus adjusted net debt).

Return on average equity
Group profit before tax plus joint venture tax divided by the average equity shareholders' funds.

Revenue profit
Profit before tax, excluding profits on the sale of non-current assets and trading properties, profits on long-term development contracts, valuation movements, fair value movements on interest-rate swaps and similar instruments used for hedging purposes, the adjustment to interest payable resulting from the amortisation of the bond exchange de-recognition, debt restructuring charges and any items of an unusual nature.

Reversionary or under-rented
Space where the passing rent is below the ERV.

Reversionary yield
The anticipated yield to which the initial yield will rise (or fall) once the rent reaches the ERV.

Scrip dividend
Land Securities offers its shareholders the opportunity to receive dividends in the form of shares instead of cash. This is known as a scrip dividend.

3.34 It is essential that the messages within the strategic report are understandable. Directors can help readers to navigate their reporting by explaining the critical issues for the entity and highlighting them (for example, in quotes, titles and bullet points).

3.35 It will not be possible (or even desirable, given the volume of explanation that would be required) to explain every technical aspect of an entity's business. Besides, the reader of the strategic report is most likely to be a person with some knowledge either of the industry or of the entity itself. So, the reader is likely to have more knowledge than a layman, and entities should take that into account when preparing the strategic report. The strategic report should not try to be 'all things to all men', although it should be aimed at shareholders. [SR guidance para 3.2].

3.35.1 It might be necessary, in some cases, to simplify the description of the entity's business. For example, the use of technical terms and scientific names might be unavoidable in an explanation of a drug development pipeline; however, additional information should be given to describe, as simply as possible, what the drug does in relation to diseases or other conditions and how development will benefit both the entity and the sufferers. Many pharmaceutical entities also include a brief description of the various stages (phases) of the approval process for new drugs. Table 3.4 shows an extract of the 'Pipeline overview' for diabetes drugs being developed by Novo Nordisk A/S.

Table 3.4 – Pharmaceutical pipeline

Novo Nordisk A/S – Annual Report and Accounts – 31 December 2010

Pipeline overview (extract)

Pipeline overview

In 2010, significant progress was made throughout Novo Nordisk's clinical development pipeline. This overview illustrates key development activities, including entries into the pipeline and progression of development compounds.

See more at novonordisk.com/investors/rd_pipeline/rd_pipeline.asp and clinicaltrials.gov.

Phase 1
Studies in a small group of healthy volunteers, and sometimes patients, usually between 10 and 100, to investigate how the body handles new medication and establish maximum tolerated dose.

Phase 2
Testing a drug at various dose levels in a larger group of patients to learn about its effect on the condition and its side effects.

Therapy area	Indication	Compound	Description
Diabetes care			
Diabetes	Type 1 and 2 diabetes	Degludec	Ultra-long-acting basal insulin. Enrolment in the phase 3a programme completed in June 2010. First phase 3a study results announced in October 2010.
	Type 1 and 2 diabetes	DegludecPlus	Ultra-long-acting basal insulin with a bolus boost. Enrolment in the phase 3a programme completed in June 2010. First phase 3a study results announced in August 2010.
	Type 2 diabetes	Semaglutide	Once-weekly GLP-1 analogue. Phase 3 initiation was postponed in June 2010 pending a long-acting portfolio development strategy decision.
	Type 2 diabetes	NN9068	GLP-1 and basal insulin combination. Phase 1 studies are ongoing.
	Type 1 and 2 diabetes	NN1218	Ultra-fast-acting insulin analogue. First phase 1 studies initiated during the second quarter of 2010.
	Type 1 and 2 diabetes	NN1952	Fast-acting oral insulin analogue. First phase 1 study completed during the fourth quarter of 2010.
	Type 2 diabetes	NN9924	Long-acting oral GLP-1 analogue. First phase 1 study initiated in the first quarter of 2010.
Obesity	Obesity	Liraglutide	Once-daily GLP-1 analogue. First phase 3a study completed during the third quarter of 2010. The remaining phase 3a studies are expected to be initiated mid-2011.

Phase 2a
Pilot clinical trials to evaluate efficacy (and safety) in selected populations of patients.

Phase 2b
Well controlled trials to evaluate efficacy (and safety) in patients with the disease. Sometimes referred to as pivotal trials.

Phase 3
Studies in large groups of patients worldwide comparing the new medication with a commonly used drug or placebo for both safety and efficacy in order to establish its risk–benefit relationship.

Phase 3a
Trials conducted after efficacy of the medicine is demonstrated, but prior to regulatory submission.

Phase 3b
Clinical trials conducted after regulatory submission, but prior to the medicine's approval and launch.

Filed/regulatory approval
A New Drug Application is submitted for review by various government regulatory agencies.

Intended clinical benefit	Phase 1	Phase 2	Phase 3	Filed/regulatory approval
Long-acting basal insulin with duration of action of 24 hours and an improved safety profile.				
A soluble fixed combination of fast-acting and long-acting insulin combining 24-hour basal insulin coverage with a distinct meal peak.				
Provide the pharmacological actions of a GLP-1 analogue with fewer injections.				
Combination of a basal insulin and a GLP-1 analogue intended to combine the benefits of the two hormones in a single preparation.				
Fast-acting insulin for improvement of glycaemic control during a meal.				
Insulin delivered as a tablet.				
A GLP-1 analogue delivered as a tablet.				
Sustainable weight loss for people with obesity, including those at risk of developing diabetes.				

3.36 The method of presentation can significantly affect the understandability of information in the strategic report. The most appropriate method of presentation will depend on the nature of the information, but it could include tabular, graphical or pictorial methods as well as text. A combination of these methods might also be appropriate. [SR guidance para 6.5]. An example of the use of clear presentation, in Table 3.5, is focused on strategy.

Table 3.5 – Strategy presentation

3i Group plc – Annual report and accounts – 31 March 2013

Our strategic priorities and progress

Strategic priorities	Progress in FY2013	Priorities for FY2014–15
1 Create a leaner organisation with a cost base more closely aligned with its income	■ Net reduction of 168 staff before Debt Management acquisitions; ahead of target reduction of more than 160 staff ■ Re-shaped international network with closure of six offices, reducing network to 13 offices ■ Achieved greater central control and business focus through removal of organisational complexity and bureaucracy ■ £51m of run-rate operating cost reduction; 28% ahead of £40m target	■ New target of £60m of cumulative run-rate operating cost reduction by 31 March 2014; 33% increase from original target of £45m ■ Cover operating costs with annual cash income by 31 March 2014 on a run-rate basis

2 Improve consistency and discipline of investment processes and asset management approach	■ Substantially implemented programme of six asset management improvement initiatives across Private Equity
	  – Investment review process
	  – People: governance and resourcing
	  – Operational capabilities, knowledge management and networks
	  – Monitoring and performance tracking
	  – Valuation process, exit strategy and planning Systems upgrade and reporting
	■ Implemented new vintage control policy
		■ Grow Private Equity investment portfolio earnings through asset management improvement initiatives
		■ Continue to re-establish investment track record through improved performance and new investment
		■ Roll-out of upgraded Private Equity system

3 Re-focus and re-shape the Private Equity business	■ Combined into single business unit ■ Re-focused Private Equity on mid-market investing in our core northern European markets. North America and Brazil ■ Continued to manage intensively the existing portfolio with total realisations of £575m, representing an uplift to opening value of 49% and a money multiple of 2.1x	■ Continue to manage intensively the existing portfolio and realise investments at values representing good uplifts to book value and strong cash-on-cash multiples, thereby optimising the value of the portfolio for 3i, its shareholders and its fund investors ■ Selective investing in our core markets using a combination of proprietary capital and third-party co-investment

4 Grow third-party AUM and income	■ Private Equity
	  – Established framework arrangements with a number of leading investors to invest alongside 3i in Europe
	  – Completed second Brazilian investment alongside co-investors
	■ Infrastructure
	  – European portfolio continued to perform well and generated a strong level of portfolio income
	■ Debt Management
	  – Substantial increase in third-party AUM from £3.3bn to £6.4bn
	  – Acquisition of Invesco European CLO management contracts
	  – Strategic transaction with Fraser Sullivan, to establish US debt management platform
	  – Launched two US CLOs, raising c.US$1bn
		■ Continue to explore opportunities to further grow and develop our three fund management platforms
		■ Grow annual operating profit from fund management activities, demonstrating additional value beyond NAV

5 Improve capital allocation, focusing on enhanced shareholder distributions and re-investment in our business	■ Announced strengthened distribution policy in May 2012 to give shareholders a direct share of our realisation proceeds ■ Achieved gearing of less than 20% and gross debt reduction ahead of schedule to less than 1bn – 44% reduction in gross debt from £1.6bn to £0.9bn by 30 April 2013 (31 March 2013; £1.1 bn) ■ Reviewed Group-wide compensation arrangements. Established new principles and designed new arrangements	■ Initiate additional shareholder distributions above the annual base dividend in respect of FY2014 ■ Reduce gross interest payable to less than £60m, excluding costs of early debt repayment ■ Implement new compensation arrangements across the Group

Strategic report

Principle 2 – Comprehensive but concise

3.37 Principle 2 states that *"The strategic report should be comprehensive but concise"*. [SR guidance para 6.7].

3.38 The directors have a duty to promote the success of the entity for the benefit of its shareholders; and the strategic report should contain only the strategic and other important information that is relevant to assessing how the directors have performed this duty.

3.39 Comprehensiveness reflects the breadth of information that should be included in the strategic report, rather than the depth of information. The strategic report does not need to cover all possible matters in detail to be considered comprehensive. [SR guidance para 6.8].

3.39.1 The strategic report should be focused, and it should include only information that is important to the entity (when taken as a whole) and is relevant to shareholders' needs. So, the application of materiality contributes to concise reporting.

3.39.2 Conciseness is achieved through the efficient communication of all material information. [SR guidance para 6.9].

3.40 Information is material if its omission from, or misrepresentation in, the strategic report might reasonably be expected to influence the economic decisions that shareholders make on the basis of the annual report as a whole; such information should therefore be included in the strategic report. Conversely, the inclusion of immaterial information can obscure key messages and impair the understandability of the information provided in the strategic report; so, immaterial information should be excluded from the strategic report. [SR guidance para 5.1].

3.41 Some entities are being more explicit about how they determine their materiality, usually aligning this to identification of key stakeholders, their material issues and how these map to the business. Table 3.5.1 shows how Halfords plc has done this.

Table 3.5.1 – Materiality and stakeholders

Halfords plc – Annual report and accounts – 3rd April 2015

STRATEGIC REPORT > OVERVIEW

MATERIAL
ISSUES

Halfords' vision is to help and inspire our customers with their life on the move by offering unique in-store services and a compelling product range with expert services. The table below identifies the key stakeholders we interact with to achieve this vision and outlines how and why we engage with them.

Why we engage	Material issues	What we are doing
Customers		
Customers want value, personalisation, and trustworthy advice and service. We want to know how we are performing so we can deliver unparalleled products and services.	• Value for money • Customer service • Convenience • Range	• Service Revolution • The 'H' Factor • Stores Fit to Shop • 21st Century Infrastructure • Click with the Digital Future
Colleagues		
Our colleagues are fundamental to the achievement of our customer experience ambitions.	• Career opportunities • Pay and conditions • Training and development • Innovation • Colleague engagement	• '3-Gears' training programme - see page 10 • Listening: surveys and colleague groups • 'Accelerate' management development courses • Recognition and reward
Suppliers		
Our brand relies heavily on the high standards of our carefully selected suppliers in order for us to deliver market-leading products and services.	• Quality management • Cost efficiency • Ethical Trading policy • Speed to market • Security of supply	• Far East trading office developing mutually beneficial relationships • Logistics efficiencies and environmental management • Supplier conferences
Investors		
As a publicly listed company we need to provide fair, balanced and understandable information to instil trust and confidence and allow informed investment decisions to be made.	• Future-orientated information • Risk information • Operating and financial performance • Dividend • Access to management	• Integrated reporting page – explained IBC • Consistent KPIs provided through clear and regular updates - see pages 22 to 24 • Responding to investor queries and meeting requests • Recognition in Social Responsibility investor indices e.g. FTSE4Good
Communities		
We aim to contribute positively to the communities and environment in which we operate.	• Impact of Group activities on the wider community • Developing future customers	• Re-Cycle partnership • Onley Prison workshops giving training and employment opportunities for ex-offenders • Free kids' holiday bike clubs - see page 5 • Cub Scouts Cyclist Activity badge workshops - see page 5 • Stores will donate payroll hours to engage with local charities
Media		
As a business-to-consumer company, we need strong omnichannel exposure to connect with customers and our wider stakeholder audience.	• Reliable range, product and pricing information • Transparency of reliable and timely Group information	• Product videos and peer reviews • TV and radio advertising campaigns • Email and PR customer engagement • Improving Twitter, Facebook and YouTube content • Monitoring and responding to comments and concerns on social media channels
Government		
Policies and regulatory changes may provide both opportunities and risk to our operations. Working closely with the Government ensures that our products and services evolve.	• Transport policies and schemes • CO_2 reduction strategies	• Cycle to work policy campaigning • DAB Radio working groups • Driver training and vehicle safety enhancements • Engaging with VOSA, DVLA, TSI, ASA and HSE

3.42 The strategic report should contain only the information that is relevant to shareholders' needs. The inclusion of too much information or detail could obscure matters of importance and will not promote a clear understanding of the entity's development, performance, position and future prospects.

3.43 Consistent with other aspects of the Corporate Governance Code, the focus on key (or principal) risks and key performance indicators indicates that reporting deals with the most relevant material. Table 3.6 highlights Cairn Energy who provide comprehensive insight into its principal risks with a detailed explanation of why they are of most concern to the board, linking this with reference to discussion elsewhere in the narrative. Coverage of other risks follows in a summary table.

Table 3.6 – Principal risks

Cairn Energy – Annual report and accounts – 31 December 2014

Principal risks and uncertainties

As the Group continues to focus on creating value and shareholder returns from disciplined capital allocation across a balance of exploration and development assets, the principal risks and uncertainties facing the Group at the end of 2014 were as follows:

Principal risks to the Group in 2014/2015

During 2014, we regularly reviewed the risks which we believed could adversely impact our business at the time. The following table provides an overview of the principal risks to the Group at the end of 2014, the potential impacts, the mitigation measures we have in place and the KPIs the risks impact on. The list is not exhaustive or set out in any order of priority and is continually subject to change.

Lack of exploration success
Exploration success is fundamental to the strategy of creating value through the discovery and development of hydrocarbon resources. Consequently, a sustained lack of exploration success may lead to limited or no value creation and a loss of investor confidence in the Group's business model. In 2014, both the Senegal operated wells discovered oil, mitigating this risk to a degree. The Group continues to actively evaluate a number of potential new exploration investment opportunities for 2015 and beyond, which are all subject to extensive external and internal peer review.

 Discover more: *Operational review* P22-27

Restriction on ability to sell Cairn India Limited (CIL) shareholding
In January 2014, Cairn received a request from the Indian Income Tax Department to provide information regarding a group reorganisation that took place during the fiscal year ended 31 March 2007 and as a result a restriction was applied to the sale of the Group's CIL shares. The restriction remains in place and the Group continues to cooperate with the Indian Income Tax Department investigation. The continued freeze of the Group's CIL shares could restrict the Group's funding capacity. The Group will take whatever steps are necessary to protect its interests.

 Discover more: *Cairn in India* P29

Operational and project performance
Delivering all operated and non-operated projects in a safe and efficient manner is a key objective for the Group. In 2014, the Morocco and Senegal drilling campaigns experienced delays as a result of unscheduled maintenance requirements on the Cajun Express rig. With safety being the principal concern, the Group ceased drilling until acceptable mitigation plans were implemented. Anticipated in 2015, offshore wells in Senegal, Western Sahara, the UK and Norway will be drilled and the Group will be working with the rig contractors to agree on a safe and efficient execution plan. In addition, the Group will work closely with JV partners to ensure the Kraken and Catcher development projects are delivered safely and efficiently.

 Discover more: *Operational review* P22-27

Kraken and Catcher development projects not executed on schedule and budget
The Kraken and Catcher development projects will provide future cash flow to sustain the Group's business plan and are part of the North West Europe portfolio which provides balance to the Group's exploration and appraisal activities in earlier stage hydrocarbon basins. Development projects of this nature can be susceptible to delays and budget increases for a variety of reasons and this may lead to increased costs and delays in future cash flow. To mitigate these risks, the Group works closely with its JV partners to support and/or influence key decisions. The Catcher and Kraken developments in the North Sea are progressing, with first oil targeted for 2017.

 Discover more: *Operational review* P22-27

3.44 The appropriate placing of information within the annual report also contributes to concise reporting. Table 3.7 illustrates how National Grid plc have moved a number of regulatory disclosures in their annual report to a section at the end of the report.

Table 3.7 – Placement of additional information

National Grid plc – Annual report and accounts – 31 March 2013

Additional Information pages 170 to 196

Additional disclosures and information, definitions and glossary of terms, summary consolidated financial information and other useful information for shareholders including contact details for more information or help.

170 Contents of additional information
190 Definitions and glossary of terms

Additional information
Business information in detail

Contents

[The next paragraph is 3.45.]

Principle 3 – Forward-looking

3.45 Principle 3 states that *"Where appropriate, information in the strategic report should have a forward-looking orientation"*. [SR guidance para 6.10].

3.46 Information on how a fact or circumstance might affect the entity's future development, performance or position should be included in the strategic report where it is material to an assessment of the development, performance, position or future prospects of the entity. The provision of this information does not require disclosure of a forecast of future results. [SR guidance para 6.11].

3.47 No rules dictate the forward-looking information that an entity must provide in its strategic report. Directors must decide which information to include on the basis of their own business dynamics and those of the industry sectors in which they operate.

3.48 Topics might include:

■ An explanation of the resources, principal risks and uncertainties and relationships that might affect the entity's long-term value (for example, development of new products or services).

■ An analysis of the trends and factors that the directors believe are likely to impact future prospects (for example, introduction of new technology).

■ Information on future targets (for example, for key performance indicators).

3.49 There will be some information that, if it is disclosed, would undermine the market position of any entity; but this fact should not be used to avoid full and frank disclosure. For example, pharmaceutical entities disclose details of their products in the pipeline without disclosing the underlying patent formulations; so they provide investors with the information that they need to understand the sustainability of the entity's performance without compromising the entity's interests.

3.50 The strategic report should not concentrate solely on a single timeframe. Where relevant to an understanding of the development, performance, position or future prospects of the entity, the strategic report should give due regard to the short-, medium- or long-term implications of the fact or circumstance being described. [SR guidance para 6.12]. As illustrated in the table below, Pace plc have clearly indicated their three-year and five-year strategic priorities.

Table 3.8 – Strategic timeline

Pace plc – Annual report and accounts – 31 December 2012

Pace's strategic objectives

Grow a broader platform across hardware, software and services

1 Transform core economics

2 Build on our position as world leader in PayTV hardware

3 Widen out into Software, Services and Integrated Solutions

Three-year strategic intent

Significantly improve efficiency of our core business through:
— Opex efficiency improvement
— Cost of Goods Sold improvement
— Balance Sheet and Working Capital improvement

Build on our position as a world leading PayTV hardware company, across:
— Set-top box solutions
— Media Server solutions
— Gateway solutions

Widen out into Software, Services and Integrated Solutions, focusing on:
— Next generation content security
— Integrated solutions
— Proactive customer care

Five-year strategic intent

— Build on Software and Service platforms to become a leading provider of user experience and customer management solutions

— Leverage leading-edge position across hardware and software to drive next wave of innovation

3.51 In Table 3.9, Telus Corporation sets out in tabular form the current year performance compared with the target performance. Target performance for the next year is also included. There is accompanying narrative (not included in the table below) to explain why particular targets were not met.

Table 3.9 – Performance against targets

Telus Corporation – Annual Report – 31 December 2010

Management's Discussion and Analysis (extract)

	2010 performance			2011 targets (IFRS-IASB)	
Scorecards	Actual results and growth	Original targets and estimated growth	Result	2010 unaudited *pro forma* IFRS-based comparative results	2011 targets and estimated growth over 2010 IFRS
Consolidated					
Revenues	**$9.779 billion** **2%**	$9.8 to $10.1 billion 2 to 5%	✗	$9.792 billion	**$9.925 to $10.225 billion** **1 to 4%**
EBITDA[1]	**$3.643 billion** **4%**	$3.5 to $3.7 billion flat to 6%	✓	$3.650 billion	**$3.675 to $3.875 billion** **1 to 6%**
EPS – basic[2]	**$3.23** **3%**	$2.90 to $3.30 (8) to 5%	✓	$3.27	**$3.50 to $3.90** **7 to 19%**
Capital expenditures	**$1.721 billion** **(18)%**	Approx. $1.7 billion (19)%	✓	$1.721 billion	**Approx. $1.7 billion**
Wireless segment					
Revenue (external)	**$5.014 billion** **6.5%**	$4.95 to $5.1 billion 5 to 8%	✓	$5.014 billion	**$5.2 to $5.35 billion** **4 to 7%**
EBITDA	**$2.031 billion** **5%**	$1.925 to $2.025 billion flat to 5%	✓✓	$2.022 billion	**$2.15 to $2.25 billion** **6 to 11%**
Wireline segment					
Revenue (external)	**$4.765 billion** **(3)%**	$4.85 to $5.0 billion (1) to 2%	✗	$4.778 billion	**$4.725 to $4.875 billion** **(1) to 2%**
EBITDA	**$1.612 billion** **3.5%**	$1.575 to $1.675 billion 1 to 8%	✓	$1.628 billion	**$1.525 to $1.625 billion** **(6) to 0%**

(1) A non-GAAP measure. *See Section 11.1 Earnings before interest, taxes, depreciation and amortization (EBITDA)* for the definition.
(2) Actual EPS for 2010 includes approximately nine cents for favourable income tax-related adjustments and a 12-cent charge for early partial redemption of long-term debt that were not contemplated in the original target for EPS.

✓✓ Exceeded target
✓ Met target
✗ Missed target

3.52 In Table 3.10, Telus Corporation also describes the assumptions made in creating the 2010 targets, and it compares each of these assumptions with what actually happened (only the first few assumptions are shown).

Table 3.10 – Assumptions compared with actual experience

Telus Corporation – Annual Report – 31 December 2010

Management's Discussion and Analysis (extract)

The following key assumptions were made at the time the 2010 targets were announced in December 2009.

Assumptions for 2010 original targets	Result or expectation for 2010
Ongoing wireline and wireless competition in both business and consumer markets	Confirmed by frequent promotional offers by the primary cable-TV competitor in Western Canada (Shaw Communications), a new brand launch (Chatr) by an incumbent wireless competitor (Rogers Communications), and a brand re-launch (Solo) by an incumbent wireless competitor (Bell Canada).
Canadian wireless industry market penetration gain of approximately four percentage points for the year (approximately 3.6 percentage points in 2009)	The Company's estimate is a gain of approximately 4.4 percentage points in industry market penetration for 2010, with an increasing proportion from postpaid subscribers associated with growing data usage and smartphone adoption.
Increased wireless subscriber loading in smartphones	Smartphones represented 46% of postpaid gross additions in the fourth quarter of 2010, compared to 25% in the fourth quarter of 2009. Smartphones represent 33% of the postpaid subscriber base at the end of 2010 compared to 20% at the end of 2009.
Reduced downward pressure on wireless ARPU	Confirmed by the 1.9% year-over-year increase in wireless ARPU in the fourth quarter of 2010 and 1.4% decrease for the full year of 2010, as compared to decreases of 7.7% and 6.8%, respectively, in the fourth quarter and full year of 2009.
New competitive wireless entry in early 2010 following one competitive launch in December 2009	After its initial launch in Calgary and Toronto in December 2009, Globalive (Wind brand) launched in Edmonton and Ottawa in the first quarter of 2010, and Vancouver in the second quarter, and announced that it expects to launch in Victoria in 2011. Other new entrants began launching services in the second quarter of 2010. Mobilicity launched services in the Toronto area in the second quarter, in Edmonton, Vancouver and Ottawa in the fourth quarter, and in Calgary in early 2011. Public Mobile turned up services in the Toronto and Montreal areas. Quebecor (Videotron brand) launched its services in September 2010, initially in Montreal and Quebec City. Videotron previously offered wireless services in Quebec as a mobile virtual network operator. Shaw Communications stated it expects to begin launching wireless services in early 2012. In addition, during the third quarter of 2010, one incumbent national competitor launched a new brand and the other incumbent national competitor re-launched one of its brands.
In wireline, stable residential network access line losses and continued competitive pressure in small and medium business market from cable-TV and voice over IP (VoIP) companies	Residential access line losses moderated in the second half of 2010 when compared to the same period in 2009, due to improved bundle and retention offers. Residential access lines decreased by 8.0% in 2010, resulting from promotional activity by the primary Western cable-TV competitor Shaw for voice and Internet services, particularly in the first half of 2010. Business line losses were 2.9% in 2010 due to increased competition in the small and medium business market and conversion of voice lines to more efficient IP services. See Section 5.4.
Continued wireline broadband expansion	See Section 2: Core business and strategy.
Significant increase in cost of acquisition and retention expenses for smartphones and TELUS TV loading	Wireless cost of acquisition (COA) per gross subscriber addition was $350 in 2010, an increase of 3.9% from 2009. Retention spending as a percentage of growing network revenue was 11.6% in 2010, up from 10.9% in 2009. TELUS TV loading was 144,000 in 2010, an increase of 57% from 2009. TELUS TV programming and other costs have increased, as well, due to the 85% increase in total TV subscribers compared to 2009.
EBITDA savings of approximately $135 million from efficiency initiatives	Savings of approximately $134 million were realized in 2010.
Approximately $75 million of restructuring expenses ($190 million in 2009)	Restructuring charges were $74 million.
A blended statutory tax rate of approximately 28.5 to 29.5% (30.3% in 2009). The expected decrease is based on enacted changes in federal and provincial income tax rates	The blended statutory income tax rate was 29% and the effective income tax rate was 24%.

Cash income taxes peaking at approximately $385 to $425 million (net $266 million in 2009) due to the timing of instalment payments	Cash income tax payments net of refunds received were $311 million in 2010, comprised of instalments for 2010 and final payments for the 2009 tax year made in the first quarter, net of $41 million of refunds for the settlement of prior years' matters. The expectation for the full year was revised to a range of $300 to $350 million on November 5, 2010, and was previously revised to a range of $330 to $370 million on August 6, 2010.
A pension accounting discount rate was estimated at 5.75% and subsequently set at 5.85% (140 basis points lower than 2009). The expected long-term return of 7.25% is unchanged from 2009 and consistent with the Company's long-run returns and its future expectations. ■ Defined benefit pension plans net expenses were estimated to be $28 million in 2010 (compared to $18 million in 2009), based on projected pension fund returns ■ Defined benefit pension plans contributions were estimated to be approximately $143 million in 2010, down from $179 million in 2009, largely due to the stock market recovery in 2009 and proposed federal pension reforms.	Defined benefit pension plan expenses were $28 million in 2010 and are set at the beginning of the year. The Company's contributions to defined benefit pension plans in 2010 were $137 million. A $200 million voluntary contribution was announced in mid-December 2010 and made in January 2011. See *Assumptions for 2011 targets* in *Section 1.5*.

Principle 4 – Entity-specific

3.53 Principle 4 states that *"The strategic report should provide information that is entity-specific"*. [SR guidance para 6.13].

3.54 However, information on how a particular fact or circumstance might affect, or has affected, the development, performance or position of the entity's business, and how it is responding to the fact or circumstance, provides more insightful information that can be used in the assessment of the entity's future prospects. The inclusion of generic or 'boilerplate' information on its own is only of limited use to shareholders. [SR guidance para 6.14].

3.55 Over the last few years, the FRRP has been much more focused on challenging entities that provide 'boilerplate' disclosures, particularly around principal risks and uncertainties.

3.56 The FRC also released a discussion paper on 'Cutting Clutter', which encouraged entities to avoid immaterial detail and focus on key messages in report writing. A number of entities have been prompted by this to align their accounting policies and financial notes in order to underline their relevance. This is illustrated by Provident Financial in Table 3.11.

Table 3.11 – Alignment of accounting policies and financial notes

Provident Financial – Annual report and accounts – 31 December 2012

6 EARNINGS PER SHARE

The group presents basic and diluted EPS data on its ordinary shares. Basic EPS is calculated by dividing the profit for the year attributable to equity shareholders by the weighted average number of ordinary shares outstanding during the year. adjusted for treasury shares (own shares held). Diluted EPS calculates the effect on EPS assuming conversion of all dilutive potential ordinary shares. Dilutive potential ordinary shares are calculated as follows:

(i) For share awards outstanding under performance-related share incentive schemes such as the Performance Share Plan (PSP) and the Long Term Incentive Scheme (LTIS), the number of dilutive potential ordinary shares is calculated based on the number of shares which would be issuable if: (i) the end of the reporting period is assumed to be the end of the schemes' performance period; and (ii) the performance targets have been met at that date.

(ii) For share options outstanding under non-performance-related schemes such as the Save As You Earn scheme (SAYE), a calculation is performed to determine the number of shares that could have been acquired at fair value (determined as the average annual market share price of the company's shares) based on the monetary value of the subscription rights attached to outstanding share options. The number of shares calculated is compared with the number of share options outstanding, with the difference being the dilutive potential ordinary shares.

The group also presents an adjusted EPS, excluding the impact of any exceptional items.

Reconciliations of basic and diluted earnings per share are set out below:

| | 2012 | | | 2011 | | |
	Earnings £m	Weighted average number of shares m	Per share amount pence	Earnings £m	Weighted average number of shares m	Per share amount pence
Diluted earnings per share Group						
Earnings per share						
Shares in issue during the year		138.0			136.8	
Own shares held		(3.9)			(3.1)	
Basic earnings per share	148.0	134.1	110.4	119.8	133.7	89.6
Dilutive effect of share options and awards	–	2.5	(2.1)	–	0.3	(0.2)
Diluted earnings per share	148.0	136.6	108.3	119.8	134.0	89.4

The directors have elected to show an adjusted earnings per share prior to exceptional items in 2012 (see note1). This is presented to show the earnings per share generated by the group's underlying operations. A reconciliation of basic and diluted earnings per share to adjusted base and diluted earnings per share is as follows:

| | 2012 | | | 2011 | | |
Group	Earnings £m	Weighted average number of shares m	Per share amount pence	Earnings £m	Weighted average number of shares m	Per share amount pence
Basic earnings per share	148.0	134.1	110.4	119.8	133.7	89.6
Exceptional items, net of tax	(11.3)	–	(8.4)	–	–	–
Adjusted basic earnings per share	136.7	134.1	102.0	119.8	133.7	89.6
Diluted earnings per share	148.0	136.6	108.3	119.8	134.0	89.4
Exceptional items, net of tax	(11.3)	–	(8.2)	–	–	–
Adjusted diluted earnings per share	136.7	136.6	100.1	119.8	134.0	89.4

Adjusted basic EPS has g rown by 13.8% in 2012 due to the strong performance of Vanquis Bank in the year. This growth is higher than the 11.7% growth in profit before tax and exceptional items due to the fall in corporation tax rate from 26% to 24% on 1 April 2012.

3.57 In 2014 the FRC's Reporting Lab produced a new report, 'Towards Clear and Concise Reporting'. This document offers practical tips aimed at improving the clarity of disclosures made in annual reports but without adding to the length of the document.

Principle 5 – Highlight linkages

3.58 Principle 5 states that *"The strategic report should highlight and explain linkages between pieces of information presented within the strategic report and in the annual report more broadly"*. [SR guidance para 6.15].

3.58.1 Linkages are relationships or interdependencies between, or the causes and effects of, facts and circumstances disclosed in the annual report. [SR guidance para 6.16].

3.59 The Act sets out a list of discrete requirements which could be met in a series of independent sections in a strategic report. It is often the case, however, that there are relationships and interdependencies between the required pieces of information that, if highlighted and explained, will provide a greater insight into the entity's business. [SR guidance para 6.17]. For example, in the table below, Berendsen plc provides clear linkage between its sections on risk and on KPIs.

Table 3.12 – Linkage from risk to KPI

Berendsen plc – Annual report and accounts – 31 December 2012

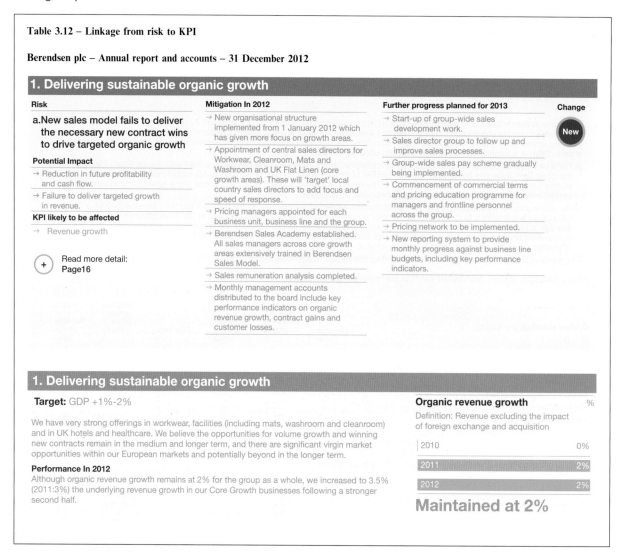

1. Delivering sustainable organic growth

Risk	Mitigation In 2012	Further progress planned for 2013	Change
a. New sales model fails to deliver the necessary new contract wins to drive targeted organic growth	→ New organisational structure implemented from 1 January 2012 which has given more focus on growth areas.	→ Start-up of group-wide sales development work.	New
Potential Impact	→ Appointment of central sales directors for Workwear, Cleanroom, Mats and Washroom and UK Flat Linen (core growth areas). These will 'target' local country sales directors to add focus and speed of response.	→ Sales director group to follow up and improve sales processes.	
→ Reduction in future profitability and cash flow.		→ Group-wide sales pay scheme gradually being implemented.	
→ Failure to deliver targeted growth in revenue.		→ Commencement of commercial terms and pricing education programme for managers and frontline personnel across the group.	
KPI likely to be affected	→ Pricing managers appointed for each business unit, business line and the group.	→ Pricing network to be implemented.	
→ Revenue growth	→ Berendsen Sales Academy established. All sales managers across core growth areas extensively trained in Berendsen Sales Model.	→ New reporting system to provide monthly progress against business line budgets, including key performance indicators.	
(+) Read more detail: Page16	→ Sales remuneration analysis completed.		
	→ Monthly management accounts distributed to the board include key performance indicators on organic revenue growth, contract gains and customer losses.		

1. Delivering sustainable organic growth

Target: GDP +1%-2%

We have very strong offerings in workwear, facilities (including mats, washroom and cleanroom) and in UK hotels and healthcare. We believe the opportunities for volume growth and winning new contracts remain in the medium and longer term, and there are significant virgin market opportunities within our European markets and potentially beyond in the longer term.

Performance In 2012
Although organic revenue growth remains at 2% for the group as a whole, we increased to 3.5% (2011:3%) the underlying revenue growth in our Core Growth businesses following a stronger second half.

Organic revenue growth %
Definition: Revenue excluding the impact of foreign exchange and acquisition

2010	0%
2011	2%
2012	2%

Maintained at 2%

3.59.1 Similarly, there are many examples where separate sources of requirements that apply to different components of the annual report result in the disclosure of related information. While each component of the annual report is independently useful, more valuable insight can be provided if the strategic report highlights and explains linkages between the information disclosed in them. [SR guidance para 6.18].

3.60 Management should consider what it needs to communicate, and what investors want to know, to prevent key messages from getting lost. For example, some form of narrative sequence or cross-referencing (and clear linkage from the entity's discussion of its markets to its strategy, key performance indicators and future goals) can be helpful. In Table 3.13, Capita Group give an example of this. An integrated structure, where important issues are linked throughout the report, can aid the reader's retention of the information provided.

Table 3.13 – Clear linkage

Capital Group – Annual Report and Accounts – 31 December 2010

Business review (extracts)

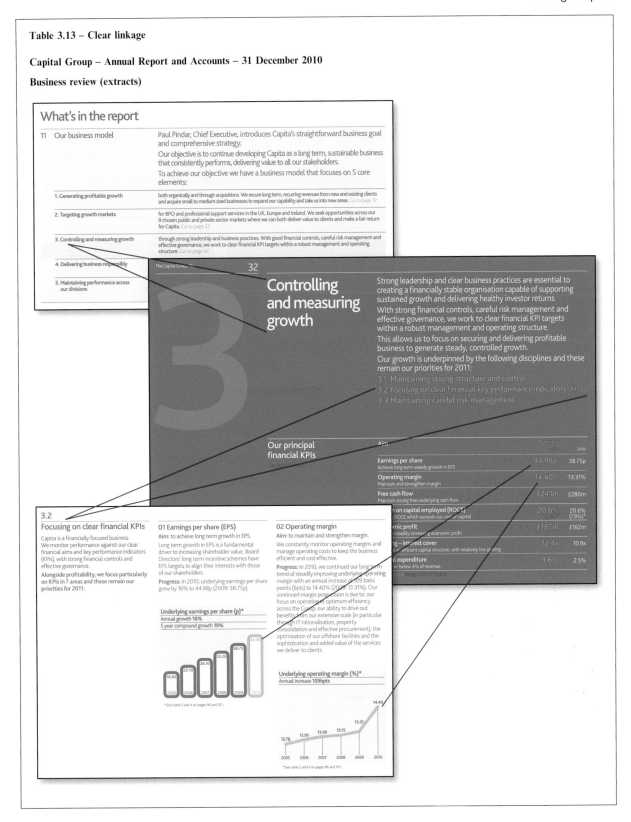

3.61 The most appropriate method of dealing with these linked requirements will depend on factors such as the nature of the information and any regulatory requirements specific to the disclosures being made. Where cross-referencing or signposting is used, care should be taken to ensure that the nature of the relationship or interdependency is adequately explained, rather than just highlighting its existence. [SR guidance para 6.19].

3.62 Clear signposting – between the strategic report and other narrative reports, the corporate governance statements, the financial statements or (where regulation allows) other material outside the annual report – will enable readers to readily 'drill down' into greater levels of detail, should they wish to do so.

Table 3.14 – Signposting

Marks & Spencer plc – Annual report and accounts – 30 March 2013

Financial overview

Group revenue	Underlying Group profit before tax	Group profit before tax
£10.0bn	£665.2m	£564.3m
↑1.3%*	↓5.8%	↓14.2%

Interim + final dividend	Underlying Group earnings per share	Group earnings per share
6.2p+ 10.8p = 17.0p	32.7p	29.2p
→level	↓6.3%	↓10.2%

UK	**Multi-channel**	**International**
Our UK turnover is split between Food (54%) and General Merchandise (46%). With 766 stores across the UK and a growing e-commerce business, we sell high-quality, great value food and remain the UK market leaders in womenswear, lingerie and menswear.	From browsing through to purchase and delivery, we aim to provide the best shopping experience for our customers. Whether in stores, online or by phone, we offer a convenient service for all our customers – however and whenever they choose to shop with us.	We are making the M&S brand even more accessible to customers around the world. We now operate in 51 territories across Europe, the Middle East and Asia and continue to grow our international presence through a multi-channel approach.
Read more on page 16	Read more on page 26	Read more on page 28

Plan A

We aim to become the world's most sustainable retailer and Plan A, our eco and ethical programme, is at the very heart of how we do business. More than five year since launch, we continue to extend the influence of Plan A – engaging our employees, suppliers and customers.

CERTIFIED CARBON NEUTRAL company

Read more on page 32

Total Plan A commitments	Commitments achieved	Commitments on plan
180	139	31

*Group revenue and International revenue increases are stated on a contstant currency basis throughout the direcotors' report. Using actual rates Group revenue was up 0.9% and International revenue was up 0.9%.

The information that fulfils the Business review requirements is incorporated by reference and can be found in the following sections:

- Chairman's statement on pages 2 to 3
- Strategic review on pages 8 to 33
- Our plan in action on pages 10 to 11
- Principal risks and uncertainties on pages 45 to 48
- Financial review on pages 34 to 37
- Social, environmental and ethical matters on pages 32 to 33.

More information is given in the How We Do Business report available on our website at marksandspencer.com/plana2013

3.63 It is probable that the information related to some disclosure requirements will be relevant to several different parts of the annual report. Where this is the case, management will need to consider how the linkages between these discrete disclosure requirements can be highlighted and explained in the most efficient and understandable way. [SR guidance para 6.20].

3.63.1 The duplication of information should generally be avoided as it usually leads to unnecessary volumes of disclosure detracting from the understandability and usefulness of the annual report as a whole. In some cases, it may be necessary to repeat certain pieces of information; however, this should be limited to circumstances when this would tell the entity's story more effectively. This may also be achieved by using signposting or cross-referencing. [SR guidance para 6.21].

Principle 6 – Annual review of structure and presentation

3.64 Principle 6 states that *"The structure and presentation of the strategic report should be reviewed annually to ensure that it continues to meet its objectives in an efficient and effective manner".* [SR guidance para 6.23].

3.65 Consistent structure, presentation and content will facilitate comparison from year to year, but the benefits of continuity should not override innovation where this will improve the relevance and understandability of the information presented. [SR guidance para 6.24].

Principle 7 – Annual review of content

3.65.1 Principle 7 states that *"The content of the strategic report should be reviewed annually to ensure that it continues to be relevant in the current period".* [SR guidance para 6.25].

3.65.2 Content that has been brought forward from previous years should be reviewed to ensure that it has continuing relevance. Any information that is no longer necessary in meeting the objectives of the strategic report should be removed. [SR guidance para 6.26].

Content elements

3.66 The guidance provides a framework for the disclosures to be included in a strategic report. The framework prescribes content elements that relate to the provisions of the Companies Act 2006; but it is for management to consider how best to use the framework to structure the strategic report, in view of the entity's circumstances. These circumstances might include:

■ The industry or industries in which the entity operates.

■ The range of products, services or processes that the entity offers.

■ The number of markets served by the entity.

3.67 The strategic report should provide information that assists members to assess not only the strategies adopted by the entity but also the potential for those strategies to succeed. The following key elements of the disclosure framework are necessary to achieve this:

■ Strategic management – how the entity intends to generate and preserve value. Includes insight into strategy and objectives and the business model. (See para 3.71 onwards.)

■ Business environment – the internal and external environment in which an entity operates. Includes trends and factors, principal risks and uncertainties and environmental, employee, social, community and human rights matters. (See para 3.96 onwards.)

■ Business performance – how the entity has developed and performed and its position at the year end. Includes analysis of performance and position, key performance indicators (KPIs) and employee gender diversity. (See para 3.125 onwards.)

3.68 To assist entities in structuring their strategic report more effectively, the FRC's guidance sets out the above framework, which can be represented in a logical flow, as shown in Table 3.15. The first column connects the main headings of the framework to our integrated reporting model (see para 3.15).

Table 3.15 – Disclosure framework

Integrated reporting model	Strategic report framework	
External drivers	Insight into the entity's business model and its main strategy and objectives (see para 3.71 onwards)	– Description of business and external environment.
Strategy*		– Objectives to generate or preserve value over the longer term. – Strategies for achieving the objectives.
Resources and relationships	A description of the principal risks that the entity faces and how they might affect its future performance (see para 3.108 onwards)	– Description of resources (tangible and intangible) available and how they are managed. – Description of principal risks and uncertainties and the directors' approach to them. – Information about significant relationships and stakeholders (other than investors) who might directly impact performance.
Performance	An analysis of the entity's past performance (see para 3.138 onwards)	– Significant features of the development and performance of the business. – Main trends and factors likely to impact future performance. – Analysis of financial position and critical accounting policies. – Discussion of capital structure. – Discussion of cash inflows and outflows, ability to generate cash to meet commitments, and fund growth. – Discussion of current and prospective liquidity.
Underpinned by the financial and non-financial KPIs used to assess progress against stated objectives (see para 3.191 onwards)		

*Strategy is affected by the risks facing the business and by management's appetite for risk.

3.69 The discussion of an issue related to any of the matters described in the paragraph above might be considered necessary for an understanding of the development, performance, position or future prospects of the entity's business; in that case, the strategic report should make it clear why it is considered necessary. The report should also include information on the entity's policies on those matters and the effectiveness of those policies.

3.70 The disclosures set out in paragraph 3.67 are only included to the extent that they are necessary to meet the objectives set out in the guidance; in other words, they are only included where they are relevant to the entity's business. Increasingly, these matters will be relevant to the business because, for example, they affect its reputation or its ability to obtain scarce resources. But the purpose of the strategic report is not to demonstrate an entity's 'green' or 'good employer' credentials, but to explain the entity's business development and performance, and so on. It is, of course, open to entities to prepare other reports to address the needs of stakeholders other than investors. In Table 3.16 the entity links its good environmental practice to its business development.

Table 3.16 – Sustainable development

Rio Tinto plc – Annual Report – 31 December 2010

Group strategy (extract)
The way we work: Governance, Sustainable Developoment and Values (extract)

The way we work is equally important to achieving our vision, as we integrate sustainable development practices into everything we do, wherever we operate: building on improvements to health and safety performance and extending leadership in areas such as community and government engagement, biodiversity and management of land, carbon, energy and water.

Success in these areas helps strengthen our licence to operate. We are recognised as a socially responsible developer, and one that builds strong relationships that bring lasting benefits to our neighbours and to the places where we work. Our approach gives us improved access to land, people and capital – all of which are essential to our future success.

> Makes the link between good environmental practice and business development.

Collectively, our strengths provide us with our strategic advantage. And this advantage is allowing us to meet responsibly the needs of a wide variety of customers while generating superior returns for our shareholders.

Sustainable Development Review (extract)

Our approach

📄 Group strategy on p.18

Sustainable development has been identified as an area crucial to the delivery of the Group's long term strategy.

> Sustainable development is key part of strategy.

The minerals and metals produced at our operations contribute to society's needs, delivering financial dividends for our shareholders, paying wages and salaries for our employees, and creating wealth to support community infrastructure, health care and education. Our activities also provide the means and opportunity to develop new approaches to the environmental and human development challenges confronting society, such as climate change and poverty.

We recognise that some aspects of our activities can lead to unavoidable impacts, such as limiting options for the future use of land and water, impacts on local communities, and greenhouse gas emissions from our operations and the use of our products. We strive to minimise these impacts through good management of our operations.

The extended timeframes associated with our operations from exploration, through development and operation to closure provide us with opportunities to plan, implement and deliver sustainable contributions to social wellbeing, environmental stewardship and economic prosperity, within our strong governance systems.

Our continued licence to operate is subject to the ever increasing expectations of society. Consequently, we have developed and implemented a structured framework to ensure that we meet our goal of contributing to the global transition to sustainable development. This framework contains the "must have" building blocks, which must all work together to achieve leading performance and manage risk effectively.

We are communicating and raising our awareness of our approach to our internal and external stakeholders.

In 2010 we commenced a review of our approach to sustainable development to ensure it remains focused on the risks most relevant to delivering our business strategy.

Sustainable development framework

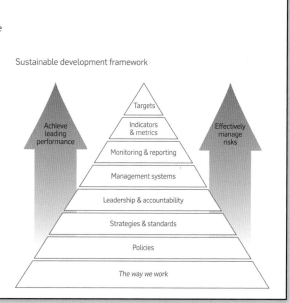

Detailed guidance within the disclosure framework

Strategic management

The entity's principal objectives and strategies

3.71 The strategic report should include a description of the entity's strategy and the objectives it is intended to achieve. [CA06 Sec 414C(8)(a); SR guidance para 7.5].

3.72 An entity will usually have a number of formal objectives that it intends to achieve in pursuit of its ultimate aim or mission. The entity will also have developed a strategy that describes the means by which it intends to achieve these objectives. A description of the strategy for achieving an entity's objectives provides insight into its development, performance, position and future prospects. The disclosure of the entity's objectives places the strategy in context and allows shareholders to make an assessment of its appropriateness. [SR guidance para 7.6].

3.73 To assess the quality and sustainability of an entity's performance, investors need to be clear about the entity's objectives, and its strategies for achieving those objectives: they need to know how management intends to address market trends, and the threats and opportunities that they represent; they also need to understand the relationship between strategic objectives, management actions and executive remuneration. (Directors' remuneration is dealt with in chapter 5.) All of this information will enable investors to judge the appropriateness and success of management actions in delivering the strategy and what to expect in the future.

3.74 Statements of objectives and strategies should provide the detail that enables investors to understand the priorities for action or the resources that must be managed to deliver results; they should also explain how success will be measured and over what period of time it should be assessed. The table below highlights an example from The Go Ahead Group, which clearly explains the specific actions to be taken against every aspect of its strategy, highlighting clear, specific and timely targets where possible.

Table 3.17 – Strategic priorities and actions

The Go Ahead Group – Annual report and accounts – 30 June 2012

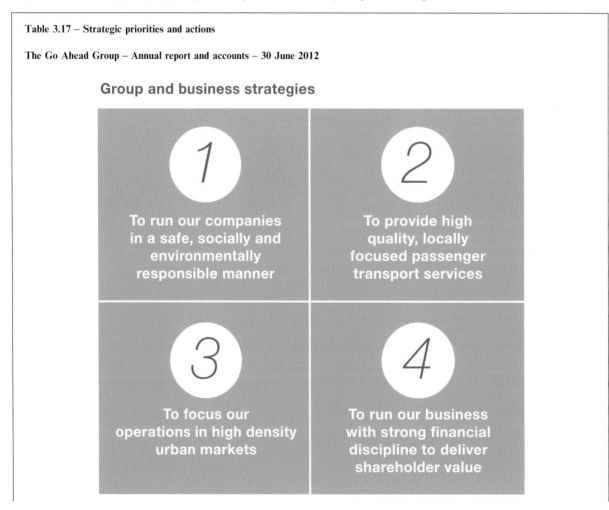

Group and business strategies

1 To run our companies in a safe, socially and environmentally responsible manner

2 To provide high quality, locally focused passenger transport services

3 To focus our operations in high density urban markets

4 To run our business with strong financial discipline to deliver shareholder value

1

To run our companies in a safe, socially and environmentally responsible manner

As a public transport operator, corporate responsibility is integral to the way we run our business. Ensuring the safety of our passengers and employees is an absolute priority for the Group. We are also committed to reducing the environmental impact of our operations. We strongly believe that a sustainable public transport network is essential to the future of the UK.

2012 progress

Safety

- Almost 90% of our bus fleet is fitted with CCTV
- There has been a significant reduction in bus accidents per million miles, down 39% on last year.
- Crime on our rail networks has reduced by 3% in the year
- Signals passed at danger (SPADs) reduced by over 20% in the year.

Driving Energy Further

- We have now achieved 14% of our target to reduce carbon emissions by 20% in 2015 with a 2% reduction in the year to 30 June 2012.

Site Energy

- Improvements such as fitting energy efficient LED lighting in outside areas have contributed to reducing site energy usage by almost 6% in the year.

Fuel efficiency

- A continued focus on driver training has helped to improve fuel efficiency in the year.

Olympic delivery

- Thorough preparation during the financial year enabled us to successfully play a key part in the transport provision of the 2012 Olympic Games. We were delighted to be involved in making the Games a great success and were pleased to have the opportunity to showcase our high quality services and staff. An estimated one in ten ticket holders travelled at least part of their journey on a Southeastern service. Punctuality on these services during the Olympics was an impressive 96%.

2013 priorities

Safety

- Improve performance against our Group targets to improve safety KPIs by at least 20% by 2015.

Environment

- Make further progress towards our targeted 20% reduction in carbon emissions per passenger journey by 2015.

Staff

- More staff to receive work-related training in order to enhance performance and development.

Community

- Continue to provide a positive contribution to the communities in which we operate.

Our key performance Indicators

The following KPIs underpin our strategic principle to be a responsible operator.

RIDDOR accidents per 100 employees

The reporting of injuries, diseases and dangerous occurrences regulation (RIDDOR) is a statutory requirement for all companies and relates to a work place incident which results in absence from work for over three days or a legally reportable incident to the Health & Safety Executive. We are pleased to report no employee fatalities this financial year.

Why it's important: Helps us to measure against our commitment to provide a safe working environment for our employees.

Aim: To reduce RIDDOR accidents by 60% by 2015[1] (previously 50%).

2012 performance: 1.01 RIDDOR accidents per 100 employees, an improvement of 11.4%

Bus accidents per million miles

The Board monitors the number of bus accidents which result in a notification to a claims handler.

Why it's important: Helps us to measure against our commitment to provide a safe and positive travel experience for our bus passengers and helps us to manage accident claim costs.

Aim: To reduce by 50% by 2015[1] (originally 20%).

2012 performance: 31.51 bus accidents per million miles, an improvement of 39.0%

SPADs per million miles[2]

Across the rail industry tram operating companies are legally required to report SPADs. Although every SPAD is treated as a serious incident, most SPADs occur at low speed where braking distance has been misjudged and the train is stopped by automatic warning systems and therefore the likelihood of an accident is very low. The industry average is 0.61[3].

Why it's important: Helps us to measure against our commitment to provide a safe rail passenger service.

Aim: To reduce SPADS by 60% by 2015[1] (previously 50%).

2012 performance: 0.58 SPADS per million miles, an improvement of 22.7%

Carbon emissions per passenger journey[4]

We monitor the carbon emissions from our operations per passenger journey.

Why it's important: Helps us to measure against our commitment to improve our energy efficiency and deliver high quality services that provide attractive alternatives to car travel.

Aim: To reduce carbon emissions per passenger journey by 20% by 2015[1].

2012 performance: 14% reduction in carbon emissions per passenger journey since 2008.

RIDDOR accidents per 100 employees

Bus accidents per million miles

SPADs per million miles

Reduction in CO_2 emissions per passenger journey (%)*

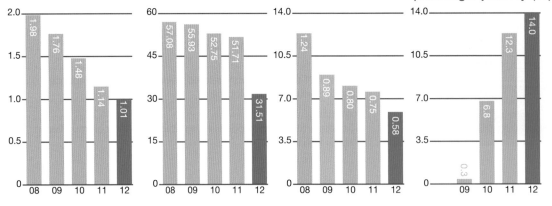

1. Target uses 2007/08 as the base year.

2. SPADs excludes those that occur in our depot, in line with industry reporting.

3. Association of Train Operating Companies (ATOC) Safety Key Performance Indicator (KPI) Report, July 2012.

4. CO_2 conversion factors used are in accordance with the most recent Department for Energy and Climate Charge guidelines 2012.

* The graph shows the cumulative reduction since 2007/08.

3.75 The description of the entity's strategy and objectives should concentrate on the high-level priorities related to its development, performance, position and future prospects. [SR guidance para 7.8].

3.76 For many businesses, financial objectives and general interests are best served by having increased regard to social, environmental and other non-financial factors. As a result, an entity's objectives, whilst generally continuing to focus on achieving returns for members, include or refer to non-financial objectives or factors, particularly in those industries that have the potential to significantly affect the environment in which they operate. The theme of increasing responsibility is now a trend or factor that influences the development of businesses. It emerges even more clearly in the development of strategies. Where creating value for the entity depends partly on the entity's response to social and environmental issues, this is built into management's strategies; and these strategies should be presented in the strategic report. In such cases, management's action in social and environmental fields is not an optional 'add-on', designed only to improve the image of the business, but it is part of core strategy to promote the quality and sustainability of business performance. Where social and environmental issues are not particularly important in delivering the entity's business objectives, they should not be included in the strategic report; this is because they will obscure the important disclosures.

3.77 Many entities now produce separate corporate social responsibility reports. So the strategic report might, in some cases, contain details of an entity's policy and performance in this area; but, in other cases, a separate report might be prepared. Sometimes, such a report is separate from the annual report and accounts, with only a summary appearing in the latter document; on other occasions, a full corporate social responsibility report is included with the annual report, either separate from the strategic report or incorporated within it.

3.78 Discussion of separate corporate social responsibility reporting is outside the scope of this chapter, but it is worth noting that a number of organisations are dedicated to improving corporate reporting in this area. Among them are Business in the Community and The Business Impact Review Group, who work together to develop a common approach to social and environmental reporting. As part of this work, they have developed guidance for disclosures under five major headings: marketplace, environment, workplace, community and human rights. For more on environmental reporting within the strategic report, see para 3.125 onwards.

3.79 Examples of where financial objectives are qualified by non-financial considerations in the extractive industry – one of the industries where such factors are most significant – are given in Table 3.18.

Table 3.18 – Social, environmental and other non-financial factors

BHP Billiton plc – Annual Report – 31 December 2010

3.2 Our strategy (extract)

Our objective and commitments are pursued through our six strategic drivers:

· *People* – the foundation of our business is our people. We require people to find resources, develop those resources, operate the businesses that produce our products, and then deliver those products to our customers. Talented and motivated people are our most precious resource.

· *Licence to operate* – we aim to ensure that the communities in which we operate value our citizenship. Licence to operate means win-win relationships and partnerships. This includes a central focus on health, safety, environment and the community, and making a positive difference to our host communities.

· *World-class assets* – our world-class assets provide the cash flows that are required to build new projects, to contribute to the economies of the countries in which we operate, to meet our obligations to our employees, suppliers and partners, and ultimately to pay dividends to our shareholders. We maintain high-quality assets by managing them in the most effective and efficient way.

· *Financial strength and discipline* – we have a solid 'A' credit rating, which balances financial flexibility with the cost of finance. Our capital management program has three priorities:
  – To return excess capital to shareholders.
  – To reinvest in our extensive pipeline of world-class projects that carry attractive rates of return regardless of the economic climate.
  – To ensure a solid balance sheet.

· *Project pipeline* – we are focused on delivering an enhanced resource endowment to underpin future generations of growth. We have an abundance of tier one resources in stable countries that provide us with a unique set of options to deliver brownfield growth.

· *Growth options* – we use exploration, technology and our global footprint to look beyond our current pipeline to secure a foundation of growth for future generations. We pursue growth options in several ways – covering the range from extending existing operations to new projects in emerging regions, through exploration, technology and, on occasion, merger and acquisition activity.

> Links strategy on people and licence to operate to key measures

3.3 Key measures (extract)

People and licence to operate

These foundational strategic drivers bring together health, safety, environment and community (HSEC) related measures. These measures are a subset of the HSEC Targets Scorecard, which can be found in each corresponding section of our Sustainability Report at *www.bhpbilliton.com*.

We monitor a comprehensive set of health, safety, environment and community contribution indicators. Two key measures are the Total Recordable Injury Frequency (TRIF) and community investment.

	2010	2009	2008
People and licence to operate – health, safety, environment and community			
Total Recordable Injury Frequency (TRIF) [1]	**5.3**	5.6	5.9
Community investment (US$M) [1]	**200.5**	197.8	141.0

[1] See section 10 for glossary definitions.

Safety – Despite strong performance improvement across the organisation, sadly we experienced the loss of five colleagues at our operations during the year.

We made an incremental improvement in Total Recordable Injury Frequency (which comprises fatalities, lost-time cases, restricted work cases and medical treatment cases per million hours worked) from 5.6 to 5.3 per million hours worked. This is over halfway towards our target of a 50 per cent reduction on 2007 TRIF performance of 7.4 by 2012.

Health – We are progressing well with our health performance objectives. We had 164 new cases of occupational disease reported in FY2010, 52 fewer new cases compared with the FY2007 base year. The overall reduction in occupational disease since FY2007 is 27 per cent, which is on track to meet our target of a 30 per cent reduction in incidences in occupational disease among our employees by June 2012.

It is mandatory for our employees who may be potentially exposed to airborne substances or noise in excess of our occupational exposure limits (OELs) to wear personal protective equipment. Compared with the FY2007 base year there was a 3.9 per cent reduction in the proportion of employees potentially exposed in excess of OELs in FY2010, which is behind schedule to meet our target of a 15 per cent reduction in potential employee exposures over our occupational exposure limits.

Environment – In FY2010, we reduced absolute greenhouse gas emissions by more than three million tonnes compared with FY2009.

We have five-year targets of a six per cent reduction in our greenhouse gas emissions intensity index and a 13 per cent reduction in our carbon-based energy intensity index, both by 30 June 2012. Our greenhouse intensity index is currently tracking at seven per cent below our FY2006 base year. Our carbon-based energy intensity index is currently tracking at six per cent below our FY2006 base year.

We have a five-year target of a 10 per cent improvement in our land rehabilitation index by 2012. This index is based on a ratio of land rehabilitated compared with our land footprint. In FY2010, the index improved by one per cent due to the development of new green and brownfield projects and the divestment of a number of operations, including Optimum Colliery in 2008, which had large areas of land under rehabilitation.

We have a five-year target of a 10 per cent improvement in the ratio of water recycled to high-quality water consumed by 30 June 2012. This water use index has improved seven per cent on our FY2007 base year.

We define a significant environmental incident as one with a severity rating of four or above based on our internal severity rating scale (tiered from one to five by increasing severity). One significant incident occurred during FY2010 at our Pinto Valley Operations (US) involving a tailings release. The majority of the eroded tailings and cover material were recovered. Metal concentrations in surface water and sediments appear to be well below levels that could present a hazard.

Community – We continue to invest one per cent of our pre-tax profits in community programs, based on the average of the previous three years' pre-tax profit publicly reported in each of those years. During FY2010, our voluntary investment totalled US$200.5 million comprising cash, in-kind support and administrative costs and includes a US$80 million contribution to BHP Billiton Sustainable Communities.

Despite the global financial crisis, our direct expenditure on community programs during the year was similar to our expenditure in FY2009.

3.80 Objectives can be financial or non-financial in nature and can be expressed in quantitative or qualitative terms. [SR guidance para 7.9].

3.81 Many strategic objectives focus on achieving value for shareholders and financial success. However, an entity's strategy should also be based on an understanding of the key areas in which an entity has competitive advantage (such as a market-leading customer base or a highly skilled workforce). The entity's success in creating value will depend on management's ability to invest resources in these areas and manage them so that they deliver the financial performance that investors expect.

3.82 In its 2011 annual report, Premier Farnell plc describes its strategy and breaks it down into areas of strategic focus. The entity describes what has happened in relation to each of these focus areas in the current year, and it sets out priorities for action in 2012. Table 3.19 shows an extract of the strategy and an extract of the related area of strategic focus.

Table 3.19 – Strategy – Priorities for action

Premier Farnell plc – Annual Report – 30 January 2011

Strategy (extract)

Focus on EDE

Central to the strategy is Electronic Design Engineering – an attractive market which offers above average gross margins and growth rates. Through providing an industry leading high service proposition together with an increasingly rich offering of design solutions, EDEs truly appreciate the value of our model and reward us with loyalty and high purchase frequency.

The global EDE market consists of customers involved in the design of electronic products and components. EDE customers have similar service requirements wherever they are located around the world – a broad product offering, latest technology, technical support, accurate design and legislative information and reliable and prompt delivery – which means we can leverage our global organisation to meet those needs. Increasingly EDEs also want to collaborate and discuss their work through social media, a trend which led us to launch the pioneering element14 community in 2009. This convergence of community with commerce is a trend we expect to increase and is central to our brand and eCommerce strategies.

We set a goal for this part of our strategy that 50% of MDD revenue would come from EDE customers by the end of 2010 and in many regions we exceeded that goal. That journey continues and we are now aiming for 50%–70% of our business to come from EDE by the end of our 2013 financial year. In the final quarter of 2011 EDE sales accounted for 53.7% of sales from our electronics distribution businesses.

Strategic report

Strategic Focus 1 (extract)

Strategic Focus 1
Profitable growth through
focusing on
EDEs globally

The world of the EDE is changing rapidly. Electronics is becoming increasingly ubiquitous across all aspects of life.

The demand for electronics in more end products is rising, while the importance of aesthetics and environmental compliance is driving an increase in the redesign of electronics. The speed-to-market requirements in the modern design world are also placing greater pressures on our core EDE customer group as they strive to take their designs from concept through to creation as quickly as possible. Such change is presenting us with much opportunity to develop solutions and enhance our proposition to meet the evolving needs of EDEs and win market share.

Designs have to work first time and comply with the latest legislation, as well as reflecting market focus on miniaturisation, green technology and the demands of aesthetics. In this climate the needs of the EDE go beyond the component – they require a wealth of data and information, design tools, software and, increasingly, the views of their global peers to inform their decisions. Once the pressure on time-to-market is factored in, the opportunity for meeting all those needs in a single converged web environment is clear. The element14 brand and our enhanced proposition are delivering just that – high service access to all the latest products, design and legislative information and the leading global EDE community.

The investments we continue to make in building such a holistic, industry leading proposition means we are able to meet more of an EDE's needs. This is reflected in our EDE active customer base growing 7.5% year-on-year as we concentrated on leveraging our powerful proposition to deliver accelerated market share gains and help to ensure customer loyalty.

During the year we enhanced the design support we provide EDEs through our own technical services department. We are continuing to invest to provide our engineering customers no matter where they are in the world, with 24 hour, five day a week access to our own dedicated technical support team. We have also introduced live chat as another method for customers to communicate with our own engineers, as we look to build a technical offering which fully complements our growing suite of services within our EDE ecosystem. Our acquisition of CadSoft, developer of the EAGLE CAD software, has enabled another step towards offering engineers a holistic solution to meet all their needs no matter what stage of the design cycle they are at. EAGLE and its ongoing development is just one aspect of our next 1,000 day services beyond product programme which is focused on introducing new technology or service based propositional enhancements that meet the needs of EDEs as they move through the design cycle. Indeed, towards the end of the year we launched a new service that combines the power of element14, the Eagle software and our franchise relationship with Pentalogix to allow customers to order a prototype directly from their virtual design environment.

EDE customers depend on our high service model to get their products to them exactly when they need them. Our delivery service is best-in-class, with 99.6% of our orders delivered either the same day or the next day, supported by our distribution facilities located in seven different locations around the world. However, to ensure we remain at the forefront of our industry, we hold numerous customer focus groups to ensure we stay in touch with and listen closely to the needs of our customers. This helps us to understand the challenges they are facing today and into the future. It also helps us to understand how we can meet those needs and where best to invest when developing our proposition to drive market share growth.

Achievements in 2011

- Our full year sales growth in the EDE sector outperformed our sales growth in the MRO sector by 20.8 percentage points, while EDE sales accounted for 52.5% of our distribution business' sales. This is within our target range of 50%–70%.

- Market launch in Asia Pacific of our enhanced value proposition and the first convergence of community and transactional web offerings under the element14 brand.

- Ongoing development of the element14 EDE community, with close to 50,000 registrants and over 1.5 million customers visiting the site in 2011. This has helped drive a 7.5% year-on-year increase in our EDE active customer base.

- Successful integration of CadSoft and the market launch of further enhancements to the EAGLE software, in conjunction with the launch of a rapid prototyping service accessible from within an EDE's CAD environment or directly on element14.

- Added 72,500 new EDE products to our stocked range, 43 new suppliers, and nearly doubled the locally stocked range in Asia Pacific to 122,000.

- Successfully enhanced our technical support services and global technology centres, located in Bangalore and Chengdu, with over 200 technical experts now employed within the organisation globally.

Priorities in 2012

- Leveraging the convergence of community, information and transaction under the element14 brand to drive customer acquisition and loyalty.

- Accelerate our services beyond product initiative to create and launch a holistic ecosystem for design engineers that offers EDEs the solutions and services they require at each stage of the design cycle.

- Build on our work in 2011 to draw together design tools, software and partners into a truly collaborative workspace for EDEs.

- Focus on customer acquisition in the world's developing markets and key high growth vertical markets globally, such as lighting, solar and wind while also targeting universities to attract tomorrow's engineers to the element14 brand.

- Provide our supplier partners with rich insights into customer behaviour from our global online environment as we seed the market with their latest technology and supporting information.

- Ensure efficient and cost effective stocking processes are in place, purchasing products around the world, making the most of Premier Farnell's global footprint.

- Continue to invest in technical skills, software and services to build a global brand with EDEs.

- Engage with customers and suppliers to find new ways to reduce our environmental footprint.

3.83 Strategies and objectives can also embed environmental, social and ethical values of particular importance to the entity, as shown in Table 3.20. In this example, Marks and Spencer Group PLC sets out how Plan A is important to its brand value, as well as helping to reduce costs.

3040

Table 3.20 – Embedding non-financial values in strategy

Marks and Spencer Group PLC – Annual Report and Financial Statements – 2 April 2011

About M&S (extract)

Plan A

Plan A is our eco and ethical programme. Our commitments help us to reduce our environmental impact, develop sustainable products and improve the lives of our employees, customers, suppliers and people in our local communities.

Seven pillars
180 commitments

P30

Involve our customers in Plan A
Make Plan A how we do business
Climate change
Waste
Natural resources
Fair partner
Health & wellbeing

Plan A DOING THE RIGHT THING

Our performance (extract)

Making Plan A how we do business   P30

Improve carbon efficiency
in tonnes CO_2e per 1,000 sq ft of salesfloor

2006/07	2010/11	Improvement	2012 target
51	38	25%	0

Store, office, warehouse, business travel and logistics carbon dioxide emissions in tonnes CO_2e per 1,000 sq ft of salesfloor. Residual emissions will be offset by 2012.

Why carbon efficiency? Improving carbon efficiency reduces greenhouse emissions and costs.

Governance: Accountability (extract)

Risk description

Mitigating activities

Brand and reputation Our founding principles of Quality, Value, Service, Innovation and Trust continue to influence how we do business and our reputation for being one of the UK's most trusted brands.

Corporate reputation
External expectations relating to our Plan A, ethical or corporate governance commitments are not adequately managed
Our brand continues to be trusted in the marketplace with Plan A being an integral component of the M&S brand. With such a strong brand comes high expectations and the need to consistently deliver quality and value to our wide stakeholder base.

– Our commitment to Plan A and becoming the world's most sustainable major retailer by 2015 continues to be a priority for the Group with one of our key objectives being for all M&S products to have at least one Plan A attribute by 2020.
– We have recently launched 'Only at Your M&S' emphasising to customers that they will find exclusive and innovative products that are unique to M&S.
– We are ensuring that adequate policies and procedures are in place to meet the requirements of the Bribery Act 2010 which comes into force in July this year.

Financial Review (extract)

Looking ahead

Plan A is an integral part of the M&S brand, which sets us apart from the competition. In the year ahead we aim to retain our leadership position and make Plan A even more relevant to our customers.

3.84 When describing an entity's strategies, directors should include information about any changes in strategies. This is particularly important where past strategies have not been successful, resulting in poor performance. In such circumstances, it is important for directors (in seeking to restore lost confidence in the entity) to spell out in detail the revised strategies for the future. In doing so, they might have particular regard, when discussing past strategy, to the principle that the strategic report should be balanced and neutral, dealing even-handedly with both good and bad aspects.

3.85 The example of Serco, set out in the table below, demonstrates direction, and transparency, from the Chairman when significant change has been required to strategic priorities.

Table 3.20.1 – Changing strategy

Serco plc – Annual report and accounts – 31 December 2014

Chairman's Statement

Since the traumatic events of 2013, when overbilling in our Electronic Monitoring contracts and misreporting of data on the Prisoner Escort & Custody Services contract was identified, I have sought to stabilise Serco with the recruitment of strong new management and Non-Executive Directors, building a much improved relationship with the UK Government; and bringing clarity to our strategic direction. During the course of 2014 we undertook a Strategy Review which reassessed the Group's future prospects, including Contract and Balance Sheet Reviews and identified the right capital structure, to which the rights issue launched on 12 March 2015 for approximately £555m is central. All of these are necessary steps in putting Serco back onto an even keel and giving our new management team the firm foundation for taking the Company forward again.

3.85.1 Transnet Limited's 2010 annual report describes the entity's new 'Quantum Leap Strategy', which sets targets for a five-year period. Table 3.21 gives an overview of the change in strategy; and Table 3.22 shows the projections for capital investment, which is one of the key areas of focus under the new strategy.

Table 3.21 – Changes in strategy

Transnet Limited – Annual Report – 31 March 2010

Review of strategy execution

Review of strategy execution

The successful turnaround of the Company laid the foundation for the Growth Strategy adopted in 2008. Achieving the targeted growth in volumes has been impacted by the global economic crisis – given the high correlation between commodity volumes and containers handled by Transnet and global economic growth. Despite the impact of the global economic crisis the outcome of the Growth Strategy is evident in the performance of the Company during the year. While operational performance has improved in many areas of the Company, the **rate of improvement has not met our expectations**. Progress has been slow and at best incremental.

During the year the Board approved a strategic shift from the Growth Strategy. This shift constitutes a number of focus areas and initiatives to be implemented in the medium-term, and will enhance Transnet's ability to deliver on its mandate and position the Company to support the long-term competitiveness of the South African economy.

The strategy going forward will be on realising a **Quantum Leap** improvement in **customer service** by improving **operational efficiency** in all areas of the business together with **volume growth** while maintaining the **financial stability** of the Company.

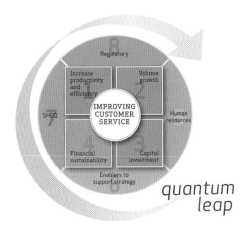

Achieving objectives within a framework of
corporate governance, internal controls, dynamic
management reporting, leading environmental practices and
legal compliance.

This is embodied in the Quantum Leap Strategy as set out below:

- Harnessing **volume growth** opportunities;
- Achieving substantial improvement in **customer service**;
- Increasing **productivity** and operating **efficiencies**;
- Implementing effective **cost-control** and reducing the cost base;
- Continuous **improvement** in **safety** and environmental compliance; and
- Improving asset utilisation to achieve **appropriate returns**.

The overarching theme for 2011 is a Quantum Leap improvement in customer service, volume growth and operational efficiency. The Quantum Leap initiatives aims to change the trajectory of performance improvement to a significantly higher level.

This will be achieved by enhancing operational efficiencies across the Company which will result in an improvement in the reliability and predictability of services while maintaining the financial sustainability for the Company.

Table 3.22 – Strategy over five-year timescale

Transnet Limited – Annual Report – 31 March 2010

Our key focus areas going forward – Quantum Leap Strategy (extract)

Capital investments#

Five-year capital investment (R93,4 billion)
(R million)

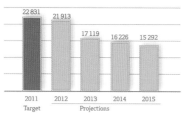

	2011 Target	2012	2013	2014	2015
	22 831	21 913	17 119	16 226	15 292
			Projections		

Five-year capital investment by commodity

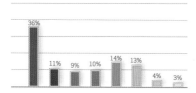

- ● General freight (R33,5 billion)
- ● Export coal (R10,1 billion)
- ● Export iron ore (R8,6 billion)
- ● Maritime containers (R9,2 billion)
- ● Pipelines liquid bulk (R12,5 billion)
- ◔ Other* (R13,7 billion)
- ◔ Bulk ports (R3,4 billion)
- ○ Break-bulk ports (R2,4 billion)

Other includes investments that support commodities that may span across sectors including the above, eg tugs and dredgers support all commodities transported.

Capacity creation – within five years

Equipment	Existing fleet	Additions
Locomotives	1 978	554
Wagons	72 643	7 231
Cranes	95	19

	Existing capacity	Future capacity
GFB	81mt	110mt
Export coal	71mt	81mt
Export iron ore	47mt	60,7mt
Containers	4,56 m TEUs	6,26 m TEUs
Pipeline (NMPP)	4,4bℓ	8,7 bℓ

Excludes capitalised borrowing costs.
million tons (mt)
billion litres (bℓ)

targets for 2011 - 2015

Transnet has formulated a **National Infrastructure Plan** (NIP) – 30 year infrastructure capacity plan.

General freight business (GFB) volume increase is supported by an investment plan of **R33,5 billion** which includes additional locomotives, wagons and upgrade to the infrastructure. OR

Studies are currently under way to increase the capacity for **export coal** to 81mt. **R10,1 billion** has been included in the five-year investment plan to support the growth of this commodity. OR

Growth of 60,7mt for **export iron ore** is aligned with customer contracts in place. Capital investment of **R8,6 billion** is included in the investment plan. Growth beyond 60,7mt is being investigated. OR

Container volume growth will remain moderate over the next year, however long-term projections indicate staggered growth of between 6% and 9% which is in line with international trends. **R9,2 billion** will be spent to support future growth. OR

Transnet will continue to implement the **CSDP** to contribute towards the competitiveness of the domestic supply chain and procurement environment.

3.85.2 Where relevant, linkage to and discussion of key performance indicators (KPIs) should be included in any descriptions given in order to allow an assessment of the entity's progress against its strategy and objectives. Similarly, emphasising the relationship between an entity's principal risks and its ability to meet its objectives might provide relevant information. [SR guidance para 7.10]. In Table 3.22.1, SEGRO draws all of these elements together in a clear strategy overview table.

Table 3.22.1 – Strategy linked to KPIs and risks

SEGRO PLC – Annual Report – 31 December 2013

Providing a clear line of sight

OVERVIEW **AT A GLANCE**

PROVIDING A CLEAR LINE OF SIGHT

OUR STRATEGIC PRIORITIES

Our strategy is founded on the two pillars of Disciplined Capital Allocation and Operational Excellence which, if underpinned by an efficient and prudent capital structure and lean overhead base, should translate into attractive shareholder returns. For more information see page 11.

In November 2011, we published our four strategic priorities to deliver our goals.

OUR PERFORMANCE

We have delivered tangible results against our strategic objectives, but recognise that there remains more to do.

OUR BUSINESS MODEL

We want to be the best European owner-manager and developer of warehouse/industrial properties and to be a leading income-focused REIT.

BUY SMART

We acquire land and buildings in European countries and regions which offer attractive income and capital growth potential.

ADD VALUE

We manage each of our assets to enhance their capital and income returns through lease initiatives, refurbishment and development.

SELL WELL

We assess the future return and risk profile of each of our assets and will sell if we believe that disposal will generate a higher risk-adjusted return than continuing to hold the asset.

1 RESHAPING THE EXISTING PORTFOLIO

To focus on high-quality, modern warehousing and light industrial assets in the strongest markets

We sold £591 million of assets at an average 4.7 per cent above December 2012 book values and at a topped-up yield of 7.2 per cent.

We generated a total property return (TPR) of 10.7 per cent. Our UK portfolio TPR was 14.0 per cent outperforming the IPD UK benchmark TPR of 12.7 per cent.

2 DELIVERING PROFITABLE GROWTH THROUGH DEVELOPMENT AND ACQUISITION

To take advantage of development and acquisition opportunities which meet or exceed our target rates of return and enhance the quality of our portfolio

We acquired £141 million of land and standing assets, the latter at a yield of 7.1 per cent.

We deployed £108 million into our development pipeline, completing 15 projects, 85 per cent let at 31 December 2013, generating £6.6 million of rent when fully let. Our pipeline contains 18 projects which are 60 per cent pre-let.

3 REDUCING NET DEBT AND INTRODUCING THIRD PARTY CAPITAL

To create a capital structure which seeks to enhance our return on equity on a sustainable basis throughout the property cycle without taking undue risk

We reduced Group net debt by £631 million, reducing our 'look-through' LTV to 42 per cent from 51 per cent at 31 December 2012.

We created the SEGRO European Logistics Partnership joint venture, seeding it with €1 billion of Continental European 'big box' logistics assets and development land.

4 DRIVING OUR OPERATIONAL PERFORMANCE

To improve total property returns through excellent asset management and customer service, whilst keeping tight control on costs

£27 million of rental income contracted compared to £21 million of take-backs (excluding Neckermann).

Like-for-like net rental income fell 1.5 per cent

Cost ratio rose to 24.2 per cent (2012: 22.9 per cent) despite a 7 per cent fall in administrative expenses.

EPRA vacancy rate is 8.5 per cent (2012: 8.2 per cent).

76 per cent of our customers rated us 'good' or 'excellent' (2012: 72 per cent).

FOR MORE DETAIL, SEE: FINANCIAL REVIEW PAGE 48 ▶

OUR KPIs

43.2%
TOTAL SHAREHOLDER RETURN

10.7% TOTAL PROPERTY RETURN | **312P** EPRA NAV PER SHARE | **42%** LTV

10.7% TOTAL PROPERTY RETURN | **17.7P** EPRA EPS | **8.5%** EPRA VACANCY RATE

42% LTV

17.7P EPRA EPS | **24.2%** TOTAL COST RATIO | **76%** CUSTOMER SATISFACTION

8.5% EPRA VACANCY RATE | **10.7%** TOTAL PROPERTY RETURN

OUR FUTURE

We will continue to manage the Group in line with our four strategic priorities.

We will deploy our asset base, capital structure and management expertise to generate attractive returns in 2014 and beyond, without taking undue risk.

We will continue to sell our non-core assets but we will also sell core assets if their risk/return profile does not meet our targets.

There were £440 million of non-core assets on the balance sheet at 31 December 2013 (2012: £725 million).

We will continue to source new acquisitions in our core markets which enhance our return and risk profile.

We have 18 development projects in our pipeline at 31 December, which are 60 per cent pre-let at 31 December 2013. We will add to our development programme in 2014.

We retain our longer-term term target of a 40 per cent 'look-through' LTV ratio.

The LTV could fluctuate depending on the timing and extent of acquisitions, disposals and development expenditure.

We aim to generate positive rent roll growth from standing assets.

We target a vacancy rate of between 6 per cent and 8 per cent over the long-term.

We retain our target total cost ratio of 20 per cent although achieving this is dependent on both cost control and the level of gross rental income.

We aim to at least maintain our level of customer satisfaction.

OUR RISK AWARENESS

Equity market volatility and relative performance of peers can impact the performance of SEGRO's shares.

Our performance is also dependent on macro-economic conditions as well as changes in government policies and in the commercial real estate environment.

The investor appetite for commercial real estate could impact the valuation of our assets, our ability to sell at prices in line with current valuation and our ability to acquire assets at prices which meet our return criteria.

A poor macro-economic environment could impact our tenants' ability to pay their rent.

We are dependent on equity and debt markets for funding, as well as on our ability to raise proceeds from disposals.

Any disruption to equity or debt capital markets could limit our ability to fund acquisitions and developments.

Our LTV is dependent both on the quantum of debt on our (and our joint ventures') balance sheet, which depends on the level of capital investment, our ability to sell assets, and on the value of our assets which depends on the health of the commercial real estate environment and the pricing of other asset classes.

Our operational performance is dependent on the financial health of our customers and other stakeholders.

A weak or uncertain economy can cause occupiers to reduce their space requirements and may impact their ability to pay rent and other property charges.

The actions of competitors can impact our operational performance, influencing rental levels and yields.

KPIs | PAGE 12 ▶ | FINANCIAL REVIEW | PAGE 48 ▶ | PRINCIPAL RISKS | PAGE 32 ▶

The entity's business model

3.86 The strategic report should include a description of the entity's business model. [CA06 Sec 414C(8)(b); SR guidance para 7.11].

3.87 The description of the entity's business model should set out how it generates or preserves value over the longer term, and how it captures that value. It should describe what the entity does and why it does it. It should also make clear what makes it different from, or the basis on which it competes with, its peers. [SR guidance para 7.12].

3.88 From the business description, a user of the financial statements can expect to gain an overall picture of the business model. It is a key disclosure for any entity that wishes to communicate effectively with investors and other interested parties: How does the business work? What does the business do to add value, and how does it do it? In Table 3.23, ARM Holdings plc gives an overview of its business model.

Table 3.23 – Business model

ARM Holdings plc – Annual Report – 31 December 2010

Overview (extract)

How ARM makes money

ARM is the world's leading semiconductor intellectual property (IP) supplier. The technology we design was at the heart of many of the digital electronic products sold in 2010.

ARM has an innovative business model. We licence our technology to a network of Partners, mainly leading semiconductor manufacturers. These Partners incorporate our designs alongside their own technology to create smart, low-energy chips suitable for modern electronic devices.

Why semiconductor companies use ARM technology

ARM designs technology that once was developed by our Partners' R&D teams, but it is cheaper for them to licence the technology from ARM. The design of a processor requires a large amount of R&D investment and expertise. We estimate that every semiconductor company would need to spend about $100 million every year to reproduce what ARM does. This represents an additional $20 billion of annual costs for the industry. By designing once and licensing many times, ARM spreads the R&D costs over the whole industry, making digital electronics cheaper.

Technologies that are suitable for the ARM business model

ARM's licensing business started in the early 1990s with the development of our first processor. The processor is like the brain of the chip; it is where the software runs and controls the functionality of the product that the chip is in. ARM designs each processor to be applicable to a broad range of end-markets to maximise the number of companies that can licence each processor. In most years ARM introduces 2-3 new processor designs.

Recently, ARM has developed other technologies suitable for a licensing and royalty business model, such as graphics processors and physical IP components.

How ARM creates value

ARM endeavours to recover its costs from the licence revenues of each technology, leaving the majority of royalties as profits. Over the medium term, we expect royalties to grow faster than licence revenues, and we expect that revenues will grow faster than costs, making ARM increasingly profitable.

As our customers are the world's largest semiconductor manufacturers, their regular royalty payments have become a highly reliable cash flow. ARM's business model is strongly cash generative. In 2010 we generated £180 million of cash. Since 2004, ARM has returned over £400 million of cash to shareholders through a combination of share buybacks and dividends.

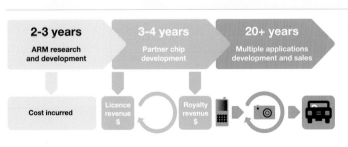

ARM business model

The companies who choose ARM technology pay an up-front licence fee to gain access to a design. They incorporate the ARM technology into their chip – a process that often takes 3-4 years. When the chip starts to ship, ARM receives a royalty on every chip that uses the design. Typically our royalty is based on the price of the chip. Each ARM processor design is suitable for a wide range of end applications and so can be reused in different chip families addressing multiple markets. Each new chip family generates a new stream of royalties. An ARM processor design may be used in many different chips and may ship for over 20 years.

3.89 The description of the business model should also provide shareholders with an understanding of how the entity is structured, the market in which it operates, and how the entity engages with those markets (for example, what part of the value chain it operates in, its main products, services and customers, and its distribution methods). [SR guidance para 7.13].

Table 3.23.1 – Business Model – place in the value chain

Croda plc – Annual report and accounts – 31st December 2014

Our Value Chain

To maximise growth opportunities we need to keep in step with all stages of the value chain: from keeping informed of the global drivers and mega trends, to understanding the priorities of our customers. In doing so, we are helping them to reach their own sustainability targets and meet the expectations of their consumers. Here are some examples of how our products have met our customers' needs to satisfy consumer demands during 2014.

	Consumer Demand	Customer Need	Croda	Customer Manufacture	Consumer Benefit
Control of Friction (p9)	Environmental concerns are boosting calls for greener transport	Companies want to produce oil and fuel that is more efficient and reduces emissions	Our ingredients reduce friction between moving parts and improve performance efficacy	Our ingredients are added to the customer's product to increase fuel efficiency and reduce wear and tear	Drivers have more environmentally friendly transport that lasts longer
Pure Health Partnership (p7)	The expanding elderly population faces multiple health challenges	Drug companies require active pharmaceutical ingredients to treat heart health issues	Our product OmeRx™ is derived from Omega 3, which is a recognised treatment for hypertriglyceridemia	Par Pharmaceuticals successfully markets OmeRx as a drug in North America	The drug supports patients with cardio vascular problems
Turning Back Time (p15)	People are continuously seeking ways to stay looking young	Personal care companies want to deliver effective anti-ageing products	We develop high performance ingredients like the Matrixyl™ range, which repairs skin	Matrixyl features in leading skin care brands to make an advanced anti-ageing claim	Consumer and beauty specialist feedback confirms that some of the products containing Matrixyl are amongst the best anti-ageing formulations ever
Sustainable Palm Oil (p33)	Consumers are concerned about the environmental impact of growing palm trees for their oil	Companies are committed to finding a sustainable source of palm oil and its derivatives	We lead our industry in offering sustainable palm oil and palm kernel oil derivatives	Companies can meet their sustainability targets by using our ingredients in their products	Discerning consumers can buy products with ingredients that support sustainable palm oil

Our Business Model

Engage → Create → Make → Sell

Our Value Chain

Consumer Demand → Customer Need → Croda → Customer Manufacture → Consumer Benefit

3.89.1 The description of the business model should provide shareholders with an understanding of the nature of the relationships, resources and other inputs that are necessary for the successful continuation of the business. [SR guidance para 7.15].

3.90 Table 3.24 shows the key inputs into Aggreko's business model – an overview view which is supported by more detail on how each of the key resources is managed.

Table 3.24 – Investing to implement business model

Business model and relationships

Aggreko plc – Annual Report – 31 December 2014

STRATEGIC REPORT CONTINUED

HOW WE CREATE VALUE
THROUGH OUR BUSINESS MODEL

 KEY INPUTS    FLEET

Human

 We have a highly skilled and professional workforce of over 7,700 employees worldwide

Supply chain

 We work with suppliers to ensure the components and services they provide comply with our quality standards

Design and manufacture

 We work closely with engine manufacturers and technology partners to design and manufacture equipment that is fuel efficient, emissions compliant and with a unique capital cost advantage

Financial

 The Group has a strong balance sheet with sufficient facilities available

Intellectual

 We invest in our technology and operating procedures to deliver better performance

Power

9,695MW   £926m
assets[1]

Chillers

1,294MW   £53m
assets[1]

Oil-free air

634cfm   £12m
assets[1]

Ancillaries

£95m
assets[1]

KEY INPUTS

Relationships
We have longstanding relationships with many of our suppliers, notably Cummins, our main engine supplier. We also have sourcing relationships across the globe where we work very closely with suppliers to ensure that the components and services provided comply with our quality standards.

1 Net asset value

Strategic report

How our strategy maximises performance
⮕ Page 22

Risks that are involved
⮕ Page 28

LOCAL BUSINESS

POWER PROJECTS

Maintain and Service

211

Sales and Service Centres worldwide operating a hub and spoke model

4

Power Projects hubs on major shipping routes

Local business revenue

£904m

Average contract value: £21k

The Local business rents power and temperature control equipment to a diverse range of customers who operate it themselves; we service and maintain it

Power Projects revenue

£625m (excluding pass-through fuel)

Average contract value: £5 million per annum

The Power Projects business sells electricity which we deliver using power plants built, owned and operated by ourselves

The value we create

 Supporting industry and commerce

 Providing power for countries and communities

 Enabling key events around the world

 Innovating to build a sustainable business

 Global employment

 Strong brand and good reputation

 Rewarding careers

 Shareholder returns

OUR PROJECT LIFE CYCLE IS EXPLAINED ON THE NEXT PAGE

 Understand the requirement

 Design and Plan

 Proposal

  Mobilise, Install and Commission

  Operate

 Service and Maintain

 Demobilise

 Service and Refurbish

STRATEGIC REPORT CONTINUED

HOW WE CREATE VALUE
USING OUR RESOURCES

 Human

Aggreko has over 6,300 permanent and 1,400 temporary employees worldwide, united by our unique culture which has developed over more than 50 years. Our people are highly skilled and are used to reacting quickly, doing a professional job in a safe manner and above all, responding effectively under pressure.

We have enormous strength and depth throughout the business. Our sales and commercial teams are highly trained and understand the financial, regulatory and environmental logistics of operating in challenging markets; our engineers and technicians are trained to problem solve in even the most difficult situations to keep our equipment operating; supported by strong back office functions.

Our people are our biggest asset. Therefore it is essential that our people are properly trained and are remunerated and incentivised appropriately. Each part of the business has training programmes in place to provide our employees with the necessary skills to perform their role; training is a combination of on-the-job learning and specific skill development through training courses.

Read more about our people
➔ Page 62

The Company's remuneration policy, set out in the Corporate governance report, is aligned with the key objectives of growing earnings and delivering strong returns on capital employed. These metrics are used for the Group's long-term incentive scheme and senior managers' annual bonuses. We also encourage all employees to own shares in the Company and currently over 2,400 people participate in the Sharesave programme.

Read more about our remuneration policy
➔ Page 92

 Supply Chain

Aggreko's supply chain capability in managing suppliers to provide goods and services in around 100 countries is a key part of our business model, including the logistics of getting equipment and supplies into and out of these countries in a short period of time. We have long standing relationships with many of our suppliers, notably Cummins, our main engine supplier. We also have sourcing relationships across the globe where we work very closely with suppliers to ensure that the components and services provided comply with Aggreko's quality standards.

Design and Manufacture

Unusually for a rental company, we design and assemble most of our power equipment. Our specialist in-house teams based in Dumbarton, Scotland, understand intimately the requirements of the environment in which the fleet operates. We operate equipment for its useful life; we do not build our equipment to sell. This gives a powerful incentive to maintain it well, which gives a longer life and better reliability.

Designing and assembling our own fleet gives us a unique competitive advantage:

- **Optimise equipment to meet our particular operational requirements**
- **Design equipment for reliability and longevity**
- **Material capital cost advantage through economies of scale and not paying the final assembly margin (20–40% over competitors)**
- **React quickly to customer requirements with lead times of only a few months from engine order to the equipment being in the fleet**

We currently purchase most of our temperature control equipment externally to suit the needs of local markets.

Fleet is managed on a real time basis across the world and is transferable across all sectors and applications, which enables us to optimise utilisation and therefore its deployment and returns.

Financial

The Group has sufficient facilities to meet our funding requirements over the medium term. These facilities have a range of maturities and are satisfied by the following covenants:

Funding Source	Covenants	Performance as at December 2014
Lenders	EBITDA ≥4x Interest	EBITDA to Interest: 27x
	Net debt/EBITDA ≤3x	Net debt to EBITDA: 0.9x

The Group does not consider these covenants restrictive and under normal business conditions looks to operate the business with net debt/EBITDA ratio of around one. The Group believes that this is the appropriate level given the characteristics of the Group, including the inherently risky nature of where we operate, in particular in the Power Projects business.

Fleet is at the heart of any rental business; it is the core of the service we offer and managing it effectively is necessary to ensure the long-term sustainability of our business

OUR DESIGN AND ASSEMBLY CAPABILITY

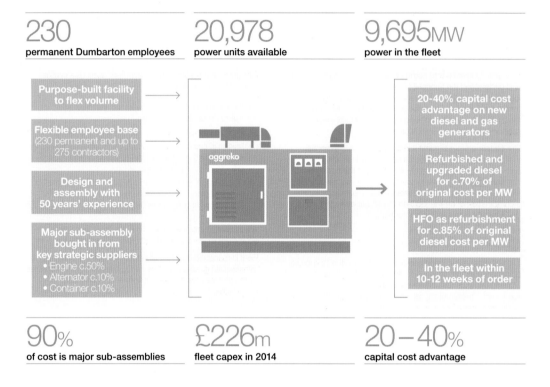

230
permanent Dumbarton employees

20,978
power units available

9,695MW
power in the fleet

Purpose-built facility to flex volume

Flexible employee base (230 permanent and up to 275 contractors)

Design and assembly with 50 years' experience

Major sub-assembly bought in from key strategic suppliers
• Engine c.50%
• Alternator c.10%
• Container c.10%

aggreko

20-40% capital cost advantage on new diesel and gas generators

Refurbished and upgraded diesel for c.70% of original cost per MW

HFO as refurbishment for c.85% of original diesel cost per MW

In the fleet within 10-12 weeks of order

90%
of cost is major sub-assemblies

£226m
fleet capex in 2014

20–40%
capital cost advantage

Intellectual

We have built a competitive advantage by designing our own equipment that is fit for purpose. Key attributes of our equipment are:

• Durable and portable – has to be lifted and transported hundreds of times during its life
• Ability to work in extreme conditions, both temperature and altitude
• Fuel efficient
• Safe
• Quiet
• Reliable
• Compliant with environmental and safety regulations

Furthermore, in recent years we have invested in the underlying technology to deliver better performance and new capability in our 1MW generators. We were the first company in the world to develop and assemble 1MW gas generators in 20 foot containers; we have increased the power output of our 1MW diesel engines by 15% whilst improving fuel consumption by 4% and we have re-engineered the same engines to allow them to run on Heavy Fuel Oil.

We have also developed a process to allow us to re-cycle and refurbish our large diesel generators at the end of their useful life, for significantly less than the cost of a new generator. At the same time, we re-engineer it to the latest specification.

Read more about generator refurbishments
See page 61

3.91   The discussion of an entity's business model should include a description of the resources available to the entity and how they are managed. It should set out the key strengths and resources, tangible and intangible, available to the business that will help it to pursue its objectives. This should include, in particular, resources that are not reflected in the balance sheet. Depending on the nature of the business, these might include:

■   Corporate reputation.

■   Brand strength.

- Natural resources.

- Employees.

- Research and development.

- Intellectual capital.

- Licences, patents, copyright and trademarks.

- Market position.

- Customer/supplier relationships.

- Strength of proprietary business processes, such as distribution systems.

- Websites and databases.

- Non-financial aspects of reputation, such as environmental reputation or strength of involvement in and identification with the community.

- Strength of geographical spread or product range.

3.92 Resources to be disclosed will depend on the nature of the business and the industry in which the entity operates. The example in Table 3.25 shows how an entity sees its brands as key assets and explains how it has developed them during the year.

Table 3.25 – Resources – brands

LVMH Group – Annual Report – 31 December 2010

Review of operations (extract)

Champagne and wines

In 2010, revenue generated by the Champagne and Wines business amounted to 1,664 million euros. Profit from recurring operations totaled 453 million euros.

Moët & Chandon consolidated its position as the world leader in champagne. The brand fully benefited from the recovery in demand in most of the major consumer countries and recorded remarkable growth in the emerging markets.

The creation of *Moët Ice Impérial*, the first champagne developed to be drunk over ice during the summer, was another illustration of the tradition of innovation and the pioneering spirit of Moët & Chandon. This new product offers a brand new experience and a radically new way to drink champagne. The introduction of the 2002 Vintage, the first since 1930 to have aged for seven years, achieving exceptional levels of maturity and harmony, was the year-end high point and illustrates the wine-making expertise of the brand.

Moët & Chandon expanded its presence and its visibility at international film festivals. The House also organized an extraordinary event at its vineyard during the harvest to celebrate its heritage and its expertise, an event attended by its international ambassador Scarlett Johansson.

Dom Pérignon, an iconic brand, showing strong growth, performed exceptionally well in the United States, Europe and Asia as retail inventories returned to normal levels. The brand organized dynamic events, including VIP dinners to highlight a history that dates back to 1668 at the Abbaye d'Hautvillers. The year 2010 was an exceptional year with the launch of four vintages (Vintage 2002, Rosé Vintage 2000, OEnothèque Vintage 1996 and OEnothèque Rosé Vintage 1990, the first of its kind), which were all received enthusiastically by the trade press. Another unique moment during the year was the tribute to Andy Warhol, the master of Pop Art, through a limited edition produced with the assistance of Central Saint Martin's College of Art and illustrated with an international advertising campaign.

Ruinart, whose strategy is geared primarily to the development of premium cuvées, recorded solid revenue growth in France and abroad. Several new product launches marked by exciting events illustrated the innovative values of the brand, like the *Extraits* box designed by India Mahdavi and the *Fil d'Or*, created by Patricia Urquiola. In the second half of the year, Ruinart launched the "Integrale" case holding its six vintages in France. True to its long -standing ties with the world of art, the brand continued to be present at major contemporary art exhibits and maintained its partnership with the magazine Connaissance des Arts.

Mercier, a brand which has geared its strategy primarily to the French market where it is highly appreciated, continued to expand its presence in its traditional restaurant segment through its original program "Les Lieux de Toujours".

Taking full advantage of the improved economic environment Veuve Clicquot grew substantially in all its markets. The sharp recovery seen in the major traditional countries went hand in hand with the appearance of solid prospects in emerging markets such as Brazil and Russia.

The performance of Veuve Clicquot is based on the constancy of its value strategy, the quality of its wines recognized by excellent ratings, and its tradition of daring and innovation, which was particularly illustrated in 2010 by the success of the *Fridge*, a designer case that suggests both "vintage" and the avant-garde.

Veuve Clicquot also relied on an international event platform that was set up and on a publicity campaign in the new media (internet sites and social networks, expanded relations with bloggers).The end of the year was marked by the happy discovery,

---

reported by the international press, of the oldest bottles of Veuve Clicquot champagne known to date. The intact bottles, found on a wreck off the Alan Islands in the Baltic Sea, date from the mid-19th century and still have admirable organoleptic qualities.

Capitalizing on its fundamentals, Krug implemented a tasting program paying homage to the Grande Cuvée, its emblematic champagne which embodies the values of generosity, excellence and non-conformity. This initiative was highly successful worldwide. The Krug champagnes again earned the top international ratings. The brand focused on giving an opportunity to discover or rediscover its universe and the excellence of its champagnes to representatives from the general and trade press and to preferred consumers during trips to Reims and during an amazing gastronomical evening in Paris prepared by six famous chefs from around the world.

The excellence of the wines developed throughout the world by Estates & Wines has regularly been recognized by many international critics. These wines recorded strong growth in 2010 in all their markets, with a special mention for the Asia-Pacific and Latin American regions.

The Chandon sparkling wines achieved remarkable growth in their domestic markets, and consolidated their leadership position in the super premium category. After its successful launch in Japan and in Asia, the brand continued its internationalization strategy.

The still wine brands of Cloudy Bay (New Zealand) and Terrazas de los Andes (Argentina) recorded excellent results in all markets, as did Newton (California), Numanthia (Spain), Cheval des Andes (Argentina) and Cape Mentelle (Australia) in more selective markets.

Château d'Yquem offered the first sale of a classic vintage, the 2009, which was enthusiastically received by international experts and buyers, particularly in the Asian market. Out of a desire to place its brand within its era, Château d'Yquem created its own blog called "mYquem" and joined its fans in the social networks.

3.93 A further example is given in Table 3.26, where an entity reports on the key resources that it must manage in order to deliver operational scale and capability. Table 3.27 identifies the factors contributing to the difference between the market capitalisation and the net asset value of another entity.

Table 3.26 – Resources

Capita Group Plc – Annual Report and Accounts – 31 December 2010

4.2

Building scale and capacity and optimising our infrastructure

Aim: to have the right resources in place, both in terms of infrastructure and people, to satisfy clients that we have the operational scale and capability to deliver their requirements.

Progress: We have built up an extensive operational infrastructure and depth of capabilities which enable us to fully support our clients, provide flexible operating models and share economies of scale.

We continuously assess the needs of each business unit to ensure that we have the necessary people, infrastructure and resources for current and future development. Each month we review comprehensive operational management information through the MOB review process enabling us to manage our resources in a way that meets the needs of our clients and delivers our key financial targets. See page 33.

Wherever possible, we migrate and integrate systems, share resources and rationalise premises to optimise our infrastructure while maintaining and enhancing services. In 2010, we increased our focus on this and took significant steps forward, investing further in IT platforms in our life and pensions and registrar businesses and announcing the creation of a new business centre in Europe.

Sharing scale benefits

Our substantial scale and broad capability enable us to put forward compelling propositions to clients and are integral to us winning major integrated service transformation contracts.

The delivery of progressively larger contracts, with common processes and substantial numbers of transferring employees, fuels the growth of our operations and resources. As we increase scale, we are able to deliver more services and contracts through shared ICT platforms and operating structures, providing greater benefits to clients. They benefit not only from cost efficiencies but also from greater access to specialist skills and flexible service delivery models.

Our business centres, where we are able to run a broad range of shared services, form a central part of our service delivery infrastructure. At the end of 2010, we had 64 business centres onshore in the UK, nearshore in Ireland, the Channel Islands and Europe, and offshore in India.

Blended service delivery

Our infrastructure allows us to offer clients an onshore/nearshore/offshore blended delivery model structured to meet their individual needs. By combining onshore, nearshore and offshore resources we can deliver maximum service flexibility, quality and cost effectiveness. Our comprehensive security and quality assurance systems ensure consistent service quality across the entire infrastructure.

India

We established our offshore operations in India in 2004. We now have 3 sites in Mumbai, 1 site in Pune and 1 site in Bangalore. At the end of 2010, our Indian operations represented approximately 10% of our overall headcount. These operations play an important role in our business and long term growth strategy, providing high quality, cost effective English language based services.

Capita India is fully integrated into the Group and operates like any other Capita business with the same values, technical infrastructure and operating model. The sites share a combined management team to ensure they all benefit from their collective skills. We proactively recruit from the highly skilled graduate workforce that is available in these locations. Their skills, knowledge and excellent work ethic help us meet our objectives of delivering a first class service to our clients. Capita is widely regarded in India as a first class employer who will encourage and help employees grow and develop their careers. We therefore benefit from being able to attract and retain a highly skilled and professional workforce.

In addition to being the largest offshore operation for UK life and pensions administration, we continue to grow our BPO capability across other sectors such as general insurance, finance and accounting. Recently, we have expanded our service capability in India incorporating IT application development and testing, infrastructure consultancy and research and analytical services for UK based pharmaceutical companies.

"By combining onshore, nearshore and offshore resources we can deliver maximum service flexibility, quality and cost effectiveness."

Vic Gysin Joint Chief Operating Officer

Table 3.27 – Resources – brand value and other intangibles

SAP AG – Annual report – 31 December 2010

Management Report (extract)

Competitive Intangibles

The assets that are the basis for our current as well as future success do not appear on the Consolidated Statements of Financial Position. This is apparent from a comparison of the market capitalization of SAP AG, which was €46.7 billion at the end of the year (2009: €40.5 billion), with the equity on the Consolidated Statements of Financial Position, which was €9.8 billion (2009: €8.5 billion). The difference is mainly due to certain intangible assets that the applicable accounting standards do not allow to be recorded (at all or at fair value) on the Consolidated Statements of Financial Position. They include customer capital (our customer base and customer relations), employees and their knowledge and skills, our ecosystem of partners, software we developed ourselves, our ability to innovate, the brands we have built up – in particular, the SAP brand itself – and our organization. On December 31, 2010, SAP was the fourth most valuable company in Germany in terms of market capitalization. In 2010, the SAP brand ranked 26th on the Interbrand and *BusinessWeek* scoreboard of *100 Best Global Brands*, compared to 27th in the previous year. Our brand's ranking is now at an all-time high. Against other German brands, the SAP brand ranked third behind Mercedes-Benz and BMW, and globally against other IT brands ours ranked 10th. In 2009, Interbrand determined a value of US$12.8 billion (2009: US$12.1 billion) for the SAP brand.

Our investment in research and development, including R&D investment in the past, is also a significant element in our competitive intangibles.

Our customer capital continued to grow in 2010. We gained approximately 14,000 new customers in various market segments and strengthened our existing customer relationships. With the help of an independent service provider, IMAGIN AG, we regularly measure the satisfaction and loyalty of our customers. In 2010, overall customer satisfaction remained almost flat in comparison to the prior year, but our recommendation rate improved slightly. For more information about our new customers, see the *Customers* section. For more information about customer satisfaction, see our *Sustainability Report* at www.sapsustainabilityreport.com.

Employee-related and R&D activities increased the value of our employee base and our own software. For more information, see the *Employees* and *Research and Development sections*.

We also increased the value of our partner ecosystem by continuing to develop sales and development partnerships.

3.94 An entity will often create value through its activities at several different parts of its business process. The description of the business model should focus on the parts of the business processes that are most important to the generation, preservation or capture of value. [SR guidance para 7.14]. In Table 3.28, Coca Cola demonstrates the various capitals that are key to its business model.

Table 3.28 – Business model

Coca Cola HBC AG – Integrated Report – 5 June 2012

waters, sports and energy dirnks and
ready to drink teas. Together these respresents

Coca-Cola Hellenic

PRODUCT PORTFOLIO

BOTTLING & DISTRIBUTION
value created

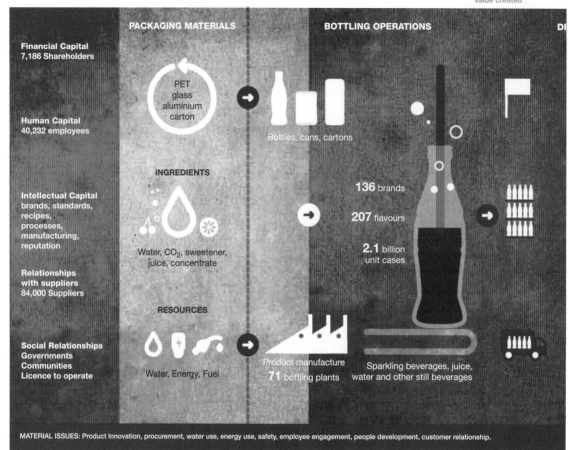

MATERIAL ISSUES: Product Innovation, procurement, water use, energy use, safety, employee engagement, people development, customer relationship.

[1]In the Coca-Cola System, sales volume is typically reported in unit cases equating to approximately 5.678 litres or 24 x 8 ounce servings.

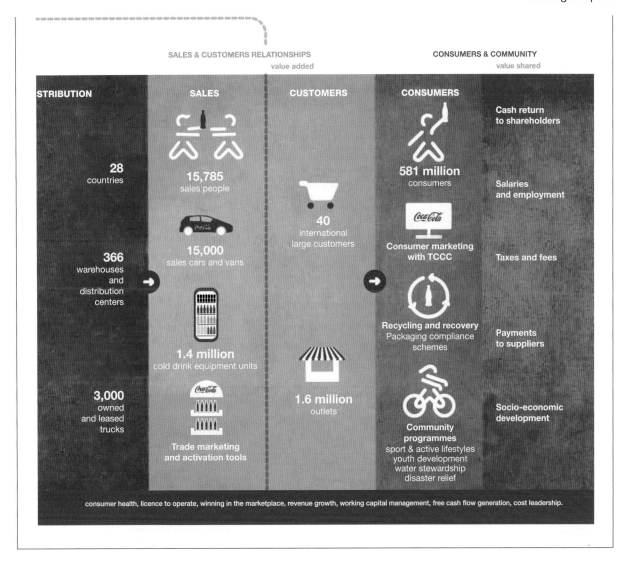

3.95 The description of the business model should provide context for the strategic report and the annual report more broadly. [SR guidance para 7.16]. In the table below, Derwent London sets out its business model as a way to provide context for its strategic priorities which ultimately link to both KPIs and key risks.

Table 3.29 – Business model providing context

Derwent London – Annual report and accounts – 31 December 2012

Our business model	Acquiring properties and unlocking their potential	Creating well-designed office space
Our strategies to achieve this	■ Using our detailed understanding of the London market to buy at modest capital values in emerging locations, taking advantage of market cycles	■ Combining exciting and innovative architecture with environmentally friendly, high quality construction
	■ Holding a variety of types and sizes of properties, primarily in the West End and the borders of the City	■ Harnessing the design flair of a range of architectural, design and engineering practices to create inspiring spaces
	■ Building a portfolio with a variety of regeneration opportunities, both in terms of timing and scale	■ Avoiding over-specification of buildings to provide attractive, adaptable offices
	■ Restructuring ownership interests where necessary to unlock development opportunities	■ Adjusting the scale of the development pipeline depending on market conditions, tenant demand and the mix of the rest of the portfolio
	■ Maintaining a strong balance sheet with flexible financing to allow us to act quickly when opportunities arise	■ Adapting existing structures where possible, saving embodied carbon and reducing the use of new materials
	■ Avoiding the core of the City of London as we believe it has a more extreme property cycle	■ Investing in public realm to provide attractive spaces for our tenants and the wider local community
Current areas of focus	■ Adding to our portfolio in core areas of operation	■ Demonstrating the design of the White Collar Factory concept, including concrete core cooling
		■ Accelerating development pipeline
Key risks that we take into account in implementing our strategy ▤ p30	■ Inconsistent strategy ■ Breach of financial covenants	■ Inconsistent development programme ■ Reduced development returns ■ Inconsistent strategy ■ Shortage of key staff ■ Reputational damage
Key performance indicators that measure our performance ▤ p26	■ Total return ■ Total property return ▤ p42	■ Total property return ■ BREEAM ratings ▤ p44

Optimising income	Recycling capital	Maintaining robust and flexible financing
■ Providing attractive space at mid-market rents that appeal to a wide range of tenants	■ Reviewing the status and options for each property in the portfolio regularly	■ Basing our assessment of sustainable gearing on a minimum level of interest cover and a maximum level for the Group's loan-to-value ratio
■ Working closely with tenants and other stakeholders to understand tenants' needs	■ Disposing of assets where we believe future growth is limited when market conditions are favourable	■ Varying our sources of funding in accordance with the lending environment
■ Altering lease lengths, building in fixed minimum rental uplifts or finding new space from elsewhere in the portfolio to accommodate those needs if necessary	■ Disposing of assets that are deemed non-core when market conditions are favourable	■ Maintaining excellent long-term relationships with our lenders and refinancing facilities well in advance of expiry
■ Building "green" features into our developments to minimise the property's environmental impact	■ Keeping the proportion of the portfolio suitable for refurbishment or redevelopment at around 50%	■ Using Interest rate hedging to provide adequate protection against unpredictable changes in short-term interest rates
■ Generating sufficient income from the portfolio to maintain comfortable Interest cover and recurring profits		
■ Replacing upward-only rent reviews with fixed minimum uplifts where practicable	■ Identifying assets suitable for recycing	■ Diversifying sources of funds
■ Tenant default	■ Breach of financial covenants	■ Breach of financial covenants
■ Reduced development returns	■ Sub-optimal financing structure	■ Higher interest rates
■ Shortage of key staff		■ Sub-optimal financing structure
■ Reputational damage		■ Reputational damage
■ Void management	■ Total property return	■ Interest cover ratio
■ Tenant receipts		
▤ p38	▤ p43	▤ p58

Business environment

Trends and factors likely to affect the future development, performance and position of the business

3.96 To the extent necessary for an understanding of the development, performance or position of the entity's business, the strategic report should include the main trends and factors likely to affect the future development, performance or position of the business. [CA06 Sec 414C(7)(a); SR guidance para 7.17].

3.97 To understand and evaluate an entity's strategy and performance, investors need a clear grasp of its business environment and the impact that this has on the entity. Frequently, when management discusses market conditions and other factors, it does so only to explain past behaviour and performance. Management should also discuss its expectations for the future and how this will impact on the delivery of business strategy. Often, performance is reported in isolation, with only high-level commentary on the business environment such as *"... against intensifying competition ..."* or *"... prospects are good ..."*.

3.98 Investors who are familiar with the entity are interested in management's interpretation of market developments and trends; investors who are less familiar with the entity might need the information to judge performance and the logic of the entity's strategies.

3.99 Trends and factors affecting the business may arise either as a result of the external environment in which the entity operates or from internal sources. [SR guidance para 7.18]. As illustrated in the table below, Shanks Group plc explicitly highlight the impact of external factors and management activities on their overview of the drivers of trading profit.

3059

Table 3.30 – Market drivers – impact on profit

Shanks Group plc – Annual report and accounts – 31 March 2012

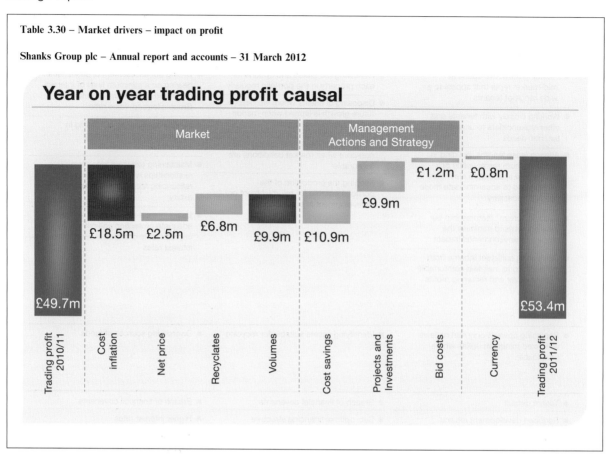

3.100 The strategic report should include a description of the entity's major markets and its competitive position within those markets. It should also cover other significant features of its external environment (such as the legal, regulatory, macro-economic and social environment) and how these influence the business. The strategic report should set out the directors' analysis of the potential effect of the trends or factors identified on the development, performance, position or future prospects of the entity. [SR guidance para 7.19]. In table 3.30.1, Rexam explores a number of aspects of its market environment and supports its disclosure with quantified data.

Table 3.30.1 – Market environment

Rexam plc – Annual report – 31st December 2014

THE GLOBAL BEVERAGE MARKET

While the average consumer drinks around 270 litres of beverages a year, consumption levels and growth rates differ widely by beverage category and region. North America remains the largest market for beverages, with consumption at 577 litres per capita while average rates in Africa, the Middle East and Asia (AMEA) are well below the global average. The low consumption regions are expected to achieve the strongest growth in coming years, especially AMEA.

Carbonated soft drinks (CSD) and beers are well established beverage categories and one of the largest globally in terms of consumption along with packaged water, milk and hot drinks. In 2014, the beer category continued to grow at an annual rate of around 2%, while CSD volumes increased by less than 1%. The fastest growth rates over the next three years are expected from smaller categories such as energy drinks, iced ready to drink (RTD) tea and coffee and flavoured alcoholic beverages (FABs), but also from the large and high growth packaged water category. (See charts 1 and 2 opposite.)

Globally, more than 1.5 trillion units of beverage packaging were sold in 2014, an increase of 5% versus 2013. Glass still accounts for the biggest share of the market closely followed by PET and then beverage cans, with the remainder packaged in a mix of cartons, pouches, sachets and other pack types. Cans and PET have been growing fast at respectively 3% and 7% per year over the past five years, gaining share over glass. (See chart 3 opposite.)

THE GLOBAL BEVERAGE CAN MARKET

The beverage can market comprises about 90% aluminium cans and 10% steel cans. There is a continued move from steel to aluminium, and steel cans are now only used in some parts of AMEA and Brazil. Moreover, nearly all beverage cans used in North America and Europe are two piece cans but some three piece beverage cans are still used in China and South East Asia.

Rexam estimates that around 310 billion beverage cans were consumed globally in 2014. Beer and CSD account for the vast majority of consumption, but an increasing number of consumers are drinking other beverage categories such as energy drinks, cider, iced RTD tea and coffee, FABs, flavoured and sparkling water and milk from a can. Craft beer is also growing strongly, especially in North America and Europe. (See chart 3 opposite.)

Industry trends vary significantly region to region according to different market dynamics. The world's largest two piece market by far, North America, continues to show a slow controlled decline in the CSD market. This is being partially offset by the growth in cans for beer, energy, RTD tea, and specialty categories. Brand owners seek pack differentiation and shelf appeal in the more mature markets of North America, Europe and Japan and we can expect an increase in niche markets for specialty cans (such as Sleek, Big Cans and sizes other than standard 12oz cans).

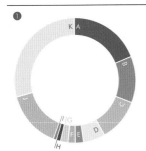

① 2014 Global consumption by beverage category
1.9 trillion litres

- A: Packaged water
- B: CSD
- C: Beer & cider
- D: Juice drinks
- E: Iced/RTD tea & coffee
- F: Spirits (incl FABs)
- G: Squash & fruit powders
- H: Wine
- I: Energy & sports drinks
- J: Milk & dairy drinks
- K: Hot drinks

Source: Canadean

② 2014–17(e) Global beverage volume growth CAGR
Soft drink and alcoholic drinks

Energy drinks	10%
Sports drinks	8%
Packaged water	7%
Flavoured milk	7%
Iced/RTD tea	7%
Still drinks	6%
Spirits	6%
Iced/RTD coffee	4%
FABs	4%
Beer & cider	3%
Wine	2%
Juice & nectar	2%
Squash & fruit powder	2%
CSD	2%

Source: Canadean

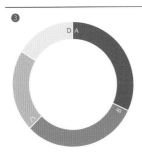

③ 2014 Global beverage pack mix
1.5 trillion units

- A: Glass
- B: Plastic
- C: Cans
- D: Other

Source: Rexam estimates

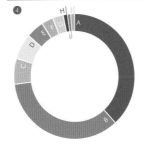

④ 2014 What's in a can

- A: Beer
- B: CSD
- C: Still drinks
- D: Energy drinks
- E: Iced/RTD coffee drinks
- F: Iced/RTD tea drinks
- G: FABs
- H: Sports drinks
- I: Nectars (25–99%)
- J: Juices (100%)

Source: Rexam estimates

⑤ 2014 Global can volumes by region
c310 billion cans

- Middle East & Africa
- South & Central America
- Europe
- Asia
- North America (incl Mexico)

2014

Source: Rexam estimates

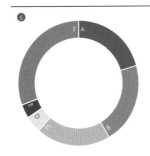

⑥ 2014 Can makers' market share
c310 billion cans

- A: Rexam
- B: Ball
- C: Crown
- D: MCC
- E: Can-Pack
- F: Other

Source: Rexam estimates

3.101 From the business description, a user of the financial statements can expect to gain an overall picture of the business. For example:

- Whether it operates internationally.

- Whether it operates in unstable economic and political regions.

- The entity's relative strength in the markets/industry compared to its competitors, including its strongest and weakest business and geographic areas.

- Whether the entity is highly regulated, or subject to significant legal actions against it.

- The performance and outlook for the economies, markets and sectors in which the business operates.

- The environmental and social factors that influence the business.

- The products or services that the entity provides, whether they involve significant R&D or advertising support and the product risk involved; whether there is significant dependency on a small number of customers or suppliers, or scarcity of sources of supply for raw materials that affect the business.

- Whether there are significant factors involved in manufacturing or distributing the entity's products.

- How the business is organised and monitored by the board (for example, by business and/or geographic sector).

- Whether the business is run centrally, or the individual units have a high degree of autonomy.

- Where the main operating facilities are located, giving an idea of the size of the business.

3.102 Where practicable and relevant, the trend or factor should be quantified and the source of the evidence underpinning it identified. [SR guidance para 7.21]. Table 3.31 shows how Anglo American use industry data from a variety of different sources, both internal and external.

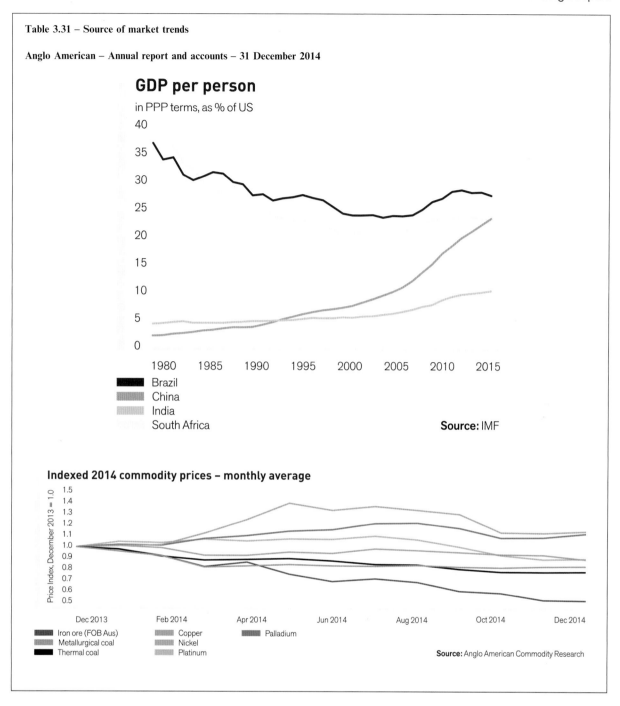

Table 3.31 – Source of market trends

Anglo American – Annual report and accounts – 31 December 2014

GDP per person

in PPP terms, as % of US

Brazil
China
India
South Africa

Source: IMF

Indexed 2014 commodity prices – monthly average

Iron ore (FOB Aus) Copper Palladium
Metallurgical coal Nickel
Thermal coal Platinum

Source: Anglo American Commodity Research

3.103 The discussion of internal trends and factors will vary according to the nature of the business, but could, for example, include the development of new products and services or the benefits expected from capital investment. [SR guidance para 7.20].

3.104 Management should consider the potential future significance of trends and factors in deciding whether or not to include an analysis of them in the strategic report.

3.105 In Table 3.32, Logica plc's 2010 annual report discusses current and potential future trends within the group's market. It uses graphics to support the narrative discussion in respect of market concentration and market position. The table sets out extracts only; considerable further detail is included in the report. In addition, the annual report refers to an online annual report, which includes videos of members of the management team speaking on the main subjects of interest.

Table 3.32 – Business trends

Logica plc – Annual report – 31 December 2010

Our markets in 2010 (extracts)

Throughout 2010 we have seen signs of the market returning to growth. The IT Services market has continued to evolve with growth in global IT spend expected to be solid in 2011 and the European IT services sector is now expected to total £134 billion. Outsourcing continues to be the driver of growth across Europe.

Our market share

We grew revenue ahead of the market and our major European peers in 2010.

Within the European markets where we operate, we maintain a strong position as one of the top five suppliers with particularly good market share in the Nordics, France and Portugal. In the UK, our market position remains solid based on our position with the UK government. In 2010, we were one of the 19 key suppliers invited to sign the government's Memorandum of Understanding.

In Europe, buying patterns varied by country and this has played to our strength of local presence, allowing us to tailor solutions locally for our clients with a blended delivery of services. Such a specialist offering will be paramount to remaining competitive and maintaining market share as all geographies return to growth.

Our approach to clients

As outlined on pages 10 to 15, we approach our clients by industry but organise ourselves by geography.

Growth patterns in different geographies are closely related to GDP growth, so 2010 was a mixed year. Despite recovery in the Northern and Central European and French economies, the UK, Benelux and Portuguese economies remained weaker. Across all geographies the blended delivery model has proved successful this year in creating efficiency for both us and our clients while still maintaining service close to them.

We have seen significant growth in Morocco, for example, from where we support the relationships with our French clients.

Similarly, as the industry remains fragmented, clients increasingly want IT suppliers with good vertical industry knowledge. This is one of our strengths. Our contracts in energy and utilities, transport and logistics and the public sector give us good visibility for 2011.

The Public Sector represented 31% of Group revenue in 2010. This sector declined as a result of the elections held in a number of countries. Following the change in UK government in May, we saw a reduction in short-term demand. But the signing of our £157 million, 10-year contract with the UK Serious Organised Crime Agency at the beginning of 2011 was a welcome sign that high quality IT solutions remain important in the government's agenda. We expect demand to improve as government departments absorb spending reductions and allocate their spending priorities. Clients such as the UK Crown Prosecution Service remain focused on reducing costs, using shared services for front and back office to deliver savings, and want suppliers with a reputation for security. Throughout this, Logica has been well-placed as a valued and trusted supplier and we remain confident that there are significant medium-term opportunities.

In the Energy & Utilities sector, we have continued to develop long-term partnerships. Our contract with EDP in Portugal is a good example of how we can successfully evolve and how our client intimacy approach produces best in class, innovative solutions.

Financial services has seen a return to growth as a result of improving conditions in the sector and client need for systems improvements and upgrades. Revenue drivers include consulting work around payments, risk and regulation, and integration support resulting from disposals and acquisitions. Within this, Logica remains a top three supplier for key clients in managing their risk.

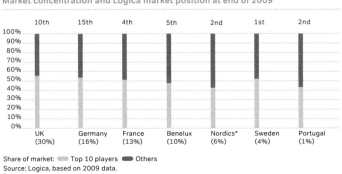

Market concentration and Logica market position at end of 2009

Share of market: Top 10 players Others
Source: Logica, based on 2009 data.
Number in brackets indicates size of country market.
* Nordics includes Finland, Norway and Denmark. Sweden is excluded.

3.106 Given the influence that trends and factors might have on many aspects of the entity's development, performance or position, the linkage of this type of information to other aspects of the strategic report, and the annual report more widely, will be particularly important. [SR guidance para 7.22].

3.107 In their 2012 report, International Airlines Group clearly explain the external trends impacting on their market place alongside their strategic and business model reporting. The table below sets this out.

Table 3.33

International Airlines Group – Annual report and accounts 2012

Business model and strategy
Creating value for our stakeholders

Mission

To be the leading international airlines group in future industry consolidation on a regional and a global scale.

Business model

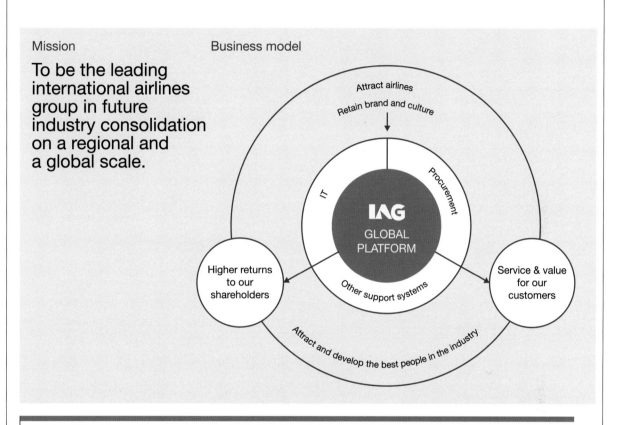

The airline industry is consolidating rapidly due to:

- Cost pressures, such as high oil price, driving airlines to search for greater economies of scale
- Marked reduction in access to cheap sources of capital
- Continued privatisation
- Gradually eroding regulatory hurdles
- Increased potential for partnerships between airlines, such as alliance membership and the establishment of joint businesses

Airline consolidation has the potential to bring the following advantages to airline shareholders and customers:

- Reduced exposure to single-region risk
- Elimination of excess capacity, and the ability to adjust capacity to meet changing demand
- Ability to streamline costs
- A wider choice of product for customers
- More integrated and higher quality customer experience (eg lounges and customer loyalty programmes)

IAG is designed to lead the consolidation in the industry but also to create optimal value for shareholders and customers in this changing environment:

- Central team focused on driving revenue and cost synergies between the operating companies
- Simple structure to enable other airlines to plug into
- Dedicated management of core airlines
- Direct management of areas of business which benefit strongly from scale effects, such as cargo and customer loyalty programmes
- A platform for further entities to join the Group with minimal integration cost

Principal risks and uncertainties

3.108 The strategic report should include a description of the principal risks and uncertainties facing the entity, together with an explanation of how they are managed or mitigated. [CA06 Sec 414C(2)(b); SR guidance para 7.23].

3.109 The risks and uncertainties included in the strategic report should be limited to those considered by the entity's management to be material to the development, performance, position or future prospects of the entity. They will generally be matters that the directors regularly monitor and discuss because of their likelihood, the magnitude of their potential effect on the entity, or a combination of the two. [SR guidance para 7.24].

3.110 Table 3.34 illustrates an entity reporting its risk discussion in the context of its overall business drivers. National Grid shows a clear flow of actions from business drivers, through risk and opportunities, and links to strategic objectives and key performance indicators. A concise diagram makes the information easy to absorb. The diagram cross-refers to a detailed analysis of the risks (not shown here).

Table 3.34 – Risks, business drivers and objectives

National Grid plc – Annual Report and accounts – 31 March 2010

Operating and Financial Review (extract)

Operating and Financial Review

Business drivers, principal risks and opportunities

Business drivers

There are many factors that influence the success of our business and the financial returns we obtain. We consider the factors described here to be our principal business drivers.

Price controls and rate plans

The prices we charge for use of our electricity and gas transmission and distribution networks are determined in accordance with regulatory approved price controls in the UK and rate plans in the US. These arrangements include incentive and/or penalty arrangements. The terms of these arrangements have a significant impact on our revenues.

Multi-year contracts

Revenues in our Long Island electricity distribution and generation operations are subject to long-term contracts with the Long Island Power Authority. In addition, revenues in our Grain LNG importation terminal are determined by long-term contractual arrangements with blue chip customers.

People

The skills and talents of our employees, along with succession planning and the development of future leaders, are critical to our success. We believe that business success will be delivered through the performance of all current and future employees, and enhanced by having a workforce that is diverse in its cultural, religious and community influences.

Principal risks and opportunities

There are a number of risks that might cause us to fail to achieve our vision or to deliver growth in shareholder value. We can mitigate many of these risks by acting appropriately in response to the factors driving our business. The principal risks are described here. For more detail on risks, see pages 91 to 93.

Regulatory settlements and long-term contracts

Our ability to obtain appropriate recovery of costs and rates of return on investment is of vital importance to the sustainability of our business. We have an opportunity to help shape the future of the regulatory environment, for example in our rate filings in the US. If we fail to take these opportunities, we risk failing to achieve satisfactory returns.

Financial performance

Financial performance and operating cash flows are the basis for funding our future capital investment programmes, for servicing our borrowings and paying dividends, and for increasing shareholder value. Failure to achieve satisfactory performance could affect our ability to deliver the returns we and our stakeholders expect.

Talent and skills

Harnessing and developing the skills and talent of our existing employees, and recruiting, retaining and developing the best new talent, will enable us to improve our capabilities. Failure to engage and develop our existing employees or to attract and retain talented employees could hamper our ability to deliver in the future.

Objectives

We have developed the Company strategy and objectives to address the key business drivers and risks, ensuring we manage the business appropriately so as to mitigate risks and optimise opportunities. For more detail on objectives, see pages 38 and 39.

Delivering strong, sustainable regulatory and long-term contracts with good returns

Building trust, transparency, and an inclusive and engaged workforce

Developing our talent, leadership skills and capabilities

Key performance indicators (KPIs)

We use a variety of performance measures to monitor progress against our objectives. Some of these are considered to be key performance indicators and are set out here. For more detail on performance, see pages 40 to 69.

Adjusted earnings per share

Group return on equity

Total shareholder return

Employee engagement index

3.111 In Table 3.35, Taylor Wimpey plc links its risk discussion directly to its strategy and key performance indicators. Only four of the areas of risk are shown here.

Table 3.35 – Risks linked to strategy and KPIs

Taylor Wimpey plc – Annual report – 31 December 2013

Risks linked to strategy and KPIs (extract)

Principal Risks and Uncertainties

The table below summarises the Group's principal risks and uncertainties. We also maintain a Sustainability and Climate Change Risk and Opportunity Register to monitor other non-financial issues that could affect the Group. More information is available in our Corporate Responsibility Report at www.taylorwimpey.co.uk/corporate/corporate-responsibility/cr-reports

	Relevance to strategy	Potential impact on KPIs	Mitigation	Progress in 2013
Government policy and planning regulations The implementation of recent legislation (the Localism Act, National Planning Policy Framework and the Community Infrastructure Levy (CIL)) is having a significant impact on the planning system and with the recovering housing market it could lead to a change in government policy. **Responsibility** – Chief Executive – Director of Land and Planning – Other members of our senior management team – Managing Directors of our regional businesses	Our ability to build homes is dependent on obtaining the necessary planning permissions to develop communities which is dependent on our ability to meet the relevant regulatory and planning requirements. Although the new planning system is in place, it is still a relatively new system with the powers within the processes still being tested. This could result in extended timescales for gaining planning consents or increased legal challenges. These factors increase uncertainty and increase the commercial risk of projects.	– Inability to obtain suitable consents, or unforeseen delays, could impact on the number or type of homes that we are able to build. We could also be required to fund higher than anticipated levels of planning obligations, or incur additional costs to meet increased regulatory requirements. – The locally produced CIL charge schedules could increase costs and therefore impact on the viability of current developments. All of these would have a detrimental impact on the contribution per plot.	We have responded to the changes in planning policy by introducing a comprehensive community led planning strategy which improves communications with all parties but especially local communities therefore enhancing our ability to deliver developments that meet local requirements. We consult with Government agencies and opposition parties on housing policy, both directly and indirectly as a member of industry groups, to highlight potential issues and to understand any proposed changes to regulations.	We continue to make significant strides in the implementation of our customer and community engagement planning strategy and have been encouraged by the feedback and successes that we have achieved. We are participating in the local Plans Management Group (PMG) via the HBF to ensure local plans are robust and CIL charge schedules are appropriate.
Impact of market environment on mortgage availability and demand Mortgage availability is a key constraint on demand in the UK housing market. In 2013 mortgage availability has improved with the return of high loan to value mortgages initially via the Government backed Help to Buy initiative and latterly by general mortgage products. However there is still uncertainty on how and what the impact will be when the Help to Buy initiative for new build is removed by the Government. **Responsibility** – Group Management Team – UK Sales and Marketing Director – Regional Sales and Marketing Directors	The majority of the homes that we build are sold to individual purchasers who take on significant mortgages to finance their purchases. A change in business confidence or employment opportunities can therefore impact on their demand for housing. In particular the ability of first time buyers and investors to purchase homes is impacted by any change in the mortgage availability at the higher loan to value levels as it would impact on the level of deposits required.	– A reduction in effective demand for new homes below normal levels could negatively impact on both profitability and cash generation. This would have an adverse effect on return on net operating assets and net debt.	Our local teams select the locations and home designs that best meet the needs of the local community and customer demand in the present and future. We evaluate new outlet openings on the basis of local market conditions and regularly review the pricing and incentives that we offer. We work closely with the financial services industry to ensure customers receive good advice on the procurement of mortgage products.	We were amongst the first in the industry to offer the Government backed Help to Buy scheme when it launched in March 2013 and we have seen strong interest in the scheme amongst our customers. We launched a new Taylor Wimpey website to provide best in industry customer experience and better insight into the Taylor Wimpey products.
Ability to attract and retain high-calibre employees Recruiting employees with inadequate skills or in insufficient numbers, or not being able to retain key staff with the right skills for the future, could have a detrimental impact on our business. **Responsibility** – Chief Executive – Group HR Director – Every employee managing people	Our value cycle requires significant input from skilled people to deliver quality homes and communities for our customers. The recovery in the housing market and the recent changes in the planning system have meant that the retention of high-quality trained employees is key to achieving our strategic goals.	– Not having the right teams in place could lead to delays in build, quality issues, reduced sales levels, poor customer care and reduced profitability.	We closely monitor employee turnover levels on a monthly basis and conduct exit interviews, as appropriate, to identify any areas for improvement. We benchmark our remuneration to ensure we are competitive within the industry and have succession plans in place for key roles within the Group. We hold regular development reviews to identify training requirements.	During 2013, we have committed to delivering 1.5 days of training per salaried employee and extended our development initiatives to improve key skills. This included the introduction of a mentoring programme for key staff and the development of a modular training programme for production and technical employees. We have also extended our apprentice and graduate training programmes.

3.112 Management should consider the full range of business risks, including those that are financial and those that are non-financial. Principal risks should be disclosed and described, irrespective of how they are classified or whether they result from strategic decisions, operations, organisation or behaviour, or from external factors over which the board might have little or no direct control. The assessment should include threats to solvency and liquidity. [SR guidance para 7.25].

3.113 The purpose of disclosing risks and risk management policies is to enable investors and other users of the financial statements to assess the sustainability of the entity's current performance. Future performance might be vulnerable to factors that the entity cannot control. Investors need to be aware of the risk appetite of management; this is because their investment risk is linked to the risks being borne by the entity. In Table 3.36, Potash Corporation describes its risk management policies.

Table 3.36 – Risk management

Potash Corporation of Saskatchewan – Financial Review Annual Report – 31 December 2010

Risk Management (extract)

Risk Management

Managing Risks to Our Fertilizer Enterprise

We must effectively manage all risks associated with our business goals and activities, which have been established to successfully execute our corporate strategy. After evaluating risks for their severity and likelihood to adversely affect the company, we prioritize them and determine the most appropriate responses among accept, control, share, transfer, diversify or avoid.

Global Risk Environment

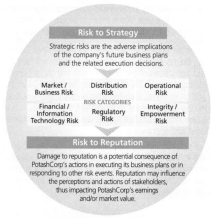

The risks that can threaten our business are integrated, and affect each other. Only by understanding the inherent risks within each risk category can we design and implement mitigation activities so we can execute our strategies and meet our business goals within acceptable residual risk tolerances.

Six categories of risks have been identified within our global environment: market/business, distribution, operational, financial/information technology, regulatory and integrity/empowerment. However, damage to our reputation is the most severe risk faced by

PotashCorp, and it could ultimately impede our ability to execute our corporate strategy. To mitigate this risk, we strive continually to build goodwill through a commitment to sustainability, transparency, effective communication and corporate governance best practices.

Risk Methodology and Ranking Matrix

After identifying an inherent risk, we assess it against our risk ranking matrix as if no mitigation measures had been taken. Through the matrix, we weigh the severity and likelihood of such a potential event, and establish relative risk levels from A through E to guide our mitigation activities.

A Extreme: Initiate mitigation activities immediately to reduce risk. If such activities cannot sufficiently reduce risk level, consider discontinuation of the applicable business operation to avoid the risk.

B Major: Initiate mitigation activities at next available opportunity to reduce risk. If such activities cannot sufficiently reduce the risk level, board approval is required to confirm acceptance of this level of risk.

C Acceptable: Level of risk is acceptable within tolerances of the risk management policy. Additional risk mitigation activities may be considered if benefits significantly exceed cost.

D Low: Monitor risk according to risk management policy requirements, but no additional activities required.

E Negligible: Consider discontinuing any related mitigation activities so resources can be directed to higher-value activities, provided such discontinuance does not adversely affect any other risk areas.

We can lower risk by reducing the likelihood of the initiating event occurring or by reducing the significance of the consequence if it does occur.

Residual risk remains after mitigation and control measures are applied to an identified inherent risk. We endeavor to be fully aware of all potential inherent risks that could adversely affect PotashCorp, and to choose appropriately the levels of residual risk we accept.

PotashCorp Risk Management Ranking Methodology							
Risk Ranking Matrix			SEVERITY OF CONSEQUENCE				
			1	2	3	4	5
			Negligible	Low	Acceptable	Major	Extreme
LIKELIHOOD OR FREQUENCY	5	**Probable** (0-6 months)	C	B	B	A	A
	4	**High** (6 months-2 years)	D	C	B	B	A
	3	**Medium** (2-10 years)	D	D	C	B	B
	2	**Low** (10-50 years)	E	D	D	C	B
	1	**Remote** (> 50 years)	E	E	D	D	C

Strategic report

3.113.1 In Table 3.36.1, Fresnillo plc describes its risk appetite for each type of risk and the risk rating (that is, likelihood of risk occurring), followed by an explanation of the risk change.

Table 3.36.1 – Risk Appetite

Fresnillo plc – Annual Report – 31 December 2013

Managing our risks (extract)

Our approach to managing risk is underpinned by our understanding of our current risk exposures, risk appetite and how our risks are changing over time.

Current Order (change from 2012)	Risk	Risk appetite	Risk rating 2012	Risk rating 2013	Change	Description of risk change
1. (was 2)	Impact of global macro-economic developments	High	High	Very high	↑	Most industry and financial analysts who follow metal prices predict lower average silver and gold prices, with continued high volatility. The sharp fall in precious metal prices in 2013 has put the industry under more pressure than it has known for almost a decade.
2. (was 4)	Access to land	Medium	High	Very high	↑	Negotiations for land, in Mexico and globally, combined with an increase in land requirements, remain a challenge. Foreign mining companies in general, and Canadian ones in particular, have set certain precedents for future negotiations in their agreements with members of agrarian communities (ejidos). A number of ejidos have disavowed previous agreements, seeking to renegotiate agreed, upon terms and conditions; such actions are often driven by special interests. Their demands have increased significantly compared to previous years and this trend is expected to continue.
3. (was 1)	Security	Low	Very high	Very high	↑	Although we have not experienced a material negative impact on our operations this year, the number of security incidents in areas near our operations and exploration projects increased in 2013.
4. (was 5)	Potential actions by the government e.g. implementation of a tax on mining companies in Mexico, more stringent regulations for obtaining permits, etc.	Low	High	Very high	↑	As part of the Tax Reform approved by the Mexican Congress in 2013, the tax burden that mining companies will face includes reduced deductions of exploration costs and social benefits, and new mining duties (7.5% of a base similar to EBITDA and 0.5% of gold and silver sales). Detailed rules on the implementation of these new mining duties are yet to be defined. Additionally, it is expected that a new more restrictive mining law with higher burdens will be discussed and approved in 2014. Another potential government action that may impact on us is the increase in regulations on the use and handling of explosives, driven by the new administration and the increased concern about misuse of explosives by drug cartels; the length of time to obtain permits is longer and the requirements more stringent.

3.114 In Table 3.37, Great Portland Estates plc sets out how it manages risk, discloses the principal risks and uncertainties that it faces, and links the commentary on each risk to its broader discussion of its business activities.

Table 3.37 – Management and disclosure of principal risks

Great Portland Estates plc – Annual Report – 31 March 2011

Risk management (extract)

Risk management (extract)

The successful management of risk is essential to enable the Group to deliver on its strategic priorities. Whilst the ultimate responsibility for risk management rests with the Board, the foundation of effective day-to-day management of risk is in the way we do business and the culture of our team. Our flat organisational structure, with close involvement of senior management in all significant decisions combined with our cautious and analytical approach, is designed to align the Group's interests with those of shareholders.

Board oversight

Board meetings
Audit Committee
Remuneration Committee

Operational Committees

Executive Committee – weekly

Leasing co-ordination weekly	Investment weekly	Financial management weekly
Asset management weekly	Environmental policy bi-monthly	Corporate responsibility monthly

Policies for highlighting and controlling risk

Investment return benchmarks	Regular review of business plans	Development appraisal parameters
Debt leverage, covenant compliance and liquidity limits	Occupancy targets	Leasing objectives and tenant covenant testing

Procedures and internal controls

High level risk assessment framework	Extensive documentation to support decisions	Defined performance indicators with sensitivity analysis
Strict approval requirements	Formal policies and procedures consistently applied	External review of key controls

People and culture

Focused market expertise	Integrity in business conduct	Conservative attitude to capital deployment
Open communication	Interests aligned with shareholders	Analytical rigour
Transparent disclosure with stakeholders	Qualified and experienced personnel with specific roles	

Business risk

Strategic report

The Group views effective risk management as integral to the delivery of superior returns to shareholders. Principal risks and uncertainties facing the business and the processes through which the Company aims to manage those risks are:

Risk and impact	Mitigation	Change (From last year)	Commentary
Market risk			
Central London real estate market underperforms other UK property sectors leading to poor relative financial results	Research into the economy and the investment and occupational markets is evaluated as part of the Group's annual strategy process covering the key areas of investment, development and asset management and updated regularly throughout the year.		The central London real estate market has considerably out performed the wider UK Market during the year ended 31 March 2011, demonstrated by IPD's central TPR exceeding IPD's universe by 6.7 percentage points and the outlook continues to be favourable. Our market pages 20 to 23 ←
Economic recovery falters resulting in worse than expected performance of the business given decline in economic output	Regular economic updates received and scenario planning for different economic cycles. 46% of income from committed developments secured.		Whilst the economic environment appears to have stabilised and take up has increased markedly on last year, there remains the continued downward pressure from the Eurozone Sovereign debt crisis and the impact of the Government's austerity measures have yet to be seen. Our market pages 20 to 23 ←
Investment			
Not sufficiently capitalising on market investment opportunities through difficulty in sourcing investment opportunities at attractive prices, poor investment decisions and mistimed recycling of capital	The Group has dedicated resources whose remit is to constantly research each of the sub-markets within central London seeking the right balance of investment and development opportunities suitable for current and anticipated market conditions. Detailed due diligence is undertaken on all acquisitions prior to purchase to ensure appropriate returns. Business plans are produced on an individual asset basis to ensure the appropriate choice of those buildings with limited relative potential performance.		With independent forecasts indicating that capital values are expected to rise over the near to medium term, limited disposals were made during the year. The Group has committed in excess of £370 million since its Rights Issue in May 2009 equating to nearly a quarter of the portfolio at 31 March 2011. With the market having risen from the low of 2009, the risk of missing compelling acquisitions has lessened. Our market pages 20 to 23 ← Case studies pages 8 to 11 ←
Asset management			
Failure to maximise income from investment properties through poor management of voids, mispricing, low tenant retention, sub-optimal rent reviews, tenant failures and inappropriate refurbishments	The Group's in-house asset management and leasing teams proactively manage tenants to ensure changing needs are met with a focus on retaining income in light of vacant possession requirements for refurbishments and developments.		The Group continues to maintain a low void rate which was 2.7% at 31 March 2011. Tenant delinquencies were less than 1% of the rent roll for the year to 31 March 2011. The Group continues to actively manage the portfolio to maximise occupancy and drive rental growth. Asset management pages 26 and 27 ← Case study pages 12 and 13 ←
Development			
Poor development returns relating to: – incorrect reading of the property cycle; – inappropriate location; – failure to gain viable planning consents; – level of development undertaken as a percentage of the portfolio; – level of speculative development; – contractor availability and insolvency risk; – quality of the completed buildings; and – poor development management	See market risk above. Prior to committing to a development the Group conducts a detailed Financial and Operational appraisal process which evaluates the expected returns from a development in light of likely risks. During the course of a development, the actual costs and estimated returns are regularly monitored to signpost prompt decisions on project management, leasing and ownership. 46% of income from committed developments secured. Due diligence is undertaken of the financial stability of demolition and main contractors prior to awarding of contracts. Working with agents, potential occupiers' needs and aspirations are identified during the planning application and design stages. All our major developments are subject to BREEAM ratings with a target to achieve a rating of "Very Good" on major refurbishments and "Excellent" on new build properties.		With forecasted supply of central London office space expected to be scarce in the near to medium term, the Group has embarked on a near-term development programme to capitalise on the expected resulting rental growth. The Group's exposure to development risk has increased accordingly. Development pages 28 and 29 ← Case study pages 14 and 15 ←

Risk and impact	Mitigation	Change From last year	Commentary
Financial risks			
Limited availability of further capital constrains the growth of the business	Cash flow and funding needs are regularly monitored to ensure sufficient undrawn facilities are in place. Funding maturities are managed across the short, medium and long term. The Group's funding measures are diversified across a range of bank and bond markets. Strict counterparty limits are operated on deposits.	↓	Since 31 March 2010, the Group has refinanced all of its 2012 debt maturities. Pro forma undrawn cash and committed credit facilities are £518 million. Our financial position pages 32 to 35 ← Note 16 forming part of the Group financial statements pages 74 to 77 →
Adverse interest rate movements reduce profitability	Formal policy to manage interest rate exposure by having a high proportion of debt with fixed or capped interest rates through derivatives.	→	With the strength of economic recovery still uncertain, the timing of interest rate rises remains unclear. Our financial position pages 32 to 35 ← Note 16 forming part of the Group financial statements pages 74 to 77 →
Inappropriate capital structure results in suboptimal NAV per share growth	Regular review of current and forecast debt levels.	→	The Group's existing capital structure is well placed to take advantage of opportunities as they arise and to deliver our near-term development programme. Our financial position pages 32 to 35 ←
People			
Correct level, mix and retention of people to execute our Business Plan. Strategic priorities not achieved because of inability to attract, develop, motivate and retain talented employees	Regular review is undertaken of the Group's resource requirements. The Company has a remuneration system that is strongly linked to performance and a formal appraisal system to provide regular assessment of individual performance and identification of training needs.	→	With increased levels of activity, the Group has strengthened and broadened its team and the process to appoint a new Finance Director is ongoing. At the 2010 AGM, shareholders approved a new Long Term Incentive Plan. Our people pages 38 to 42 ← Remuneration report pages 102 to 112 →
Regulatory			
Adverse regulatory risk including tax, planning, environmental legislation and EU directives increases cost base and reduces flexibility	Senior Group representatives spend considerable time, using experienced advisers as appropriate, to ensure compliance with current and potential future regulations. Lobbying property industry matters is undertaken by active participation of the Executive Directors through relevant industry bodies.	↑	During the year new Building Regulations came into effect requiring further reductions on carbon emissions whilst the risk to the Group from increasing regulation having unforeseen consequences and the impact of certain EU directives including the AIFM directive continues to be uncertain. Property industry representation page 47 → Corporate responsibility targets pages 48 to 51 →
Health and safety incidents Loss of or injury to employees, contractors or tenants and resultant reputational damage	The Company has dedicated Health & Safety personnel to oversee the Group's management systems which include regular risk assessments and annual audits to proactively address key Health & Safety areas including employee, contractor and tenant safety. On developments, the Group operates a pre-qualification process to ensure selection of competent consultants and contractors.	↑	The Group had no reportable accidents during the year, however, as a result of our near-term development programme we have increased exposure to health and safety incidents on our development sites. Corporate responsibility targets pages 52 and 53 →

3.115 Significant risks and uncertainties include both financial risks and non-financial risks. Indeed, the two types are often indistinguishable; this is because non-financial risk (for example, the risk that a product might be faulty) could have serious financial consequences, such as the cost of withdrawing the product, penalties on long-term contracts, or damage to the entity's reputation. Other non-financial risks, which are increasingly referred to, reflect trends in consumer and social behaviour and potential regulatory actions. Examples include the health hazards of cigarettes, obesity risk, and possible health risks from the use of mobile phones. So, product risk (in addition to many other risks) is often significant for such businesses.

3.116 Risk interdependency disclosure is used by some entities to draw attention to the fact that most key risks do not sit in isolation and that failure in one area may trigger other risks. Similarly whilst some smaller risks are not noted as key when sat in isolation, could well be identified as such when interdependencies are acknowledged. Marks & Spencer in table 3.37.1 summarises its risk interdependencies and visually represent them with a diagram.

Table 3.37.1 – Risk Interdependencies

Marks & Spencer plc – Annual report and financial statements 28 March 2015

RISK INTERDEPENDENCY

We recognise that there is significant interdependency between our key risks. This diagram, based on our current Group Risk Profile, highlights how changes to one risk could impact on those connected to it, and therefore on the Group Risk Profile as a whole. By understanding the relationship between our key risks, if they were to materialise, we are better placed to ensure that we are managing them appropriately and to understand the entirety of our risk exposure.

The highlighted risks illustrate potential interdependent risk scenarios:

The success of our business is highly influenced by our ability to retain quality individuals ❿. The loss of key product developers would impact our ability to provide a point of difference against our competitors in terms of quality, value and innovation ❸, whilst maintaining expertise in our Food technology team enables us to maintain high standards of food safety and integrity across our products and supply chain in an increasingly challenging environment ❷. Our customers tell us

that they trust us to do the right thing. By maintaining these high standards of food safety and integrity, we continue to stand out from our competitors ❸.

Strong GM customer engagement ❶ is influenced by our ability to maximise product availability and provide customers with an efficient and reliable delivery proposition ⓬. The robustness of the online business ❼ will also impact this supply chain and logistics network, as well as having a direct influence on customer engagement through the provision of a reliable online experience.

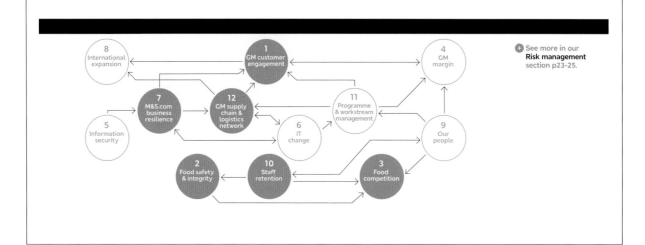

➕ See more in our **Risk management** section p23-25.

3.117 The descriptions of the principal risks and uncertainties facing the entity should be specific, so that a shareholder can understand why they are material to the entity. This might include a description of the likelihood of the risk, an indication of the circumstances under which the risk might be most relevant to the entity and its possible effects. An explanation of how the principal risks and uncertainties are managed or mitigated should also be included to enable shareholders to assess the impact on the future prospects of the entity. [SR guidance para 7.26].

3.118 Significant changes in principal risks, such as a change in likelihood or possible effect, or the inclusion of new risks, should be highlighted or explained. [SR guidance para 7.27].

3.118.1 In Table 3.38, Anglo American provide a clear summary of how their key risks have changed in the period and also provide more commentary on why this is when exploring each individual risk in more detail.

Table 3.38 – Change in risk

Anglo American plc – Annual Report – 31 December 2013

Key risks

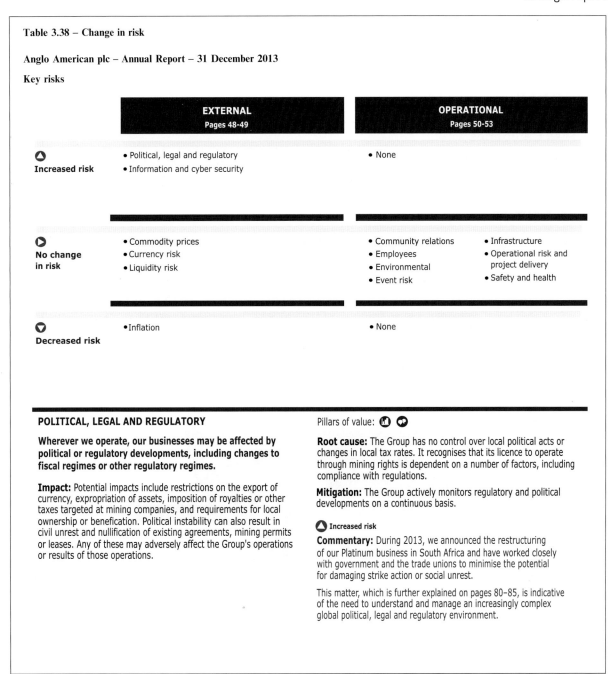

	EXTERNAL Pages 48-49	OPERATIONAL Pages 50-53
Increased risk	• Political, legal and regulatory • Information and cyber security	• None
No change in risk	• Commodity prices • Currency risk • Liquidity risk	• Community relations • Infrastructure • Employees • Operational risk and project delivery • Environmental • Event risk • Safety and health
Decreased risk	• Inflation	• None

POLITICAL, LEGAL AND REGULATORY

Wherever we operate, our businesses may be affected by political or regulatory developments, including changes to fiscal regimes or other regulatory regimes.

Impact: Potential impacts include restrictions on the export of currency, expropriation of assets, imposition of royalties or other taxes targeted at mining companies, and requirements for local ownership or benefication. Political instability can also result in civil unrest and nullification of existing agreements, mining permits or leases. Any of these may adversely affect the Group's operations or results of those operations.

Pillars of value:

Root cause: The Group has no control over local political acts or changes in local tax rates. It recognises that its licence to operate through mining rights is dependent on a number of factors, including compliance with regulations.

Mitigation: The Group actively monitors regulatory and political developments on a continuous basis.

Increased risk

Commentary: During 2013, we announced the restructuring of our Platinum business in South Africa and have worked closely with government and the trade unions to minimise the potential for damaging strike action or social unrest.

This matter, which is further explained on pages 80–85, is indicative of the need to understand and manage an increasingly complex global political, legal and regulatory environment.

3.118.2 Table 3.39 is an example of an entity presenting its risks diagrammatically to indicate the relationship between likelihood and impact. It also shows how the risks have changed during the year.

Table 3.39 – Risk radar

Wärtsilä Corporation – Annual Report – 31 December 2010

Corporate governance

Risks and Risk Management (Extract)

Risk Categories

The relevant risks for Wärtsilä have been classified in four sections; strategic, operational, hazard and financial risks. Risk is defined as the outcome of the probability and the loss exposure of the occurrence. The outcome or potential loss expectancy is highest with strategic and operational risks, and lowest with hazard and financial risks.

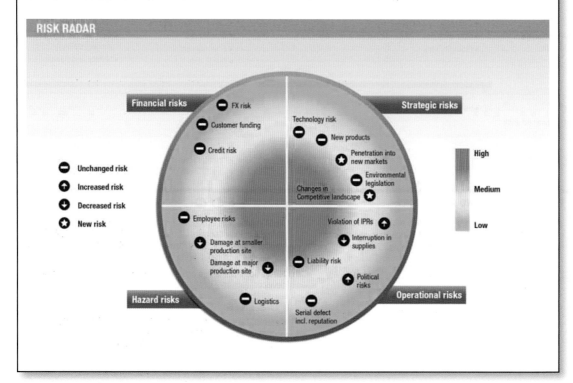

3.119 In Table 3.40, the risk diagram shows the relative likelihood and impact of each key risk. Included in the entity's annual report immediately after this diagram (but not shown here) is an explanation of each risk, how it is being managed and how it has changed since the prior year. Each risk is cross-referenced to a specific strategic priority and performance measure. The member of management responsible for managing each risk is also disclosed.

Table 3.40 – Likelihood and impact of risks

Afren plc – Annual Report and Accounts – 31 December 2013

Risk profile map (extract)

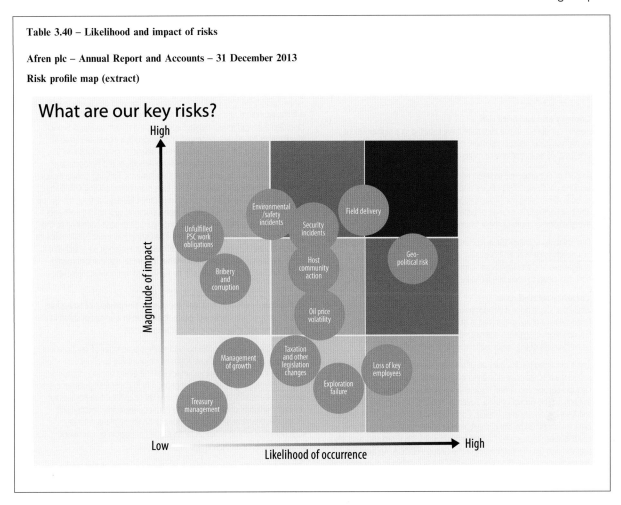

3.120   Management should disclose uncertainties as well as risks. These could include contingent liabilities relating to specific operational uncertainties (such as outstanding litigation) or market uncertainty (for example, whether a new product will be successful). There are also inherent uncertainties that surround the preparation of the financial statements, which might require significant estimates and judgements. These can be referred to in the description of risk factors, but are more often dealt with in the description of critical accounting policies. (For the disclosure of critical accounting policies, see para 3.187.) In addition, under IFRS, significant judgements made by directors, as well as key sources of estimation uncertainty, are required to be disclosed in the financial statements. [IAS 1 paras 113, 116].

3.121   A risk or uncertainty might be unique to the entity, a matter that is relevant to the market in which it operates, or something that applies to the business environment more generally. Where the risk or uncertainty is more generic, the description should make clear how it might affect the entity specifically. [SR guidance para 7.28].

3.122   As highlighted by the FRC report, 'An Update for Directors of Listed Companies: Responding to increased country and currency risk in financial reports', country and/or currency risks are among the principal risks that many entities face. Of particular note are the risks arising from regime change in the Middle East, the funding pressures on some European countries, and the curtailment of capital spending programmes. The outcome of these events remains uncertain. The austerity measures being widely adopted in Europe might result in significant changes to growth rates and demand for consumer products in those countries. In addition, entities might be affected significantly if one or more countries are forced to exit the euro area. In Table 3.41, Vodafone plc describes its eurozone risk.

Table 3.41 – Eurozone risk

Vodafone plc – Annual Report – 31 March 2012

Principal risk factors and uncertainties (extract)

Eurozone risk

Country and currency risk

Recent conditions in the eurozone have resulted in a higher risk of disruption and business risk from high currency volatility and/or the potential of an exit of one or more countries from the euro.

As part of our response to these conditions we have reviewed our existing processes and policies, and in places, evolved them with the aim of both minimising the Group's economic exposure and to preserve our ability to operate in a range of potential conditions that may exist in the event of one or more of these future events.

Our ability to manage these risks needs to take appropriate account of our needs to deliver a high quality service to our customers, meet licence obligations and the significant capital investments we may have made and may need to continue to make in the markets most impacted.

Currency related risks

While our share price is denominated in sterling, the majority of our financial results are generated in other currencies. As a result the Group's operating profit is sensitive to either a relative strengthening or weakening of the major currencies in which it transacts.

The "Operating results" section of the annual report on pages 40 to 49 sets out a discussion and analysis of the relative contributions of the Group's Europe and AMAP regions and the major geographical markets in each, to the Group's service revenue and EBITDA performance. Our markets in Italy, Ireland, Greece, Portugal and Spain have been most directly impacted by the current market conditions and in order of contribution, represent 17% (Italy), 8% (Spain), 3% (Portugal) and 3% (Ireland and Greece combined) of the Group's EBITDA. An average 3% decline in the sterling equivalent of these combined geographical markets due to currency revaluation would reduce Group EBITDA by £0.1 billion. The Group's foreign currency earnings are diversified through its 45% equity interest in Verizon Wireless, which operates in the United States and generates its earnings in US dollars. Verizon Wireless, which is equity accounted, contributed 42% of the Group's adjusted operating profit for the year ended 31 March 2012.

The Group employs a number of mechanisms to manage elements of exchange rate risk at a transaction, translation and economic level. At the transaction level our policies require foreign exchange risks on transactions denominated in other currencies above certain de minimis levels to be hedged. Further, since the Company's sterling share price represents the value of its future multi-currency cash flows, principally in euro, US dollars and sterling, we aim to align the currency of our debt and interest charges in proportion to our expected future principal multi-currency cash flows, thereby providing an economic hedge in terms of reduced volatility in the sterling equivalent value of the Group and a partial hedge against income statement translation exposure, as interest costs will be denominated in foreign currencies.

In the event of a country's exit from the eurozone, this may necessitate changes in one or more of our entities' functional currency and potentially higher volatility of those entities' trading results when translated into sterling, potentially adding further currency risk.

A summary of this sensitivity of our operating results and our foreign exchange risk management policies is set out within "Financial risk management – Market risk – Foreign exchange management" within note 21 to the consolidated financial statements.

Operational planning

We have worked to develop operational plans to use as a basis for continuity planning across the Group in the event of significant exchange rate volatility and/or the withdrawal of one, or a small number of countries, from the euro. We have categorised "at risk" countries into three categories based on risk profile and identified three broad areas of operational risks for the Group where work has been focused, being:

Financial/investment risk: Our activities are focused on counterparty risk management and in particular the protection and availability of cash deposits and investments. Exposures in relation to liquid Group investments have been reviewed and actions have been taken to reduce counterparty limits with certain financial institutions and to convert a significant proportion of euro denominated holdings and deposits into sterling and US dollar investments. Existing Group policy requires cash sweep arrangements, to ensure no operating company has more than €5 million on deposit on any one day. Further, the Group has had in place for a number of years collateral support agreements with a significant number of its counterparties to pass collateral to the Group under certain circumstances. The Group has a net £980 million of collateral assets in its statement of financial position at 31 March 2012. Further information is provided within "Financial risk management – Credit risk" within note 21 to the consolidated financial statements.

Trading risks: We have investigated the structure of existing procurement contracts and we have started the process of amending certain contractual clauses to place the Group in a better position in the event of the exit of a country from the eurozone.

Business continuity risks: We have identified a number of key business continuity priorities which are focused on planning to allow migration to a more cash-based business model in the event banking systems are frozen, developing dual currency capability in contract customer billing systems or ensuring the ability to move these contract customers to prepaid methods of billing, and the consequential impacts to tariff structures. We have also put in place contingency plans with key suppliers that would assist us to continue to support our network infrastructure, retail operations and employees.

The Group continues to maintain appropriate levels of cash and short-term investments in many currencies and, with a carefully controlled group of counterparties, to minimise the risks to the ongoing access to that liquidity and therefore to the ability of the Group to settle debts as they become due. Further information is provided within "Financial risk management – Liquidity risk" within note 21 to the consolidated financial statements.

Risk of change in carrying amount of assets and liabilities

The main potential short-term financial statement impact of the current economic uncertainties is the potential impairment of non-financial and financial assets.

The Group has significant amounts of goodwill, other intangible assets and plant, property and equipment allocated to, or held by, companies operating in the eurozone. We have performed impairment testing for each country in Europe as at 31 March 2012 and identified aggregate impairment charges of £4.0 billion in relation to Vodafone Italy, Spain, Greece and Portugal. Further detail on this exercise together with the sensitivity of the results of this assessment to reasonably possible adverse assumptions is set out in note 10 to the consolidated financial statements.

Our operating companies in Italy, Ireland, Greece, Portugal and Spain have billed and unbilled trade receivables totalling £2.0 billion. IFRS contains specific requirements for impairment assessments of financial assets. We have a range of credit exposures and provisions for doubtful debts that are generally made by reference to consistently applied methodologies overlaid with judgements determined on a case-by-case basis reflecting the specific facts and circumstances of the receivable. Detailed disclosures made in relation to provisions against loans and receivables as well as disclosures about any loans and receivables that are past due at the end of the period, concentrations of risk and credit risk more generally as set out in "Financial risk management – Credit risk" within note 21 to the consolidated financial statements.

3.123 Table 3.42 illustrates an entity presenting a SWOT (strengths, weaknesses, opportunities and threats) analysis. MTU Aero Engines Holding AG includes this analysis in its 'Risk Report', where it describes its risk management system and risks.

Table 3.42 – SWOT analysis

MTU Aero Engines Holding AG – Annual Report – 31 December 2010

Group Management Report (extract)

SWOT analysis

SWOT analysis of the MTU group

Corporate	Market
Strengths	**Opportunities**
Technological leadership – OEM: Excellence in engine modules: low-pressure turbines, high-pressure and IP compressors – MRO: Excellence in advanced repair techniques	Market environment of business units on a long-term growth trend
Balanced mix of production and after-market business, covering all stages from development and manufacturing to maintenance	Increasing technological complexity of future engines
Focus on high-profit-margin engine business	Good market opportunities for fuel-efficient engine designs (geared turbofan) in the event of steadily rising oil prices
Presence in fast-growing Asian market (MTU Maintenance Zhuhai)	Solid financing structure and technological leadership open the way to program investments
Long-term contracts in the OEM business, involvement in consortia and cooperative ventures	Growth of MRO in newly industrializing countries
Quality and on-time delivery form basis for reliable partnerships	Airline outsourcing in order to concentrate on core activities offers additional opportunities for MRO business
Proximity of MRO sales network to customers	Greater exploitation of synergies between areas of commercial business
Solid financing structure opens up opportunities for M&A activities and program investments	Positive changes in U.S. dollar exchange rate
Weaknesses	**Threats**
High dependency on U.S. dollar	Low, volatile profitability on the part of end customers (airlines); possible spending cuts in the event of an economic downturn
Cyclic business	Inherent risk of advanced technology development with regard to estimated schedules and costs
Small company by comparison with OEMs	Competition from low-cost PMA parts
	Entry of newly industrializing nations into the aerospace industry
	Restrained public spending may lead to defense budget cuts and structural reform of the German armed forces
	Difficulty of obtaining licenses in the MRO business
	Negative changes in U.S. dollar exchange rate

3.124 The guidance recommends the disclosure of risks and uncertainties, including financial risks; in addition, IFRS 7 and FRS 29 (its UK equivalent) require such disclosure for financial policies and risks. An entity should disclose information that enables users of its financial statements to evaluate the nature and extent of risks arising from financial instruments to which the entity is exposed at the end of the reporting period. [IFRS 7 para 31]. Potentially, the combination of IFRS 7's requirements and the recommendations in the guidance could result in information being duplicated in an annual report. However, IFRS 7 recognises this issue and states that the information regarding the nature and risks arising from financial instruments must either be given in the financial statements, or be incorporated by cross-reference from the financial statements to some other statement (such as a management commentary or risk report) that is available to users of the financial statements on the same terms and at the same time as the financial statements. [IFRS 7 para B6]. The Manual of accounting – IFRS for the UK deals with these requirements.

Environmental and social matters

3.125 To the extent necessary for an understanding of the development, performance or position of the entity's business, the strategic report should include information about the following:

■ environmental matters (including the impact of the entity's business on the environment);

■ the entity's employees; and

■ social, community and human rights issues.

The information should include a description of any relevant policies in respect of those matters and the effectiveness of those policies.

[CA06 Sec 414C(7)(b); SR guidance para 7.29].

3.125.1 Information on any of the matters described in paragraph 3.125 that is not considered necessary for an understanding of the development, performance, position or future prospects of the entity's business should not be included in the strategic report. Where the directors wish to put this information in the public domain, it should be located outside the strategic report – for example, in a separate sustainability or corporate social responsibility report which could be located online. [SR guidance para 7.37].

3.126 There could be a strong relationship between the development, performance, position or future prospects of the entity and the matters described in the above paragraph, particularly over the longer term. This might be because a particular matter gives rise to a principal risk or uncertainty or because the entity has gained a competitive advantage from its policies and responses to such matters. The relative importance of the matters will depend on the sector in which the entity operates and its strategy and business model. [SR guidance para 7.30].

3.127 A clear way of demonstrating the importance of this information is to consider if these aspects are part of overall group strategy; if so, they should be incorporated into group priorities. As shown in Table 3.43, for example, The British Land Company include 'people' as a key strategic theme.

Table 3.43

The British Land Company – Annual report and accounts – 31 March 2013

	PROPERTY PERFORMANCE		
PRIORITIES	Grow income	Grow value	Incremental value

OUR LONG-TERM DECISIONS

Our macro calls on property cycles, our sector and asset selection and our capital structure.

We focus on UK retail and London offices because they are large and liquid markets with the best growth potential for rents and capital values.

Across our portfolio, we are increasing our exposure to London and the South East in particular reflecting its growing status as one of the most important cities in the world. In Retail, we are focusing on owning and creating the best experiential convenience or functional shopping destinations which

dominate their catchment areas. In Offices, we operate across London but with an increasing emphasis on infrastructure hubs and the West End.

The security and stability of our business means we are able to invest in highly profitable activities such as development. We look for 'incremental' activity such as development, repositioning, buying and selling properties to meaningfully add to the returns we generate for our shareholders.

OUR SHORT-TERM ACTIONS

The individual actions we take which support our long-term decisions.

SHARPENING OUR FOCUS ON INCOME

Our focus on creating the right environments and world-class customer service means we continue to attract and retain occupiers even in today's difficult markets. At Broadgate, we have extended 1.5 million sq ft of leases with existing occupiers and signed 0.1 million sq ft of leases for new space over the last two years. All of this has helped keep occupancy high (96.8%) and leases long (10.7 years).

RENT SECURED THROUGH PRE-LETS

£49m

DEVELOPING THE RIGHT SPACE TO SATISFY DEMAND

We are one of only a few companies with the financial resources and expertise to have been able to exploit the shortage of high-quality space in retail and London offices. Our early decision to start a major development programme in 2010 has already delivered significant value to shareholders with £49 million of rent already secured through pre-lets and a capital value uplift of £312 million, equivalent to a 31.2 pence contribution to our net asset value per share.

SECURING THE RIGHT DEALS

We are able to do smart deals because we have the expertise and financial firepower to take on more complex transactions and have a proven track record meaning people trust us. This means we have been able to take advantage of the increased flow of attractive opportunities coming to market over the last year. Our acquisitions include the Clarges Estate, an exciting office/residential development in Mayfair, Ealing Broadway Shopping Centre and two in-town retail/leisure developments in Hereford and Lancaster.

HOW WE MEASURE OURSELVES

KPI

- Property returns
- Gross income growth
- Development commitment
- Customer satisfaction

→ See KPIs
P28–29

→ See Remuneration Policy
P94–99

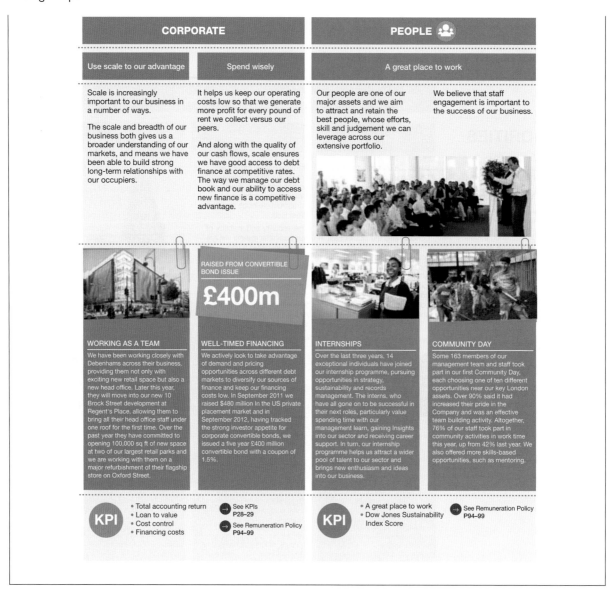

3.128 African Barrick Gold have a clear focus throughout their report on their licence to operate. This is clearly stated as part of their business model, and it is developed further in a specific section. The entity also discusses their human rights policy and their training in this area.

Table 3.44

African Barrick Gold – Annual report and accounts – 31 December 2012

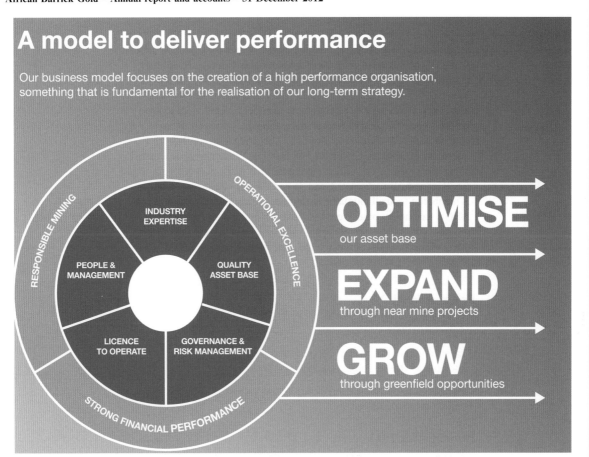

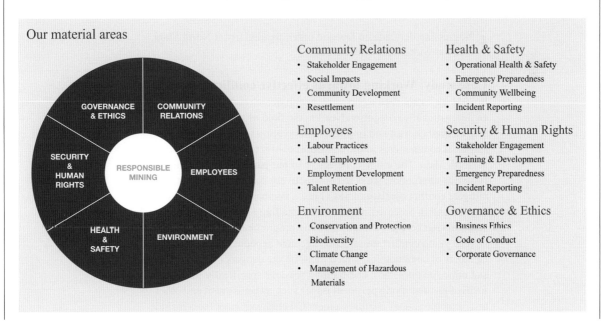

Our material areas

Community Relations
- Stakeholder Engagement
- Social Impacts
- Community Development
- Resettlement

Employees
- Labour Practices
- Local Employment
- Employment Development
- Talent Retention

Environment
- Conservation and Protection
- Biodiversity
- Climate Change
- Management of Hazardous Materials

Health & Safety
- Operational Health & Safety
- Emergency Preparedness
- Community Wellbeing
- Incident Reporting

Security & Human Rights
- Stakeholder Engagement
- Training & Development
- Emergency Preparedness
- Incident Reporting

Governance & Ethics
- Business Ethics
- Code of Conduct
- Corporate Governance

In the context of human rights, in addition to Voluntary Principles training, we continued to progress the roll out of our human rights policy and compliance programme, notably with the further implementation of reporting and investigations procedures for suspected human rights violations.

In conjunction with ABG training initiatives, Search for Common Ground ("SFCG") continued to progress its human rights training and conflict resolution programme, building on progress made in 2011. During the year, SFCG held 95 training sessions with communities surrounding ABG mine sites, involving 1,428 community members overall, in order to progress understanding of the Voluntary Principles on Security and Human Rights. In addition to this, SFCG held 60 youth conflict management sessions, in which 1,868 community members participated, 55 sessions focused on conflict management as it affects women, in which 1,570 individuals participated, and 76 participatory theatre productions. A number of football tournaments, aimed at relationship building across ABG's stakeholder base, were also held. All of these initiatives aim to progress discussion, communication and understandings as regards the effect of conflict and conflict related issues within communities.

Progress in 2012

- Completing enhancements to security systems across all ABG operations

- Increasing training on the Voluntary Principles on Security and Human Rights across ABG stakeholders

- Progressing implementation of our human rights compliance programme

Priorities for 2013

- Maintaining training levels on the Voluntary Principles on Security and Human Rights

- Progressing dialogue on law and order, particularly at North Mara, with our wider stakeholder group

Case study: Working towards effective conflict management

In 2011 we established a partnership with Search for Common Ground, an internationally recognised NGO in the field of conflict resolution, to help strengthen trust and improve collaboration between ABG operations and local communities in the context of conflict management, particularly at North Mara. The ultimate objective of our partnership is to find culturally appropriate ways to constructively deal with conflicts in order to mitigate conflict escalation. SFCG use a number of methods of community engagement in order to progress understanding of conflict resolutions. In addition to general community training programmes, SFCGs activities include youth conflict training management sessions aimed at younger members of communities, which focus on the dangers of illegal mining and mine site intrusions; and training sessions specifically for women, focused on identifying pertinent issues such as harassment and other unacceptable actions against women. Other engagement tools include the creation and distribution of educational materials, such as comics, to discuss topics including the Voluntary Principles on Security and Human Rights, UN guidelines on use of force by law enforcement officials, universal human rights and sexual harassment. SFCG also uses theatre productions in order to highlight conflict scenarios in context and sporting activities, such as football tournaments involving players from local communities, the authorities and members of the ABG workforce, which aim to build relations and teamwork.

3.129 The strategic report should include information on a matter described in 3.125 when its influence, or potential influence, on the development, performance, position or future prospects of the entity's business is material to shareholders. [SR guidance para 7.31]. The table below sets out an extract from Unilever's annual report, which itself has a big sustainability section, but explicitly cross-refers to more detail in the separate sustainability report.

Table 3.45

Unilever plc – Annual report and accounts – 31 December 2012

UNILEVER SUSTAINABLE LIVING PLAN

IMPROVING HEALTH AND WELL-BEING

By 2020 we will help more than a billion people take action to improve their health and well-being.

REDUCING ENVIRONMENTAL IMPACT

By 2020 our goal is to halve the environmental footprint of the making and use of our products as we grow our business.^

1 HEALTH AND HYGIENE

By 2020 we will help more than a billion people to improve their hygiene habits and we will bring safe drinking water to 500 million people. This will help reduce the incidence of life-threatening diseases like diarrhoea.

AROUND 220 MILLION PEOPLE REACHED BY END 2012 THROUGH OUR PROGRAMMES ON HANDWASHING, SAFE DRINKING WATER, ORAL HEALTH AND SELF-ESTEEM†

2 NUTRITION

We will continually work to improve the taste and nutritional quality of all our products. By 2020 we will double the proportion of our portfolio that meets the highest nutritional standards, based on globally recognised dietary guidelines. This will help hundreds of millions of people to achieve a healthier diet.

18% OF OUR PORTFOLIO BY VOLUME MET THE CRITERIA IN 2012†º

3 GREENHOUSE GASES

Our commitment is to halve the greenhouse gas impact of our products across the lifecycle by 2020.^

OUR GREENHOUSE GAS IMPACT HAS REDUCED BY AROUND 6% SINCE 2010‡‡

4 WATER

Our commitment is to halve the water associated with the consumer use of our products by 2020.^*

OUR WATER IMPACT HAS REMAINED BROADLY UNCHANGED SINCE 2010‡‡

 OUR UNILEVER SUSTAINABLE LIVING PLAN IN ACTION PROGRESS AGAINST OUR PLAN IS DETAILED IN THE SUSTAINABLE LIVING SECTION OF WWW.UNILEVER.COM/SUSTAINABLE-LIVING AND IN OUR UNILEVER SUSTAINABLE LIVING PLAN: PROGRESS REPORT 2012, TO BE PUBLISHED IN APRIL 2013.

3.130 A number of entities have traditionally reported this type of information within their sustainability report. In these cases, it might be worthwhile considering if any information required under the new regulations would be better placed in the strategic report. For example, RBS Group have a clear human rights statement in their sustainability report.

Table 3.46

RBS Group – Sustainability report – 2012

Business and human rights

RBS Group is committed to upholding and respecting human rights, and is signatory to the United Nations Global Compact (UNGC). which includes commitments to support and respect the protection of human rights, and ensure we are not complicit in human rights abuses. The UNGC is formally incorporated into our ESE policies and our Ethical Code for Suppliers. The RBS Position Statement on Human Rights protects the human rights of all RBS employees as well as ensuring that human rights are a key consideration in our lending decisions. These are available on our website at rbs.com/sustainable.

In 2012, we engaged with stakeholders on human rights issues through involvement in the Equator Principles, UNEP FI, and other industry organisations. RBS has also worked with other multinational banks to contribute to a sectoral discussion paper around the UN Guiding Principles for Business and Human Rights (also known as the 'Ruggie Principles' after creator Professor John Ruggie).

Human rights modules have been built into relevant compulsory online training programmes for RBS employees. In addition, client specific human rights risk training is delivered to risk professionals and appropriate employees across the Group. Additional workshops are available for relationship managers with exposure to sensitive clients or countries. The approach to human rights is continually reviewed, and the Board level Group Sustainability Committee receives updates on human rights from across the business.

3.131 The information should make clear how any matters identified under paragraph 3.125 might affect the development, performance, position or future prospects of the entity's business. [SR guidance para 7.32].

3.132 The influence, or potential influence, of the matters described in paragraph 3.125 on the development, performance, position or future prospects of the entity's business might sometimes be better described through the integration of the relevant information with other content elements, rather than through the use of a separate 'corporate social responsibility' section of the strategic report; but, in any case, clear linkage should be provided. [SR guidance para 7.33].

3.133 In the extract below, Johnson Matthey is clear from the outset of its report that it considers sustainability an integrated part of its overall approach to business, with insights on this located throughout the annual report.

Table 3.47 – Sustainability reporting

Johnson Matthey – Annual report – 2014

Integrating sustainability

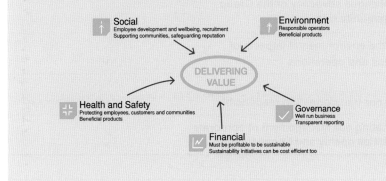

JOHNSON MATTHEY IS A LEADING SPECIALITY CHEMICALS COMPANY.

As a business, we always aim to deliver what we promise. We work together, applying our expertise in advanced materials and technology to innovate and improve solutions that:

- are valued by our customers;
- optimise the use of natural resources; and
- enhance the quality of life for the people of the world, both today and for the future.

To us, good performance is not just about profit. It's about running our business in the most sustainable way and we have five elements of sustainability which have a material impact on our business. In this report we will update you on our progress.

BUILDING A SUSTAINABLE BUSINESS

Social
Employee development and wellbeing, recruitment
Supporting communities, safeguarding reputation

Environment
Responsible operators
Beneficial products

DELIVERING VALUE

Health and Safety
Protecting employees, customers and communities
Beneficial products

Governance
Well run business
Transparent reporting

Financial
Must be profitable to be sustainable
Sustainability initiatives can be cost efficient too

3.134 Royal Mail, in the extract below, have taken the opposite approach, having a specific CSR section but being clear in the introduction how the corporate responsibility objectives are aligned to overall business priorities.

Table 3.48 – Sustainability reporting

Royal Mail – Annual report – 2014

Corporate responsibility linked to priorities

Royal Mail makes a major contribution to the UK's social and economic infrastructure. As the designated provider of the Universal Service, we play a vital role in connecting millions of customers, businesses, organisations and communities – including those in the most remote rural areas.

Our corporate responsibility strategy is an integral part of realising our core strategic priorities. The objectives at the heart of our business and corporate responsibility strategies are the same – to ensure a sound and sustainable Universal Service and to generate sustainable shareholder value.

The links between our corporate responsibility aims and our core strategic priorities are shown in the table below.

Corporate responsibility objective	Being a successful parcels business	Managing the decline in letters	Being customer focused
Delivering economic and social benefit to the communities we serve	✓	✓	✓
Driving colleague advocacy of the Group and its community role	✓		✓
Managing the environmental impacts of our business and operations	✓		✓
Delivering our transformation responsibly	✓	✓	✓
Communicating our management of corporate responsibilities openly and transparently	✓		✓

3.135 Where information on a specific matter described in paragraph 3.125 is considered necessary for the understanding of the development, performance, position or future prospects of the entity's business, a description of some or all of the following items could be included in the strategic report, where they are considered relevant:

- The entity's policy in respect of the matter, together with a description of any measures taken to embed the commitment within the organisation.

- The process of due diligence through which the entity:

    - assesses the actual or potential impacts arising from its own activities and through its business relationships;

    - integrates the findings from these assessments and takes actions to prevent or mitigate adverse impacts;

    - tracks the effectiveness of its efforts; and

    - communicates it efforts externally, in particular to affected stakeholders.

- The entity's participation in any processes intended to remediate any adverse effects that it has caused or contributed to. [SR guidance para 7.34].

3.136 In the extract below, African Barrick Gold provide insight into their positive contributions in one of their most active regions.

Table 3.49 – Sustainability reporting

African Barrick Gold plc – Annual report – 2013

Positive regional contribution

Responsible mining
Investing in Tanzania

We contribute to the economic growth of our host communities, regions and countries to assist the progression of sustainable socio-economic development

ABG's direct economic contribution is made up of the economic value we add by paying our employees, governments, suppliers, shareholders, contractors and communities. However, our true economic contribution is far greater once the wider effects of our presence are considered. These include indirect effects of people spending their wages, governments distributing tax and royalty revenues, and neighbouring communities using the infrastructure developed for our operations. Our direct economic contribution in 2013 was US$959 million, compared to US$1,073 million in 2012.

The distribution of ABG taxes includes royalties, indirect taxes (VAT and fuel levies), payroll taxes (inclusive of social security payments and other taxes such as withholding taxes), stamp duties and environmental levies. Geographically, the majority of our taxes are paid in Tanzania, being the location of our operating mines, followed by South Africa, where certain administrative, financial and technical functions are located, followed by the UK, being the location of our corporate headquarters. Our net taxation contribution was US$203 million in 2013, compared to US$159 million in 2012.

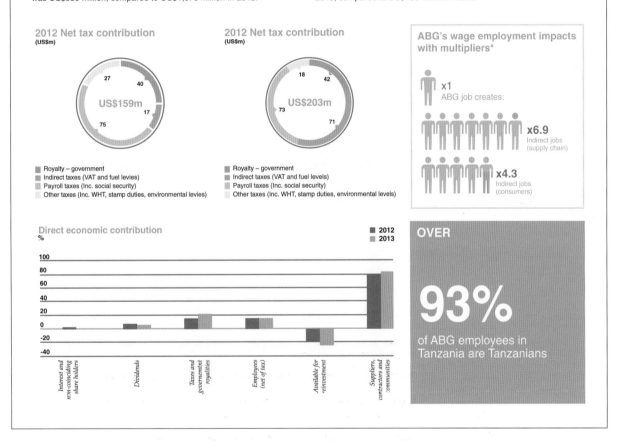

2012 Net tax contribution (US$m)

US$159m — 27, 40, 17, 75

- Royalty – government
- Indirect taxes (VAT and fuel levies)
- Payroll taxes (Inc. social security)
- Other taxes (Inc. WHT, stamp duties, environmental levies)

2012 Net tax contribution (US$m)

US$203m — 18, 42, 73, 71

- Royalty – government
- Indirect taxes (VAT and fuel levels)
- Payroll taxes (Inc. social security)
- Other taxes (Inc. WHT, stamp duties, environmental levels)

ABG's wage employment impacts with multipliers*

x1 ABG job creates:

x6.9 Indirect jobs (supply chain)

x4.3 Indirect jobs (consumers)

Direct economic contribution %

- 2012
- 2013

Interest and non-coinciding share holders / Dividends / Taxes and government royalities / Employees (net of tax) / Available for reinvestment / Suppliers, contractors and communities

OVER

93%

of ABG employees in Tanzania are Tanzanians

3.137 The Berkeley Group Holdings, shown below, have provided some clear context for their sustainability disclosures and provided good detail in each area of their commitments, including an assessment of performance against targets.

Table 3.50 – Sustainability reporting

The Berkeley Group Holdings plc – Annual report – 2013

Sustainability commitments

Berkeley is aware that it needs to balance its aim to be successful with a will to operate sustainably and with a social purpose. Creating exceptional places that stand the test of time is at the forefront of this, as is its role in creating new jobs, working in partnership with local communities and contributing to the communities in and around each of its developments.

Berkeley is respectful of the inherently cyclical nature of the property market and is protective of the business's capacity to operate safely, sustainably and at an optimal size, now and in the future.

OPERATIONS

Running our business efficiently and considerately and working with our supply chain.

Our Vision for 2020

First

major housebuilder to sign up to the Prompt Payment Code

35.9/40

(2012:35.7) average Considerate Constructors Scheme score (May to December)

7%

reduction in operational carbon emissions per site operative

"Sustainability remains fully integrated into our business strategy and operations. We have developed excellent partnerships with our supply chain to ensure high quality materials and services are consistently provided, and environmental, social and ethical impacts are minimised. We will continue to conduct our operations in an environmentally efficient manner and with consideration to our neighbours."

Progress at a Glance: Against key two year commitments 2012-2014

Supply Chain	Integrate an assessment of the sustainability of products, suppliers and contractors into the formal selection process	✓
	Ensure that all wood purchased by Berkeley is certified by a timber certification scheme	✓
Community Relations	Register all sites with the Considerate Constructors Scheme and achieve a minimum of 35 points out of 50 in site audits (32 out of 40 prior to January 2013)	✓
Environmental Management	Reduce average site carbon dioxide emissions by 3% per site operative by May 2014	✓
	Reduce average site water consumption by 3% per site operative by May 2014	✖
	Re-use or recycle over 85% of construction, demolition and excavation waste	✓

Key: ✓ Currently on target to achieve ✖ Not currently on target to achieve

3.137.1 Where an entity uses KPIs to monitor its performance in respect of any of the matters described in paragraph 3.125, the most efficient way of communicating information on the effectiveness of its policies on those matters will often be through reference to those measures. [SR guidance para 7.35].

3.137.2 Directors could refer to a source of guidance (such as the UN Guiding Principles on Human Rights) or a voluntary framework that provides advice on how the entity should conduct its business, suggests ways of monitoring or tracking performance, or provides examples of disclosure that might be helpful in communicating information to the entity's stakeholders. In preparing the strategic report, the directors might choose to comply fully or partially with that guidance or voluntary framework, or take a more general regard of its content. Where such an approach is taken, directors should nevertheless ensure that only information that is necessary for an understanding of the development, performance, position or future prospects of the entity's business, or that otherwise required by law, is included in the strategic report. [SR guidance para 7.36].

3.137.3 The Global Reporting Initiative (GRI) is one organisation that has developed a specific sustainability reporting framework to assist entities. Their G4 guidelines are designed to help entities disclose their most critical impacts on the environment, society and economy. The guidelines are universally applicable to all types and sizes of entities. Historically, the influence of these guidelines has driven the separate sustainability report, but as more entities bring sustainability disclosures into the strategic report GRI insights may also become more commonplace.

3.137.4 Rio Tinto, in its disclosure of human rights policies (shown below), makes clear reference to its consistency with the UN Declaration of Human Rights.

Table 3.51 – Human rights reporting

Rio Tinto plc – Annual report – 2013

Human rights

Human rights

Rio Tinto has diverse operations across more than 40 countries with very different social, economic, political and cultural landscapes. The actions we take to respect and support human rights help us build enduring and active relationships with local communities, employees and business partners.

We respect and promote fundamental human rights consistent with the United Nations Universal Declaration of Human Rights. Our human rights approach is founded in *The way we work*, voluntary commitments and our Human Rights policy. It draws together relevant internal controls that incorporate the broad range of issues encompassed by human rights. This includes those associated with communities, security, human resources, procurement, and health, safety and the environment. Our approach is consistent with the human rights due diligence process in the UN Guiding Principles on Business and Human Rights. We understand this includes avoiding involvement in human rights harm by others, including business partners.

We integrate human rights into our risk analysis, impact assessment complaints, disputes and grievance processes. At locations that are high risk, we may conduct additional human rights risk analyses and impact assessments.

In implementing our policies, we are subject to the local laws of the many countries in which we operate. We build on compliance with local laws and, where our policy and procedures are more stringent, we operate to these standards.

To ensure our employees and other key stakeholders understand how these tools work together, we developed a Human Rights guidance note, which will replace our 2003 guidance. We also rolled out updated human rights e-learning across the company and developed site-specific human rights training. In 2013 a human rights section was included in mandatory training for *The way we work*. To continue to build internal networks and identify Group-wide challenges, we refreshed the mandate of our multi-function and cross-product group human rights working group.

Rio Tinto has made voluntary commitments to the OECD Guidelines for Multinational Enterprises and the UN Global Compact, and is a member of its Human Rights Working Group. We also participate in the Voluntary Principles on Security and Human Rights. We are committed to avoiding violations of fundamental human rights through our security arrangements and to taking steps to avoid complicity in such violations by private and public security personnel. This includes training for security personnel and conducting security and human rights assessments at all critical risk sites. To assist sites in this regard we have also developed a security and human rights toolkit.

We strive to achieve the free, prior and informed consent of Indigenous communities as defined in the 2012 International Finance Corporation Performance Standard 7 and supporting guidance. Because we must respect the law of the countries in which we operate, we seek consent as defined in relevant jurisdictions, and ensure agreement-making processes are consistent with such definitions. We respect the land connection of Indigenous communities and seek agreements with affected communities in the development and performance of our operations.

Business Performance

Analysis of the development and performance of the business

3.138 The strategic report should provide an analysis of the development and performance of the business in the financial year and of its position at the end of that year. [CA06 Sec 414C(3); SR guidance para 7.38].

3.139 An entity's financial position (for example, plans for future capital expenditure and acquisitions, and the robustness of its funding position to achieve those plans) is often contained in a separate section of the annual report. In larger entities with diversified operations, additional financial information might be given elsewhere – for example, by dividing reporting into sections that describe the operations and financial position of each of the main business segments. Even where that form of presentation is adopted, however, there is usually a separate financial review dealing with the group's overall financial position.

3.140 The analysis should complement the financial statements, where relevant providing additional explanations of amounts recognised in the financial statements and the conditions and events that shaped the information contained within them. [CA06 Sec 414C(12); SR guidance para 7.39]. It should aim to answer the questions that are commonly asked by shareholders at an annual general meeting (AGM) or at results presentations.

3.141 Even though the analysis is based on the financial statements, it should supplement the disclosures required by accounting standards, and it should comment on events that impacted the entity's financial position during the year. This is particularly relevant where a large part of the entity operates in an area of economic instability. The analysis should also comment on factors that are likely to affect the financial position in the future. There can be significant volatility in the reported results arising from the use of derivatives and the requirement under the standards to fair value some types of instrument. The requirement to classify as debt some instruments and arrangements involving shares could also have a significant effect on the balance sheet presentation. This is why particular emphasis is placed on the need to further explain the entity's policies and practices. The guidance contained in the Manual of accounting – IFRS for the UK might be useful when preparing disclosure in this area.

3.141.1 The development and performance of the business should be analysed in the context of the strategy applied by the entity during the financial performance year. Segmentation of the analysis of the development, performance or position should be consistent with the segments identified in the financial statements. [SR guidance para 7.40].

3.142 A number of the measures used to monitor the entity's financial position can be taken directly from the financial statements, but management often supplements these with other measures common to their industry, in order to monitor their progress towards stated objectives. For more information on key performance indicators, see paragraph 3.191. Such disclosure might reflect non-GAAP measures and might include sensitivity analysis (for example, in respect of financial instrument values where volatility can have a significant impact on the entity's financial position).

3.143 The strategic report should include information on the entity's key strengths, and tangible and intangible resources. This should include those items that are not reflected in the financial statements. Depending on the nature of the business, these might include: corporate reputation and brand strength; natural resources; employees; research and development; intellectual capital; licences; patents; copyrights and trademarks; and market position. [SR guidance para 7.42].

3.144 The following sections look at different elements of financial disclosure, some of which are not specifically recognised by the strategic report guidance but would, in our view, help entities to provide a clear picture of the development and performance of their business.

Cash flows

3.145 Where necessary for an understanding of the development, performance, position or future prospects of the entity, the analysis should make reference to cash flows during the year and factors that might affect future cash flows. Where appropriate, the strategic report should discuss the entity's current and prospective liquidity and its ability to fund its stated strategy. [SR guidance para 7.41].

3.146 The entity should comment on any special factors that have influenced cash flows in the period and that might have a significant effect on future cash flows. This could include the existence and timing of commitments for capital expenditure and other known or probable cash requirements; an example of the latter might be the need to repay a large tranche of debt at a particular date in the future. Unusual or non-recurring cash flows (such as proceeds of a sale and leaseback or the termination of an interest rate swap) should be highlighted, where material.

3.147 Where an entity has cash that is surplus to its future operating requirements and its current levels of distributions to members, the strategic report should discuss the entity's plans for making use of the cash. Table 3.52 illustrates an entity reporting on its uses of surplus cash.

Table 3.52 – Uses of surplus cash

Deutsche Lufthansa AG – Annual Report – 31 December 2010

Financial strategy (extract)

Dividend policy keeps the balance between sharing profit and preserving capital.

Our dividend policy follows a clear logic and is embedded in our financial strategy: dividend payments are primarily oriented towards the Group's operating profit as reported under IFRS. After successful financial years we have distributed between 30 and 40 per cent of operating profit as a dividend in the past. However, this is subject to the ability to pay a dividend from the net profit for the year reported in the individual financial statements for Deutsche Lufthansa AG under HGB. The proposed amount of the dividend also considers the continued or successive achievement of our financial objectives. The continuity of this dividend policy means that our shareholders share in the success of the Lufthansa Group and we maintain the financial substance of the Company.

Dividend in €

2010	2009	2008	2007	2006
0.60	–	0.70	1.25	0.70

3.148   Cash flow is real; whether an entity has more or less cash is not a matter of judgement. So, for many users of financial statements, cash flow is a key measure of performance, and entities often develop KPIs that relate to cash flow. Some measures focus on cash flow from operations after meeting the entity's obligations for interest, tax and dividends and after capital expenditure; this is sometimes termed 'free cash flow'. But definitions of 'free cash flow' (a non-GAAP measure) often vary from entity to entity, and so they should be fully explained. An example of disclosure of free cash flow is provided in Table 3.53.

Table 3.53 – Free cash flow

British American Tobacco plc – Annual Report – 31 December 2010

Business review (extract)

Cash flow – free cash flow

Free cash flow is defined as net cash from operating activities (including dividends from associates, restructuring costs and taxation) less net interest, net capital expenditure and dividends to minorities.

Free cash flow is defined.

A specific target is set each year for free cash flow. The target for 2010 was exceeded.

£ million

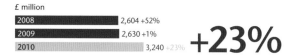

2008	2,604	+52%
2009	2,630	+1%
2010	3,240	+23%

+23%

Cash flow

The IFRS cash flow statement on page 112 includes all transactions affecting cash and cash equivalents, including financing. The alternative cash flow statement is presented to illustrate the cash flows before transactions relating to borrowings.

The IFRS cash flow statement on page 112 includes all transactions affecting cash and cash equivalents, including financing. The alternative cash flow statement is presented to illustrate the cash flows before transactions relating to borrowings.

Links to IFRS cash flow statement and explains purpose of alternative cash flow statement.

Operating cash flow increased by £584 million or 14 per cent to £4,901 million, reflecting growth in underlying operating performance. Taking into account outflows relating to taxation, which were £83 million higher than last year due to higher taxable profits, an increase in restructuring costs due to the timing of payments and an increase in restructuring activities, as well as an increase in inflows relating to dividends received from associates, the Group's free cash flow was £610 million, or 23 per cent higher at £3,240 million.

The ratio of free cash flow per share to adjusted diluted earnings per share was 92 per cent (2009: 86 per cent), with free cash flow per share increasing by 23 per cent (2009: increasing by 2 per cent).

Below free cash flow, the principal cash outflows for 2010 comprise the payment of the prior year final dividend and the 2010 interim dividend. Proceeds on disposal of subsidiaries of £12 million which arose from the sale of the Group's Belgian distribution business, Lyfra NV, have been offset by a cash outflow of £12 million arising from the acquisition of non-controlling interests in subsidiaries.

The year ended 31 December 2009 included a net outflow of £382 million in respect of the purchase of Bentoel and Tekel, the proceeds from the ST trademark disposals and £2 million refunded from the original purchase consideration paid in 2008.

The other net flows principally relate to the impact of the level of shares purchased by the employee share ownership trusts and outflows in respect of certain derivative financial instruments.

The above flows resulted in net cash inflows of £1,070 million (2009: £433 million inflow). After taking account of exchange rate movements, net debt disposed and the change in accrued interest and other, total net debt was £7,841 million at 31 December 2010, down £1,001 million from £8,842 million on 31 December 2009.

Cash flow and net debt movements

	2010 £m	2009 £m
Adjusted profit from operations	4,984	4,461
Depreciation, amortisation and impairment	442	446
Other non-cash items in operating profit	59	25
Profit from operations before depreciation and impairment	5,485	4,932
Increase in working capital	(61)	(100)
Net capital expenditure	(523)	(515)
Gross capital expenditure	(584)	(554)
Sale of fixed assets	61	39
Operating cash flow	4,901	4,317
Net interest paid	(491)	(499)
Tax paid	(1,178)	(1,095)
Dividends paid to non-controlling interests	(234)	(234)
Restructuring costs	(219)	(187)
Dividends from associates	461	328
Free cash flow	3,240	2,630
Dividends paid to shareholders	(2,093)	(1,798)
Net investment activities	–	(196)
Purchases of subsidiaries and non-controlling interests	(12)	(383)
Disposal of subsidiaries and trademarks	12	187
Net flow from share schemes and other	(77)	(203)
Net cash flow	1,070	433
External movements on net debt		
Exchange rate effects*	(41)	672
Net debt disposed/(acquired)	11	(84)
Change in accrued interest and other	(39)	28
Change in net debt	1,001	1,049
Opening net debt	(8,842)	(9,891)
Closing net debt	(7,841)	(8,842)

*Including movements in respect of debt related derivatives

Capital structure and treasury policies

3.149 The strategic report could discuss the entity's capital structure, and it should set out the entity's treasury policies and objectives.

3.150 This could include:

- Type of capital instruments used.

- Balance between equity and debt.

- Regulatory capital.

- Maturity profile of debt.

- Currency.

- Interest rate structure.

3.151 The discussion could include comments on short- and long-term funding plans to support the directors' strategies to achieve the entity's objectives. In addition, the discussion could comment on why the entity has adopted its particular capital structure.

3.152 For many listed entities, this section of the strategic report could be relatively complex. Discussion could include reference to inter-linking issues. For example, a discussion could:

- Start with a description of the gearing and capital structure at the beginning of the year.

- Observe that the gearing level was lower or higher than normal.

- Discuss capital expenditure plans.

- Explain that ten-year debt was raised to finance that expenditure.

- Explain that long-term debt was raised because the investment was in long-term assets, but also acknowledge that:

    - the group was overly reliant on short-term debt; and

    - the group wanted to take advantage of the historically low rate of interest on long-term debt.

Finally, this could lead to a discussion of the group's policy regarding fixed or floating rate finance. If interest rate swaps had been taken out as part of this policy, this fact could be explained.

3.153 In another example, a group might have overseas subsidiaries and might have changed the way in which these subsidiaries are financed. For example, the discussion could deal with the opening position (which might be that all funding was in sterling) and explain that the directors had decided during the year that, particularly in the light of their ambitions for overseas expansion, this gave rise to unduly high exchange rate exposure. The discussion could add that the directors had, therefore, decided to finance the overseas operations by a mixture of US dollar and euro borrowings. Alternatively, it might explain that the group had retained its sterling borrowings, but taken out derivative contracts to hedge the overseas investments.

3.154 An example of disclosure relating to funding strategy is provided in Table 3.54.

Table 3.54 – Insights into funding

The British Land Company – Annual report and accounts – 31 March 2013

FINANCING

The scale of our business combined with the security and stability of our rental income means we are able to finance our business on competitive terms from a broad range of sources.

Finance contributes to our success, most importantly by providing the liquidity and resources to grow and develop the business.

We aim to ensure that the Group and its joint ventures and funds are financed with sufficient resources and flexibility to pursue and execute their strategy, covering additional requirements and opportunities which may arise. We use debt to enhance returns, provide flexibility and grow the business.

Access to capital and to the debt markets is a competitive advantage, allowing us to exploit opportunities when they arrive. Our access to finance has also made us one of a relatively few companies able to invest in major London development.

We have five guiding principles that we employ in managing our debt book:
1 Diversify our sources of finance;
2 Maintain liquidity; 3 Extend and stretch maturity of debt portfolio; 4 Maintain flexibility; and 5 Maintain strong balance sheet metrics.

We aim to finance the business from a diverse range of sources with a broad mix of maturities. Our joint ventures and funds are financed separately on the strength of their assets and without recourse to British Land for repayment.

Our debt financing includes long-term securitisations, unsecured private placements, convertible bonds, debentures and secured bank facilities as well as shorter-term revolving unsecured facilities available for immediate drawdown.

DEBT PROFILE -
PROPORTIONALLY CONSOLIDATED
(AS AT 31 MARCH 2013)

Determining the optimal level of gearing for the business is a very important judgement for us, and one which involves weighing up the risk and rewards from owning a larger portfolio and having more debt on our balance sheet. Our preferred range of gearing is between 40% and 50% on a proportionally consolidated basis.

In addition to the £493 million raised from our share placing in March 2013, over the last 24 months we have raised £2.8 billion of debt, all on competitive terms and from a range of different sources. By borrowing at a low cost we are able to deliver enhanced returns to shareholders.

Liquidity

3.155   The strategic report could discuss the entity's current and prospective liquidity. This could include, where relevant, a commentary on the level of borrowings, the seasonality of borrowing requirements (indicated by the peak level of borrowings during the period), and the maturity profile of borrowings and undrawn committed borrowing facilities.

3.156   The discussion could cover the entity's ability to fund its current and future operations and stated strategies. This is consistent with the increased emphasis on the need for a forward-looking orientation.

[The next paragraph is 3.158.]

3.158   Our research has shown that investors also want, beyond information on liquidity, a clear picture of an entity's debt position; this is so that they can understand management's plans for servicing it and any risks associated with it. Entities are required to give information about how they are funded, but this can be scattered throughout the annual report – both in the strategic report and in the financial statements. In addition, some of the information relating to debt is not provided in the annual report at all – that is, investors receive the information outside the regulatory model. In Table 3.55, ITV plc presents its debt maturity profile diagrammatically to accompany the narrative commentary.

Table 3.55 – Maturity profile of debt

ITV plc – Annual Report – 31 December 2010

Financial and performance review (extract)

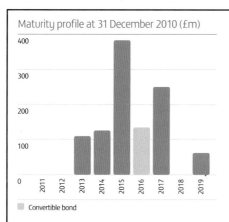

Maturity profile at 31 December 2010 (£m)

☐ Convertible bond

Funding

ITV is aware of the perceived inefficiency of holding £860 million of cash and cash equivalents and over £1 billion of gross debt, but it is important to note the speed at which the net debt has reduced over the past two years. The extent of decline of the television advertising market in 2008 and 2009, and then the subsequent recovery in 2010, was unexpected. This recovery, combined with tight cash control, has allowed net debt to reduce significantly over two years from £730 million at 31 December 2008 to £188 million at 31 December 2010. In addition to net debt of £188 million at 31 December 2010, the Group also has an IAS 19 Pension Deficit of £313 million.

In 2010 ITV bought back €63 million (£54 million) nominal of the 2011 bonds, £42 million nominal of 2015 bonds and repaid the £50 million May 2013 loan. As at 31 December 2010, ITV's net sterling position after the impact of cross currency swaps against the remaining €54 million 2011 Eurobond is a receivable of £16 million. This receivable has arisen due to large positive swap values arising from favourable currency movements; when ITV exchanged or bought back these series of bonds it was more efficient to enter into new swaps to protect this position rather than terminate existing swaps.

In October 2010 ITV increased the size of its undrawn, covenant free bilateral bank facility secured on advertising receivables from £75 million to £125 million and the maturity of this facility was extended from March 2013 to September 2015. This facility remains undrawn. ITV is financed using debt instruments with a range of maturities. Borrowings at 31 December 2010 (net of currency hedges and secured gilts) are repayable as follows:

Amount repayable	£m	Maturity
€54 million Eurobond*	(16)	October 2011
£110 million Eurobond	110	March 2013
€188 million Eurobond*	126	June 2014
£383 million Eurobond	383	October 2015
£135 million Convertible bond	135	November 2016
£250 million Eurobond	250	January 2017
£200 million bank loan**	62	March 2019
Finance leases	61	Various
Total repayable	**1,111**	

* Net of cross currency swaps.
**Net of £138 million (nominal) Gilts secured against the loan.

At 31 December 2010 ITV had £860 million of cash and cash equivalents. This figure includes £89 million of cash equivalents whose use is restricted to finance lease commitments and unfunded pension commitments. Cash and cash equivalents also include £47 million held principally in overseas and part owned subsidiaries.

As explained above, steps have been taken to repurchase some of the more expensive debt. The remaining debt now held is not expensive given our credit rating (at an average gross cost of debt of 7%), is an appropriate mix of medium to long-term debt and has no financial covenants. As ITV drives forward the Transformation Plan it is also important that some flexibility is maintained to invest in the business.

3.159 The problem of determining an entity's credit risk profile is even greater if it has a number of subsidiaries. In this case, investors need a clear debt profile of the group and its individual business units, as well as an understanding of any restrictions on the transfer of funds between business units. Such internal sources of liquidity should be discussed. If there are restrictions on the group's ability to transfer funds from one part of the group to meet the obligations of another part of the group (for example, as a result of exchange controls or tax consequences of transfers), this should be discussed. The restrictions could be in the form of legal barriers, such as exchange controls, that preclude or limit repatriation of profits; or they could be commercial obstacles, such as where funds could be repatriated but unduly high rates of withholding or other taxes would have to be paid.

3.160 Investors, when looking at debt, do not stop at financial instruments or borrowings; they want to know about other debt-like liabilities. These could include revenues paid in advance by customers, operating leases, pensions, or other liabilities (such as decommissioning costs) that could trigger major cash outflows in the future.

3.161 We suggest that entities should include an analysis of net debt that incorporates financial debt, operating debt in off balance sheet leases and other debt-like liabilities. Investors have indicated that they value such disclosure, even though it is not required. Generally, investors believe that all instruments that the entity views as debt, including instruments that accounting standards classify as equity, should be incorporated in this statement. By the same token, instruments classified by accounting standards as debt, but which the entity sees as equity, should be excluded. A comprehensive maturity table of all components, analysis by currency and by subsidiary, as well as details of any collateral or other restrictions, are also highly desirable to investors.

3.162 Net debt analyses are common amongst UK entities, and are often included in the notes to the financial statements. Table 3.56 shows an entity's separate 'analysis of net debt' after its 'consolidated cash flow statement' and cross-references to other financial statement notes for further details of, for example, cash and cash equivalents.

Table 3.56 – Analysis of net debt

Home Retail Group plc – Annual Report & Financial Statements – 1 March 2014

Consolidated Cash Flow Statement (extract)

Analysis of net cash/(debt)

At 1 March 2014

Non-GAAP measures	Notes	1 March 2014 £m	2 March 2013 £m
Financing net cash:			
Cash and cash equivalents	21	**331.0**	396.0
Total financing net cash		**331.0**	396.0
Operating net debt:			
Off balance sheet operating leases		**(2,046.2)**	(2,361.7)
Total operating net debt		**(2,046.2)**	(2,361.7)
Total net debt		**(1,715.2)**	(1,965.7)

The Group uses the term 'total net debt' to highlight the Group's aggregate net indebtedness to banks and other financial institutions together with debt-like liabilities, notably operating leases. The capitalised value of these leases is £2,046.2m (2013: £2,361.7m), based upon discounting the existing lease commitments at the Group's estimated long-term cost of borrowing of 5.0% (2013:4.2%).

3.163 Our research has shown that investors consider a net debt reconciliation to be a particularly useful disclosure. A net debt reconciliation is intended to show how an entity's indebtedness has changed over a period as a result of cash flows and other non-cash movements. A net debt reconciliation allows investors to see how business financing has changed over the year. It is a way of identifying whether an entity that, for instance, seems to have had a significant increase in cash has achieved this only by taking on a corresponding increase in debt. It can also highlight:

- Debt acquired or disposed of in business combinations.

- Foreign exchange movements arising on debt.

- Information that is not always obvious elsewhere in the statements.

3.164 In providing a net debt reconciliation, entities should explain clearly what they mean by 'net debt', preferably with an accompanying analysis. Table 3.57 is an example of a net debt reconciliation.

Table 3.57 – Net debt reconciliation

GlaxoSmithKline plc – 31 December 2013

Financial position and resources (extract)

Net debt

	2013 £m	2012 £m
Cash, cash equivalents and liquid investments	5,600	4,265
Borrowings – repayable within one year	(2,789)	(3,631)
Borrowings – repayable after one year	(15,456)	(14,671)
Net debt	(12,645)	(14,037)

Movements in net debt

	2013 £m	2012 £m
Net debt at beginning of year	(14,037)	(9,003)
Increase/(decrease) in cash and bank overdrafts	1,473	(1,607)
Cash inflow from liquid investments	(15)	(224)
Net increase in long-term loans	(1,913)	(4,430)
Net repayment of short-term loans	1,872	816
Debt of subsidiary undertakings acquired	(6)	(3)
Exchange movements	(34)	(385)
Other movements	15	29
Net debt at end of year	(12,645)	(14,037)

3.165 In Table 3.58, Diageo plc gives information on contractual obligations. Post-employment benefits are not included in the table, but the narrative explains their position.

Table 3.58 – Contractual obligations

Diageo plc – Annual Report – 30 June 2010

Business review (extract)

Contractual obligations

	Less than 1 year £ million	1-3 years £ million	3-5 years £ million	More than 5 years £ million	Total £ million
				Payments due by period	
As at 30 June 2010					
Long term debt obligations	439	2,124	2,666	3,205	8,434
Interest obligations	461	829	600	1,335	3,225
Credit support obligations	80	–	–	–	80
Operating leases	95	147	108	322	672
Finance leases	8	16	12	80	116
Deferred consideration payable	3	25	–	–	28
Purchase obligations	776	585	142	17	1,520
Provisions and other non-current payables	134	113	52	138	437
	1,996	3,839	3,580	5,097	14,512

Long term debt obligations comprise the principal amount of borrowings (excluding foreign currency swaps) with an original maturity of greater than one year. Interest obligations comprise interest payable on these borrowings. Where interest payments are on a floating rate basis, rates of each cash flow until maturity of the instruments are calculated based on the forward yield curve at the last business day of the year ended 30 June 2010. Credit support obligations represent liabilities to counterparty banks in respect of cash received as collateral under credit support agreements. Purchase obligations include various long term purchase contracts entered into for the supply of certain raw materials, principally bulk whisky, grapes, cans and glass bottles. The contracts are used to guarantee supply of raw materials over the long term and to enable more accurate predictions of future costs. Provisions and other non-current payables exclude £14 million in respect of vacant properties and £75 million for onerous contracts, which are included in operating leases and purchase obligations, respectively.

Potential income tax exposures included within corporate tax payable of £391 million (2009 – £532 million) and deferred tax liabilities are not included in the table above, as the ultimate timing of settlement cannot be reasonably estimated.

Post employment benefit liabilities are also not included in the table above. The group makes service-based cash contributions to the UK Pension Scheme which in the year ending 30 June 2011, are expected to be approximately £50 million. The company has agreed a deficit funding plan with the trustee of the UK Scheme based on the trustee's actuarial valuation at 31 March 2009 under which annual income of approximately £25 million will be generated by the new funding structure for the UK Pension Scheme, commencing in the year ended 30 June 2011. The company also agreed to make conditional contributions of up to £338 million if an equivalent reduction in deficit is not achieved over the 10 year term of the funding plan. In addition, Diageo has provisionally agreed a deficit funding arrangement in respect of the Guinness Ireland Group Pension Scheme (the Irish Scheme) which is expected to result in additional annual contributions to the Irish Scheme of €21 million (£17 million) for the next 18 years. The company also provisionally agreed to make conditional contributions of up to €188 million (£154 million) if an equivalent reduction in deficit is not achieved over the next 18 years. Annual contributions to the GrandMet Irish Pension Fund of €6 million (£5 million) have been agreed with the Irish trustee for the next seven years. Contributions to other plans in the year ending 30 June 2011 are expected to be approximately £128 million.

Capital commitments at 30 June 2010 are excluded from the table above.

[The next paragraph is 3.167.]

3.167 Management should disclose the existence of borrowing covenants that restrict the use of financing arrangements or credit facilities; management should also explain where a breach of covenant has occurred, or is expected to occur, and it should outline the measures that the entity has taken to recover the situation. In Table 3.59, an entity discloses its financial covenants.

Table 3.59 – Financial covenants

Great Portland Estates plc – Annual Report – 31 March 2014

Notes to the financial statements (extract)

The Group meets its day-to-day working capital requirements through the utilisation of its revolving credit facilities. The availability of these facilities depends on the Group complying with a number of key financial covenants; these covenants and the Groups' compliance with these covenants are set out in the table below:

Key covenants	Covenant	March 2014 actuals
Group		
Net debt/net equity	< 1.25x	0.30x
Inner borrowing (unencumbered asset value/unsecured borrowings)	> 1.66x	3.43x
Interest cover	> 1.35x	4.32x

The Group has undrawn credit facilities of £488.0 million and has substantial headroom above all of its key covenants. As a result the directors consider the Group to have adequate liquidity to be able to fund the ongoing operations of the business.

3.168   There is some judgement involved in addressing whether a breach of covenant is expected to occur. But disclosure should be made when negotiations are being held, perhaps to change the covenants, in a situation where there is neither a breach nor any expectation of a breach. An example might be where a covenant is being renegotiated, not because of financial difficulty but following the introduction of a new accounting standard that alters the ratios without any change in the underlying economic position.

3.169   An example of disclosure of a breach of covenant is given in Table 3.60.

Table 3.60 – Breach of covenant

Thomas Coffey Limited – 30 June 2010

Directors' Report (extract)

Notes to the financial statements (extract)

Note 1 Significant accounting policies (extract)

GOING CONCERN

As at 30 June 2010, the consolidated entity was in breach of its borrowing covenants with respect to its banking facilities. Subsequent to year end the consolidated entity received a waiver from the financier and amended covenants are to apply during the year ending 30 June 2011. Further details regarding the breach of the borrowing covenants, waiver and amended covenants are detailed in the note 1 of the financial statements.

Accordingly, no adjustments have been made to the financial report relating to the recoverability and classification of recorded asset amounts and classification of liabilities that might be necessary should the consolidated entity not continue as a going concern.

Going concern

As at 30 June 2010, the consolidated entity was in breach of its borrowing covenants with respect to its banking facilities. As a result, the consolidated entity classified $12.5m of borrowings for which the facility expires in excess of 12 months from the reporting date as current liabilities on the statement of financial position, reflecting at that time the lender had the right to call these funds immediately. As a result the consolidated entity had a net current asset deficiency of $10,106,000.

Subsequent to the 30 June 2010 the consolidated entity's financier agreed to a borrowing covenant waiver as at 30 June 2010 and amended the covenants to apply during the year ending 30 June 2011.

The ongoing viability of the consolidated entity and its ability to continue as a going concern and meet its debts and commitments as they fall due are mainly dependent upon the consolidated entity being successful in:

1. receiving the continuing support of its financiers; and
2. achieving forecast operational performance and generate sufficient future cash flows to meet its business objectives and financial obligations.

The directors believe that the consolidated entity will be successful in the above matters and, accordingly, have prepared the financial report on a going concern basis. At this time, the directors are of the opinion that no asset is likely to be realised for an amount less than the amount at which it is recorded in the financial report at 30 June 2010. This is mainly due to the following factors:

1. the directors expect the consolidated entity will achieve positive operating cash flows;
2. since the 30th June 2010, the consolidated entity's banker has provided a waiver for the 30 June covenant breaches and amended the financial covenants to apply during the year ending 30 June 2011. (refer to note 19 for further details of the amended facility). The directors expect the consolidated entity to comply with these covenants;
3. the directors have announced that a number of capital raising initiatives are also being considered;
4. if required the consolidated entity will sell non-core assets in line with the strategic direction of the consolidated entity.

In addition and as a result of the loss for the year and the classification of borrowings as current the consolidated entity has not met financial requirements under certain licensing regulatory criteria at year end. Steps are being taken to ensure the licenses are maintained and renewed.

Accordingly, no adjustments have been made to the financial report relating to the recoverability and classification of recorded asset amounts and classification of liabilities that might be necessary should the consolidated entity not continue as a going concern.

3.170 FRS 18 and IAS 1 require disclosure (by all entities) of any material uncertainties, of which directors are aware, that might cast significant doubt on the entity's ability to continue as a going concern. [FRS 18 para 61; IAS 1 para 23]. In addition, IFRS 7 requires disclosure of any defaults and breaches of principal, interest, sinking fund or redemption provisions on loans payable, and of any other breaches of loan agreements where the breaches can permit the lender to demand repayment (except where the breaches have been remedied before the balance sheet date). [IFRS 7 paras 18, 19]. The Manual of accounting – IFRS for the UK deals with these requirements.

[The next paragraph is 3.175.]

Current and future development and performance

Development and performance in the year

3.175 The strategic report could describe the significant features of the development and performance of the business in the financial year, focusing on business (including geographical) segments that are relevant to an understanding of the development and performance as a whole. The example in Table 3.61 shows performance by region and by product type, together with a high-level explanation of that performance (only one region and one product type are shown here).

Table 3.61 – Financial performance

Unilever PLC – Annual Report and Accounts – 31 December 2011

Financial review (extract)

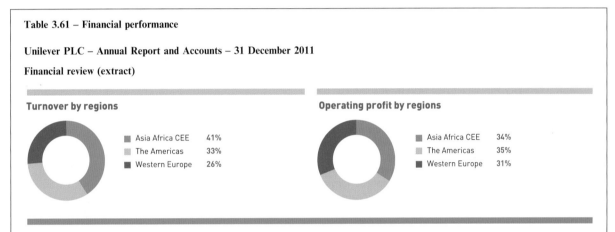

Turnover by regions

■ Asia Africa CEE	41%
■ The Americas	33%
■ Western Europe	26%

Operating profit by regions

■ Asia Africa CEE	34%
■ The Americas	35%
■ Western Europe	31%

Asia Africa CEE

	€ million 2011	€ million 2010	% Change
Turnover	18,947	17,685	7.1
Operating profit	2,216	2,253	(1.6)
Underlying operating margin (%)	12.7	13.4	(0.7)
Underlying sales growth (%)	10.5	7.7	
Underlying volume growth (%)	4.5	10.2	
Effect of price changes (%)	5.8	(2.2)	

Key developments
- Market growth remained strong throughout the region, with high single digit increases particularly in buoyant markets across East and South Asia. Conditions in Russia and CEE, however, were more subdued.
- Underlying sales growth of 10.5% was ahead of our markets and well balanced between volume and price. China and India both contributed double digit volume growth; South Africa, Turkey and Indonesia also performed strongly.
- Value market shares were up for the region as a whole, driven by strong growth in Home Care, while Foods value shares were slightly down. Share gains were seen across many key markets, including China, Indonesia, the Philippines and South Africa. Volume shares were flat.
- Underlying operating margin was down 0.7%, primarily reflecting the impact of higher commodity costs.
- Other key developments included further progress on the roll-out of the regional IT system and the acquisition of the Concern Kalina business in Russia.

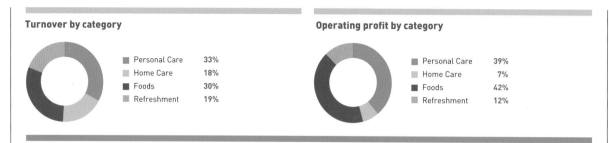

Turnover by category

■ Personal Care	33%
■ Home Care	18%
■ Foods	30%
■ Refreshment	19%

Operating profit by category

■ Personal Care	39%
■ Home Care	7%
■ Foods	42%
■ Refreshment	12%

Personal Care

	€ million 2011	€ million 2010	% Change
Turnover	15,471	13,767	12.4
Operating profit	2,536	2,296	10.5
Underlying operating margin (%)	18.0	18.0	–
Underlying sales growth (%)	8.2	6.4	
Underlying volume growth (%)	4.2	7.9	
Effect of price changes (%)	3.8	(1.4)	

Key developments
- Personal Care grew strongly in 2011 to become Unilever's largest category, with underlying sales growth of 8.2%. The acquisitions of Alberto Culver and the Sara Lee brands started to contribute positively.
- Growth was well balanced between volume and price, and reflected strong performance across the portfolio, particularly in deodorants, hair care and skin cleansing.
- Value market shares were up overall, with strong gains in North America where hair care and deodorants performed well, and in China where skin cleansing and hair care saw strong gains.
- Underlying operating margin was stable at 18.0%.

3.176 Where trends and factors in development and performance are evident from an analysis of current and previous financial years, these should be highlighted. Development and performance should be described in the context of the business' strategic objectives and the entity's key performance indicators.

3.177 Comparison over a number of years might be appropriate where, for example, the entity has a particular strategic objective with a duration of several years.

3.178 Table 3.62 shows a graphical explanation of the revenue and profit from operations included in the financial statements. There is a clear indication of reasons for changes in these figures from one period to the next. Further information on each element of the movement is given in detailed narrative explanations of financial performance.

Table 3.62 – Explaining financial performance

Intu plc – Annual Report – 31 December 2013

The principal components of the change in underlying earnings are as follows

— while increasing overall due to the impact of the acquisitions of Midsummer Place and Parque Principado, like-for-like net rental income reduced by 1.9 per cent largely due to the impact of tenant administrations in the first half of the year. This has been partially offset by the favourable impact of new lettings and rent reviews at intu Trafford Centre, Manchester Arndale and intu Lakeside

— as detailed in the table below the Group's net rental income margin has remained in line with the 87 per cent achieved in 2012 with property operating expense reducing, despite the acquisitions in the year, offsetting higher void costs. Property operating excesses in the year ended 31 December 2013 includes £10 million (2012 – £10 million) in respect of car park operating costs and the Group's contribution to shopping centre marketing of £8 million (2012 – £8 million)

	Year ended 31 December 2013 £m	Year ended 31 December 2012 £m
Gross rental income	**448**	442
Head rent payable	**(24)**	(25)
	424	417
Net service charge expense and void rates	**(16)**	(13)
Bad debt and lease incentive write-offs	**(9)**	(10)
Property operating expense	**(29)**	(31)
Net rental income	**370**	363
Net rental income margin	**87%**	87%

— underlying net finance costs, which exclude exceptional items, reduced by £1 million due to the favourable impact of lower interest rates following the debt refinancings that were completed in the year offsetting the slightly higher debt levels

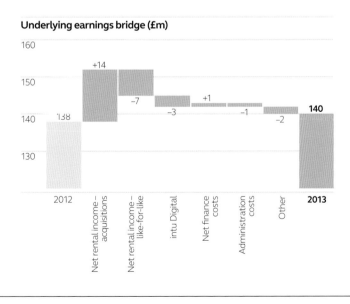

Underlying earnings bridge (£m)

3.179   The introduction of new products or services is often a factor that affects an entity's performance. Table 3.63 gives an entity's explanation of the impact of new products.

Table 3.63 – Effect of new products on performance

Johnson & Johnson – Annual Report – 2 January 2011

Management's Discussion and Analysis of Results of Operations and Financial Condition (extract)

> **MANAGEMENT'S OBJECTIVES**
> The Company manages within a strategic framework aimed at achieving sustainable growth. To accomplish this, the Company's management operates the business consistent with certain strategic principles that have proven successful over time. To this end, the Company participates in growth areas in human health care and is committed to attaining leadership positions in these growth areas through the development of high quality, innovative products and services. New products introduced within the past five years accounted for approximately 25% of 2010 sales. In 2010, $6.8 billion, or 11.1% of sales, was invested in research and development. This investment reflects management's commitment to the importance of ongoing development of new and differentiated products and services to sustain long-term growth.

3.180   Where an entity operates in a number of different territories and has a number of different product lines that are affected by different trends and factors (either economic or non-economic), analysis of performance showing this level of detail should be given. In Table 3.64, Group Five Limited explains the geographic drivers of its business, and it presents information about each of those geographic areas (only West Africa is shown here).

Table 3.64 – Geographic drivers

Group Five Limited – Annual Report – 30 June 2010

Contents

OUR STRATEGY / Pg 4 and 84

The group's strategy is to secure growth and reduce earnings volatility within the construction sector by capturing multiple margin streams across the infrastructure value chain. This is achieved through product and geographic diversity and optimising the materials supply chain.

Relevant geographic drivers

The next few pages outline relevant geographies we monitor in the execution of our strategy.

NORTH AMERICA
Characteristics
- Developed, mature industrialised markets
- Expected average GDP growth of 3.1% for 2010 and 2011

WESTERN EUROPE
Characteristics
- Developed, mature industrialised markets
- Expected average GDP growth of 1.6% for 2010 and 2011

EASTERN EUROPE
Characteristics
- Rapidly emerging industrialised economies
- High skills base
- Improving political stability
- Under-developed infrastructure
- Growing membership of European Union
- Expected average GDP growth of 3.6% for 2010 and 2011

MIDDLE EAST AND NORTH AFRICA
Characteristics
- Good infrastructure
- Relatively politically stable
- High-growth countries diversifying their economies
- Energy, water and transport constraints to growth in certain countries
- Democratic standards are low, with monarchies or long term one-party rulers
- Expected average GDP growth of 6% for Middle East and 3.6% for North Africa for 2010 and 2011

INDIA, AUSTRALASIA AND CHINA
Characteristics
- Rapidly emerging industrialised economies with strong mining and manufacturing base
- Large populations with expanding spending power and skills base
- Increasing political stability
- Under-developed infrastructure in power, transport, water and waste
- Long term economic planning
- Expected average GDP growth of 5.1% for Australasia, 9.3% for China and 8.3% for India for 2010 and 2011

SOUTH AMERICA
Characteristics
- Rapidly emerging industrialising economies, with strong mining and manufacturing bases
- Large population with expanding spending power and skills base
- Improving political stability
- International expansion of manufacturing, mining and construction
- Expected average GDP growth of 4.1% for 2010 and 2011

WEST AFRICA
Characteristics
- Relatively poor infrastructure
- Improving political stability
- Rapidly growing average per capita wealth
- Energy, water and transport constraints to growth
- Improving governance, but still high levels of corruption
- Expected average GDP growth rate of 7.4% for 2010 and 2011

CENTRAL AND EAST AFRICA
Characteristics
- Poor infrastructure
- Improving governance and political stability, but still high levels of corruption
- Relatively poor, with high unemployment, but potential for growth driven by resources
- Energy, water and transport constraints to growth
- Expected average GDP growth of 5.1% for East Africa and 7.3% for Central Africa for 2010 and 2011

SOUTHERN AFRICA
Characteristics
- Relatively good infrastructure
- Politically stable in most countries, although increasing levels of corruption
- Dichotomy of growing average wealth, with high unemployment
- Energy, water and transport constraints to growth
- Expected average GDP growth of 3.3% for 2010 and 2011

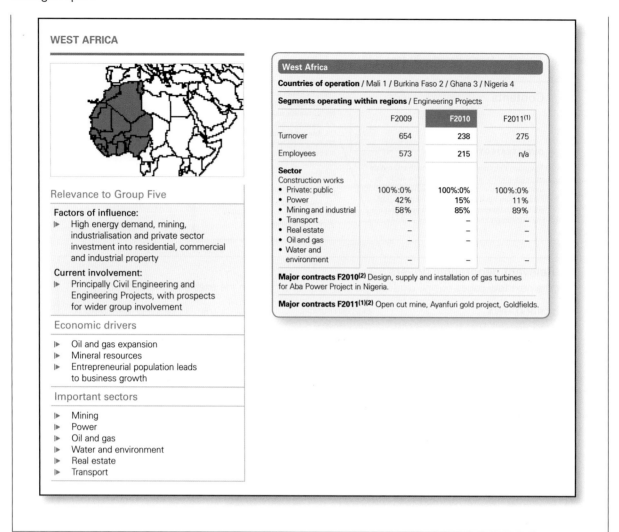

WEST AFRICA

Relevance to Group Five

Factors of influence:

▷ High energy demand, mining, industrialisation and private sector investment into residential, commercial and industrial property

Current involvement:

▷ Principally Civil Engineering and Engineering Projects, with prospects for wider group involvement

Economic drivers

▷ Oil and gas expansion
▷ Mineral resources
▷ Entrepreneurial population leads to business growth

Important sectors

▷ Mining
▷ Power
▷ Oil and gas
▷ Water and environment
▷ Real estate
▷ Transport

West Africa

Countries of operation / Mali 1 / Burkina Faso 2 / Ghana 3 / Nigeria 4

Segments operating within regions / Engineering Projects

	F2009	F2010	F2011[1]
Turnover	654	238	275
Employees	573	215	n/a
Sector Construction works			
• Private: public	100%:0%	100%:0%	100%:0%
• Power	42%	15%	11%
• Mining and industrial	58%	85%	89%
• Transport	–	–	–
• Real estate	–	–	–
• Oil and gas	–	–	–
• Water and environment	–	–	–

Major contracts F2010[2] Design, supply and installation of gas turbines for Aba Power Project in Nigeria.

Major contracts F2011[1][2] Open cut mine, Ayanfuri gold project, Goldfields.

Acquisitions and disposals

3.181 Changes resulting from acquisitions or disposals represent another factor that can have a significant impact on an entity's current development and performance. Investors want to know the rationale for any acquisitions, and whether those acquisitions have delivered value to the entity. In Table 3.65, United Business Media plc describes the basis for selecting targets for acquisition and what the entity expects from its investments.

Table 3.65 – Acquisition strategy and returns on investment

United Business Media plc – Annual Report and Accounts – 31 December 2010

UBM Strategy (extract)

2.
Growth through acquisition
We invest in strategic acquisitions in order to strengthen our existing portfolio or provide exposure to markets we feel are attractive.

Target selection

We select targets which are complementary to our existing business in terms of geography, segment or community. Below is a table showing the acquisitions made in 2010.

Integration process

In order to facilitate a smooth process, executives are given responsibility for integration. The integration of the Canon acquisition, completed in October, is progressing well.

Strict financial discipline

A target acquisition also has to satisfy financial criteria with projected post tax ROI* exceeding 8% within the first full year of ownership.

	Consideration £m	Pre tax return on investment %		
		2008	2009	2010
2008 acquisitions	49.9	12.4	6.5	7.8
2009 acquisitions	26.5	–	14.8	4.5[1]
2010 acquisitions[2]	258.0	–	–	10.6
Total	**334.4**			**10.0**

2010 acquisitions	Geography	Segment	Community	Initial consideration net of cash acquired* £m	Expected contingent and deferred consideration £m	Estimated total consideration £m
E Commerce Expo	UK	Events	Technology	0.4	1.2	1.6
Sign China	China	Events	Other	6.3	4.3	10.6
DesignCon	USA	Events	Technology	0.9	–	0.9
Sienna – Concrete show	Brazil	Events	Built Environment	6.5	6.8	13.3
NavalShore	Brazil	Events	Trade & Transport	1.2	0.1	1.3
Children – Baby – Maternity – Expo	China	Events	Lifestyle	6.3	4.2	10.5
The Routes Development Group	UK	Events	Trade & Transport	6.8	1.3	8.1
Canon Communications	USA	Events	Technology/Health	182.9	–	182.9
Publishing Expo	UK	Events	Other	0.2	–	0.2
DNA-13	Canada	TD&M	News Distribution	4.0	0.6	4.6
PR Newswire do Brasil	Brazil	TD&M	News Distribution	0.7	0.1	0.8
PR Newswire Argentina	Argentina	TD&M	News Distribution	0.0	–	0.0
Corporate360	Hong Kong	TD&M	News Distribution	0.2	0.7	0.9
Hors Antenne	Europe	TD&M	News Distribution	5.3	2.7	8.0
SharedVue	USA	DS	Technology	0.2	4.9	5.1
CenTradeX	USA	DS	Trade & Transport	0.3	0.1	0.4
UM Paper	China	DS	Paper	0.1	0.2	0.3
JOC Exchange (Triton)	USA	DS	Trade & Transport	0.3	1.7	2.0
Lead-In Research	UK	DS	Built Environment	0.9	0.3	1.2
Game Advertising Online	New Zealand	Online	Technology	0.6	3.0	3.6
Astound	USA	Online	Technology	0.1	1.0	1.1
OBGYN.net	USA	Online	Health	0.5	0.1	0.6
Total				**224.7**	**33.3**	**258.0**

1 Performance reflects reported results for The Fuel Team which was integrated into PR Newswire in 2010. Excluding it, the pre tax return on acquisition would have been 8.6% for 2009 acquisitions.
2 2010 return on investment calculated on a full year pro-forma basis.
* See explanation of UBM's business measures on page 51.

3.182 The example in Table 3.66 illustrates how acquisitions impact on performance for a drinks entity, in total and by division. The performance of the acquired businesses is set out separately, and the divisional analysis of results distinguishes between the organic and the acquired businesses (only the distribution segment is shown here).

Table 3.66 – Acquisitions

C&C Group Plc – 28 February 2010

Operations Review (extract)

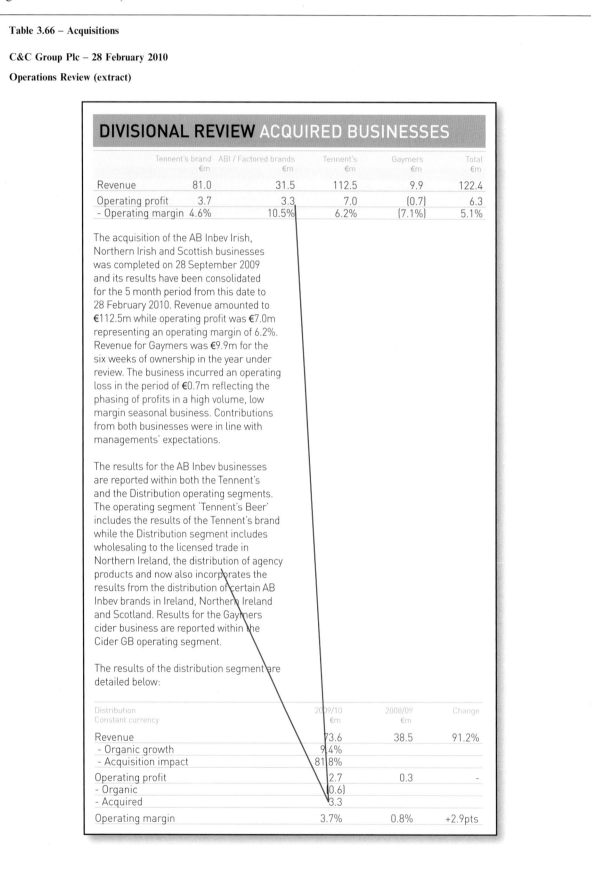

DIVISIONAL REVIEW ACQUIRED BUSINESSES

	Tennent's brand €m	ABI / Factored brands €m	Tennent's €m	Gaymers €m	Total €m
Revenue	81.0	31.5	112.5	9.9	122.4
Operating profit	3.7	3.3	7.0	(0.7)	6.3
- Operating margin	4.6%	10.5%	6.2%	(7.1%)	5.1%

The acquisition of the AB Inbev Irish, Northern Irish and Scottish businesses was completed on 28 September 2009 and its results have been consolidated for the 5 month period from this date to 28 February 2010. Revenue amounted to €112.5m while operating profit was €7.0m representing an operating margin of 6.2%. Revenue for Gaymers was €9.9m for the six weeks of ownership in the year under review. The business incurred an operating loss in the period of €0.7m reflecting the phasing of profits in a high volume, low margin seasonal business. Contributions from both businesses were in line with managements' expectations.

The results for the AB Inbev businesses are reported within both the Tennent's and the Distribution operating segments. The operating segment 'Tennent's Beer' includes the results of the Tennent's brand while the Distribution segment includes wholesaling to the licensed trade in Northern Ireland, the distribution of agency products and now also incorporates the results from the distribution of certain AB Inbev brands in Ireland, Northern Ireland and Scotland. Results for the Gaymers cider business are reported within the Cider GB operating segment.

The results of the distribution segment are detailed below:

Distribution Constant currency	2009/10 €m	2008/09 €m	Change
Revenue	73.6	38.5	91.2%
- Organic growth	9.4%		
- Acquisition impact	81.8%		
Operating profit	2.7	0.3	-
- Organic	(0.6)		
- Acquired	3.3		
Operating margin	3.7%	0.8%	+2.9pts

3.183 Similarly, the disposal of operations will affect an entity's development and performance. Table 3.67 shows an entity that made disposals of businesses during the year, including the impact of one of the disposals on the relevant division.

Table 3.67 – Disposal of operation

Greencore Group plc – Annual Report and Accounts – 24 September 2010

Chairman's statement (Extract)

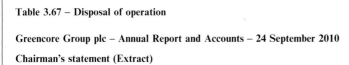

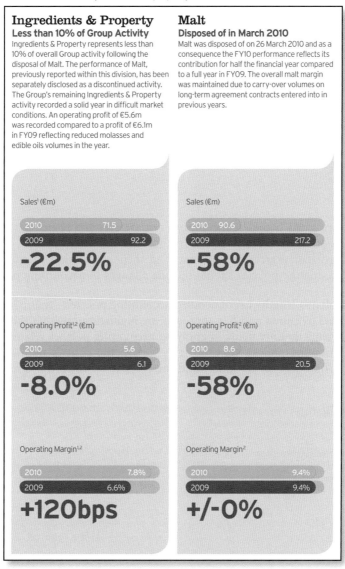

3.184 Where an entity undertakes a significant volume of transactions in foreign currencies, the impact of currency exchange rates might be a useful disclosure.

3.185 Table 3.68 illustrates the effect of changes in exchange rates on net income.

Table 3.68 – Impact of foreign exchange

Potash Corporation of Saskatchewan – Annual Report – 31 December 2010

Financial Review (extract)

Impact of Foreign Exchange

Due to the international nature of our operations, we incur costs and expenses in foreign currencies other than the US dollar. The exchange rates of such currencies have varied substantially over the last three years. The sharp movements in the US dollar have had a significant impact on costs and expenses incurred in other currencies, which are translated into US dollars for financial reporting purposes. In Canada, our revenue is earned and received in US dollars while the cost base for our potash operations is predominantly in Canadian dollars.

We are also affected by the period-end change in foreign exchange rate on the translation of our monetary net assets and liabilities, and on treasury activities.

The following table shows the impact of foreign exchange on net income. Positive numbers represent an increase to net income while numbers in brackets are a decrease to net income.

Impact on Net Income

Dollars (millions), except per-share amounts

	2010	2009
Foreign exchange impact on operating costs before income taxes [1]	$ (15.7)	$ (42.1)
Foreign exchange impact on conversion of balance sheet and treasury activities before income taxes	(16.8)	35.4
Net income decrease before income taxes	(32.5)	(6.7)
Diluted net income per share decrease before income taxes	(0.04)	–

[1] Assumes the 2010 exchange rate had remained at the 2009 year-end rate of 1.0466 (compared to 0.9946 at December 31, 2010), and the 2009 exchange rate had remained at the 2008 year-end rate of 1.2246.

3.186 Many entities express figures in the strategic report in terms of constant currency; this enables them to show the trends in performance, excluding the effect of exchange rates.

Accounting policies

3.187 The strategic report could highlight the entity's critical accounting policies. The critical accounting policies are key to understanding the entity's performance and financial position. The focus should be on those that require the particular exercise of judgement in their application to which the results are most sensitive. Discussion of accounting policies should include changes in accounting policies during the year.

3.188 This disclosure is often a lengthy list of detailed accounting policies – that is, similar to those found in risk disclosures. But Table 3.69 shows another approach, by highlighting within the financial statements the key areas in which judgements that are made in applying accounting policies relate to the balance sheet. As with risks, where the accounting policies that are truly key to the entity's performance and position are emphasised, investors can find it easier to understand the context in which those results are presented.

Table 3.69

Cairn Energy – Annual report and accounts – 31 December 2012

Section 5 – Results for the Year

This section focuses on the results and performance of the Group, with disclosures including segmental information, components of the operating loss, results from discontinued operations, taxation and earnings per share.

Significant accounting judgements in this section:
Deferred taxation
The deferred tax liablity relating to the Group's investment in Cairn India Limited, classified as an available-for-sale financial asset, is provided on the assumption that any future disposal will result in a tax liability.

Details of the impairment of intangible exploration/appraisal assets can be found in section 2.2.

Key estimates and assumptions in this section:
Deferred taxation
Deferred tax liabilities relating to North Sea assets are measured using the tax rates and laws that are expected to apply to the period when the assets are realised, based on the conditions that existed at the balance sheet date. Deferred tax liabilities are not adjusted for Field Allowances that certain assets in the UK may qualify for in future periods, but which are subject to Government approval of respective field development plans which did not exist at the Balance Sheet date.

Details of impairment of Goodwill and Share-based Payments can be found in sections 4.1 and 6.4 respectively.

5.1 Segmental Analysis
Operating Segments
For management purposes, the operations of the Cairn Group are organised based on geographical regions. The Cairn Group's operations currently focus on new exploration activities in four key operating segments: North West Europe - North Sea, Atlantic Margin - Greenland, Atlantic Margin - Morocco and the Mediterranean.

Geographical regions may be combined into regional business units. Each business unit is headed by its own regional director and management monitors the results of each separately for the purposes of making decisions about resource allocation and performance assessment.

North West Europe - North Sea
The corporate acquisitions in the year, with primary interests in the UK and Norwegian North Sea, provide Cairn with a core platform for growth from organic near-term exploration, appraisal and development activities, ultimately leading to sustainable cash flow.

Atlantic Margin - Greenland
Cairn's Greenland assets have been the focus of much of the Groups exploration activity in recent years. Further exploration drilling is planned in 2014 subject to the necessary approvals being received.

Other
The Atlantic Margin - Morocco and Mediterranean operating segments results have been combined into the "Other Cairn Energy" reportable segment together with the Group's remaining exploration and corporale assets. New exploration opportunities in Morocco have been added through corporate acquisitions and farm-in agreements during the year. Cairn's presence in the Atlantic Margin has increased post year end with the Senegal farm-in. The discontinued operations of the Cairn India Group were a separate business unit up to the point of disposal in 2011.

5.1 Segmental Analysis Continued
Geographical information: Non-current assets

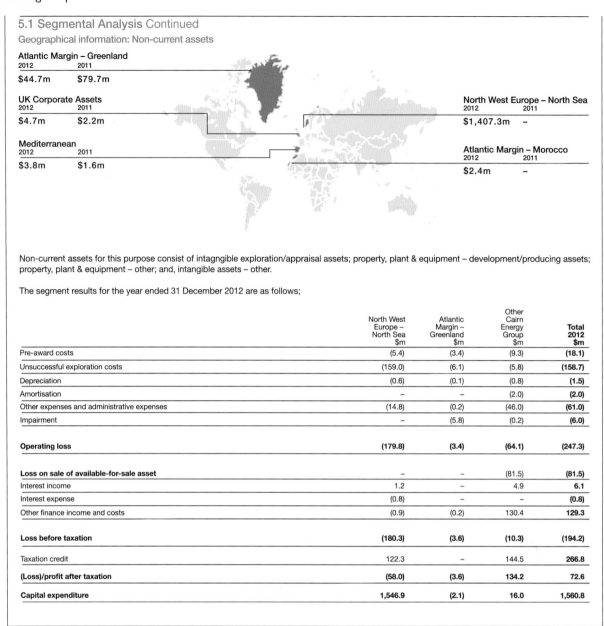

Atlantic Margin – Greenland

2012	2011
$44.7m	$79.7m

UK Corporate Assets

2012	2011
$4.7m	$2.2m

Mediterranean

2012	2011
$3.8m	$1.6m

North West Europe – North Sea

2012	2011
$1,407.3m	–

Atlantic Margin – Morocco

2012	2011
$2.4m	–

Non-current assets for this purpose consist of intangible exploration/appraisal assets; property, plant & equipment – development/producing assets; property, plant & equipment – other; and, intangible assets – other.

The segment results for the year ended 31 December 2012 are as follows;

	North West Europe – North Sea $m	Atlantic Margin – Greenland $m	Other Cairn Energy Group $m	Total 2012 $m
Pre-award costs	(5.4)	(3.4)	(9.3)	(18.1)
Unsuccessful exploration costs	(159.0)	(6.1)	(5.8)	(158.7)
Depreciation	(0.6)	(0.1)	(0.8)	(1.5)
Amortisation	–	–	(2.0)	(2.0)
Other expenses and administrative expenses	(14.8)	(0.2)	(46.0)	(61.0)
Impairment	–	(5.8)	(0.2)	(6.0)
Operating loss	**(179.8)**	**(3.4)**	**(64.1)**	**(247.3)**
Loss on sale of available-for-sale asset	–	–	(81.5)	(81.5)
Interest income	1.2	–	4.9	6.1
Interest expense	(0.8)	–	–	(0.8)
Other finance income and costs	(0.9)	(0.2)	130.4	129.3
Loss before taxation	**(180.3)**	**(3.6)**	**(10.3)**	**(194.2)**
Taxation credit	122.3	–	144.5	266.8
(Loss)/profit after taxation	**(58.0)**	**(3.6)**	**134.2**	**72.6**
Capital expenditure	**1,546.9**	**(2.1)**	**16.0**	**1,560.8**

3.189 The accounting policies disclosed and discussed will vary from one entity to another and between industries. Critical accounting policies might include the following:

- Revenue recognition – particularly in assessing revenue and profit to be recognised on long-term contracts and multiple-component sales.

- Impairment – where choice of discount rates and other assumptions can have significant effects on calculations.

- Taxation – particularly where the entity has international operations and engages in significant tax planning activities.

- Provisions – some types of provisions, particularly for long-term environmental obligations, require significant judgements and estimates.

- Pensions – similar to provisions above, but there is also additional volatility owing to the effects of stock market fluctuations.

- Intangible assets, including goodwill and development expenditure – goodwill and intangibles might comprise a large element of an entity's net assets, particularly in industries such as advertising and publishing. Significant estimates and judgements are often required in assessing recoverability of such intangibles.

3.190 Although the critical accounting policies could be outlined in the strategic report, it might be appropriate to cross-refer to the detailed descriptions that are contained in the notes to the financial statements.

Tax disclosure

3.191 A number of new reporting initiatives are driving changes to tax reporting for EU extractive and banking entities.

3.192 Country by country tax reporting will become a requirement for EU extractive and banking entities for financial years beginning on or after 1 January 2016. Disclosure includes corporate taxes paid, royalties, fees, production entitlements, bonuses, dividends and payments for infrastructure improvements.

3.193 The Extractive Industries Transparency Initiative (EITI), The Dodd-Frank Wall Street Reform and Consumer Protections Act (The Dodd-Frank Act) and the EU Accounting and Transparency Directives (ATD) relate to companies in the extractive sector, with ATD also applying to companies active in the logging of primary forests.

3.194 The ATD requires companies to disclose the payments they make to governments in each country where they operate, and for each project where the payment has been attributed to a certain project, when material to the recipient government.

3.195 The following types of payments made to government should be reported: production entitlements; taxes on income, production or profits; royalties; dividends; signature, discovery and production bonuses; licence fees, rental fees, entry fees and other considerations for licences and / or concessions; payments for infrastructure improvements.

3.196 Payments below €100,000 (whether made as a single payment or as a series of related payments) do not need to be disclosed.

3.197 Article 89 of the EU Capital Requirements Directive (CRD) IV applies to banks, other credit institutions and certain investment firms.

3.198 Institutions are required to disclose profits and turnover, profit taxes, government subsidiaries, number of employees and the geographical location of activities.

3.199 Two ongoing developments could have more general relevance: the OECD's Base Erosion Profit Shifting initiative (or 'BEPS') and the proposed Shareholder Rights Directive (SRD). BEPS will apply to any multi-national corporation with revenues of over £500million on a consolidated basis. The SRD would (if it goes through with country by country reporting (CBCR) intact) apply to EU public interest entities and other large companies and groups as defined in the Accounting Directive (number of employees 250; turnover £35m; assets £18m).

3.200 In terms of when these apply, the ATD and CRD are already in place (the ATD from this year). The BEPS reporting to the HMRC was enabled in the UK in the 2015 Budget. It will be required for periods beginning on or after 1 Jan 2016, with the first reports due by December 2017.

3.201 The SRD is still going through the EU institutions. Once it is finalised, there will be an 18 month period to transpose it for Member States, so the expectation is that 2018 year ends will be the first accounting period affected.

3.202 These initiatives involve some form of public disclosure of information, on websites or annual reports. BEPS, however, only requires information to be shared with HMRC.

3.203 The types of information also vary. BEPS and the SRD, and also the disclosures for banks under the ATD, are focused on tax on profit by country, with various measures, such as number of employees, revenues or value of assets to compare the tax. The initiatives in the extractives industry focus on payments to governments more generally (though including profit taxes), so would include royalties, licence fees and a host of other payments. Interestingly, the EITI involves an independent party reconciling the payments the company reports to those that the government reports receiving.

3.204 CRD IV information needs to be audited, and there are some proposed audit responsibilities in the draft SRD. It's not clear whether the CBCR element of the SRD will survive into EU law (and the UK implementation process) but, if it does, this will change the tax reporting landscape in this area fundamentally.

3.205   Table 3.69.1 below sets out the voluntary tax contribution disclosure of SAB Miller in its separately produced tax report.

Table 3.69.1 – Country by country tax reporting

SAB Miller – Our approach to tax 2015

Our contribution to government tax revenues

By running businesses successfully, we create employment, stimulate the local economies that supply us with crops, services and retail distribution, and generate tax revenues of all kinds for governments.

Total tax contribution by region
%

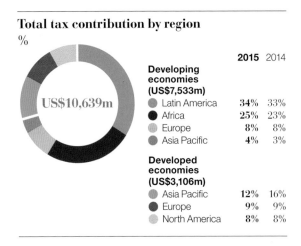

US$10,639m

	2015	2014
Developing economies (US$7,533m)		
Latin America	34%	33%
Africa	25%	23%
Europe	8%	8%
Asia Pacific	4%	3%
Developed economies (US$3,106m)		
Asia Pacific	12%	16%
Europe	9%	9%
North America	8%	8%

Total tax contribution by category
%

US$10,639m

	2015	2014
Taxes on production	58%	57%
VAT collected	18%	17%
Employment taxes	7%	7%
Taxes on profits	13%	14%
Other indirect taxes	2%	3%
Tax withheld at source	2%	2%
Taxes on property	0%	0%

How much we pay and where

We are a major contributor to tax in most markets we operate in. In the year ended 31 March 2015, our total tax contribution, including both our own taxes and those we collect on behalf of governments, was US$10,639 million. This represents cash taxes directly generated by our economic activity in each country and is thus a fair reflection of our tax footprint and what we contribute to government tax revenues. As well as corporate income tax on our profits, it also includes excise, value-added tax (VAT) collected from customers, employee taxes, and other taxes.

Total tax contribution

	2015 US$m	2014 US$m
Payments to tax authorities	7,035	7,203
Payments by MillerCoors joint venture (our share) to tax authorities	657	672
Payments of VAT collected	1,959	1,876
Payments of employment taxes collected	703	714
Payments of other sundry taxes	285	285
Total tax contribution	**10,639**	10,750

Total tax contribution by country and region

	2015 US$m	2014 US$m	Organic, constant currency growth %
Colombia	1,773	1,750	11
Ecuador	314	309	2
El Salvador	114	112	2
Peru	1,177	1,165	6
Others[1]	212	180	26
Total Latin America	**3,590**	3,516	9
Mozambique	239	231	12
South Africa[2]	1,665	1,517	20
Tanzania	301	269	18
Zambia	154	134	34
Others[1]	320	272	31
Total Africa	**2,679**	2,423	21
Australia	1,225	1,671	(22)[3]
India	392	367	9
Others[1]	13	12	8
Total Asia Pacific	**1,630**	2,050	(16)
Czech Republic	288	291	8
Hungary	102	109	1
Italy	238	245	2
Poland	640	637	4
Romania	130	137	(2)
United Kingdom	299	267	10
Others[1]	189	198	2
Total Europe	**1,886**	1,884	4
USA[4]	854	877	(3)
Total North America	**854**	877	(3)
Total tax contribution	**10,639**	10,750	5

Financial and non-financial key performance indicators (KPIs)

3.206 A number of regulatory bodies are in the process of drafting guidance in this area, which will be reflected in the next version of this manual.

3.207 The analysis in the strategic report should include the financial and non-financial key performance indicators (KPIs). [CA06 Sec 414C(4); SR guidance para 7.43].

3.208 The KPIs used in the analysis should be those that the directors judge to be the most effective in assessing progress against objectives or strategy, monitoring principal risks, or are otherwise used to measure the development, performance or position of the entity. [SR guidance para 7.44].

3.209 Non-financial KPIs can be indicators of future financial prospects and progress in managing risks and opportunities. They could include, for example, measures related to product quality, customer complaints, or environmental, employee or social matters. [SR guidance para 7.45].

3.210 In Table 3.70, Centrica clearly sets out its non-financial KPIs, and aligns them to strategic priorities through the use of symbols. It is also worth noting that Centrica has had some of these measures assured by a third party.

Table 3.70 – Non-financial indicators

Centrica – Annual report and accounts – 31 December 2013

Unless otherwise stated, all references to operating profit or loss, taxation and earnings numbers throughout the report are adjusted figures, as reconciled to their statutory equivalents in the Group Financial Review on page 35.
Deloitte LLP review our non-financial key performance indicators, providing limited assurance using the International Standard on Assurance Engagements (ISAE) 3000.

→ See our performance measures on pages 185 and 186

Non-financial indicators

LOST TIME INJURY FREQUENCY RATE (LTIFR)
Safety remains a core priority at Centrica. Our work to build a safety-first culture has helped drive consistent improvements in the safety of our activities.

Our Group LTIFR in 2013 reduced by 45% to 0.11 per 100.000 hours worked.

Strategic priorities

Innovate Integrate Increase

LTIFR per 100,000 hours worked

0.11

2013	0.11
2012	0.20
2011	0.25

Target for 2014
Continue to grow a best practice safety culture and at least maintain and if possible further improve our LTIR performance.

PROCESS SAFETY
Process safely focuses on the integrity of operating systems and processes that handle hazardous substances in order to prevent the potential for major incidents.

There were no significant process safety events in 2013.

Strategic priorities

Innovate Integrate

Significant events

0

(2012:0)

Target for 2014
Continue to improve process safety awareness and performance metrics.

CUSTOMER TRUST
We use net promoter scores (NPS) to measure customer satisfaction in British Gas in the UK and Direct Energy in North America.

British Gas NPS decreased, primarily due to the price announcement and in common with other suppliers. British Gas' score was +15. which is in the low performance range. Direct Energy NPS increased to +40. which is in the high performance range.

Strategic priorities

Innovate

Net promoter scores

British Gas
| 2013 | +15 |
| 2012 | +30 |

Direct Energy
| 2013 | +40 |
| 2012 | +39 |

Target for 2014
British Gas:
Return to the high performance range.
Direct Energy:
Remain within the high performance range.

EMPLOYEE ENGAGEMENT
The employee survey allows us to measure engagement and receive feedback from across the Group on how we are progressing in making a positive work environment.

In 2013 we achieved a score at 4.81 out of 6 in the survey, placing us within the median performance range.

Strategic priorities

Innovate Integrate Increase

Employee engagement

4.81 out of 6

| 2013 | 4.81 |
| 2012 | 4.72 |

Target for 2014
To continue to strive towards top quartile performance, measured against an independent high performance benchmark range.

3120

3.211   Where possible, KPIs should be generally accepted measures that are widely used, either within the entity's industry sector or more broadly. However, the comparability of the KPIs between industry peers should not override the effectiveness of the KPIs for assessing the performance or position of the entity's own business. [SR guidance para 7.46].

3.212   Entities should ensure that the KPIs currently presented to the board are those that allow the board to assess progress against stated strategies and (where reported externally) that allow readers to make a similar assessment. If this is not the case, is it because the information is simply not available, or has it not yet escalated to the board but might instead be assessed by the management of individual business units.

3.213   In addition, the KPIs will vary according to the industry in which an entity operates. Comparability will be enhanced if the KPIs are accepted and widely used; but management should not feel compelled to create KPIs to match those reported by the entity's peers. The overriding need is for the KPIs to be relevant to that particular entity. Management should explain its choice of KPIs in the context of the chosen strategies and objectives, and it should provide sufficient detail on measurement methods so that readers can make comparisons with other entities' choices.

3.214   Where multiple performance measures are disclosed, management should explain which of those measures are key to managing the business. The choice of which ones are key is unique to each entity and its strategy; it is impossible to specify how many KPIs an entity should have. However, in practice, entities typically report between four and ten measures.

3.215   Management should reflect on whether the chosen KPIs continue to be relevant. Strategies and objectives develop over time, so it is sometimes inappropriate to continue reporting the same KPIs as in previous periods. Equally, more information might become available to management, so it can report new KPIs that provide a deeper understanding of the business, or it can change how an existing KPI is calculated.

3.216   Comparatives should be included for KPIs, and the reasons for any significant changes from year to year explained. Consistency in the presentation of KPIs is a desirable quality. [SR guidance para 7.47].

3.217   In Table 3.71, BP clearly explain the changes that they have made to their KPIs year on year, and they identify where further information on previous KPIs can still be found.

Table 3.71 – Change in KPIs

BP – Annual report and accounts – 31 December 2013

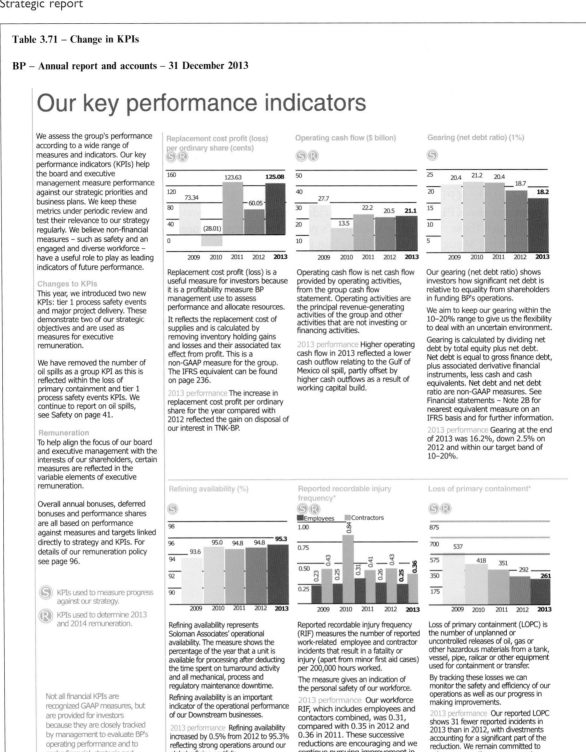

3.218 Measurement of performance in isolation, over a single period, does not provide the reader with useful information. An indication of how performance has changed over time is much more valuable in assessing the success of management's strategies. It is also beneficial to explain to the reader what a particular trend in the data means (for example, an increasing measure is not always a sign of strength), and to explain management's actions to address or maintain such trends.

3.219 Management might sometimes be concerned about the reliability of some of the information reported on KPIs, particularly where it is encouraged to move beyond traditional financial KPIs that are usually the output of established systems and controls processes and routine audit. There is no specific narrative reporting requirement for KPIs to be reliable, but the nature of the information should be clear to the users of narrative reports.

3.220 In order to address this issue, and to provide readers with useful information, it is important that the limitations of the data (and any assumptions made in providing it) are clearly explained. Readers can then judge the reliability for themselves, and they can make any necessary adjustments in their own analysis. Where data has been specifically assured by independent third parties, it might assist the reader if this fact is identified (see Table 3.70 above).

Reporting KPIs – a model for effective communication

3.221 The guidance does not prescribe either the KPIs to be used or the methods of calculating them. However, it does set out a model for effective communication of KPIs, recommending the disclosures listed below to be given for each KPI reported in the strategic report; this is to ensure that the KPIs can be understood by readers and properly used by them to assess the strategies adopted by the entity and the potential for those strategies to succeed:

■ The KPI definition and its calculation method. In view of the rapidly increasing use of industry-specific terminology, clear definitions of performance indicators add greatly to the reader's understanding of exactly what is being measured, and they allow comparisons between entities within an industry. An explanation of a metric's components, and how it is calculated, should be included; this is because there are no standards for the measurement of many industry-specific indicators, and many entities apply their own indicators.

■ The KPI's purpose. Management should explain why it believes that a performance indicator is relevant (for example, because it measures progress towards achieving a specific strategic objective).

■ The source of underlying data and any significant assumptions made. To enable readers to make their own assessment of the reliability of the information, management should identify the sources of the data used in calculating performance indicators and any limitations on that data. Any assumptions made in measuring performance should be explained, so that readers can reach an informed view of judgements made by management.

■ Any changes in the calculation method used, compared to previous financial years, should be identified and explained, including significant changes in the underlying accounting policies adopted in the financial statements which might affect the KPI. [SR guidance para 7.48].

3.222 Where a line-item from the financial statements, or a commonly used KPI, has been adjusted for inclusion in the strategic report, the term used for that adjusted measure should be clear; and, where practicable, a reconciliation to an appropriate financial statement line-item and explanation of any adjustments should be provided. [SR guidance para 7.49].

3.223 Performance indicators could be financial or non-financial. Where the amounts measured are financial, but are not 'traditional' measures required by accounting standards (that is, GAAP measures), it is good practice to explain any differences. So, a reconciliation should be provided between accounting measures and non-GAAP measures.

3.224 Similar KPIs should be clearly distinguishable from each other. [SR guidance para 7.50].

3.225 In June 2015, the European Securities and Markets Authority (ESMA) released guidelines for the disclosure of alternative performance measures (APMs) designed to encourage European issuers to publish transparent, unbiased and comparable information on their financial performance. These principles include providing an explicit definition of the APM along with the calculation method used and ensuring that component parts are clearly labelled and not misleading. For more information see Chapter 2 para 2.33.

3.226 The following information is also useful to investors and management when considering reporting in relation to KPIs:

■ Link to strategy: the primary reason for including performance indicators in corporate reporting is to enable readers to assess the strategies adopted by the entity and their potential to succeed. KPIs presented in isolation from strategies and objectives, or vice versa, cannot fulfil this requirement, and they will not provide the reader with the level of understanding that they need.

■ Quantification or commentary on future targets: some performance indicators are best suited to a quantification of future targets; but expectations and aims for other indicators might be better explained in commentary. Either way, a forward-looking orientation is essential for readers, to enable them to assess the potential for strategies to succeed and to give them a basis on which to assess future performance.

■ Segmental: management should consider how KPIs are collated and reported internally; it should also consider whether the KPIs make sense when aggregated and reported at a group level, or whether they would be more usefully reported at business segment level. Users of the strategic report might need more detailed segmental information to enable them to assess progress towards specific segmental strategic aims. So, performance indicators that are relevant to a specific segment's industry or strategy should be provided in addition to those with a more group-wide focus.

■ Benchmarking: performance benchmarked against a relevant peer group, with an explanation of why these peers were chosen, is valuable to users. It clearly indicates management's view of the entity's competitors, and sets the entity's own performance in the context of a well-defined peer group.

3.227 Tables 3.72, 3.73 and 3.74 show how three entities have aligned their KPIs with specific group strategies and objectives, and they illustrate a variety of content aspects. Note also that the disclosure of risks provided by the first two entities reflects on the link with KPIs.

Table 3.72 – Key performance indicators

Taylor Wimpey plc – Annual report – 31 December 2010

Business Review (extracts)

Strategy

Vision and goal
Taylor Wimpey is a focused community developer. We aim to be the developer of choice for customers, employees, shareholders and communities.

Our Group strategy
We create value through active management of our land portfolio and deliver this value through building high quality communities that meet the needs of local residents and our customers.

Long term objectives

- Provide growth in earnings per share, in light of market conditions.
- Deliver a return on capital employed above the level of our cost of funding.
- Return the Group to an investment-grade credit rating.
- Attract and retain the highest calibre of employees and strive to be a company that people want to work for.

Short term priorities

- Enhance the Group's profitability in both of our main markets through:
  - Focusing on sales price increases rather than volume growth.
  - Continued focus on operating efficiency.
  - Maintaining a tight control on overhead costs.
- Active management of our land portfolio.
- Evaluate proposals for our North American business.
- Maximise the potential of our employees through training and development programmes.

Group key performance indicators

Our Group KPIs provide a measure of our performance against our strategy

Adjusted earnings/(loss) per share

0.6p
for 2010

Objective
We seek to provide growth in earnings per share in light of market conditions.

Definition
The basic earnings per share from continuing operations based upon the profit attributable to ordinary shareholders before exceptional items divided by the average number of shares in issue during the year.

Why is it key to our strategy?
The generation of earnings is essential to deliver share price growth and dividends to shareholders and to fund future growth in the business. This measure is also commonly used by stock market analysts in assessing the value of companies.

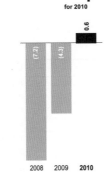

Return on average capital employed

8.2%
for 2010

Objective
We aim to deliver a return on capital employed above the level of our cost of funding.

Definition
Profit on ordinary activities before finance costs, exceptional items and amortisation of brands but including share of results of joint ventures, divided by the average of opening and closing tangible net worth.

Why is it key to our strategy?
Developing communities is a capital-intensive business due to the need to fund our landbank, so it is essential to ensure that this capital is used as effectively as possible.

Tangible net assets per share

56.9p
for 2010

Objective
To deliver growth in tangible net assets per share as market conditions allow.

Definition
The net asset value of the Group, as reported on the consolidated Balance Sheet, less goodwill and other intangible assets, divided by the number of shares in issue at the period end.

Why is it key to our strategy?
The Group must meet its financial covenants in order to retain access to its debt funding.

Please note this key performance indicator has been amended following the Group's refinancing in December 2010, which removed the requirement to meet the cash flow covenant test as set out in the previous financing arrangement.

Employee turnover

9%
for 2010

Objective
We endeavour to attract and retain the highest calibre of employees and strive to be a company that people want to work for.

Definition
The number of employees leaving the Group (excluding redundancies) expressed as a percentage of the average number of employees across the Group during the year.

Why is it key to our strategy?
Having high quality teams in place is essential to developing communities and delivering high quality homes that our customers want to live in, on time and to budget.

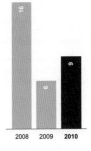

Table 3.73 – Key performance indicators

National Grid plc – Annual Report and Accounts

Operating and Financial Review (extract)

Key performance indicators (KPIs)

Financial KPIs

Company strategy and objectives	Financial KPIs	Definitions
Sustainable growth and superior financial performance	Adjusted earnings per share	Adjusted earnings* divided by the weighted average number of shares
	Total shareholder return	Growth in share price assuming dividends are reinvested
Delivering strong, sustainable regulatory and long-term contracts with good returns	Group return on equity	Adjusted earnings* with certain regulatory based adjustments divided by equity
Becoming more efficient through transforming our operating model and increasingly aligning our processes	Regulated controllable operating costs	Regulated controllable operating costs as a proportion of regulated assets

Our performance and the progress we have made against our strategic aims and against the objectives we have set ourselves are described below and on the following pages. Commentary on our overall financial results can be found on pages 38 to 45, and information on the performance and financial results of each line of business is set out on pages 46 to 73.

We measure the achievement of our objectives both through the use of qualitative assessments and through the monitoring of quantitative indicators. To provide a full and rounded view of our business, we use non-financial as well as financial measures. Although all these measures are important, some are considered to be of more significance than others, and these more significant measures are designated as KPIs. Our financial and non-financial KPIs are highlighted here. KPIs are used as our primary measures of whether we are achieving our principal strategic aims of sustainable growth and superior financial performance. We also use KPIs to measure our performance against our objectives; the relationships between the objectives and the KPIs is explained above.

Adjusted earnings per share*+†

Total shareholder return

Group return on equity^

Regulated controllable operation costs ‡

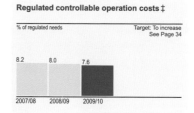

* Adjusted earnings excludes exceptional items, remeasurements and stranded cost recoveries
+ 2007/08 data includes continuing operations acquired with KeySpan for the period from 24 August 2007 to 31 March 2008 or as at 31 March 2008
^ 2007/08 results include KeySpan operations on a pro forma financial performance basis assuming the acquisition occurred on 1 April 2007
† Comparative data has been restated for the impact of the scrip dividend issues
‡ Comparative data has been restated to present information on a consistent basis with the current year

Non-financial KPIs

Company objectives	Non-financial KPIs	Definitions
Modernising and extending our transmission and distribution networks	Network reliability targets	Various definitions appropriate to the relevant line of business
Driving improvements in our safety, customer and operational performance	Customer satisfaction	Our position in customer satisfaction surveys
	Employee lost time injury frequency rate	Number of employee lost time injuries per 100,000 hours worked on a 12 month basis
Building trust, transparency and an inclusive and engaged workforce	Employee engagement index	Employee engagement index calculated using responses to our annual employee survey
Positively shaping the energy and climate change agenda with our stakeholders in both regions	Greenhouse gas emissions	Percentage reduction in greenhouse gas emissions against our 1990 baseline

Network reliability targets

	Performance					Measure	Target
	05/06	06/07	07/08	08/09	09/10		09/10
Electricity transmission – UK	99.9999	99.9999	99.9999	99.9999	99.9999	%	99.9999
Gas transmission – UK	100	100	100	100	100	%	100
Gas distribution – UK	99.999	99.999	99.999	99.9999	99.999	%	99.999
Electricity transmission – US	348	259	437	266	147	MWh tosses	<253
Electricity distribution – US	141	121	110	114	114	Mins of outage	<122

See pages 50, 58 and 66 for additional details on network reliability

Customer satisfaction

	Performance		Measure	Target
	08/09	09/10		
Gas Distribution – UK	4th quartile	**Not yet available**	Quartile ranking	To improve
Gas Distribution – US: Residential	4th quartile	**3rd quartile**	Quartile ranking	To improve
Gas Distribution – US: Commercial	3rd quartile	**2nd quartile**	Quartile ranking	To improve
Electricity Distribution & Generation: Residential	4th quartile	**4th quartile**	Quartile ranking	To improve
Electricity Distribution & Generation: Commercial	4th quartile	**3rd quartile**	Quartile ranking	To improve

Employee lost time injury frequency rate

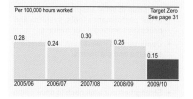

Per 100,000 hours worked — Target Zero See page 31
0.28 (2005/06), 0.24 (2006/07), 0.30 (2007/08), 0.25 (2008/09), 0.15 (2009/10)

Employee engagement index

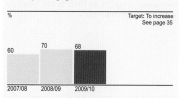

% — Target: To increase See page 35
60 (2007/08), 70 (2008/09), 68 (2009/10)

Greenhouse gas emissions–#

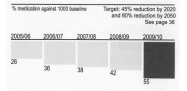

% medication against 1000 baseline — Target: 45% reduction by 2020 and 80% reduction by 2050 See page 36
2005/06: 26, 2006/07: 36, 2007/08: 38, 2008/09: 42, 2009/10: 55

− 2007/68 restated due to improved baseline data relating to KeySpan. Previously published figure excluding KeySpan was 30%
Our greenhouse gas emissions for 2009/10 are not fully verified at the date of this Report Fuly verified data will be published on cur website in July 2010

Table 3.74 – Industry-specific key performance indicators

InterContinental Hotels Group PLC – Annual Report and Financial Statements – 31 December 2013

Key performance indicators (KPIs)

We measure our performance through a holistic set of carefully selected KPIs to monitor our success in achieving our strategy and the progress of our Group to deliver high-quality growth. The KPIs are organised around the elements of our strategy – our Winning Model and Targeted Portfolio, and Disciplined Execution.

Winning Model and Targeted Portfolio

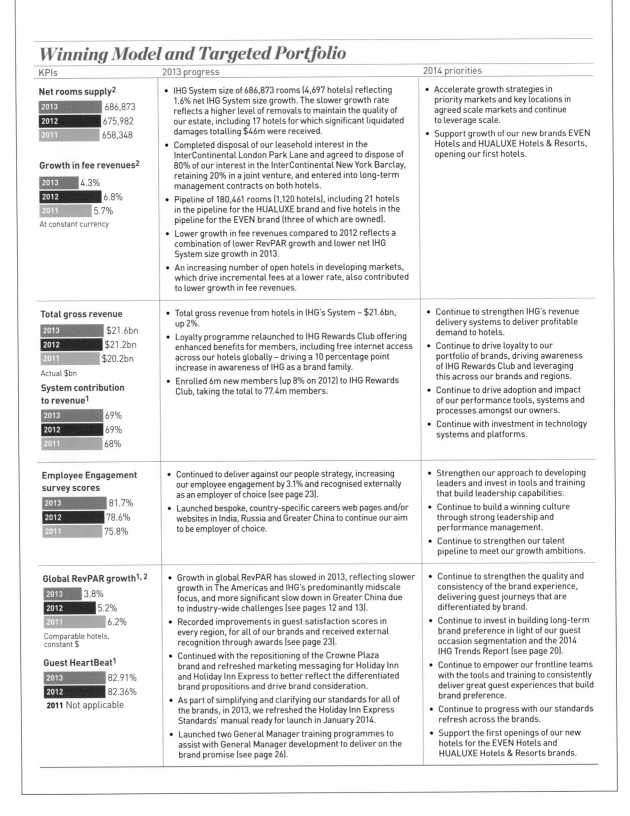

KPIs	2013 progress	2014 priorities
Net rooms supply[2] 2013 686,873 2012 675,982 2011 658,348 **Growth in fee revenues[2]** 2013 4.3% 2012 6.8% 2011 5.7% At constant currency	• IHG System size of 686,873 rooms (4,697 hotels) reflecting 1.6% net IHG System size growth. The slower growth rate reflects a higher level of removals to maintain the quality of our estate, including 17 hotels for which significant liquidated damages totalling $46m were received. • Completed disposal of our leasehold interest in the InterContinental London Park Lane and agreed to dispose of 80% of our interest in the InterContinental New York Barclay, retaining 20% in a joint venture, and entered into long-term management contracts on both hotels. • Pipeline of 180,461 rooms (1,120 hotels), including 21 hotels in the pipeline for the HUALUXE brand and five hotels in the pipeline for the EVEN brand (three of which are owned). • Lower growth in fee revenues compared to 2012 reflects a combination of lower RevPAR growth and lower net IHG System size growth in 2013. • An increasing number of open hotels in developing markets, which drive incremental fees at a lower rate, also contributed to lower growth in fee revenues.	• Accelerate growth strategies in priority markets and key locations in agreed scale markets and continue to leverage scale. • Support growth of our new brands EVEN Hotels and HUALUXE Hotels & Resorts, opening our first hotels.
Total gross revenue 2013 $21.6bn 2012 $21.2bn 2011 $20.2bn Actual $bn **System contribution to revenue[1]** 2013 69% 2012 69% 2011 68%	• Total gross revenue from hotels in IHG's System – $21.6bn, up 2%. • Loyalty programme relaunched to IHG Rewards Club offering enhanced benefits for members, including free internet access across our hotels globally – driving a 10 percentage point increase in awareness of IHG as a brand family. • Enrolled 6m new members (up 8% on 2012) to IHG Rewards Club, taking the total to 77.4m members.	• Continue to strengthen IHG's revenue delivery systems to deliver profitable demand to hotels. • Continue to drive loyalty to our portfolio of brands, driving awareness of IHG Rewards Club and leveraging this across our brands and regions. • Continue to drive adoption and impact of our performance tools, systems and processes amongst our owners. • Continue with investment in technology systems and platforms.
Employee Engagement survey scores 2013 81.7% 2012 78.6% 2011 75.8%	• Continued to deliver against our people strategy, increasing our employee engagement by 3.1% and recognised externally as an employer of choice (see page 23). • Launched bespoke, country-specific careers web pages and/or websites in India, Russia and Greater China to continue our aim to be employer of choice.	• Strengthen our approach to developing leaders and invest in tools and training that build leadership capabilities. • Continue to build a winning culture through strong leadership and performance management. • Continue to strengthen our talent pipeline to meet our growth ambitions.
Global RevPAR growth[1, 2] 2013 3.8% 2012 5.2% 2011 6.2% Comparable hotels, constant $ **Guest HeartBeat[1]** 2013 82.91% 2012 82.36% **2011** Not applicable	• Growth in global RevPAR has slowed in 2013, reflecting slower growth in The Americas and IHG's predominantly midscale focus, and more significant slow down in Greater China due to industry-wide challenges (see pages 12 and 13). • Recorded improvements in guest satisfaction scores in every region, for all of our brands and received external recognition through awards (see page 23). • Continued with the repositioning of the Crowne Plaza brand and refreshed marketing messaging for Holiday Inn and Holiday Inn Express to better reflect the differentiated brand propositions and drive brand consideration. • As part of simplifying and clarifying our standards for all of the brands, in 2013, we refreshed the Holiday Inn Express Standards' manual ready for launch in January 2014. • Launched two General Manager training programmes to assist with General Manager development to deliver on the brand promise (see page 26).	• Continue to strengthen the quality and consistency of the brand experience, delivering guest journeys that are differentiated by brand. • Continue to invest in building long-term brand preference in light of our guest occasion segmentation and the 2014 IHG Trends Report (see page 20). • Continue to empower our frontline teams with the tools and training to consistently deliver great guest experiences that build brand preference. • Continue to progress with our standards refresh across the brands. • Support the first openings of our new hotels for the EVEN Hotels and HUALUXE Hotels & Resorts brands.

3.228 It might be appropriate to disclose other quantified measures that management uses to monitor trends and factors and that can provide further context to the narrative reporting. But, if they are not considered by management to be KPIs and/or are outside the entity's control, the level of information about each measure should be less than for a KPI.

3.229 In June 2015 the Institute of Chartered Accountants in Scotland (ICAS) published guidance on the provision of greater assurance and transparency in KPI reporting designed to help audit committees and boards select suitable KPIs for their entity. It also recommends the clear communication to users of the degree of confidence gained over the reliance and reliability of the KPIs and the process taken to acquire this confidence.

Diversity

3.230 The strategic report should provide a breakdown showing, as at the end of the financial year:

i.   the number of persons of each sex who were directors of the entity;

ii.   the number of persons of each sex who were senior managers of the entity (other than persons falling within subparagraph i); and

iii. the number of persons of each sex who were employees of the entity.

[CA06 Sec 414C(8)(c); SR guidance para 7.51].

3.231 A 'senior manager' is an employee who has responsibility for planning, directing or controlling the activities of the entity or a strategically significant part of it. In the strategic report of a consolidated group, directors of subsidiary entities that are included in the consolidated financial statements are also considered 'senior managers'. [CA06 Sec 414C(9), (10); SR guidance para 7.52].

3.232 In Table 3.75, BP clearly differentiate between group leaders and subsidiary directors – both which can be considered senior managers.

Table 3.75 – Diversity disclosure

BP – Annual Report – 31 December 2013

Diversity

Diversity

We are a global company and aim for a workforce that is representative of the societies in which we operate.

We have set out our ambitions for diversity and our group people committee reviews performance on a quarterly basis. We aim for 25% of our group leaders – the most senior managers of our businesses and functions – to be women by 2020.

Workforce by gender

Numbers as at 31 December	Male	Female	Female %
Board directors	12	2	14
Group leaders	477	105	18
Subsidiary directors	494	107	18
All employees	58,500	25,400	30

At the end of 2013, 22% of our group leaders came from countries other than the UK and the US. We continue to increase the number of local leaders and employees in our operations so that they reflect the communities in which we operate and this is monitored at a local, business or national level.

We support the UK government-commissioned Lord Davies review which recommends increasing gender diversity on the boards of listed companies. See page 70 for information on our board composition.

3.233 Clear articulation of how an entity has defined the 'senior manager' grade within its reporting is encouraged, to ensure clarity and comparability of disclosures. Table 3.76 shows the approach that Smith and Nephew have taken to achieving this.

Table 3.76 – 'Senior manager' definition

Smith and Nephew – Annual Report – 31 December 2013

Diversity disclosure

At 31 December 2013, Smith & Nephew had the following breakdown of employees:

	Number of Employees[1]
Directors	
Male	9
Female	3
Total	**12**
Senior Managers and above [2]	
Male	484
Female	140
Total	**624**
Total employees	
Male	7,203
Female	4,821
Total	**12,024**

1   Number of employees as at 31 December 2013 including part time employees and employees on leave of absence.
2   Senior managers and above includes all employees classed as Directors, Senior Directors, Vice Presidents and Executive Officers and includes all statutory Directors of our subsidiary companies.

3.234 In referring to a 'strategically significant' part of an entity, and by including directors of all subsidiaries, the definition of a 'senior manager' above is wider than the definition of 'key management personnel' in IAS 24 and FRS 102. [SR guidance para 7.53].

3.235 An entity might not consider that including all directors of all of the subsidiaries that are included in the consolidated financial statements within the statutory definition of 'senior managers' accurately reflects its executive pipeline. This might be the case, for instance, where a subsidiary is insignificant in the context of the group as a whole. In such cases, it might be appropriate to provide an enhanced analysis of the statutory 'senior manager' category. [SR guidance para 7.54].

3.236 William Hill, in the example below, have provided clear commentary on their reasons for setting out their statutory directors separately from other senior managers.

Table 3.77 – 'Senior manager' definition

William Hill – Annual Report – 31 December 2013

Diversity disclosure

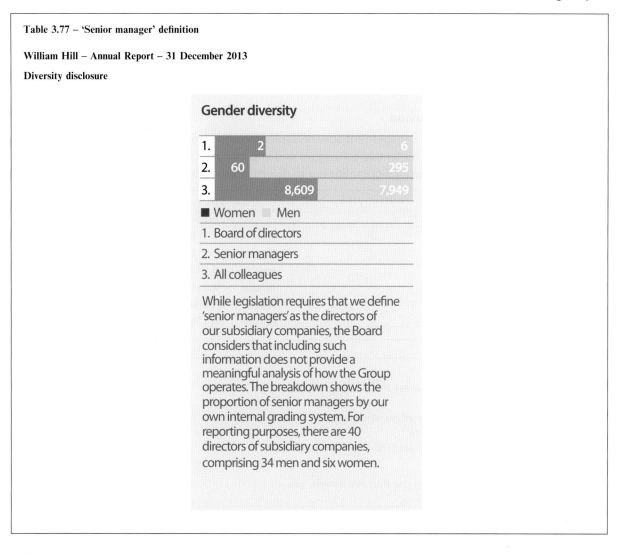

Gender diversity

	Women	Men
1.	2	6
2.	60	295
3.	8,609	7,949

■ Women   Men

1. Board of directors

2. Senior managers

3. All colleagues

While legislation requires that we define 'senior managers' as the directors of our subsidiary companies, the Board considers that including such information does not provide a meaningful analysis of how the Group operates. The breakdown shows the proportion of senior managers by our own internal grading system. For reporting purposes, there are 40 directors of subsidiary companies, comprising 34 men and six women.

3.237 Where the strategic report includes an enhanced analysis (such as that suggested in para 3.198), a description of how employees included in any non-statutory category have been identified should be provided. Information on other executive pipeline or general employee diversity matters should also be provided where it is necessary to put the diversity statistics into context. While percentages of male and female directors and employees can be informative, numbers must also be provided. [SR guidance para 7.55].

3.238 In Table 3.78, Lloyds Banking Group clearly show gender diversity alongside other relevant diversity measures for their business.

Table 3.78 – Diversity and inclusion

Lloyds Banking Group – Annual Report – 31 December 2013

Diversity and inclusion

Diversity and inclusion

Our 2013 Colleague Engagement Survey results showed significantly higher engagement scores for female colleagues and improvements in colleagues' perceptions of the Group's commitment to diversity and inclusion.

		2013		2012
Gender		Number	%	%
Board	Male	8	73	73
	Female	3	27	27
Senior managers	Male	5,911	73	74
	Female	2,217	27	26
Colleagues	Male	38,860	41	41
	Female	55,150	59	59

	2013	2012
Disability[1]		
% of colleagues who disclose they have a disability	1.5%	1.5%
Ethnic background[1]		
% of colleagues from an ethnic minority	6%	7%
Ethnic minority managers	6%	6%
Ethnic minority senior managers	3%	3%
Sexual orientation[1]		
% of colleagues who disclose they are lesbian, gay, bisexual or transgender	1%	1%

[1] Data source: HR system (HRIS). Apart from gender data, all diversity information is based on colleagues' voluntary self-declaration. As a result this data is not fully representative; our systems do not record any diversity data for the proportion of colleagues who have not declared this information.

3.239 The analysis of senior managers should enable shareholders to ascertain the number of persons of each sex who might, in due course, attain a position that would be classified as 'director' or an equivalent position.

Other content elements

3.240 To the extent that matters are considered to be of strategic importance to the entity, the strategic report should include information that would otherwise be disclosed in the directors' report. [CA06 Sec 414C(11); SR guidance para 7.56].

3.241 There are a number of directors' report disclosure requirements that are closely related to matters that should be considered for inclusion in the strategic report. Where this information is also necessary for an understanding of the development, performance, position or future prospects of the entity, it should be included as part of the strategic report. However, where the information is not necessary for that purpose, these disclosures should be included in the directors' report. In such cases, a signpost enabling shareholders to drill down to this information should be considered where it is related to matters covered in the strategic report. [SR guidance para 7.57].

3.242 Where information that is required to be disclosed in the directors' report is included in the strategic report, it does not also need to be included in the directors' report. However, where this is the case, the directors' report should cross-refer to information that has been included in the strategic report instead of the directors' report. [SI 2008/410 'Large and Medium-sized Companies and Groups (Reports and Accounts) Regulations 2008' 7 Sch Part 1(1A); SR guidance para 7.58].

Chapter 4

Corporate governance

Chapter 4

Corporate governance

History and development of corporate governance in the UK

Introduction

4.1 In 1992 the Cadbury Committee defined corporate governance in its report 'The financial aspects of corporate governance' as *"the system by which companies are directed and controlled. Boards of directors are responsible for the governance of their companies. The shareholders' role in governance is to appoint the directors and the auditors and to satisfy themselves that an appropriate governance structure is in place. The responsibilities of the board include setting the company's strategic aims, providing the leadership to put them into effect, supervising the management of the business and reporting to shareholders on their stewardship. The board's actions are subject to laws, regulations and the shareholders in general meeting"*. In 2014, the latest version of the UK Corporate Governance Code (the 'Code') still quoted this as the classic definition of the context of the Code.

4.1.1 In the preface to its Principles of Corporate Governance published in 2004, the OECD provided the following statement of what corporate governance involves and achieves:

> *"Corporate governance involves a set of relationships between a company's management, its board, its shareholders and other stakeholders. Corporate governance also provides the structure through which the objectives of the company are set, and the means of attaining those objectives and monitoring performance are determined. Good corporate governance should provide proper incentives for the board and management to pursue objectives that are in the interests of the company and its shareholders and should facilitate effective monitoring. The presence of an effective corporate governance system, within an individual company and across an economy as a whole, helps to provide a degree of confidence that is necessary for the proper functioning of a market economy. As a result the cost of capital is lower and firms are encouraged to use resources more efficiently thereby underpinning growth."*

4.2 Most UK companies have a single 'unitary' board. Unlike a number of other countries, executive and non-executive directors sit on the same board, rather than separate management and supervisory boards. In terms of directors' legal responsibilities, the courts will expect all directors to exercise the same level of care, skill and diligence, taking into account their particular skill-sets and expertise.

4.2.1 Corporate governance in the UK corporate sector is, therefore, primarily concerned with:

- The procedures adopted by the board and its committees to discharge its duties (for example, membership of the board; frequency of, and procedures at, board meetings; the role of non-executive directors; constitution and terms of reference of board committees; and the role of the company secretary).

- The board's accountability to shareholders and other stakeholders (for example, annual reporting; use of AGMs; and shareholder voting rights).

- The manner in which the board controls the company or group (for example, management structures; group legal structure; and risk management and internal control).

The development of corporate governance disclosures

4.3 Corporate governance in its modern sense is a relatively new discipline that began as a response to the scandals and failures of the late 1980s with a series of committees, reports and recommendations. The first of these was the Committee on the Financial Aspects of Corporate Governance, generally referred to as the Cadbury Committee, after its chairman Sir Adrian Cadbury. Its report was issued in December 1992 and, as a result, major changes occurred in the way in which governance was viewed by companies as well as in the disclosures that they give.

4.4 Whilst board remuneration was one of the issues addressed by Cadbury, it was not the main focus. Nonetheless, the level of board remuneration continued to attract a high profile, particularly in relation to levels of pay in privatised utilities. In response to this a separate group was set up to study the matter and the result was 'Directors' remuneration: report of a study group chaired by Sir Richard Greenbury'. This is known as the Greenbury report and was published in July 1995. The Greenbury report led to additional disclosure requirements around directors' pay being included in the Listing Rules. The latest remuneration disclosures are discussed in chapter 5.

4.5   One of Cadbury's recommendations was that a successor body should be set up to review progress and it identified a number of issues which that body might consider. The successor body, 'The Committee on Corporate Governance' (the 'Hampel committee') was set up in November 1995 under the chairmanship of Sir Ronald Hampel.

4.6   The final version of the Hampel report was published in January 1998. The recommendations aimed to ensure a balance between business prosperity and accountability.

4.7   Following the completion of its report, the Hampel Committee co-operated with the London Stock Exchange in producing 'The Combined Code – Principles of Good Corporate Governance and Code of Best Practice' in June 1998 – referred to here as the 'Combined Code' (1998); this embraced the Cadbury and Greenbury Reports, and took into account the Hampel Committee's Report and changes made by the London Stock Exchange, with the committee's agreement.

4.8   The Combined Code (1998) was appended to the Listing Rules (although it did not form part of those rules), and a new listing rule required companies to include a two-part disclosure statement in their annual report describing how they had applied the principles of the Combined Code (1998), whether or not they had complied with its detailed provisions throughout the accounting period and details of any non-compliance – the so-called 'comply-or-explain' reporting mechanism which still lies at the heart of the UK governance framework.

4.9   In February 2002 the government announced that Sir Derek Higgs was to carry out a review of the role and effectiveness of non-executive directors, at a time when company accounting scandals and collapses, predominantly in the USA, were shocking investors and the public. Shortly after Higgs' review was announced, the government also formed a co-ordinating group to consider the implications of the US scandals for the arrangements for financial reporting and auditing in the UK. This group requested the Financial Reporting Council ('FRC') to set up a working group to consider whether the remit of audit committees under the existing Combined Code (1998) needed to change. The working group was chaired by Sir Robert Smith and worked closely with Higgs. The group's output was known as the 'Smith guidance'. The group suggested new provisions for the Combined Code (1998) around the role and responsibilities of audit committees. These were incorporated into the revised draft Combined Code published as part of the Higgs Report in January 2003. The FRC approved the new Combined Code on Corporate Governance in July 2003.

4.10   A major overhaul of company law occurred with the Companies Act 2006. Part 43 of the Companies Act 2006 (sections 1269 and 1273) includes provisions on corporate governance. These give powers to a 'competent authority' to implement European transparency obligations and, therefore, it is the Financial Conduct Authority ('FCA', previously known as the Financial Services Authority) that has created the UK corporate governance rules, through the Disclosure Rules and Transparency Rules ('DTR') and the Listing Rules (which require companies to report against the UK Corporate Governance Code). In June 2008 the FCA implemented the EU 4th and 8th Company Law Directives requiring companies to have an audit committee (or similar body) and to publish a corporate governance statement. The corporate governance compliance statement requirement of the Listing Rules was restricted to compliance with the main principles of the Code only and not the supporting principles as previously required (the requirement to explain departures from the Code's provisions remained).

4.11   In 2010, the FCA's Listing Regime was restructured into two new segments (premium and standard listed companies) with the objective of providing more clarity about the regime for market participants. The FCA rules are discussed further in paragraph 4.30 onwards but, in essence, they applied the Code to all premium listed companies regardless of their country of incorporation.

4.12   The 2008 financial crisis triggered widespread reappraisal of the governance systems which might have helped to alleviate it. In the UK, Sir David Walker was appointed by the UK government to review the governance of banks and other financial industry entities (BOFIs), and the FRC brought forward its regular review of the Combined Code so that corporate governance for other sectors could be assessed at the same time. The final report by Sir David Walker, published in November 2009, included 39 recommendations. The

FCA was given responsibility for implementing those recommendations specific to BOFIs. The recommendations that applied to all listed companies were implemented by the FRC as part of its review of the Combined Code.

4.13   The 2009-10 FRC review of the Combined Code resulted in publication of the revised UK Corporate Governance Code in May 2010.

4.14   The overriding view emerging from the 2009-10 FRC review was that the Code was effective and that the 'comply-or-explain' approach was sufficiently flexible to embrace different companies' circumstances. However, the FRC also concluded that much more attention needed to be paid to following the spirit of the Code as well as its letter and that the quality of corporate governance ultimately depends on board behaviour not process.

4.15   The FRC, therefore, made structural and wording changes, aimed at changing the 'tone' of the Code by giving more prominence to factors that underpin an effective board, such as the pivotal role of the chairman in leading the board, the responsibility of the non-executive directors to provide constructive challenge, the directors' expected time commitment, the board's composition and the board's responsibility for risk. Additionally, there were strengthened provisions on director development and two new provisions for FTSE 350 companies: externally facilitated performance reviews of boards at least every three years and annual re-election of all directors.

4.16   The FRC also took responsibility for a Stewardship Code for institutional investors to enhance shareholder engagement following Sir David Walker's recommendations. The purpose of the Stewardship Code is to improve the quality of corporate governance through promoting better dialogue between shareholders and company boards, and more transparency about the way in which investors oversee the companies they own. Paragraph 4.271 onwards deals further with the UK Stewardship Code.

4.17   Following the release of the 2010 Code, a number of the FRC's guidance documents were subject to review. The FRC commissioned the Institute of Chartered Secretaries and Administrators ('ICSA') to develop new guidance to replace the Higgs guidance issued in 2006 and the FRC published the resulting 'Guidance on Board Effectiveness' in March 2011 "*to help boards of UK companies avoid some of the problems that contributed to significant value destruction during the recent financial crisis*". [Guidance on Board Effectiveness, March 2011]. The guidance is designed to stimulate boards' thinking on how they can carry out their role most effectively and, therefore, addresses sections A and B of the UK Corporate Governance Code on leadership and effectiveness of the board. See paragraph 4.100 onwards for more information.

4.18   An updated version of the 'Smith' guidance on audit committees was released in December 2010 and included changes around the policy on appointing the external auditor to carry out non-audit services as well as enhancing disclosure around how objectivity and independence of the external auditor are safeguarded.

4.19   Now on a cycle of two-yearly reviews of the Code, in September 2012 the FRC published a version focused principally on the outcomes of its 'Effective Company Stewardship' initiative around enhancing the accountability of directors to shareholders. The main changes in this version of the Code were that the directors should confirm that the annual report and accounts taken as a whole were 'fair, balanced and understandable', that audit committees should report more fully on their activities, and that FTSE 350 companies should put the external audit contract out to tender at least every ten years. The requirement for companies to report on their boardroom diversity policies, first announced in 2011, also came into effect. The FRC 'Guidance on audit committees' was also updated.

4.19.1   The UK Stewardship Code was also revised in September 2012, although its seven principles were not changed. The extent of the revisions partly reflects the fact that the Stewardship Code is still in its infancy, and that the experience of implementing it had identified a number of respects in which it was insufficiently clear what was expected of signatories.

4.20   Following another of its two-yearly reviews, the FRC published its latest version of the Code in September 2014. In response to the 2008 financial crisis, this version focuses principally on embedding the management of risks to solvency and liquidity in the day-to-day processes of companies and boards, and was accompanied by a new set of FRC 'Guidance on risk management, internal control and related financial and business reporting'. In particular, under the 2014 Code directors are required to confirm that they have carried out a 'robust assessment' of the principal risks and to make a statement as to how they have assessed the prospects for the company, over what period they have done so, and why they consider that period to be appropriate – this has become known as the 'viability statement'. See paragraph 4.186 onwards for more details.

4.20.1   In September 2015, as part of the process of implementing the European Union's Audit Regulation 537/2014 & Directive 2014/56/EU, the FRC issued for consultation updates to the Code which would appear in the 2016 version and an updated version of the 'Guidance on audit committees'. See paragraph 4.296 for more information.

Corporate governance concepts

4.21   The concepts of the Hampel Report that led to the original Combined Code (1998) are still applicable to the UK Corporate Governance Code issued in 2012. The key concepts are discussed below.

Avoidance of 'box ticking'

4.22   Hampel argued for flexibility when considering corporate governance standards and a proper regard for the individual circumstances of the companies concerned. Too often, companies' experience of Cadbury and Greenbury was as sets of prescriptive rules with shareholders and their advisers following a 'box ticking' approach focusing only on whether a rule had been complied with rather than considering the particular circumstances involved.

4.23   In Hampel's view this 'box ticking' approach did not take account of the diversity of circumstances and experience among different companies and within the same company. Although Hampel agreed with Cadbury that there are guidelines that are appropriate in most cases, Hampel considered that there will often be valid reasons for exceptions and companies should not be penalised for this. A focus by those considering corporate governance arrangements on 'box ticking' draws attention away from the diligent pursuit of corporate governance objectives and becomes an objective in itself.

'Comply-or-explain'

4.24   As noted above, it was recognised that not all listed companies would be able to comply with all the provisions of the Code, given their different circumstances, and that there would be valid reasons for such non-compliance. Therefore the 'comply-or-explain' mechanism was adopted so that, if a company had not complied with the Code's provisions during the year, it could provide an explanation in respect of those provisions with which it did not comply. This mechanism allows companies to demonstrate proper consideration of the Code without forcing them to adopt a 'box ticking' approach to compliance and is a key characteristic of a code-based (as opposed to legislation-based) governance framework.

4.25   Listing Rule 9.8.6 requires a premium listed company to give a two-part compliance statement in its annual financial report; first to explain how it has *applied* the Code's main principles and, secondly, how it has *complied* with its provisions. This is supported by companies, investors and regulators in the UK and has increasingly been adopted as a model in other financial markets.

4.26   Although it is a cornerstone of the UK corporate governance framework, 'comply-or-explain' comes under regular scrutiny, particularly when corporate governance arrangements have arguably failed. It is significant that the EU has recently been much more willing to recognise it in its governance pronouncements than was the case in the past. See paragraph 4.61.1 for more information.

4.27   There is, however, a growing recognition that 'comply-or-explain' faces particular challenges where a company has a controlling shareholder or a group of shareholders acting in concert. In such cases the minority will usually have insufficient influence to bring the company back into line with the Code. The FCA issued rules for the protection of minority shareholders that apply from May 2014, including a requirement that there should be a formal relationship agreement in place between the company and its controlling shareholders to govern their interaction. See paragraph 4.67 onwards for further details.

Shareholder/stakeholder engagement

4.28   The theme of the directors having a dialogue with investors based on mutual understanding of objectives appeared in the Higgs Report and has continued to be developed since then. Though their primary responsibility is to shareholders, the directors are also encouraged to 'recognise the contribution made by other providers of capital' in the Preface to the 2014 version of the Code.

4.29   This underlying philosophy is responsible for the inclusion of a section in all four Combined Codes (1998, 2003, 2006 and 2008) on institutional shareholders. Transparency and openness are less effective if the communication is a one-way process. Investors have duties and responsibilities too. Included in Section 2 of each Combined Code are three main principles relating to institutional shareholders. These cover dialogue with companies, evaluation of governance disclosures and shareholder voting. In 2010 this section "was replaced by the UK Stewardship Code for institutional investors published by the FRC, which is discussed in paragraph 4.271 onwards.

FCA Corporate Governance Rules

FCA Corporate Governance Rules – impact of Disclosure Rules and Transparency Rules

4.30 In June 2008, the FCA released revisions to the Listing Rules and the DTR to implement amendments to the EU 4th and 8th Company Law Directives and chapter 7 of the DTR became the FCA Corporate Governance Rules.

4.31 The advent of the DTR/FCA Corporate Governance Rules added another set of rules governing parts of the front end of the annual report to the principles and provisions of the Code, the Listing Rules, and the legislative requirements of the Companies Act 2006 and its accompanying regulations and instruments.

4.32 The table below summarises the corporate governance requirements under the Code, Listing Rules and DTR for each type of listed company.

	UK premium	UK standard	Overseas premium	Overseas standard
Listing Rule 9.8.6 (5) and (6) (Compliance statement) (see para 4.53 onwards)	✓	✗	✓	✗
The UK Corporate Governance Code ('comply-or-explain') (also see para 4.53 onwards)	✓	✗	✓	✗
Listing Rule 9.8.6 (3) (Going concern and viability statements) (see para 4.222 onwards)	✓	✗	✗	✗
FCA Corporate Governance Rules				
● DTR 7.1 Audit Committee (see para 4.37 onwards)	✓	✓	✗	✗
● DTR 7.2 Corporate Governance Statement (see para 4.40 onwards, and para 4.33 onwards for standard listed companies and companies with only listed debt)	✓	✓	✓	✓
Auditors' Report (LR 9.8.10) (13 Code provisions) (see para 4.251 onwards)	✓	✗	✓ (excluding going concern and viability statements)	✗

AIM companies are not required to comply with the DTR (see para 4.76 onwards), but may voluntarily elect to do so.

Corporate governance reporting requirements for companies with only listed debt

4.33 The corporate governance reporting requirements of the Listing Rules and most of those in DTR 7.2 do not apply to companies that have only listed debt (that is, no equity listing).

4.34 Although Listing Rule 9.8.6 refers to 'listed companies', LR 9.1.1 states at the start of the Continuing Obligations chapter of the Listing Rules that: *"This chapter applies to a company that has a premium listing of equity shares"*.

4.35 Similarly, although DTR 7.2 refers to 'issuers' in general (which would include issuers of debt) and might therefore mean that a corporate governance statement is still needed, DTR 1B.1.6 states that: *"The* *rules in DTR 7.2.2R, 7.2.3R and 7.2.7R do not apply to an issuer which has not issued shares which are admitted to trading unless it has issued shares which are traded on an multilateral trading facility ('MTF')".*

4.36 The DTR exemption does not, therefore, extend to DTR 7.2.5R and 7.2.6R, so companies with listed debt *are* required to give the disclosures regarding internal control and risk management systems and information on share capital structures (although the 7.2.6R disclosures will only be required if the company is required under the Companies Act to give the equivalent Takeover Directive disclosures). As there will normally be no separate corporate governance statement in the annual report of such a company, the disclosures should be included in the directors' report (or cross-referenced from it). The DTR 7.2.5R and 7.2.6R reporting requirements also apply to a company that has a standard listing of equity shares but does not apply any corporate governance code (and therefore does not otherwise report on corporate governance).

Corporate governance reporting requirements for companies with only a standard listing of shares

4.36.1 The whole of DTR 7.2 applies to companies with a standard listing of shares but, where a standard listed company does not apply a governance code, there will usually be little to report in respect of DTR 7.2.2R and 7.2.3R. Where a standard listed company does apply a governance code, it must comply with the reporting requirements in those provisions of the DTR. This typically affects companies that have previously had a premium listing and move to a standard listing but undertake to maintain their existing corporate governance arrangements. Under DTR 7.2, such companies will in effect continue to report against the code that they apply on a 'comply-or-explain' basis, even though the Listing Rules do not require this.

Requirement to have an audit committee (DTR 7.1)

4.37 The DTR require certain companies to have an audit committee (or a body performing equivalent functions). At least one member must be independent, and at least one member (who may, but need not, be the same person) must have competence in accounting and/or auditing. [DTR 7.1.1R].

As a minimum the relevant body must:

- Monitor the financial reporting process.

- Monitor the effectiveness of the internal control, internal audit where applicable and risk management systems.

- Monitor the statutory audit of the annual and consolidated financial statements.

- Review and monitor the independence of the statutory auditor and, in particular, the provision of additional services. [DTR 7.1.3R].

The FCA has indicated that there are a number of overlaps between the Code and the DTR. These have been summarised in paragraph 4.50.

4.38 DTR 7.1 applies to companies with transferable securities admitted to trading on either the London Stock Exchange or the PLUS-listed markets that are required to appoint a statutory auditor as defined in section 1210 of the Companies Act 2006. The FCA has therefore effectively applied DTR 7.1 to UK incorporated issuers only, and not to overseas issuers.

4.39 There are exemptions from the DTR 7.1 requirements for:

- A listed company whose parent is subject to this rule (or an equivalent rule of any EEA State).

- An issuer whose sole business is to act as the issuer of asset-backed securities, provided that the issuer makes a public statement explaining why it is not appropriate to have an audit committee.

- A credit institution whose shares are not admitted to trading if the total nominal value of its listed debt securities is less than €100 million and the company has not prepared a prospectus in accordance with section 85 of the Financial Services and Markets Act 2000.

4.39.1 The FCA consulted in Consultation Paper CP15/28 (September 2015) on changes to the DTR to implement the EU Audit Regulation and Directive which would mean that a majority of the audit committee will need to be independent (not just one member as is currently the case). This would apply to periods beginning on or after 17 June 2016.

Requirement to present a corporate governance statement (DTR 7.2)

4.40   Under DTR 7.2, companies are required to present a corporate governance statement in one of the following ways. It may be included: as part of the directors' report (or incorporated by reference into the directors' report); separately issued to accompany the annual report and financial statements; or made available on the company's website, but with cross-references from the directors' report. Where a company chooses to present its corporate governance statement separately, there are specific Companies Act requirements in respect of the approval, signing and filing of the separate governance statement. These requirements are discussed further in paragraph 4.263.

4.41   At the present time, however, the corporate governance report must be included in the 'annual financial report' to comply with Listing Rule 9.8.6. This effectively removes for listed companies the flexibility that the DTR would allow.

4.42   DTR 7.2 applies to all companies with shares admitted to trading on the London Stock Exchange or PLUS-listed markets or traded on a multi-lateral trading facility. [DTR 1B.1.5, 1B.1.6]. In this respect, it is different from DTR 7.1, which applies only to UK incorporated issuers under the FCA Corporate Governance Rules.

4.43   The DTR contain a number of disclosures that must be given in the corporate governance statement. Many of those requirements are also dealt with elsewhere in UK legislation or guidance. The requirements are listed below, together with any overlap with other legislation or the Code.

4.44   The corporate governance statement must contain a reference to:

■   Any corporate governance code to which the company is subject.

■   Any corporate governance code which the company may have voluntarily decided to apply.

■   All relevant information about the corporate governance practices applied beyond the requirements under national law.

■   Where any corporate governance code that is applied (either mandatorily or voluntarily) is publicly available.

■   An explanation of any departure from a corporate governance code applied. (This overlaps with the 'comply-or-explain' rule in LR 9.8.6R(5) – see further paras 4.24 and 4.58 onwards).

[DTR 7.2.2R, 7.2.3R].

4.45   In addition, the corporate governance statement must contain:

■   A description of the main features of the company's internal control and risk management systems in relation to the financial reporting process. [DTR 7.2.5R].

■   The information required to be included in the directors' report by paragraph 13(2)(c), (d), (f), (h) and (i) of Schedule 7 to the Large and Medium-sized Companies and Groups (Accounts and Reports) Regulations 2008, resulting from the EU Takeover Directive, where the issuer is subject to the requirements of that paragraph. [DTR 7.2.6R]. Whilst these disclosures now need to be made in both the corporate governance statement *and* the directors' report, the disclosure may continue to be given once and appropriate cross-reference made.

■   A description of the composition and operation of the company's administrative, management and supervisory bodies and their committees. [DTR 7.2.7R].

4.46   The FCA has indicated that compliance with provisions A.1.1, A.1.2, B.2.4, D.2.1 and C.3.8 (was C.3.3) of the Code will ensure compliance with DTR 7.2.7R. See the summary table of overlapping provisions in paragraph 4.50 for more details.

4.47   Over and above the recommendations of the Code, there is a requirement in DTR 7.2.5R for a *description* of the main features of the company's internal control and risk management systems *in relation to the financial reporting process*. The FRC has indicated that, while this requirement in DTR 7.2.5R differs from the recommendation in Code provision C.2.1, the FRC envisages that both the Code and the DTR can be satisfied by a single internal control statement.

4.48   For a group, there is also a requirement to include a *description* of the main features of the group's internal control and risk management systems *in relation to the process for preparing consolidated financial statements*. [DTR 7.2.10R].

Table 4.1 – Description of internal control over financial reporting (DTR 7.2.5R)

Stagecoach plc – Annual Report and Financial Statements – 30 April 2012

Corporate governance report (extract)

5.13 Process for preparing consolidated financial statements

The Group has established internal control and risk management systems in relation to the process for preparing consolidated financial statements. The key features of these internal control and risk management systems are:

- The Risk Assurance function and management conducts various checks on internal financial controls periodically.

- Management regularly monitors and considers developments in accounting regulations and best practice in financial reporting, and where appropriate, reflects developments in the consolidated financial statements. Appropriate briefings and/or training are provided to key finance personnel on relevant developments in accounting and financial reporting. The Audit Committee is also kept appraised of such developments.

- A written certificate is provided annually by the management of each business unit confirming that the internal financial controls have been reviewed and highlighting any departures from the controls system that the Group has determined to be appropriate practice.

- The financial statements of each business unit are subject to review by a local finance manager prior to being submitted to the Group Finance function.

- The financial statements of each business unit are subject to review by the Group Finance function for unusual items, unexplained trends and completeness. Any unexplained items are referred back to local management to explain.

- The Group Finance function compares the financial statements of each business unit to the management accounts received during the year and obtains explanations for any material differences.

- The Group's consolidation, which consolidates the results of each business unit and makes appropriate adjustments, is subject to various levels of review by the Group Finance function.

- The draft consolidated financial statements are reviewed by an individual independent from those individuals who were responsible for preparing the financial statements. The review includes checking internal consistency, consistency with other statements, consistency with internal accounting records and arithmetical accuracy.

- The Audit Committee and the Board review the draft consolidated financial statements. The Audit Committee receives reports from management and the external auditors on significant judgements, changes in accounting policies, changes in accounting estimates and other pertinent matters relating to the consolidated financial statements.

- The financial statements of all material business units are subject to external audit.

Interaction between the DTR and the UK Corporate Governance Code

4.49 Although many of the DTR requirements overlap with provisions of the Code, the FRC has indicated that, where a company chooses to 'explain' rather than 'comply' with any of the overlapping provisions, it will need to ensure that it, nonetheless, meets the requirements in the DTR. It is possible to comply with Code provision C.2.1 but still be in breach of DTR 7.2.5R and, therefore, the Listing Rules. Conversely, if a smaller listed company has only one independent non-executive director on the audit committee, the company will need to explain a departure from Code provision C.3.1, but it will have complied with DTR 7.1.1R. In this case, non-compliance with the Code does not necessarily mean a breach of the DTR.

4.50 The table below shows the overlapping provisions between the DTR and the Code:

DTR	UK Corporate Governance Code
DTR 7.1.1R: Minimum requirements on composition of the audit committee or equivalent body.	Provision C.3.1: Recommended composition of the audit committee.
DTR 7.1.3R: Minimum functions of the audit committee or equivalent body.	Provision C.3.2: Recommended minimum terms of reference for the audit committee.
DTR 7.1.5R: Disclosure of composition and function of audit committee (or equivalent) in the annual report. DTR 7.1.7R states that compliance with Code provisions A.1.2, C.3.1, C.3.2 and C.3.8 (was C.3.3) will result in compliance with DTR 7.1.1R to DTR 7.1.5R.	Provision A.1.2: The annual report should identify members of the board and board committees. Provision C.3.1 and C.3.2: See above. Provision C.3.8: The annual report should describe the work of the audit committee (also see further recommendations in the FRC 'Guidance on audit committees').
DTR 7.2.5R: The corporate governance statement must include a description of the main features of the company's internal control and risk management systems in relation to the financial reporting process. While this requirement differs from the Code requirement, it is envisaged that both could be met by a single internal control statement.	Provision C.2.3 (was C.2.1): The Board must monitor the company's risk management and internal control systems and annually report on their review of the effectiveness of the risk management and internal control systems. Further recommendations on the content of the internal control statement are set out in the FRC 'Guidance on risk management, internal control and related financial and business reporting' (2014).
DTR 7.2.7R: The corporate governance statement must include a description of the composition and operation of the administrative, management and supervisory bodies and their committees. DTR 7.2.8G states that compliance with Code provisions A.1.1, A.1.2, B.2.1,C.3.8 (was C.3.3) and D.2.1 will result in compliance with DTR 7.2.7R.	This requirement overlaps with a number of different provisions of the Code: A.1.1: the annual report should include a statement of how the board operates. A.1.2: the annual report should identify members of the board and board committees. B.2.4: the annual report should describe the work of the nomination committee. C.3.8: the annual report should describe the work of the audit committee. D.2.1: a description of the work of the remuneration committee should be made available. [Note: in order to comply with DTR 7.2.7R this information will need to be included in the corporate governance statement.]

Governance reporting

UK premium listed companies – Listing Rules – two-part statement

4.51   A premium listed company is required to include in its annual report and accounts a two-part statement on corporate governance. The first part of the statement requires the company to explain how it has applied the main principles of the Code. This statement is to provide sufficient information to enable the company's shareholders to evaluate how the principles have been applied. [LR 9.8.6R(5)].

4.52   The second part of the statement is the 'comply-or-explain' report, which sets out whether or not the company has complied throughout the accounting period with the provisions set out in the Code. [LR 9.8.6R(6)].

Statement 1 – Applying the main principles of the Code

4.53   The main principles in the Code are included in the following table. These must all be applied by a listed company to comply with the 2014 Code. The supporting principles and specific Code provisions are discussed later in this chapter, and are designed to assist the preparer in addressing each of the main principles. The table below also shows the paragraph number where they are discussed in more detail in this chapter.

Section	Area	Main principle
A Leadership	A.1 The role of the board	Every company should be headed by an effective board which is collectively responsible for the long-term success of the company. (See para 4.92.)
	A.2 Division of responsibilities	There should be a clear division of responsibilities at the head of the company between the running of the board and the executive responsibility for the running of the company's business. No one individual should have unfettered powers of decision. (See para 4.92.)
	A.3 The chairman	The chairman is responsible for leadership of the board and ensuring its effectiveness on all aspects of its role. (See para 4.92.)
	A.4 Non-executive directors	As part of their role as members of a unitary board, non-executive directors should constructively challenge and help develop proposals on strategy. (See para 4.92.)
B Effectiveness	B.1 The composition of the board	The board and its committees should have the appropriate balance of skills, experience, independence and knowledge of the company to enable them to discharge their respective duties and responsibilities effectively. (See para 4.119.)
	B.2 Appointments to the board	There should be a formal, rigorous and transparent procedure for the appointment of new directors to the board. (See para 4.132.)
	B.3 Commitment	All directors should be able to allocate sufficient time to the company to discharge their responsibilities effectively. (See para 4.132.)
	B.4 Development	All directors should receive induction on joining the board and should regularly update and refresh their skills and knowledge. (See para 4.140.)
	B.5 Information and support	The board should be supplied in a timely manner with information in a form and of a quality appropriate to enable it to discharge its duties. (See para 4.92.)
	B.6 Evaluation	The board should undertake a formal and rigorous annual evaluation of its own performance and that of its committees and individual directors. (See para 4.109.)
	B.7 Re-election	All directors should be submitted for re-election at regular intervals, subject to continued satisfactory performance. (See para 4.104.)
C Accountability	C.1 Financial and business reporting	The board should present a fair, balanced and understandable assessment of the company's position and prospects. (See para 4.176.)
	C.2 Risk management and internal control	The board is responsible for determining the nature and extent of the principal risks it is willing to take in achieving its strategic objectives. The board should maintain sound risk management and internal control systems. (See para 4.189.)
	C.3 Audit committee and auditors	The board should establish formal and transparent arrangements for considering how they should apply the corporate reporting and risk management and internal control principles and for maintaining an appropriate relationship with the company's auditor. (See para 4.148.)
D Remuneration	D.1 The level and components of remuneration	Executive directors' remuneration should be designed to promote the long-term success of the company. Performance-related elements should be transparent, stretching and rigorously applied. (See para 4.231.)
	D.2 Procedure	There should be a formal and transparent procedure for developing policy on executive remuneration and for fixing the remuneration packages of individual directors. No director should be involved in deciding his or her own remuneration. (See para 4.231.)

E Relations with shareholders	E.1 Dialogue with shareholders	There should be a dialogue with shareholders based on the mutual understanding of objectives. The board as a whole has responsibility for ensuring that a satisfactory dialogue with shareholders takes place. (See para 4.237.)
	E.2 Constructive use of general meetings	The board should use the general meetings to communicate with investors and to encourage their participation. (See para 4.244.)

Statement 2 – compliance throughout the period

4.54 In the second part of the corporate governance statement required by the Listing Rules, premium listed companies have to report whether or not the company has complied throughout the accounting period with the provisions set out in the Code. Where a company has not complied with the Code provisions, or has only complied with some of these provisions, or (in the case of provisions whose requirements are of a continuing nature) has complied for only part of an accounting period, the compliance statement must identify the Code provisions with which the company has not complied, for what part of the period such non-compliance continued (where relevant) and give reasons for any non-compliance. [LR 9.8.6R(6)].

4.55 There is no requirement in the Code specifying where the statement of compliance should be located within the annual report. Such statements are commonly included within the corporate governance report, and increasingly within the chairman's introduction to the governance report.

4.56 For a company that complies with the provisions of the Code in their entirety, it is reasonable to assume that, in doing so, they have applied the main principles.

4.57 In support of the compliance statement, boards or audit committees may expect to see a paper that sets out how the company complies with each aspect of the Code, supported by relevant documentation. It is advisable for the board or audit committee to minute its approval of such a paper.

Statements of non-compliance with Code provisions

4.58 Any element of non-compliance with Code provisions for any part of the period must be identified, giving reasons. The specific aspect of the Code must be identified. This does not mean that the paragraph number in the Code must be used, although some companies might do so and this is generally helpful. It would not be adequate simply to list the paragraph numbers of the Code, because the reader would have to refer elsewhere to discover the significance of the statement.

4.59 In February 2012 the FRC issued a paper entitled 'What constitutes an explanation under 'comply-or-explain'?' in response to questions raised at that time by the European Commission about the operation of 'comply-or-explain', with the aim of ensuring that the explanations provided are as full as is necessary to meet shareholder expectations. The information in the introductory section of the Code on 'comply-or-explain' has been updated in the 2014 edition to state that: *"In providing an explanation, the company should aim to illustrate how its actual practices are consistent with the principle to which the particular provision relates, contribute to good governance and promote delivery of business objectives. It should set out the background, provide a clear rationale for the action it is taking, and describe any mitigating actions taken to address any additional risk and maintain conformity with the relevant principle. Where deviation from a particular provision is intended to be limited in time, the explanation should indicate when the company expects to conform with the provision".*

4.60 As discussed in paragraph 4.49 it is necessary to bear in mind that, where a company is explaining a departure from any of the Code's provisions that overlap with that disclosure requirement of the DTR, this departure from the Code may result in a breach of the DTR.

4.61 Strictly speaking, all instances of non-compliance for provisions of an ongoing nature should be included in the compliance statement required under Listing Rule 9.8.6(6), but we believe that it is adequate for them to be mentioned in the narrative statement under LR 9.8.6(5) provided that the non-compliance is clearly described and the governance report identifies those provisions that have still not been complied with at the end of the period.

4.61.1 In 2014 the European Commission issued a Recommendation on the quality of corporate governance reporting, which focused on the quality of 'comply-or- explain' explanations and is consistent with the FRC's earlier guidance. After a sometimes challenging history, 'comply-or-explain' appears now to be established at the centre of the European governance framework.

UK standard listed companies

4.62 UK standard listed companies are required to comply with both DTR 7.1, 'Audit Committees', and DTR 7.2, 'Corporate governance'. UK standard listed companies are not, however, required to report under the Code. See paragraph 4.30 onwards for details of the DTR requirements.

Overseas companies – standard and premium listed companies

4.63 As discussed above, from 6 April 2010, the Listing Rules were amended to reclassify listed entities from having either 'primary' or 'secondary' listings to 'premium' or 'standard'. One effect of the changes in the Listing regulations is that overseas companies, which did not previously have to comply with the Code, are now required under the Listing Rules to report against it if they have a premium listing.

4.64 Whilst only premium listed companies (both UK and overseas) are required to comply with the Code, all listed companies, whether standard or premium, are required to comply with the DTR requirements in respect of corporate governance statements (DTR 7.2).

4.65 Where a standard listed overseas company applies any corporate governance code, even on a voluntary basis, DTR 7.2.2R and 7.2.3R require it effectively to 'comply-or-explain' against that code. This could significantly increase the scope of its governance disclosures in some cases.

4.66 The FCA has not applied Listing Rule 9.8.6(3), which requires *"statements by the directors on (a) the appropriateness of adopting the going concern basis of accounting (containing the information set out in provision C.1.3 of the UK Corporate Governance Code); and (b) their assessment of the prospects of the company (containing the information set out in provision C.2.2 of the UK Corporate Governance Code)"* to overseas incorporated premium listed companies (and Listing Rule 9.8.6(3) does not apply to any standard listed company). However, any failure to provide a going concern or viability statement would need to be explained under Listing Rule 9.8.6(6) by an overseas premium listed company.

Companies with controlling shareholders

4.67 The FCA published Listing Rules (Listing Regime Enhancements) Instrument 2014 (FCA 2014/33) in May 2014, following its earlier Consultation Papers CP13/15 and CP12/25. The revised rules came into effect on 16 May 2014, subject to a number of transitional provisions. The most significant impact is on premium listed companies with 'controlling shareholders' (defined as shareholders who, individually or with any of their concert parties, exercise or control 30% or more of the votes able to be cast on all or substantially all matters at the company's general meeting).

4.68 FCA 2014/33 affects the corporate governance arrangements of premium listed companies with controlling shareholders in a number of ways. In particular:

- Companies have to enter into a relationship agreement with their controlling shareholder which includes undertakings that transactions and relationships will be conducted on an arm's length basis on normal commercial terms.

- The election of independent non-executive directors needs to be approved both by the shareholders as a whole and by the independent shareholders under a new dual voting structure. If this does not happen, a resolution for a second vote must be tabled between 90 and 120 days after the original vote; the second vote involves all the shareholders, and so the resolution is still likely to be passed, but not without a clear message having been sent to the market by the independent shareholders.

4.69 An earlier – very controversial – proposal to mandate a majority of independent non-executive directors on the board of a company with a controlling shareholder was dropped after CP12/25.

4.70 The transitional provisions in FCA 2014/33 allow six months for companies other than new applicants to comply with the relationship agreement rules, and until the next AGM to put in place dual voting for independent non-executive directors (or the AGM after next, where the meeting is due soon after the requirement becomes relevant to the company). There are also a number of specific disclosure requirements for annual reports in respect of compliance with the relationship agreement. See chapter 2 for more information.

Other aspects of reporting and compliance

Use of cross-references and 'incorporation by reference'

4.71   Where it is not a subsection of the directors' report, companies may 'incorporate by reference' the governance statement within the directors' report. In this situation, the mechanism used to link the two should be more formally worded than a simple cross-reference and should include a phrase such as *"the governance statement is incorporated by reference into"* or *"the governance statement forms part of"* the directors' report. Whether this mechanism would bring with it the safe harbour protections of section 463 of the Companies Act 2006 is a legal matter on which companies may wish to take advice.

4.72   Companies may also incorporate by reference into the governance statement parts of other components of the front end of the annual report. For instance, the risk management and internal control disclosures may be given in the strategic report, but certain parts may relate to the FRC 'Guidance on risk management, internal control and related financial and business reporting' and allow the company to comply with the related Code provision on internal control. These specific parts may be incorporated by reference into the governance statement.

Differences for smaller and FTSE 350 listed companies

4.73   The Code provides a small number of concessions specific to smaller listed companies (those below the FTSE 350 for all of the preceding year):

- The board, the audit committee and the remuneration committee should have at least two independent non-executive directors. [B.1.2, C.3.1, D.2.1].

- The company chairman may be a member of, but not chair, the audit committee so long as he or she was considered independent on appointment as chairman. This appointment would be in addition to the existing independent non-executive members of the committee. [C.3.1].

4.74   The 2010 Code also introduced two new provisions that apply only to FTSE 350 companies:

- Evaluation of the board of FTSE 350 companies should be externally facilitated at least every three years. A statement should be made available of whether an external facilitator has any other connection with the company. [Code B.6.2].

- All directors of FTSE 350 companies should be subject to annual election by shareholders. All other directors should be subject to election by shareholders at the first annual general meeting after their appointment, and to re-election thereafter at intervals of no more than three years. Non-executive directors who have served longer than nine years should be subject to annual re-election. The names of directors submitted for election or re-election should be accompanied by sufficient biographical details and any other relevant information to enable shareholders to take an informed decision on their election. [Code B.7.1].

4.75   In addition, the 2012 version of the Code introduced the requirement that FTSE 350 companies put the external audit contract out to tender at least every ten years. See paragraph 4.167 for further information on audit tendering.

Non-listed organisations and AIM

4.76   Where non-listed or AIM organisations choose voluntarily to report on compliance with the Code, we recommend that they report fully as though they were listed. We therefore generally advise against phrases such as: *"We comply with all aspects of the UK Corporate Governance Code relevant to the organisation"*.

4.76.1   In 2013, the Quoted Companies Alliance ('QCA'), which is a not-for-profit organisation that works with small and mid-size quoted companies in the UK, published its 'Corporate Governance Code for Small and Mid-Size Quoted Companies'; the QCA Code can be helpful to refer to when preparing to register on AIM, and it is a good reference point when applying the Code in any smaller quoted company environment.

4.77 Companies that are considering the possibility of a listing will need to consider establishing appropriate governance procedures well in advance of coming to the market. In particular, they should review and, if necessary, improve their systems of internal control. In seeking a listing, companies are expected to make a statement of 'support' for the principles of the relevant Code. It is also usual to describe the steps the company has taken to comply in the areas of non-executive directors, audit, remuneration and nomination committees (describing their composition and principal functions), even if they have only recently been appointed or established. The sponsors will also normally expect to see significant moves toward compliance in other areas. In their first period following listing, the UK Listing Authority has generally permitted new registrants to make a statement of compliance for the period from the date of listing only, rather than for the full accounting period. Nevertheless, it will be important to be well prepared, because certain procedures can take some time to implement.

4.78 Companies that are considering registering on AIM should also consider establishing appropriate governance procedures. AIM companies are not required to comply with the DTR or Code but may voluntarily elect to do so.

4.79 During 2014 the London Stock Exchange amended AIM Rule 26 to encourage AIM companies to provide more insight into their corporate governance arrangements. Rule 26 now requires companies to make available on their websites *"details of the corporate governance code that the AIM company has decided to apply, how the AIM company complies with that code, or if no code has been adopted this should be stated together with its current corporate governance arrangements"*. This is in addition to the existing Rule 26 requirement for the website to include a description of the responsibilities of the board and of any committees. AIM companies were required to update their website disclosures, if necessary, by 11 August 2014.

4.79.1 The effect of this might be that more AIM companies elect to follow a governance code and, if they do, they might also want to report against it in their annual reports rather than online only. While a number of AIM companies report in full against the UK Corporate Governance Code, this remains quite unusual and it is perhaps more likely that companies will look to report against the QCA Code.

Other codes and governance requirements

4.80 A number of other codes have been issued, often adapting the UK Corporate Governance Code or its predecessors for particular industries or situations. The Association of Investment Companies ('AIC') Code has been endorsed by the FRC for externally managed investment companies and includes an appendix with suggested text for a preamble to an investment company's corporate governance report when applying the AIC Code.

4.81 It is outside the scope of this chapter to deal with the specific and/or additional governance requirements that apply to particular industries or sectors, including financial services companies.

The UK Corporate Governance Code (2014)

Introduction

4.82 The 2014 edition of the Code applies to all premium listed companies for financial years beginning on or after 1 October 2014, including overseas companies.

4.83 The changes to the Code in 2014 implement the recommendations of the Sharman Inquiry into companies' going concern assessments, and seek to embed the management of risks to solvency and liquidity in the day-to-day processes of companies and boards.

4.84 The principal amendments in relation to risk, 'viability' and going concern are set out below:

- The directors should confirm in the annual report that they have carried out a robust assessment of the principal risks facing the company, including those that would threaten its business model, future performance, solvency or liquidity. The directors should describe those risks and explain how they are being managed or mitigated. [2014 Code C.2.1].

- Taking account of the company's current position and principal risks, the directors should explain in the annual report how they have assessed the prospects of the company, over what period they have done so and why they consider that period to be appropriate. The directors should state whether they have a reasonable expectation that the company will be able to continue in operation and meet its liabilities as they fall due over the period of their assessment, drawing attention to any qualifications or assumptions as necessary. [2014 Code C.2.2].

■ The board should monitor the company's risk management and internal control systems and, at least annually, carry out a review of their effectiveness, and report on that review in the annual report. The monitoring and review should cover all material controls, including financial, operational and compliance controls.[2014 Code C.2.3].

■ In annual and half-yearly financial statements, the directors should state whether they considered it appropriate to adopt the going concern basis of accounting in preparing them, and identify any material uncertainties to the company's ability to continue to do so over a period of at least twelve months from the date of approval of the financial statements. [2014 Code C.1.3].

4.84.1 As well as the matters discussed above there are a number of other areas of change in the 2014 Code. These are summarised briefly below:

■ Greater emphasis is placed on ensuring that remuneration policies are designed with the long-term success of the company in mind, and that the lead responsibility for doing so rests with the remuneration committee;

■ Companies are expected to have in place arrangements that will enable them to recover or withhold variable pay when appropriate to do so, and should consider appropriate vesting and holding periods for deferred elements of pay; and

■ Companies should explain when publishing AGM (and any other general meeting) results how they intend to engage with shareholders when a significant percentage of them have voted against any resolution (not only a resolution related to remuneration).

4.84.2 The remuneration-related changes largely bring the Code up to date with developments that have taken place in remuneration practice in recent years, many of which are reflected in the revised remuneration reporting regulations that came into force in 2013. The change relating to engaging with shareholders is intended only to have companies indicate that they believe that there was a significant vote against a resolution and how they will engage – not what they may or may not do in response. The FRC has provided no defined percentage threshold for 'significant', though the group of General Counsels of the FTSE 100 (GC100) has indicated that a 20% 'no' vote should be regarded as significant.

Overview of the contents of the UK Corporate Governance Code (2014)

4.85 The 2014 Code's structure is as follows:

■ Preamble covering: Governance and the Code; Preface; Comply-or-Explain.

■ The main principles of the Code.

■ Section A – Leadership.

■ Section B – Effectiveness.

■ Section C – Accountability.

■ Section D – Remuneration.

■ Section E – Relations with shareholders.

4.86 Sections A to E contain the main principles and provisions to be reported against in the two-part compliance statement required by the Listing Rules (discussed in para 4.53 onwards).

Schedules forming part of the UK Corporate Governance Code

4.87 Two schedules provide further information on Code provisions:

■ Schedule A – The design of performance-related remuneration for executive directors

■ Schedule B – Disclosure of corporate governance arrangements

4.88 Schedule B summarises the corporate governance requirements that generate specific disclosures, including the FCA Listing Rules and the Disclosure Rules and Transparency Rules. Schedule B also summarises the information that should be 'made available' (which may be met by placing it on the company's web site) and the information that should be set out to shareholders in AGM papers in relation to election/re-election of directors and appointment/re-appointment of an external auditor.

Structure of sections that follow

4.89 Key areas of governance covered by the Code are set out below. For each area, the following information is provided, where applicable:

■ The main and supporting principles.

■ Specific disclosure requirements.

■ Other related provisions that do not necessarily generate disclosures.

■ Trends in good practice disclosure. Such disclosures, while not mandatory, may help to avoid a 'box-ticking' approach to governance reporting.

■ Details of any other guidance that should be considered when dealing with the relevant area.

Disclosures required under DTR 7 are not included below, other than for comparative purposes against Code disclosures. See paragraph 4.30 onwards for details of these.

The board and its committees

Introduction

4.90 The Code's principles on leadership cover the role of the board, division of responsibilities, and the responsibilities of the chairman and non-executive directors.

4.91 One of the main topics of discussion in the corporate governance reviews during 2009/10 concerned the role and activity of the board and whether there was sufficient oversight from the non-executive directors. Questions were raised such as:

■ Was the board effective in its decision making?

■ Was sufficient attention paid to risk management?

■ What did the board spend their time discussing at their board meetings?

■ What role were the non-executive directors expected to fill and did they spend enough time getting to know the business?

Personal behaviours by directors underpin this area. The FRC, therefore, made structural changes at the time of the 2010 Code by splitting the previous section 'Directors' into two separate sections ('Leadership' and 'Effectiveness'), and revising the principles and provisions within them. This was to give more prominence to the factors that underpin an effective board.

Principles

4.92 The main principles that should be applied in relation to the board are as follows:

■ Every company should be headed by an effective board which is collectively responsible for the long-term success of the company. [Code Main principle A.1].

■ There should be a clear division of responsibilities at the head of the company between the running of the board and the executive responsibility for the running of the company's business. No one individual should have unfettered powers of decision. [Code Main principle A.2].

■ The chairman is responsible for leadership of the board and ensuring its effectiveness on all aspects of its role. [Code Main principle A.3].

■ As part of their role as members of a unitary board, non-executive directors should constructively challenge and help develop proposals on strategy. [Code Main principle A.4].

- The board should be supplied in a timely manner with information in a form and of a quality appropriate to enable it to discharge its duties. [Code Main principle B.5].

4.93 The supporting principles relevant to the board go on to explain that:

- The board's role is to provide entrepreneurial leadership of the company within a framework of prudent and effective controls that enables risk to be assessed and managed. The board should set the company's strategic aims, ensure that the necessary financial and human resources are in place for the company to meet its objectives and review management performance. The board should set the company's values and standards and ensure that its obligations to its shareholders and others are understood and met. [Code Supporting principle A.1].

- All directors must act in what they consider to be the company's best interests, consistent with their statutory duties. [Code Supporting principle A.1].

- The chairman is responsible for setting the board's agenda and ensuring that adequate time is available for discussion of all agenda items, in particular strategic issues. The chairman should also promote a culture of openness and debate by facilitating the effective contribution of non-executive directors in particular and ensuring constructive relations between executive and non-executive directors. [Code Supporting principle A.3].

- The chairman is responsible for ensuring that the directors receive accurate, timely and clear information. The chairman should ensure effective communication with shareholders. [Code Supporting principle A.3].

- Non-executive directors should scrutinise the management's performance in meeting agreed goals and objectives and monitor the reporting of performance. They should satisfy themselves on the integrity of financial information and that financial controls and systems of risk management are robust and defensible. They are responsible for determining appropriate levels of remuneration of executive directors and have a prime role in appointing and, where necessary, removing executive directors, and in succession planning. [Code Supporting principle A.4].

- The chairman is responsible for ensuring that the directors receive accurate, timely and clear information. Management has an obligation to provide such information, but directors should seek clarification or amplification where necessary. [Code Supporting principle B.5].

- Under the direction of the chairman, the company secretary's responsibilities include ensuring good information flows within the board and its committees and between senior management and non-executive directors, as well as facilitating induction and assisting with professional development as required. [Code Supporting principle B.5].

- The company secretary should be responsible for advising the board through the chairman on all governance matters. [Code Supporting principle B.5].

Disclosure requirements

4.94 Disclosures in relation to the board that are required within the annual report are as follows:

- A statement should be made about how the board operates, including a high-level statement of which types of decisions are to be taken by the board and which are to be delegated to management. [Code A.1.1].

- Code provision A.1.2 requires that the annual report should identify:
  - The chairman.
  - The deputy chairman (where applicable).
  - The chief executive.
  - The senior independent director.
  - The chairmen and members of each of the nomination, audit and remuneration committees.

  This provision also requires the annual report to set out the number of meetings of the board and each committee and individual attendance by directors.

4.95 There are a number of Code provisions that overlap with the requirements of the DTR, as noted in paragraph 4.50. The DTR confirm that, if a company provides the information specified by Code provisions A.1.1, A.1.2, B.2.4, C.3.1, C.3.2, C.3.8 (was C.3.3) and D.2.1, it will satisfy the relevant requirements of DTR 7.1.5R and 7.2.7R.

Other related provisions

4.96 The following provisions are not disclosure provisions. However, it is usually the case that compliance with these detailed provisions will mean that the main principle has been applied.

■ The board should meet sufficiently regularly to discharge its duties effectively. There should be a formal schedule of matters specifically reserved for its decision. [Code A.1.1].

■ The roles of chairman and chief executive should not be exercised by the same individual. The division of responsibilities between the chairman and chief executive should be clearly established, set out in writing and agreed by the board. [Code A.2.1].

■ The company should arrange appropriate insurance cover in respect of legal action against its directors. [Code A.1.3].

■ Where directors have concerns which cannot be resolved about the running of the company or a proposed action, they should ensure that their concerns are recorded in the board minutes. On resignation, a non-executive director should provide a written statement to the chairman, for circulation to the board, if they have any such concerns. [Code A.4.3].

■ The terms of reference of the nomination, audit and remuneration committees, including each committee's role and authority delegated to it by the board, should be made available. This can be met by making the information available on the company's website. [Code B.2.1, C.3.3, D.2.1].

■ All directors, especially non-executive directors, should have access to independent professional advice at the company's expense, where they judge it necessary to discharge their responsibilities as directors. Committees should be provided with sufficient resources to undertake their duties. [Code B.5.1].

■ All directors should have access to the advice and services of the company secretary, who is responsible to the board for ensuring that board procedures are complied with. Both the appointment and removal of the company secretary should be a matter for the board as a whole. [Code B.5.2].

Good practice disclosures

4.97 Current disclosures in this area tend to focus on the division of responsibilities between chairman and chief executive, with good practice examples showing clear explanations of the responsibilities of the respective roles, in a manner tailored to the circumstances of the business. The chairman/chief executive relationship is a vital aspect of the governance framework.

4.98 As the role of the chairman has been brought under a specific main principle, it would also be helpful for disclosures to highlight the chairman's pivotal role in defining the board's 'culture' and ensuring its effectiveness. The FRC is encouraging chairmen to report personally in their annual reports how the Code's principles relating to the board's role and effectiveness have been applied, so most companies now include at least a brief introduction to the governance report from the chairman and many have the chairman emphasise the company's key governance messages. A number have also taken up the suggestion to personalise committee reporting.

Table 4.2 – Personal reporting by the Chairman

Berendsen plc – Report and Accounts – 31 December 2011

Chairman's overview (extract)

What good governance means to Berendsen

At Berendsen, we do not view corporate governance as an isolated exercise in compliance but as a core and vital discipline that complements our desire continually to improve upon the long-term growth and success of the group on behalf of shareholders. Good governance is an evolving process and our aim is to consistently be at the forefront of corporate governance best practice in order to deliver effectively on the company's strategic objectives. During 2011 we were pleased that once again our focus on good governance was recognised with Berendsen being shortlisted for the Investor Relations Society 2011 Best Practice Awards for 'Best Communication of Governance and Risk in the Annual Report'. At Berendsen, we believe that effective governance is realised through leadership and collaboration resulting in consistently focused and sensible business decisions.

As Chairman, my primary responsibility is to ensure that the board has the right mix of skills, knowledge and experience so that it works effectively as a team, supporting management to formulate and execute the corporate strategy, whilst encouraging the nonexecutive directors to bring fresh perspectives to the table and, where appropriate, to hold management to account. In this way the Berendsen board comprises a team of experienced individuals with the complementary skills and talents to carry out their duties to the best of their abilities, which we hope engenders the trust and respect of all stakeholders.

New business line organisation structure

During 2011, the board has liaised with executive management to ensure that our governance systems are appropriate for our new business line structure which is effective from 1st January 2012. This has included updating the group's vision and values and the group's delegated authorities, ensuring that responsibility and accountability for all business areas are agreed and communicated and that the risk management systems and group's key policies and procedures have been reviewed and updated. The board has met the entire executive board three times during 2011 and has also received presentations, in August from Christian Ellegaard on Sales Effectiveness, in October from Chris Thrush (the newly appointed Group Director, Human Resources) on Management Development and Succession, and in December from Steve Finch on Procurement.

Board achievements during 2011

The key responsibilities of the Berendsen board are to set the strategy, monitor what management are doing, hold them accountable for performance against agreed targets and challenge their thinking to ensure that they remain focused on achieving our strategic aims and objectives.

2011 has been a very busy and exciting year for the group. The board has been committed to ensuring that the key recommendations from our 2010 strategic review are implemented and that we have the right incentive schemes to motivate (and arguably, as importantly, retain) key management. This involved an additional board meeting in March 2011 and liaison with our major shareholders in respect of changes to management shortterm incentive arrangements.

In order to gain a better understanding of our business strategy and also to meet local management, two board meetings were held outside the UK, in May in Norway and in September in Poland. This provided the board with an excellent insight into the challenges facing these businesses.

Board evaluation

We have recently completed our first external board evaluation, which was conducted by Dr Tracy Long of Boardroom Review. The findings were presented at our board meeting on 21st February 2012 and the key actions agreed by the board are detailed on page 55.

Shareholder engagement

As Chairman, I am responsible for ensuring that there is ongoing and effective communication between the board and its shareholders. During 2011, I have kept in contact with our major shareholders and in December arranged a dinner where all our major shareholders had the opportunity to meet the non-executive directors. Feedback received from shareholders was that this was a very useful event and we will arrange a similar dinner during the last quarter of 2012.

Appointment of new Chairman

As announced on 7th December 2011, I have decided to retire after this year's Annual General Meeting. Iain Ferguson has been appointed to replace me and I am sure he will be a worthy successor. I wish him every success in his new role.

Christopher Kemball
Chairman

4.99   Other good practice trends in this area include:

- Providing insight into the organisation's underlying culture and purpose, which underpins the governance arrangements.

- Explaining how appropriate board behaviours and dynamics are encouraged, acknowledging behavioural aspects of a successful board.

- Describing the actual activities undertaken by the board as well as matters reserved for it; this is a recurring feature of good practice reporting on governance – listing out the responsibilities of the board or its committees does not represent best practice in any area.

- Giving a breakdown of the time spent on particular parts of the board or committee's role – for example, strategy, performance, risk. This can be done using diagrams, and comparatives are also helpful.

Other guidance

4.100   The FRC 'Guidance on Board Effectiveness' aims to assist companies in applying the sections of the Code that deal with leadership and board effectiveness. As with the FRC's separate 'Guidance on audit committees', it *"is not intended to be prescriptive. It does not set out the 'right way' to apply the Code. Rather it is intended to stimulate boards' thinking on how they can carry out their role most effectively"*.

4.101   The 'Guidance on Board Effectiveness' focuses on board behaviours rather than process. It covers areas such as: the roles of the chairman, senior independent director, other directors and the company secretary; decision-making policies and processes; board composition and succession planning; and performance evaluation.

4.102   The Guidance explains that the board's role is to provide entrepreneurial leadership and it lists a number of behaviours that it should follow to be effective. These include:

■   Providing direction for management.

■   Demonstrating ethical leadership, displaying behaviours consistent with the culture and values it has defined for the organisation.

■   Creating a performance culture that drives value creation without exposing the company to excessive risk of value destruction.

■   Making well-informed and high-quality decisions based on a clear line of sight into the business.

■   Creating the right framework for helping directors meet their statutory responsibilities.

■   Being accountable, particularly to those that provide the company's capital.

■   Thinking carefully about governance arrangements and embracing evaluation of their effectiveness.

[Guidance on Board Effectiveness, FRC, March 2011].

4.103   The 'Guidance on Board Effectiveness' also discusses the chairman's role and suggests the role should include:

■   Demonstrating ethical leadership.

■   Setting a board agenda which is primarily focused on strategy, performance, value creation and accountability, and ensuring that issues relevant to these areas are reserved for board decision.

■   Making certain that the board determines the nature, and extent of the significant risks the company is willing to embrace in implementing its strategy, and that there are no 'no-go' areas that prevent directors from operating effective oversight in this area.

■   Regularly considering succession planning and the board's composition.

■   Developing productive working relationships with all executive directors, and the CEO in particular, providing support and advice while respecting executive responsibility.

■   Ensuring effective communication with shareholders and other stakeholders and, in particular, that all directors are made aware of the views of those who provide the company's capital.

[Guidance on Board Effectiveness, FRC, March 2011].

Re-election of directors

Principles

4.104   The main principle that should be applied in relation to the re-election of directors is as follows:

■   All directors should be submitted for re-election at regular intervals, subject to continued satisfactory performance. [Code Main principle B.7].

Disclosure requirements

4.105   None for the annual report, but see provisions B.7.1 and B.7.2 below.

Other related provisions

4.106   The following detailed provisions should be implemented:

■   All directors of FTSE 350 companies should be subject to annual election by shareholders. All other directors should be subject to election by shareholders at the first annual general meeting after their appointment, and to re-election thereafter at intervals of no more than three years. Non-executive directors who have served longer than nine years should be subject to annual re-election. [Code B.7.1].

- The board should set out to shareholders in the papers why they believe an individual should be elected as a non-executive director. When proposing re-election, the chairman should confirm to shareholders that, following formal performance evaluation, the individual's performance continues to be effective and to demonstrate commitment to the role. [Code B.7.2].

Other guidance

4.107   To enhance accountability to, and the influence of, shareholders the Walker review recommended the annual re-election of the board chairman and the re-election of the remuneration committee chair if the remuneration report fails to secure 75% support. In the 2010 Code the FRC extended these Walker recommendations by introducing a new provision requiring re-election for all directors of FTSE 350 companies on the basis that it is appropriate for shareholders to have an annual opportunity to express their views on the performance of all the directors. The FRC recognised the concern that smaller companies with a more concentrated shareholder base might be exposed to disagreements between their major shareholders and therefore limited the new provision to FTSE 350 companies. [Code B.7.1].

4.108   It is now very unusual for FTSE 350 companies not to comply with the annual re-election provision, and the instability that it was feared the new provision would cause has not happened.

Performance evaluation

Principles

4.109   The main principle that should be applied in relation to evaluation of the board is as follows:

- The board should undertake a formal and rigorous annual evaluation of its own performance and that of its committees and individual directors. [Code Main principle B.6].

4.110   The supporting principles set out that:

- Evaluation of the board should consider the balance of skills, experience, independence and knowledge of the company on the board, its diversity, including gender, how the board works together as a unit, and other factors relevant to its effectiveness. [Code Supporting principle B.6].

- Individual evaluation should aim to show whether each director continues to contribute effectively and to demonstrate commitment to the role (including commitment of time for board and committee meetings and any other duties). [Code Supporting principle B.6].

Disclosure requirements

4.111   Disclosures relevant to performance evaluation are as follows:

- The board should state in the annual report how performance evaluation of the board, its committees and its individual directors has been conducted. [Code B.6.1].

- Where an external facilitator has been used, they should be identified in the annual report and a statement made as to whether they have any other connection to the company. [Code B.6.2].

Other related provisions

4.112   The following related detailed provisions should be addressed:

- All FTSE 350 companies should engage an external party to evaluate the board's performance at least every three years. [Code B.6.2].

- The chairman should hold meetings with the non-executive directors without the executive directors present. The non-executive directors, led by the senior independent director, should be responsible for the chairman's performance evaluation, taking into account the views of executive directors. [Code A.4.2, B.6.3].

Good practice disclosures

4.113 Board evaluation disclosures are increasingly an area of focus for companies. Existing good practice includes:

- Giving details of the outcome of the evaluation and any follow up action proposed; although the Code provision relates only to *how* the evaluation was conducted, discussing the outcomes indicates commitment to improvement and transparency.

- Following up on progress against recommendations carried forward from previous years.

- Indicating what use the company makes, or plans to make in future, of externally facilitated performance reviews; where one has not been done in the year describe where the company is in the recommended three-year cycle.

- Giving some indication of how external facilitators are selected.

The 2012 Code added diversity as one of the criteria that the board evaluation should take into account. National Grid responded to this direction by using a diversity and inclusion 'lens' for their March 2013 evaluation.

The board evaluation is generally a good way of providing evidence for what might otherwise be simply assertions of good governance practice. In particular, the 'softer' aspects of board effectiveness can be assessed and reported on as part of the evaluation.

Table 4.3 – Board evaluation outcomes, actions and progress

GlaxoSmithKline plc – Annual Report – 31 December 2014

2014 External evaluation of the Board

The Board carries out an evaluation of its performance and that of its Committees every year and the evaluation is facilitated externally every third year. The 2014 evaluation was carried out by an independent external facilitator, Dr Tracy Long of Boardroom Review Limited, who has no other connection with the company.

The in-depth process involved Dr Long:

- conducting individual interviews with each of the current Directors (with the exception of Sir Philip Hampton and Urs Rohner who joined the Board on 1 January 2015), the Company Secretary and other key senior executives who regularly attend Board and Committee meetings;

- reviewing past papers and minutes;

- attending the Board and Committee meetings in September and October, which included the annual Board and CET strategy session; and

- compiling the output from the external evaluation into a report that contained her findings and recommendations.

She also held:

- individual feedback sessions with each Director;

- a session led by the SID with the Non-Executive Directors and the CEO without the Chairman present;

- a session with the Chairman only; and

- finally, a collective feedback session with the entire Board, during which her areas of principal focus and recommended action points were discussed in detail before they were formally considered and agreed by the Board at its December meeting.

Dr Long's report focused principally on the culture and environment of the Boardroom, together with the composition and tenure of the Board and succession planning arrangements.

The overall view of the Board's performance was positive and confirmed that the Board was effective at dealing with the challenges it faced. The quality of decision making and contribution of Board members was influenced by:

- the open culture and strong support for the Board's senior roles;

- a thoughtful and disciplined approach to the use and management of time, and

- improving risk, control and remuneration oversight.

Dr Long's report had noted that there was good engagement on issues and management interacted well with the Board and its Committees, responding positively to constructive challenge and enquiry. This was an aspect of Board dynamics that was considered to be outstanding compared to other Boards.

However, Dr Long's report stressed that it was a time of significant transition for the company and the Board. The context within which the Board operated was changing and the Board's modus operandi would need to evolve with it. Future challenges included the Board's ability to:

- anticipate changes to the external landscape;

- manage the transition from Sir Christopher to Sir Philip; and

- refresh the composition of the Board, including some of the most senior roles on the Board.

The agreed action points from Dr Long's report focused mainly on addressing these challenges and they are disclosed on page 81.

Extract page 81

Board performance action points for 2015

The main findings and agreed action points arising from the 2014 Board evaluation review, externally facilitated by Dr Tracy Long of Boardroom Review Limited, against which progress will be disclosed in GSK's 2015 Annual Report, are set out below:

Key findings	Agreed action points
The composition of the Board is due to change over the next two to three years which will require a carefully planned and thoughtfully executed refreshment programme.	The Chairman Designate, together with the Nominations Committee, will seek to enhance the governance processes relating to Board composition, tenure and size. They will review and seek to develop objective specifications and plans for all the Board's roles in alignment with our strategy, the external landscape, and the company's evolving circumstances.
The Directors have identified gaps in the Board's current composition relating to US pricing and healthcare, emerging markets and consumer healthcare knowledge.	Closing these knowledge and experience gaps will be considered as part of the process of recruitment of new Non-Executive Directors combined with the refreshment of designated specialist roles on the Board, such as medical and scientific expertise and the Senior Independent Director (SID).
Given the speed and complexity of the external landscape changes, and potential for surprises, highly experienced Non-Executive Directors are a crucial component of the Board's composition.	The critical skill sets of potential candidates, such as international markets and cultural experience, crisis and stakeholder management, will be considered and the composition choices of peer group Boards will be benchmarked.
The replacement of the current SID who is due to retire at the 2016 AGM is a priority issue.	The Chairman Designate is leading the search involving internal and external candidates for this role. A SID specification is being developed that balances the replacement of existing knowledge with the ability to work well with the Chairman Designate, conduct robust Board evaluations, interact well with shareholders and be able to commit the necessary time to the role.
Consideration should be given to reducing the size of the Board, if it is judged to have a strong enough composition and dynamic.	This aspiration will be considered against a refreshed Board competence/skills matrix that is being used as part of the Board refreshment programme, and is linked to the company's strategy.
Consideration should be given to enhancing the Non-Executive Director evaluation process. The Chairman Designate will lead this process and consider best practice techniques, such as a combination of annual individual and peer evaluations.	

[The next paragraph is 4.115.]

Other guidance

4.115 The updated FRC 'Guidance on Board Effectiveness' issued in March 2011 includes guidance on evaluating the performance of the board and directors. The guidance includes a list of areas which may be considered as part of any internal or external evaluation process, including the mix of skills, experience, knowledge and diversity on the board. The list is not exhaustive, but aims to give guidance on the types of considerations to expect. The guidance also suggests that the outcome of the evaluation should be shared with the whole board and should be used to help design induction and development programmes. A 'review loop' may also be useful for the company to consider how effective the board evaluation process has been.

Forms of performance evaluation

4.116 The most common forms of board evaluation are paper questionnaires and interviews. An externally facilitated evaluation will generally involve one-to-one interviews with each member of the Board and, possibly, senior management or other third parties who interact with the Board. Interviews may be complemented by the completion of questionnaires or may be based around high-level questions. An internal board evaluation will most commonly involve the completion of a questionnaire or checklist, which will be facilitated by the chairman. However, in some cases, board evaluation is simply an informal discussion of the board's strengths and weaknesses and its achievements and shortcomings. Companies may also consider a similar approach for committee reviews.

4.117 A formal externally facilitated board evaluation will usually include one-to-one interviews, completion of questionnaires (with examples to support responses), desk-top review of board papers and constitution and observation of board and/or committee meetings. For individual director (and chairman) performance evaluation, peer evaluation questionnaires are often used which require individual directors to assess their performance and the performance of their peers on a number of different criteria.

Board balance and independence

Introduction

4.118 One focus of recent governance reviews has been the importance of having an appropriate balance of skills, experience, independence and knowledge amongst the directors. The FRC has made this the main principle to replace the former one on the balance of executive and non-executive directors to emphasise that the over-riding consideration for assessing board composition is that the board is fit for purpose rather than simply independence criteria.

Principles

4.119 The main principle that should be applied in relation to board balance and independence is as follows:

■ The board and its committees should have the appropriate balance of skills, experience, independence and knowledge of the company to enable them to discharge their respective duties and responsibilities effectively. [Code Main principle B.1].

4.120 The supporting principles relevant to board composition are:

■ The board should be of sufficient size that the requirements of the business can be met and that changes to the board's composition and that of its committees can be managed without undue disruption, and should not be so large as to be unwieldy. [Code Supporting principle B.1].

■ The board should include an appropriate combination of executive and non-executive directors (and, in particular, independent non-executive directors) such that no individual or small group of individuals can dominate the board's decision taking. [Code Supporting principle B.1].

■ The value of ensuring that committee membership is refreshed and that undue reliance is not placed on particular individuals should be taken into account in deciding chairmanship and membership of committees. [Code Supporting principle B.1].

■ No one other than the committee chairman and members is entitled to be present at a meeting of the nomination, audit or remuneration committee, but others may attend at the invitation of the committee. [Code Supporting principle B.1].

Disclosure requirements

4.121 Disclosures in relation to board balance and independence that are required within the annual report are:

■ The annual report should identify each non-executive director that the board considers to be independent. If the board considers a director to be independent, but circumstances or relationships exist that may appear relevant to that decision, disclosure should be made of the reasons for determining that director to be independent. [Code B.1.1].

Other related provisions

4.122 The following are the other detailed provisions related to the principles above:

■ Circumstances that could appear to affect a director's independence will include:

    ■ employment with the company or group within the last five years;

- a material business relationship within the last three years between the company and the director, or a body of which he/she is a partner, shareholder, director or senior employee;

- any entitlement to remuneration from the company other than a director's fee or participation in the company's share option or a performance-related pay scheme or membership of the company's pension scheme;

- close family ties between the director and any of the company's advisers, directors or senior employees;

- a cross-directorship or significant links with other directors through involvement in other companies or bodies;

- representing a significant shareholder; or

- more than nine years' service on the board from the date of their first election.

[Code B.1.1].

- At least half the board, excluding the chairman, should comprise independent non-executive directors. A smaller company (that is, a company below the FTSE 350 throughout the year immediately prior to the reporting year) should have at least two independent non-executive directors. [Code B.1.2].

- An independent non-executive director should be appointed by the board as the senior independent director. This director should provide a sounding board for the chairman and serve as an intermediary for the other directors. This director should also be available to shareholders if they have concerns that contact through the normal channels of chairman, chief executive or other executive director has failed to resolve or for which such contact is inappropriate. [Code A.4.1].

- A chief executive should not go on to be chairman of the same company. If exceptionally a board decides that a chief executive should become chairman, the board should consult major shareholders in advance and should set out its reasons to shareholders at the time of the appointment and in the next annual report. [Code A.3.1].

- The chairman should on appointment meet the independence criteria set out in B.1.1. [Code A.3.1].

- The board should establish both an audit committee and a remuneration committee of at least three, or in the case of smaller companies (that is, those below the FTSE 350 throughout the year immediately prior to the reporting year) two independent non-executive directors. [Code C.3.1, D.2.1].

- The company chairman may also be a member of, but not chair, the remuneration committee if he or she was considered independent on appointment as chairman. [Code D.2.1].

- For smaller companies, the company chairman may be a member of, but not chair, the audit committee if he or she was considered independent on appointment as chairman. This is in addition to the independent non-executive directors. [Code C.3.1].

4.123 Although the main principle is now wider than independence, provision B.1.2 still requires that at least half the board (excluding the chairman) should comprise independent non-executive directors. Thus a board that comprises a chairman, three executive directors and three independent non-executive directors would comply with this provision as at least half the board excluding the chairman (that is, three independent directors out of six directors) are independent.

4.124 This provision does not apply to smaller companies (defined as those companies categorised as falling outside of the FTSE 350 throughout the year immediately prior to the reporting year), which instead should have at least two independent non-executive directors. These recommendations can be difficult for smaller companies to comply with, given the practical difficulty of attracting and retaining high quality independent non-executives.

Good practice disclosures

4.125 The Companies Act 2006 introduced a duty to avoid a conflict of interest: a director must avoid any situation where he or she has a conflict, although such conflicts can be authorised by non-interested directors as long as there is authority in the company's Articles for this to happen. It is recommended that companies include a transparent disclosure in their corporate governance statement, confirming to shareholders that the conflicts authorisation procedures have been followed. [CA 06 Secs 171-177].

4.125.1 Other good practice disclosures in this area include:

- Clear information on the tenure of directors; diagrams including all the directors are helpful in understanding the balance of the board.

- A description of succession planning to ensure ongoing balance is appropriate.

- An indication of future plans for succession for non-executives serving more than nine years (which remains relevant despite the new provision for FTSE 350 directors to be subject to annual re-election), and also for those directors that have served between six and nine years (who are also subject to a particularly rigorous review of their commitment and performance under provision B.2.3).

- A description of the criteria used for independence judgements, not simply a conclusion that the director is independent.

Table 4.4 – Explanation of independence of non-executive directors

Ocado Group plc – Annual Report – 1 December 2013

Statement of Corporate Governance (extract)

Independence

Scrutiny by the Board

The Board has scrutinised the factors relevant to its determination of the independence of the Chairman, Sir Stuart Rose, and the Non-Executive Directors, Jörn Rausing and Robert Gorrie. The question of independence arises in connection with the Main Principle B.1 of the 2012 Code that a board should have "the appropriate balance of skills, experience, independence and knowledge of the company to enable them to discharge their respective duties and responsibilities effectively."

Sir Stuart Rose

Sir Stuart Rose's remuneration includes an initial one-off award of 452,284 Ocado shares. This award was approved by shareholders at the 2013 annual general meeting. The Board believes that Sir Stuart's remuneration aligns his interests with those of the Company and does not believe that the share award compromises his independence. Relevant considerations are that (i) the award of shares was conditional on Sir Stuart acquiring at least an equal number of shares at market value (Sir Stuart acquired 750,000 of the Company's ordinary shares on his own account); (ii) that any share award will not vest until after three years of service as Chairman, that is 10 May 2016, provided that, on that date, he remains a Director of the Company; and (iii) even then, that Sir Stuart will not be entitled to sell any shares awarded to him until a year after he eventually leaves the Board. The Board does not consider the share award to be equivalent to participation in the Company's share option or performance-related pay scheme, since there are no performance conditions attached to the receipt of the shares (only continued service). There is also no possibility of any conflict arising between the terms for receipt of these shares and determination of the achievement or otherwise of any performance related scheme for the Executive Directors and senior management.

Accordingly, Sir Stuart was considered independent on appointment to the Board and to the role of Chairman.

Jörn Rausing

Jörn Rausing is a beneficiary of the Apple II Trust, a material (approximately 11%) shareholder of the Company. In addition he has been a Board Director for 11 years, although less than four of these have been in the era of the Company as a listed company.

As the Board concluded and reported in the 2012 annual report and accounts, his continued membership of the Board is considered to be beneficial to the Company and supports the principles of the 2012 Code. His significant business experience at Tetra Laval enhances the balance of skills and experience on the Board, and reinforces the long-term perspective of the Board's decision making.

The Board considers Jörn to be independent in character and judgement and does not believe that the size of the Apple II Trust's shareholding or the length of Jörn's tenure on the Board amounts to a relationship or circumstance which affects his judgement. Jörn is not a representative of the Apple II Trust, nor does the Apple II Trust have any contractual or other right to appoint a Director to the Board. While Jörn benefits from the shareholding of the Apple II Trust, this is no different from the position of each of the other Non-Executive Directors, all of whom benefit from their own respective shareholdings. Jörn remains a Director of the Company because the Board believes that is in the best interests of the Company.

Robert Gorrie

Robert Gorrie has been a Director of the Company for 14 years, but less than four of these have been in the era of the Company as a listed company. Robert chairs the Ocado Council, an employee representative forum that was set up to provide primarily hourly paid employees with direct access to the Board. He received an additional £11,000 annually for performing this role (2012: £8,000). Robert was previously employed in an executive role as the Logistics Director of the Company but more than five years ago, the period of time that the 2012 Code notes as relevant.

The Board does not consider the Ocado Council services to constitute a material business relationship with the Company, nor this additional remuneration to be material in the context of impacting Robert's judgement. Moreover, the Board considers his role on the Ocado Council to be a positive asset in the promotion of good governance. It provides the Non-Executive Directors with a direct channel of communication to employees and enhances the system of checks and balances that underpins good corporate governance. The Board believes it increases their understanding of the business, increases the effectiveness of the Board and thereby reduces risk; it therefore augments the Company's compliance with the provisions of the 2012 Code. Robert's knowledge of the Company's complex IT and logistics operations assists the Board in its formulation of strategy, and also supports the Main Principle B.1. As with Jörn Rausing, the Board does not believe that Robert's length of tenure on the Board affects his judgement.

Other guidance

4.126 The corporate governance reviews following the financial crisis questioned the role and activity of the board and whether there was sufficient oversight from the non-executive directors. The FRC, therefore, aimed in the 2010 version of the Code to emphasise the responsibility of non-executives and encourage appropriate behaviours by bringing the existing material on the role of the non-executives from supporting principle A.1 of the Combined Code (2008) under a new main principle A.4 stating that non-executives should constructively challenge and help develop proposals on strategy. In addition, the FRC adopted the Walker recommendation to expand the role of the Senior Independent Director (SID) to provide a sounding board for the chairman and serve as intermediary for other directors.

4.127 The recommendation that a senior independent non-executive director should be identified in the annual report provides an additional route for concerns to be conveyed to the board and/or an early warning system.

4.128 FRC guidance on the role of the non-executive director is included in the FRC's 'Guidance on Board Effectiveness' issued in March 2011. The non-executive director should:

■ Devote sufficient time to any induction process as well as ongoing development and refreshing of his/her knowledge.

■ Make sufficient time available to be able to discharge his/her responsibilities.

■ Uphold standards of integrity and probity, and assist the chairman and executive directors in instilling the appropriate culture, values and behaviours in the board room and beyond.

■ Insist on receiving high quality information sufficiently in advance of board meetings, to enable thorough consideration of the issues.

■ Take into account the views of shareholders and other stakeholders.

[Guidance on Board Effectiveness, FRC, March 2011].

4.129 Good practice disclosures in connection with matters raised in the FRC guidance might include:

■ Personal statements or examples from non-executive directors to demonstrate commitment to good board behaviours and constructive challenge of the executives.

■ Clear explanation of why the senior independent director is suitable for the role including any explanations around independence.

Appointments to the board

Time commitment

4.130 One of the areas of focus in recent governance reviews was whether non-executive directors spend enough time to fulfil their role, and it is clearly important that they can make the necessary commitment prior to appointment. The Walker recommendations discussed minimum time commitments, suggesting 30 to 36 days for a non-executive director in a major bank and, for a chairman of a major bank, around two-thirds of his or her time. The FRC has steered away from stipulating a minimum time commitment for non-executive directors, but the theme of time commitment from previous supporting principle A.4 of the Combined Code (2008) was elevated to new main principle B.3 in the 2010 Code, emphasising the importance of this area.

Diversity

4.131 Under the 2010 Code, the FRC encouraged boards to avoid 'group think' by considering diversity when making board appointments. It also amended supporting principle B.2 by explicitly providing that due regard must be had to the benefits of diversity on the board, including gender, when searching for board candidates and making appointments.

4.131.1 In February 2011, Lord Davies published his initial report entitled 'Women on boards'. It suggested a voluntary, business-led approach consisting of ten specific recommendations to increase the representation of women on the boards of listed companies, with a target of 25% (for the FTSE 100 initially) by 2015. The five year summary report of the Davies Review, 'Improving the Gender Balance on British Boards', was published at the end of October 2015. The headlines of this report are that *"There are more women on FTSE 350 boards than ever before, with representation of women more than doubling since 2011 – now at 26.1% on FTSE 100 boards and 19.6% on FTSE 250 boards. We have also seen a dramatic reduction in the number of all-male boards. There were 152 in 2011. Today there are no all-male boards in the FTSE 100 and only 15 in the FTSE 250"*.

4.131.2   The report calls for the UK's voluntary approach to be continued (as opposed to compulsory measures from Europe or other regulators), with a new minimum target of 33% women on FTSE 350 boards within the next five years. It also calls for a focus on appointing women to chairman, senior independent director and executive roles and on developing the 'pipeline' within companies. It is further recommended that a new independent steering group be established, to come back with more detailed recommendations in 2016.

Principles

4.132   The main principles that should be applied in relation to appointments to the board are as follows:

- There should be a formal, rigorous and transparent procedure for the appointment of new directors to the board. [Code Main principle B.2].

- All directors should be able to allocate sufficient time to the company to discharge their responsibilities effectively. [Code Main principle B.3].

4.133   The supporting principles relevant to appointments to the board state that:

- The search for board candidates should be conducted, and appointments made, on merit, against objective criteria and with due regard for the benefits of diversity on the board, including gender. [Code Supporting principle B.2].

- The board should satisfy itself that plans are in place for orderly succession for appointments to the board and to senior management, so as to maintain an appropriate balance of skills and experience within the company and on the board and to ensure progressive refreshing of the board. [Code Supporting principle B.2].

Disclosure requirements

4.134   Disclosures should be made to the board of the chairman's other significant commitments before his/ her appointment and included in the annual report. Any changes to these should be reported to the board as they arise and their impact explained in the annual report. [Code B.3.1].

Other related provisions

4.135   The following detailed provisions should be addressed:

- There should be a nomination committee that should lead the process for board appointments and make recommendations to the board. [Code B.2.1].

- The nomination committee should have a majority of independent non-executive directors. The chairman or an independent non-executive director should chair the committee. The chairman should not chair the nomination committee when it is dealing with the appointment of a successor to the chairmanship. [Code B.2.1].

- Non-executive directors should be appointed for specified terms subject to re-election and to statutory provisions relating to the removal of a director. Any term beyond six years for a non-executive director should be subject to particularly rigorous review, and should take into account the need for progressive refreshing of the board. [Code B.2.3].

- The nomination committee should prepare a job specification for the appointment of a chairman, including an assessment of the time commitment expected, recognising the need for availability in the event of crises. [Code B.3.1].

- The terms and conditions of appointment of non-executive directors should be made available for inspection (at the company's registered office during business hours and at the AGM for 15 minutes before the meeting and during the meeting). This information may be made available on the company's website. [Code B.3.2].

■ Letters of appointment should set out the expected time commitment. Non-executive directors should undertake that they will have sufficient time to meet what is expected of them. Their other significant commitments should be disclosed to the board before appointment, and upon subsequent changes. [Code B.3.2].

■ The board should not agree to a full time executive director taking on more than one non-executive directorship in a FTSE 100 company nor the chairmanship of such a company. [Code B.3.3].

Good practice disclosures

4.136 Current good practice reporting in this area includes:

■ Explanation proportionate to the company's circumstances around the commitments of directors and the chairman; where there is a potential challenge, this should be dealt with transparently.

■ Appropriate insight on the subject of diversity; different aspects of diversity are particularly relevant for specific companies and age, nationality and other factors may be equally as important as gender. Companies often stress that their principal concern remains selecting the right candidate for the role.

Table 4.5 – Diversity disclosures

Johnson Matthey Plc – Annual Report and Accounts – 31 March 2012

Corporate governance report (extract)

Appointments to the Board and its Committees
The board, through the Nomination Committee, follows a formal, rigorous and transparent procedure for the selection and appointment of new directors to the board. The processes are similar for the appointment of executive and of non-executive directors.

The Nomination Committee leads the process for board appointments and makes recommendations to the board. Further information on the Nomination Committee and its work is set out in the Nomination Committee Report.

In considering board composition, the Nomination Committee assesses the range and balance of skills, experience, knowledge and independence on the board, identifies any gaps or issues, and considers any need to refresh the board. If it is determined in light of such evaluation that it is necessary to appoint a new non-executive director, the Committee prepares a description of the role and of the capabilities required for the appointment and sets objective selection criteria accordingly. In doing so it has regard for the benefits of diversity on the board, including gender diversity. This is discussed more fully under 'Boardroom Diversity' below.

The Committee considers any proposed recruitment in the context of the company's strategic priorities, plans and objectives as well as the prevailing business environment. The Committee also takes into account succession plans in place (and this is discussed further under 'Succession Planning' below). The Committee seeks prospective board members who can make positive contributions to the board and its committees, including the capability to challenge on such matters on strategy. This is balanced with the desire to maintain board cohesiveness.

The Committee uses external search consultancies to assist in the appointment process. Appointments are ultimately made on merit against the agreed selection criteria.

The board recognises the importance of developing internal talent for board appointments as well as recruiting externally. In this regard, the company has in place various mentoring arrangements and various types and levels of management development programmes.

The board also recognises the importance of recruiting non-executive directors with the necessary technical skills and knowledge relevant to the work of its committees and who have the potential to take over as committee chairmen.

Statement on Board Diversity
In response to the Davies Report, on 28th November 2011 the board published the following statement on board diversity. It is set out in the Investor Relations / Corporate Governance section of the company's website.

"The board of Johnson Matthey has followed the important debate around the recommendations of Lord Davies' review on Women on Boards and the question of boardroom diversity. We do not think quotas, for the proportion of women on the board or otherwise, are appropriate for a number of reasons. We believe all appointments should be made on merit rather than through positive discrimination. We are clear, however, that maintaining an appropriate balance around our board table through a diverse mix of skills, experience, knowledge and background is of paramount importance. Gender diversity is a significant element of this.

At present the board has one woman member in a board of nine. When we next make an appointment to the board, our brief to search consultants in the selection process as regards external candidates will be to review candidates from a variety of backgrounds and perspectives. The consultants will be asked to work to a specification which will include the strong desirability of producing a long-list of possible candidates which fully reflects the benefits of diversity, including gender diversity. Any appointment of an internal candidate, while similarly based on merit, will also take into account the benefits of diversity, including gender diversity.

Looking beyond the board to our wider workforce, we recognise the importance of diversity, including gender diversity, and the benefits this can bring to our organisation. With regard to gender diversity specifically, Johnson Matthey faces challenges similar to

---

those faced by other organisations in the chemical, technology and manufacturing sectors. To address these, we have policies and processes in place which are designed to support gender diversity in employee recruitment, development and promotion and we are committed to ensuring that women have an equal chance with men of developing their careers within our business. Finally, we encourage gender diversity at the early career stage by working outside Johnson Matthey to encourage women to enter scientific and industrial fields."

Gender Diversity Statistics

	Number	Proportion
The board	1 woman on the board as at the date of publication of this annual report	11% of board membership
Senior management	32 women out of 196 total as at 31st March 2012	16% of senior management
Graduate intake	–	30% of graduate intake
The group	2,205 women employees as at 31st March 2012	22% of group employees

The company has taken, and continues to take, several steps to promote diversity, including gender diversity, at senior management level and in the boardroom. The basis of these measures is in developing policies and processes that prevent bias in relation to recruitment and promotion, but the key to progress is in actively promoting diversity, ensuring that other positive measures are taken. These include requesting balanced shortlists when recruiting, looking at diversity mix in company events and conferences, actively discussing diversity in succession planning, promoting industrial and scientific careers to young women and developing family friendly and flexible employment policies. There are challenges to overcome, particularly in respect of gender diversity, given the sector within which the group operates but the group is making good progress.

Boardroom Diversity Policy
Following the publication of the Davies Report, in October 2011 the FRC confirmed its intention to include revisions in the next version of the amended Code to be published in 2012 in order to accommodate the Davies Report recommendation in respect of diversity policy. These revisions will require companies to include in the section of the annual report describing the work of the nomination committee a description of the board's policy on diversity, including gender, any measurable objectives that it has set for implementing the policy and progress on achieving the objectives. The changes will formally apply to companies with a financial year commencing on or after 1st October 2012, and so for Johnson Matthey's year ending 31st March 2014.

The board is in the process of reviewing the broad question of diversity within the group and is considering a policy for diversity.

Board Evaluation Process
The FRC also announced in October 2011 that a new supporting principle would be included in the Code to the effect that evaluation of the board should consider the balance of skills, experience, independence and knowledge of the company on the board, its diversity, including gender, how the board works together as a unit and other factors relevant to its effectiveness. Again, this change will be incorporated in an updated version of the Code to be published in 2012. The board is following this principle in its board and committee evaluation process which is underway as at the date of publication of this annual report. Further information is set out under '2011/12 Evaluation Process'.

Appointments to the Board
As described under 'Appointments to the Board and its Committees', the search for board candidates is conducted, and appointments made, on merit, against objective selection criteria having due regard for the benefits of diversity on the board, including gender. Further information on diversity in the context of board appointments is contained in the Nomination Committee Report.

Nomination Committee Report (extract)

Boardroom Diversity
The search for board candidates is conducted, and appointments made, on merit, against objective selection criteria having due regard, amongst other things, to the benefits of diversity on the board, including gender. Diversity is considered by the Nomination Committee on behalf of the board in considering board composition and in its process for making board appointments, including in setting selection criteria. This is referred to further in the board's statement on board diversity dated 28th November 2011 which is published in the Investor Relations / Corporate Governance section of the company's website and is set out in the Corporate Governance Report.

In respect of the proposed recruitment of a new non-executive director, at its meeting on 29th March 2012 the Committee considered a specification which set out certain essential characteristics for the role, while stating the desirability of diversity.

4.137 The Johnson Matthey extract above includes data on the number of directors, senior managers and employees by gender, addressing the requirements that applied for quoted companies from 30 September 2013 year ends in their strategic reports. Companies frequently keep the various diversity-related disclosures together, and cross-refer as necessary between parts of the annual report.

Other guidance

4.138   Directors might wish to refer to the guidance note issued in May 2011, 'ICSA guidance on joining the right board: due diligence for prospective directors', which gives questions that individuals should consider before taking up a board position.

4.138.1   The FRC issued a discussion paper in October 2015 canvassing the views of interested parties on 'UK Board Succession Planning'. This is based on preliminary work with directors and others and sets out a number of issues and questions under six headings: business strategy & culture; the nomination committee; board evaluation; the 'pipeline' (for executives and non-executives); diversity; and the role of institutional investors.

Induction, training and ongoing professional development

Introduction

4.139   Another point of focus of the 2009/10 governance reviews was the extent of the induction, training and ongoing professional development of non-executive directors. If the non-executive directors are expected to challenge constructively and question sensibly, they need to have sufficient knowledge and understanding of the business and its issues. The FRC therefore split a previous main principle into two main principles, 'Development' and 'Information and support', to recognise that they are two separate activities of an effective board. Within the development section the FRC also included:

■   A new provision that the chairman should regularly review and agree with each director their training and development needs.

■   A new supporting principle recognising the importance of directors acquiring appropriate knowledge of the company. This recognises that non-executive directors would be better able to provide constructive challenge if they spent more time in the operational parts of the business to gain a better understanding of its activities and challenges.

Principles

4.140   The main principle that should be applied is as follows:

■   All directors should receive induction on joining the board and should regularly update and refresh their skills and knowledge. [Code Main principle B.4].

The related supporting principles are:

■   The chairman should ensure that the directors continually update their skills and the knowledge and familiarity with the company required to fulfil their role both on the board and on board committees. The company should provide the necessary resources for developing and updating its directors' knowledge and capabilities. [Code Supporting principle B.4].

■   To function effectively, all directors need appropriate knowledge of the company and access to its operations and staff. [Code Supporting principle B.4].

4.141   The following detailed provisions should be addressed:

■   The chairman should ensure that new directors receive a full, formal and tailored induction on joining the board. As part of this, directors should avail themselves of opportunities to meet major shareholders. [Code B.4.1].

■   The chairman should regularly review and agree with each director their training and development needs. [Code B.4.2].

Good practice disclosures

4.142   Companies may wish to explain as part of good practice disclosures:

■   The specific arrangements for tailored induction and ongoing professional development for directors. Some companies provide a précis of the programme provided for specific directors.

■ Opportunities provided for non-executives to understand the business more fully. Examples of site visits or meetings with people around the business can bring this reporting to life.

■ How executive directors take on non-executive roles to enhance their experience and development.

Report of the nomination committee

Introduction

4.143 The nomination committee is responsible for board composition, new appointments and succession planning; it therefore fulfils a vital role in creating an effective board.

Disclosure requirements

4.144 A separate section of the annual report should describe the work of the nomination committee, including the process it has used in relation to board appointments; a description of the board's policy on diversity, including gender; any measurable objectives that it has set for implementing the policy; and progress on achieving the objectives. An explanation should be given if neither an external search consultancy nor open advertising has been used in the appointment of a chairman or a non-executive director. Where an external search consultancy has been used, it should be identified and a statement made as to whether it has any connection with the company. [Code B.2.4].

4.144.1 The above disclosure provision overlaps with the DTR and the guidance in DTR 7.2.8G confirms that, if a company provides the information specified by Code provision B.2.4 above, it will satisfy the requirements of DTR 7.2.7R in respect of this committee.

Other related provisions

4.145 The following are the relevant detailed provisions:

■ The nomination committee should lead the process for board appointments and make recommendations to the board. The majority of the committee should be independent non-executive directors. The chair of the nomination committee should be either the chairman or an independent non-executive director. The chairman should not chair the committee when dealing with the appointment of a successor to the chairmanship. [Code B.2.1].

■ The nomination committee should evaluate the balance of skills, independence, knowledge and experience on the board. In the light of this evaluation, the committee should prepare a description of the role and capabilities required for a particular appointment. [Code B.2.2].

Good practice disclosures

4.146 Current good practice disclosures and practices on nomination committees include:

■ The preparation of a skills and/or diversity matrix for the board, identifying where new appointments need to address gaps.

■ A description of the skills and experience criteria for new board appointments; these should also show due regard for diversity.

■ The setting up of a specialised nomination committee for key appointments, such as the chairman.

Audit committee and auditors

Introduction

4.147 The 2014 Code has retained the important changes introduced in the 2012 Code relating to audit committee reporting and the relationship between the company and its auditors.

Principles

4.148 The board should establish formal and transparent arrangements for considering how to apply the corporate reporting and risk management and internal control principles and for maintaining an appropriate relationship with the company's auditors. [Code Main principle C.3].

Disclosure requirements

4.149 Disclosures in relation to audit committees arising from both the Code and the FRC Guidance on Audit Committees ('ACG') are summarised below; the ACG is discussed further in paragraph 4.162 onwards. Some new disclosures are also required under the Competition and Markets Authority Final Order. These are also included below – see paragraph 4.150 onwards.

- A separate section in the annual report should describe the work of the committee in discharging its responsibilities. [ACG para 5.1; Code C.3.8].

- The audit committee section should include:

  - a summary of the role of the audit committee;

  - the names and qualifications of all members of the audit committee during the period;

  - the number of audit committee meetings;

  - the significant issues that the committee considered in relation to the financial statements and how these issues were addressed, having regard to matters communicated to it by the auditors;

  - an explanation of how the committee has assessed the effectiveness of the external audit process and the approach taken to the appointment or reappointment of the external auditor, and information on the length of tenure of the current audit firm, when a tender was last conducted, and any contractual obligations that acted to restrict the audit committee's choice of external auditors; and

  - if the external auditor provides non-audit services, how auditor objectivity and independence are safeguarded.

  [ACG para 5.2; Code C.3.8].

- The explanation of how auditor objectivity and independence are safeguarded should:

  - describe the work of the committee in discharging its responsibilities;

  - set out the audit committee's policy on the engagement of the external auditor to supply non-audit services in sufficient detail to describe each of the elements or cross-refer to where this information can be found on the company's website; and

  - set out or cross-refer to the fees paid to the auditor for audit services, audit-related services and other non-audit services; and if the auditor provides non-audit services other than audit-related services, explain for each significant engagement, or category of engagement, what the services are, why the audit committee concluded it was in the interests of the company to purchase them from the external auditor (rather than another supplier), and how auditor objectivity and independence have been safeguarded.

  [ACG para 4.46].

- Where requested by the board, the audit committee should provide advice on whether the annual report and accounts, taken as a whole, is fair, balanced and understandable and provides the information necessary for shareholders to assess the company's position and performance, business model and strategy. [Code C.3.4]. (Although this is not in itself a disclosure provision, it is likely to generate disclosures around what the committee did to advise the board. This was also encouraged by the FRC in its annual 'Developments in corporate governance and stewardship' publication at the start of 2015.)

- Where there is no internal audit function, the reasons for its absence should be explained. [ACG para 4.11; Code C.3.6].

- The audit committee should have primary responsibility for making a recommendation to the board on the appointment, reappointment and removal of the external auditors. FTSE 350 companies should put the external audit contract out to tender at least every ten years. If the board does not accept the audit committee's recommendation, the annual report should include a statement from the audit committee explaining its recommendation and the reasons why the board has taken a different position. [ACG para 4.20; Code C.3.7].

The above disclosure provisions overlap with the DTR and the guidance in DTR 7.1.7G confirms that, if a company provides the information specified by Code provisions A.1.2, C.3.1, C.3.2 and C.3.8 (was C.3.3) above, it will satisfy the requirements of DTR 7.1.1R to 7.1.5R in respect of this committee.

4.150   The Competition and Markets Authority's Final Order applies to periods beginning on or after 1 January 2015. For these periods, there are a number of additional disclosure requirements:

- Where a FTSE 350 Company has not completed a competitive tender process for auditor appointments in relation to five consecutive financial years, the audit committee must set out in the audit committee report relating to the fifth financial year in relation to which there has been no competitive tender process:

    - the financial year in which the company proposes that it will next complete a competitive tender process; and

    - the reasons as to why completing a competitive tender process in the financial year proposed is in the best interests of the company's members.

- The information specified above must also be supplied by the audit committee in each subsequent audit committee report until such time as the company completes a competitive tender process.

- Where the audit committee considers that the proposed financial year is no longer appropriate for the completion of a competitive tender process, it must provide reasons for the decision in the audit committee report published immediately subsequent to the making of the decision.

- A FTSE 350 Company must include a statement of compliance with the provisions of this order in the audit committee report (or elsewhere in the annual report in circumstances where an audit committee report is not issued) for each financial year.

[The Statutory Audit Services for Large Companies Market Investigation (Mandatory Use of Competitive Tender Processes and Audit Committee Responsibilities) Order 2014]

4.151   See paragraph 4.172 for details of procedures for audit committees to which the requirement in the final bullet above.

Other related provisions

4.152   The following detailed provisions and guidance are relevant to this area:

- The audit committee should consist of at least three or, in the case of smaller companies (that is, those below the FTSE 350 throughout the year immediately prior to the reporting year), two independent non-executive directors. (Note: the committee should not include other members in addition to independent non-executive directors, even where the minimum number of independent non-executive directors is met; independence is the key criterion for audit committee membership.)

    In smaller companies the company chairman may be a member of, but not chair, the committee in addition to the independent non-executive directors, provided he or she was considered independent on appointment as chairman.

    The board should satisfy itself that at least one member of the audit committee has recent and relevant financial experience. [Code C.3.1; ACG paras 2.1, 2.3]. See paragraph 4.154 for further discussion of 'recent and relevant' financial experience.

- The audit committee should have written terms of reference setting out its responsibilities that should include:

    - monitoring the integrity of the company's financial statements, and announcements relating to the company's financial performance and reviewing significant financial reporting judgements contained in them;

    - monitoring and reviewing the effectiveness of the company's internal audit function;

- making recommendations to the board relating to the appointment, re-appointment and removal of the external auditor and approving the remuneration and terms of engagement of the external auditor;

- reviewing and monitoring the external auditor's independence and objectivity and effectiveness of the audit process, taking into consideration relevant UK professional and regulatory developments;

- developing and implementing a policy on the engagement of the external auditor to supply non-audit services, taking into account relevant ethical guidance and reporting to the board, identifying matters where action or improvement is needed; and

- reporting to the board on how it has discharged its responsibilities.

[Code C.3.2; ACG para 2.2].

- The audit committee should monitor and review the effectiveness of the internal audit activities. Where there is no internal audit function, the audit committee should consider annually whether there is a need for one and make a recommendation to the board. [Code C.3.6; ACG para 4.11].

- The audit committee should review arrangements by which staff of the company may, in confidence, raise concerns about possible improprieties in matters of financial reporting or other matters. It should ensure the proportionate and independent investigation of such matters and follow-up action. [Code C.3.5].

Good practice disclosures

4.153   Current good practice reporting on audit committees may include:

- Specific examples of audit committee activities in the year and how these addressed developments in the business. The requirement to disclose 'significant issues' under provision C.3.8 relates to the work of the audit committee in respect of the key accounting judgements and estimates that arose in relation to the financial statements (see para 4.155 onwards); the other activities of the audit committee should also be addressed in the report.

- Details of the qualifications and experience of audit committee members to confirm their suitability and recent and relevant financial experience.

Provision C.3.1 – 'Recent and relevant' financial experience

4.154   Some companies feel that identifying one individual as having recent and relevant financial experience may increase that individual's exposure to liability and as a result choose not to identify one individual, but rather explain that audit committee members collectively have recent and relevant financial experience. If this is the case, it is a departure from the Code and requires an explanation. The FCA Rules also provide that at least one member of the audit committee (or the equivalent body) must have competence in accounting and/ or auditing (see para 4.37). The FRC's proposed changes to the Code for 2016 (see para 4.304 onwards) would replace the concept of 'recent and relevant financial experience with 'competence in accounting and/or auditing'.

Provision C.3.8 – 'Significant issues' reporting

4.155   What constitutes a 'significant issue' is a matter of judgement for audit committees. As noted above, we believe it will normally be an accounting judgement or estimate. Internal control issues may well be listed alongside these but are addressed by other Code provisions. On the face of it, any judgement or estimate that the auditor reports in their private report to the audit committee is likely to be a 'significant issue' for these purposes. Paragraph 7.3 of the ACG mentions only going concern as a specific example that should be included, but impairment reviews, revenue recognition on contracts, tax and provisioning in general are other likely topics.

4.156   Paragraph 5.4 of the ACG also suggests some exemptions from disclosure: the audit committee *"would not be expected to disclose information which, in its opinion, would be prejudicial to the interests of the company (for example, because it related to impending developments or matters in the course of negotiation)"*.

4.157 Much of the potential value in the audit committee's reporting on significant issues – and the extent to which the disclosures demonstrate the quality of the committee's stewardship – lies in the level of insight that is provided. Effective significant issues reporting clearly distinguishes the issue from how it was addressed and, within how it was addressed, describes both the process used and the actions or outcomes that resulted.

4.158 In October 2013 the FRC's Reporting Lab issued a project report on audit committee reporting which sets out the criteria that investors indicated to the Lab would be of interest in significant issues reporting by the audit committee. These included: context for the issue; what the audit committee did in relation to it; what the committee's conclusions were; and why it reached those conclusions. The Lab report also advocates cross-referencing to where other relevant information can be found within the annual report. The Lab issued a follow-up implementation study in May 2015 entitled 'Reporting of audit committees – how companies responded to investor needs identified by the Lab; experience of the first year', reiterating the criteria identified in 2013.

4.159 These disclosures will, no doubt, continue to develop over the next few years, but an extract from a current good practice example is set out below.

Table 4.6 – Significant issues reporting by the audit committee

BG Group – Annual Report and Accounts – 31 December 2013 (extract only)

KEY AREAS OF FOCUS
Set out in the table below is a summary of key matters considered by the Committee during 2013. Key issues covered by the Committee are reported the following day to the subsequent meeting of the Board, and the Board also receives copies of the minutes of each meeting.

Issue	Key considerations	The role of the Committee	Conclusion
Egypt	Throughout 2013, the Group continued to monitor the political and economic uncertainty in Egypt and the related risk of the recoverability of assets, including the position on domestic receivables and the diversion of gas to the domestic market.	The Committee, supported by the challenge of the external auditors, considered on an ongoing basis the continuing impact of the political and economic uncertainty and the volume of diversions to the domestic market and whether it remained appropriate to continue to record receivables from the Egyptian General Petroleum Corporation at full value and without provision or discounting during 2013.	In January 2014, the Group confirmed that it had elected to issue Force Majeure notices under its LNG agreements following higher than expected diversions to the domestic market during 2013. The position on domestic receivables marginally improved with the year-end balance reduced to $1.2bn and management continue to believe this is recoverable. The Committee will continue to provide robust challenge to management on their judgements in this regard.
Impairment indicators	The Group's procedures include performing a review of potential impairment triggers. During 2013, particular consideration was given to Egypt, the Lower 48 exploration and production assets, offshore Europe's Bream assets (following the agreement of sale in the second quarter) and certain other upstream assets.	The Committee reviewed and challenged assumptions made by management in their assessment of impairment indicators. They also sought assurances from EY that they concurred with assumptions underpinning management's judgement in each case and that all judgements had been undertaken in a timely and appropriate manner.	As part of the Group's fourth quarter and full-year results process, the Group revised its expectations of the value of its US shale gas investments and recorded a non-cash post-tax impairment of $1.1bn. A non-cash post-tax impairment of $1.3bn was realised in Egypt based on reserves revisions and revised expectations of the value of the Group's Egyptian operations.

4.160 There also needs to be an appropriate degree of consistency between the items designated as significant issues in the audit committee report, the critical accounting estimates and judgements note in the financial statements and the descriptions of audit risks, or areas of focus, that are set out in the new form of audit report for listed companies under ISA (UK&I) 700 (see para 4.257 onwards).

DTR overlap summary

4.161 Refer to paragraph 4.50 for an explanation of the overlapping provisions between the Code and the DTR requirements on audit committees.

FRC Guidance on Audit Committees 2012 ('ACG')

4.162 The ACG, originally published as the Smith guidance in 2003 and updated at the same time as the 2012 revision of the Code, is designed to assist company boards in making suitable arrangements for their audit committees and to assist directors serving on audit committees in carrying out their role. While this guidance does not form part of the Code, so that companies do not have to 'comply-or-explain' against it, it is intended to assist them when implementing the relevant provisions of the Code.

4.163 The most significant additional recommendations in the ACG relate to the external audit process:

■ *The provision of non-audit services by the external auditor* – paragraph 4.39 of the ACG states that the audit committee should set and apply a formal policy specifying the types of non-audit service (if any): for which the use of the external auditor is pre-approved (that is, approval has been given in advance as a matter of policy, rather than the specific approval of an engagement being sought before it is contracted); for which specific approval from the audit committee is required before they are contracted; and from which the external auditor is excluded.

■ As noted above, paragraph 4.46 of the ACG then recommends disclosure *"for each significant engagement, or category of engagement, what the services are, why the audit committee concluded it was in the interests of the company to purchase them from the external auditor (rather than another supplier) and how auditor objectivity and independence has been safeguarded"*. A simple cross-reference to the financial statement note that sets out the fees paid to the auditors rarely includes information of this kind.

■ The ratio of non-audit services to audit services is an area of focus for investor groups and proxy advisers so the quality of the explanation given here can help to influence their views where there might be a question around the ratio. Consistent with the APB Ethical Standards for auditors, most proxy advisers start to note the ratio when it exceeds 1:1 (auditors are required to consult with their Ethics Partner at this threshold too). Non-recurring work that creates a high ratio in any one year is generally not questioned seriously, but repeated breaches of the 1:1 ratio will eventually lead to negative comments. It should be noted that the classification of services between audit and non-audit by investors and proxy advisers does not necessarily correspond to the statutory disclosure requirements.

■ *Auditor appointment and tendering* – paragraph 4.22 of the ACG provides advice on how to carry out the annual assessment of the qualification, expertise and resources of the external auditors and the effectiveness of the audit process. For instance, it recommends that the assessment should *"include obtaining a report on the audit firm's own internal quality control procedures and consideration of audit firms' transparency reports, where available"*.

■ Paragraph 4.23 of the ACG recommends that companies should announce their intentions in advance of the commencement of a tender process, so that there is time to carry out an effective process and to allow shareholders to provide input.

4.164 *Assessing the effectiveness of the external audit process* – To supplement the ACG, the FRC issued a practice aid for audit committees on audit quality in May 2015, aiming to provide a framework to assist with assessing the quality of an audit more broadly and deeply than simply its efficiency. The practice aid presents an overview of audit quality, highlighting factors that audit committees could consider when making their assessment and steps they could take in doing so. It goes on to describe the possible inputs (sources of evidence) for the assessment, and the key professional judgments the auditor makes during the audit and how audit committees might assess them. The final section of the practice aid describes three further elements that audit committees can consider when evaluating the quality of their auditor: skills, character and knowledge; mindset and culture; and quality control. An appendix provides a number of examples of real-life procedures that committees might undertake to assess quality.

4.165 There is also specific additional guidance on audit engagement partner rotation and using the external auditor to undertake aspects of the internal audit function.

4.166 The rules around the provision of non-audit services by auditors of EU Public Interest Entities ('PIEs'), which will include most of those companies that apply the UK Corporate Governance Code, are due to change as a result of EU Regulation 537/2014 regarding the statutory audit of public interest entities. See paragraph 4.299 onwards for more details.

Audit tendering – timing

4.167 Code provision C.3.7 on tendering remains applicable. Companies of course also now need to take into account the requirements of the UK Competition and Markets Authority ('CMA') Orders and the EU Regulation and Directive on audit tendering and rotation. See paragraph 4.150 for details of the disclosure requirements that apply for periods beginning on or after 1 January 2015.

4.168 Both the FRC and CMA initially tied the timing of the first expected audit tender to the engagement partner rotation cycle. The following is an extract from the FRC's transitional arrangements published on its website:

> *"The FRC suggested that the timing of tenders might be aligned with both the cycle for rotating the audit engagement partner and the length of time since the audit contract was previously put out to tender. The FRC suggested that where a company has put the audit contract out to tender or changed audit firm in or after 2000, the tender process might be deferred until the latter stages of the incoming audit engagement partner's term (in other words, for a further five years). So, for example, under these suggested arrangements, if the current audit partner was due to complete their five year period in 2014 the company would carry out a tender in time for the successful audit firm (which could be the incumbent firm) to take up their appointment when that partner steps down. However if the company had carried out a tender or changed audit firm more recently than 2000, this could be deferred until the next partner rotation in 2019."*

4.169 These transitional arrangements are not binding, and they are not part of the Code itself. Following them does not therefore mean that a company is in line with the tendering provision unless it has had a tender within the last ten years. The FRC has indicated, however, that its principal concern is not immediate 'compliance' with the Code – in the initial stages, the emphasis should be on giving an indication of what the company's intention is.

4.170 Although the EU rules and the final version of the relevant CMA Order (see para 4.286) are not based around the engagement partner rotation cycle, many companies have adopted this approach, seeing the end of each five-year cycle as a natural point at which to reassess auditor appointment.

4.171 In its consultation on changes to the Code for 2016 the FRC has proposed to withdraw the tendering provision, but it remains in place for the 2015/16 reporting season.

Competition and Markets Authority – audit committee procedures

4.172 The Competition and Markets Authority Final Order includes a number of responsibilities for audit committees of FTSE 350 companies, including when an audit tender is carried out. These apply for periods beginning on or after 1 January 2015.

4.172.1 Only the audit committee, acting collectively or through its chairman, and for and on behalf of the board of directors, is permitted:

- to the extent permissible by law and regulations, to negotiate and agree the statutory audit fee and the scope of the statutory audit;
- to initiate and supervise a competitive tender process;
- to make recommendations to the board of directors as to the auditor appointment pursuant to the competitive tender process;
- to influence the appointment of the audit engagement partner; and
- to the extent permitted by law and regulations, to authorise an incumbent auditor or an auditor appointed to replace an incumbent auditor to provide any non-audit services to the company or the group of which that company is a part, prior to the commencement of those non-audit services.

[The Statutory Audit Services for Large Companies Market Investigation (Mandatory Use of Competitive Tender Processes and Audit Committee Responsibilities) Order 2014]

Narrative and financial reporting

4.173   The 2012 version of the Code formed part of a set of changes to reporting that also included revised narrative and remuneration reporting regulations (see chapters 2, 5 and 7). The changes covered a broad range of topics, but they all related to the 'stewardship' agenda that the FRC initiated through its 'Effective Company Stewardship' paper in 2011, and to the UK government's 'accountability' agenda. They represented a concerted attempt on the part of the FRC and the government to drive up the quality of corporate reporting, and at the centre of this was a formal confirmation by the directors that they consider the annual report, taken as a whole, to be fair, balanced and understandable. In making this formal statement, the directors confirm that narrative and remuneration reporting have been completed in a way that permits them to make this overall judgement.

4.174   The 2014 Code goes on to tackle the related issues of risk, going concern and the prospects for companies (or their 'viability'), implementing the recommendation of the Sharman Inquiry that a clearer distinction should be made between the 'accounting purpose' of the going concern concept and its broader 'stewardship purpose'. Key to the changes to the 2014 Code is the concept of embedding the management of risks to solvency and liquidity in the day-to-day processes of companies and boards.

4.175   These important changes to narrative reporting introduced by both the 2012 and 2014 Codes are considered in turn below.

2012 Code changes to narrative reporting – 'fair, balanced and understandable'

Principles

4.176   The main principle that should be applied in relation to financial reporting is as follows:

■   The board should present a fair, balanced and understandable assessment of the company's position and prospects. [Code Main principle C.1].

4.177   The supporting principle relevant to financial reporting states that the board's responsibility to present a fair, balanced and understandable assessment extends to interim and other price-sensitive public reports and reports to regulators, as well as to information required to be presented by statutory requirements. The board should establish arrangements that will enable it to ensure that the information presented is fair, balanced and understandable. [Code Supporting principle C.1].

Disclosure requirements

4.178   Disclosures in relation to financial reporting that are required within the annual report are as follows:

■   The directors should explain in the annual report their responsibility for preparing the annual report and accounts, and state that they consider the annual report and accounts taken as a whole, is fair, balanced and understandable and provides the information necessary for shareholders to assess the company's performance, business model and strategy. There should be a statement by the auditors about their reporting responsibilities. [Code C.1.1]. In practice, most companies follow provision C.3.4 of the Code and request the audit committee to advise the board on the fair, balanced and understandable statement.

■   The directors should include in the annual report an explanation of the basis on which the company generates or preserves value over the longer term (the business model) and the strategy for delivering the objectives of the company. [Code C.1.2]. See chapter 3 for more information on business model reporting; this is now required to be part of the strategic report.

4.179   There has been much debate around the meaning of the terms 'fair, balanced and understandable', which are not defined in the Code. All three of the terms in fact pre-existed (the annual report had to be fair and balanced under the 2010 Code, and the management report has to be fair under the DTR), and the FRC has made it clear that the words do not have a technical definition beyond their dictionary meaning. The FRC has indicated, however, that consistency between the financial statements and the picture painted in the front half of the annual report is a key consideration, and that its programme of corporate reporting reviews will also focus on the balance between good and bad news in companies' narrative reporting. Ultimately, what is fair, balanced and understandable is also only really determinable on a case-by-case basis, and the annual report has to be taken as a whole to make the judgement. This is not something that can be easily covered by a checklist.

4.180 Another area of considerable debate has been the process needed to support the formal fair, balanced and understandable statement by the directors. Boards have largely reviewed the quality of their year-end and annual report preparation processes before making the statement. The extent of any required changes depends on the findings of this review. In most cases, the audit committee has been asked to make the initial high-level subjective judgement about the annual report. Where this is the case, companies may wish to update the terms of reference of the audit committee to include their role in advising the board and, equally, the terms of reference of any other committee that is involved may need to be reconsidered. Where there is one, a disclosure committee might have a role in ensuring that all matters that should be included in the report are indeed covered. However this, and other existing parts of the annual report preparation process (such as the verification of facts), should be seen as the foundation on top of which the audit committee adds its high-level subjective judgement, and not a substitute for that judgement.

4.181 It is outside the scope of this chapter to advise in detail on companies' internal reporting processes. Based on experience to date, however, there are two factors that most boards and/or audit committees should take into account:

- *Time* – Ensure that enough time is built into the year-end timetable for the audit committee to review the whole annual report and for any necessary amendments to be made. Many annual reports are written by a team of individuals and may not come together until relatively late in the process. With the tight timetables and the requirement to release market-sensitive information promptly after it becomes available this will usually in effect mean that the audit committee needs to be involved earlier in the process.

- *Information* – Consider what information the audit committee will need to allow it to carry out its work. Most audit committees receive papers from management in respect of the key areas of judgement in the financial statements; it might be appropriate to supplement these with a paper explaining why management believes that the report is fair, balanced and understandable and pointing out the areas that, in their view, the audit committee should focus on. The audit committee should, of course, also review the report as a whole.

4.182 In terms of disclosure, there are a number of particular areas of annual reports that are sometimes accused of lacking fairness or balance. These include:

- *The chief executive's and chairman's statements* – these may not in themselves present a balanced view of the company's performance and prospects, or of the industry and market as a whole. The fair, balanced and understandable criteria apply to the annual report taken as a whole, so there is room, within reason, for a positive stance.

- *Highlights* – carried over from the preliminary announcement, these are often just what they say – 'highlights' – and do not capture the overall position and prospects of the company.

- *Case studies and examples* - where these are used to illustrate activities or processes, they may relate to matters that are not of strategic importance and can over-emphasise immaterial matters. It may be that they are illustrating new developments which will by definition not yet be material; again, it is the overall impression made that is the point at issue.

- *Non-GAAP measures* – any non-GAAP measures used (such as 'EBITDA') should not be given undue prominence; they should be explained and reconciled to statutory GAAP measures and they should be used consistently throughout the annual report.

Clearly, none of these points is new, but the formal statement has raised the bar on any borderline cases in these areas.

4.183 Finally, it is important to consider also the second part of provision C.1.1, which requires the directors to confirm that the annual report *"provides the information necessary for shareholders to assess the company's performance, business model and strategy"*. This is, of course, closely related to the fair, balanced and understandable criteria, but it is also a more direct reminder to companies to think again about these specific aspects of their corporate reporting. In order for shareholders really to be able to assess the company's performance, business model and strategy, they need to be able to see the links between them – in other words, to follow the story through the annual report.

4.184 All in all, though the criteria set out in provision C.1.1 were not new, and many of the relevant processes may already have been in place, most companies needed to go through a new process to make sure that they could really support the directors' high-level statement and to be able to demonstrate that they had done so.

4.185 The Code does not specify where in the annual report the statement is to be given but provision C.1.1 is the source of the directors' responsibilities statement, so it appears reasonable to include it there. Companies have, however, also made the formal statement within the main directors' report and in the audit committee report. Wherever the statement is given, it is likely that the audit committee will report that it has provided its advice to the board, but it is all of the directors (and not just the audit committee) who make the statement. We would, therefore, recommend that it be included in the directors' responsibilities statement. The wording should mirror that of the Code provision.

2014 Code changes to narrative reporting – risk, going concern and the prospects for companies

Introduction

4.186 The 2014 Code requires the board to make four formal statements or reports in the area of risk, prospects and going concern. Two of these are new: the confirmation that the directors have carried out a 'robust assessment' of the principal risks; and the 'viability statement'. The other two are amended versions of existing statements: on going concern; and on the review of the effectiveness of the risk management and internal control systems. These statements and reports are considered in detail below.

4.187 There is a clear relationship between each of the statements – they are designed to form part of a coherent overall framework, and the robust assessment of risk and viability statement provisions effectively require each other to be considered.

4.188 Alongside the 2014 Code, the FRC issued its 'Guidance on risk management, internal control and related financial and business reporting' ('GRM') in September 2014, which revised, integrated and replaced the earlier 'Internal control: Revised guidance for directors on the combined code' (known as the Turnbull Guidance) and 'Going concern and liquidity risk: Guidance for directors of UK companies' (2009). As usual, FRC Guidance is not part of the Code and is not covered by the comply-or-explain reporting requirement, but the FRC does expect companies to apply the Guidance (in a way that is proportionate to their circumstances).

4.189 The main principle under which most of the 2014 Code changes sit is:

■   The board is responsible for determining the nature and extent of the principal risks it is willing to take in achieving its strategic objectives. The board should maintain sound risk management and internal control systems. [Code Main principle C.2].

Disclosure requirements

4.190 Disclosures concerning risk and prospects are as follows:

■   The directors should confirm in the annual report that they have carried out a robust assessment of the principal risks facing the company, including those that would threaten its business model, future performance, solvency or liquidity. The directors should describe those risks and explain how they are being managed or mitigated. [Code C.2.1].

■   The board should monitor the company's risk management and internal control systems and, at least annually, carry out a review of their effectiveness, and report on that review in the annual report. The monitoring and review should cover all material controls, including financial, operational and compliance controls. [Code C.2.3].

■   Taking account of the company's current position and principal risks, the directors should explain in the annual report how they have assessed the prospects of the company, over what period they have done so and why they consider that period to be appropriate. The directors should state whether they have a reasonable expectation that the company will be able to continue in operation and meet its liabilities as they fall due over the period of their assessment, drawing attention to any qualifications or assumption as necessary. [Code C.2.2].

4.191 In the following paragraphs, these provisions are discussed and linked to the relevant aspects of the FRC's accompanying Guidance (the 'GRM'), alongside our own commentary.

Robust assessment of principal risks, and their management or mitigation [Code C.2.1]

4.192 The robust assessment of risk statement is related to, but distinct from, the review of effectiveness of the systems of risk management and internal control required by Code provision C.2.3. The most obvious distinction is that the robust assessment is focused on the principal risks alone (those that relate most closely to the company's strategy, and particularly those that would threaten the business model, solvency or liquidity), whereas the review of effectiveness is across the whole risk and control framework. The two are, however, connected: part of the review of effectiveness is to see that the risk management and internal control systems would identify the correct principal risks.

4.193 As well as describing the principal risks, most companies today provide some high-level explanation of how the risks are being managed or mitigated. However, as a result of the new formal statement, the board is likely to want to assess whether the correct principal risks have been identified and disclosed clearly enough.

4.194 Risk assessment underpins the risk management process, so the robust assessment of how well it is being done should not be left to the end of the annual cycle.

4.195 The GRM confirms that the design of a robust assessment process to determine the principal risks and consider the implications for the company should be appropriate to the complexity, size and circumstances of the company and is a matter for judgement of the board, with the support of management. Circumstances may vary over time with changes in the business model, performance, strategy, operational processes and the stage of development the company has reached in its own business cycles, as well as with changes in the external environment. [GRM para 34].

4.196 The GRM encourages companies to include a description of the likelihood of a risk, an indication of the circumstances under which it might be most relevant to the company and its possible impacts. The descriptions of the principal risks and uncertainties should be sufficiently specific that a shareholder can understand why they are important to the company. [GRM para 50].

4.197 Where there are significant changes in the principal risks, such as a change in the likelihood or possible impact or the inclusion of new risks, then this should be highlighted and explained. [GRM para 50].

4.198 GRM paragraph 35 draws attention to the need to consider the impact if risks coincide (and the same would apply to other interrelationships). The combination of non-principal risks could potentially represent a single 'compound' principal risk.

4.199 A high-level explanation of how the principal risks and uncertainties are being managed or mitigated should also be included. [GRM para 50].

Monitoring and reviewing the effectiveness of the systems of risk management and internal control [Code C.2.3]

4.200 Provision C.2.3 requires the board to report on the annual review of effectiveness. Looking at the effectiveness of the ongoing monitoring would be part of the annual review, including an assessment of whether the monitoring has been sufficiently frequent.

4.201 Paragraph 43 of the GRM sets out a number of areas that boards should consider when carrying out the annual review of effectiveness. We therefore believe it would be reasonable to discuss each of these in the report on how the review was carried out:

- the company's willingness to take on risk (its 'risk appetite'), the desired culture within the company and whether this culture has been embedded;

- the operation of the risk management and internal control systems, covering the design, implementation, monitoring and review and identification of risks and determination of those which are principal to the company;

- the integration of risk management and internal controls with considerations of strategy and business model, and with business planning processes;

- the changes in the nature, likelihood and impact of principal risks, and the company's ability to respond to changes in its business and the external environment;

- the extent, frequency and quality of the communication of the results of management's monitoring to the board which enables it to build up a cumulative assessment of the state of control in the company and the effectiveness with which risk is being managed or mitigated;

- issues dealt with in reports reviewed by the board during the year, in particular the incidence of significant control failings or weaknesses that have been identified at any time during the period and the extent to which they have, or could have, resulted in unforeseen impact; and

- the effectiveness of the company's public reporting processes.

4.202 The GRM reiterates the importance of an integrated response within companies. Where strategy, risk, finance, treasury and others are separate functions, their work may need to be coordinated to achieve a unified and effective response to the Code.

4.203 GRM paragraph 43 restates the board's responsibility for determining the company's risk appetite (a requirement in place since the 2010 version of the Code). It also explicitly makes risks appetite part of the annual review of the effectiveness of the company's risk management system. To the extent that risk appetite is not sufficiently addressed, the board may need to report a significant failing or weakness in the risk management system.

4.204 GRM paragraph 43 also specifically refers to the broader 'culture' that the board wants to instil and how this drives the right behaviours throughout the organisation. This area has been under scrutiny for some time and it is one of the strongest themes of the 2014 Code. It is already a key focus for regulators in the financial services sector and the FRC has renewed its own focus on these matters with the publication of 'Corporate culture and the role of boards' in October 2015, inviting interested parties to contribute to four work-streams – one of the aims being to update the existing FRC 'Guidance on board effectiveness'.

4.205 GRM paragraph 57 carries forwards disclosures from the Turnbull Guidance. In its statement under C.2.3, the board should, as a minimum, acknowledge that it is responsible for those systems and for reviewing their effectiveness and disclose:

- that there is an on-going process for identifying, evaluating and managing the principal risks faced by the company;

- that the systems have been in place for the year under review and up to the date of approval of the annual reports and accounts;

- that they are regularly reviewed by the board; and

- the extent to which the systems accord with the guidance in the GRM.

4.205.1 GRM paragraph 58 states that *"the board should summarise the process it has applied in reviewing the effectiveness of the system of risk management and internal control"*, which is consistent with the previous Turnbull Guidance. Also consistent with Turnbull, the board should consider whether there are any 'significant failings or weaknesses' in the risk management or internal control systems. GRM paragraph 58 goes beyond Turnbull, however, by recommending that the board *"explain what actions have been or are being taken to remedy any significant failings or weaknesses"*. This will mean that such matters are identified in the annual report (which was not required under Turnbull), although paragraph 58 also allows for an exemption from disclosure for information which, in the opinion of the directors, would be prejudicial to its interests. No guidance is provided on determining what is 'significant' for these purposes – this will need to be a case-by-case judgement.

Assessment of prospects – the 'viability statement' [Code C.2.2]

4.206 The viability statement remains perhaps the most challenging and controversial aspect of the 2014 Code changes. Companies continue to consider matters such as what period is appropriate to choose for the assessment and statement (and also how this will compare with their peers), and how to factor the principal risks into the viability assessment, including the extent of any stress testing that should be undertaken. They also should weigh up the insight that should be provided in the annual report into the internal processes undertaken to support the board in making the formal statement, as much of the information used can be commercially sensitive.

4.207 The Code provision giving rise to the viability statement states that it needs to be made taking account of the company's current position and principal risks. Conducting a robust assessment of the principal risks is therefore a prerequisite for making the viability statement.

4.208 Except in rare circumstances, the period chosen should be significantly longer than 12 months from the approval of the financial statements. The length of the period should be determined, taking account of a number of factors, including without limitation: the board's stewardship responsibilities; previous statements they have made, especially in raising capital; the nature of the business and its stage of development; and its investment and planning periods. [GRM Appendix B para 3].

4.209 Having determined the period over which to assess the company's prospects, the directors need to state that they have a 'reasonable expectation' that the company will be able to continue in operation and meet its liabilities as they fall due over the period of their assessment. This implies the existence of relatively firm forecasts for a defined period, often – but not necessarily – between two and five years, which may be the most robust way of supporting the formal statement quantitatively.

4.210 'Reasonable expectation' does not mean certainty. It does mean that the assessment can be justified. The longer the period considered, the more the degree of certainty can be expected to reduce. [GRM Appendix B para 2].

4.211 It is possible that the period chosen for the viability statement will differ from that used for other purposes in the business. For example, many financing transactions involve the production for long-term plans and many industries will have operational plans that extend out for many years (such as energy, mining or insurance companies). Thus it is important to be able to explain how the viability statement is consistent with the other relevant indicators.

4.212 It is possible that the period could change from one year to the next, especially if a particular issue affects it (such as financing arrangements, or the end of a key license agreement).

4.213 The viability statement should be based on a robust assessment of those risks that would threaten the business model, future performance, solvency or liquidity of the company. [GRM Appendix B para 4]. In our view, such risks are not limited solely to those directly related to financing. Many other principal risks have the potential to affect viability indirectly.

4.214 In assessing the prospects of the company, the directors should include its resilience to the threats to its viability posed by risks in 'severe but plausible' scenarios. Such an assessment should include sufficient qualitative and quantitative analysis, and be as thorough as is judged necessary to make a soundly based statement. [GRM Appendix B para 4].

4.215 Regarding the qualitative aspect of the assessment, the Code requires an explanation of how the assessment has been made. This is likely to focus on the internal processes used, including for instance business and strategic planning, risk management and financial forecasting.

4.216 Stress and sensitivity analysis will often assist the directors in making their statement. These simulation techniques may help in assessing both the company's overall resilience to stress and its adaptability and the significance of particular variables to the projected outcome. [GRM Appendix B para 4].

4.217 The directors should consider the individual circumstances of the company in tailoring appropriate analysis best suited to its position and performance, business model, strategy and principal risks. These should be undertaken with an appropriate level of prudence, that is, weighting downside risks more heavily than upside opportunities. This may include analysis of reverse stress, starting from a presumption of failure and seeking to identify the circumstances in which this could occur. [GRM Appendix B para 5].

4.218 Any qualifications or assumptions disclosed in connection with the viability statement should be specific and clearly related to the company; it should not be necessary to adopt an approach such as that used in 'risk factor' disclosures by SEC registrants. In our view there will almost always be assumptions to disclose. We believe that in most cases assumptions will reflect matters that are already disclosed as 'principal risks'.

Other aspects of the FRC Guidance

4.219 As was the case under the Turnbull guidance, GRM paragraph 26 confirms that "it is the role of management to implement and take day-to-day responsibility for board policies on risk management and internal controls. But the board needs to satisfy itself that management has understood the risk, implemented and monitored appropriate policies and controls, and are providing the board with timely information so that it can discharge its own responsibilities."

4.220   The board should consider the breadth of the framework when deciding whether to delegate any of its responsibilities. For example, it may not be appropriate for every audit committee to be responsible for reviewing the effectiveness of risk management and internal control across all aspects of the business. The role of the risk committee (where one exists) also needs to be considered.

4.221   The Guidance also includes a reminder that the DTR require the following additional disclosures (see para 4.45):

■   The corporate governance statement must include a description of the main features of the company's internal control and risk management systems in relation to the financial reporting process. [DTR 7.2.5R].

■   Where the issuer is required to prepare a group directors' report, it should include a description of the main features of the group's internal control and risk management systems in relation to the process of preparing consolidated financial statements. [DTR 7.2.10R].

The DTR requirements differ from the Code; however, the FRC envisages that both could be met by a single internal control statement.

Going concern [Code C.1.3]

4.222   A going concern statement has been a separate requirement of the Listing Rules for UK companies for many years. This requirement remains in the Listing Rules and the 'viability statement' has been added alongside it. [LR 9.8.6R(3)]. See paragraph 4.66 for the position regarding overseas companies in this respect.

4.223   Alongside the changes discussed above, the nature of the going concern confirmation was also amended in the 2014 Code.

4.224   The 2014 Code states that *"in annual and half-yearly financial statements, the directors should state whether they considered it appropriate to adopt the going concern basis of accounting in preparing them, and identify any material uncertainties to the company's ability to continue to do so over a period of at least twelve months from the date of approval of the financial statements".* [Code C.1.3].

4.225   The going concern confirmation made by directors under the 2014 Code now mirrors precisely the relevant IFRS accounting standard. [IAS 1 paras 25-26]:

■   When preparing financial statements, management shall make an assessment of an entity's ability to continue as a going concern. An entity shall prepare financial statements on a going concern basis unless management either intends to liquidate the entity or to cease trading, or has no realistic alternative but to do so. When management is aware, in making its assessment, of material uncertainties related to events or conditions that may cast significant doubt upon the entity's ability to continue as a going concern, the entity shall disclose those uncertainties. When an entity does not prepare financial statements on a going concern basis, it shall disclose that fact, together with the basis on which it prepared the financial statements and the reason why the entity is not regarded as a going concern.

■   In assessing whether the going concern assumption is appropriate, management takes into account all available information about the future, which is at least, but is not limited to, twelve months from the end of the reporting period. The degree of consideration depends on the facts in each case. When an entity has a history of profitable operations and ready access to financial resources, the entity may reach a conclusion that the going concern basis of accounting is appropriate without detailed analysis. In other cases, management may need to consider a wide range of factors relating to current and expected profitability, debt repayment schedules and potential sources of replacement financing before it can satisfy itself that the going concern basis is appropriate

4.226   A going concern confirmation is required in half-year reports, but a viability statement is not. But, because the two will often arise from a single process, the difference between procedures supporting the half-year and annual report may only be in the reporting requirements.

4.227 The hurdle for departing from the going concern basis of accounting remains high because it is relatively uncommon to have no realistic alternative to liquidation or cessation of trading. However, companies must continue to disclose any material uncertainties. The GRM offers the following guidance on this: "*Events or conditions might result in the use of the going concern basis of accounting being inappropriate in future reporting periods. As part of their assessment, the directors should determine if there are any material uncertainties relating to events or conditions that might cast significant doubt upon the continuing use of the going concern basis of accounting in future periods. Uncertainties relating to such events or conditions should be considered material, and therefore disclosed, if their disclosure could reasonably be expected to affect the economic decisions of shareholders and other users of the financial statements. This is a matter of judgement. In making this judgement, the directors should consider the uncertainties arising from their assessment, both individually and in combination with others*". [FRC GRM Appendix A para 5].

4.228 In updating the 2009 Guidance on going concern, the FRC removed the suggested wording for the going concern statement, which included a reference to the company being able to continue in operational existence for the ' foreseeable future'. The 2014 Code only requires a period to be specified for the viability statement, and the provision on going concern is simply that it was appropriate to prepare the financial statements on a going concern basis, with any material uncertainties identified for a period of at least twelve months from the date of approval of the financial statements. We would not, therefore, advocate continuing to refer to an unspecified 'foreseeable future'.

4.229 If the directors conclude that the company is unlikely to continue in operational existence, a non-going concern basis will be required in preparing the financial statements and this will require disclosure. Directors will generally wish to take legal advice before making such a disclosure, in particular in relation to whether the directors may be liable for wrongful trading.

4.230 Further discussion of going concern accounting matters is included in chapter 4 of the Manual of accounting – IFRS for the UK.

Remuneration Committee

Principles

4.231 The main Code principles that should be applied in relation to remuneration are as follows:

■ Executive directors' remuneration should be designed to promote the long-term success of the company. Performance-related elements should be transparent, stretching and rigorously applied. [Code Main principle D.1].

■ There should be a formal and transparent procedure for developing policy on executive remuneration and for fixing the remuneration packages of individual directors. No director should be involved in deciding his or her own remuneration. [Code Main principle D.2].

4.232 The supporting principles relevant to remuneration are as follows:

■ The remuneration committee should judge where to position their company relative to other companies. But they should use such comparisons with caution, in view of the risk of an upward ratchet of remuneration levels with no corresponding improvement in corporate and individual performance, and should avoid paying more than is necessary. [Code Supporting principle D.1].

■ They should also be sensitive to pay and employment conditions elsewhere in the group, especially when determining annual salary increases. [Code Supporting principle D.1].

■ The remuneration committee should take care to recognise and manage conflicts of interest when receiving views from executive directors or senior management, or consulting the chief executive about its proposals. The remuneration committee should also be responsible for appointing any consultants in respect of executive director remuneration. [Code Supporting principle D.2].

■ The chairman of the board should ensure that the committee chairman maintains contact as required with its principal shareholders about remuneration. [Code Supporting principle D.2].

Disclosure requirements

4.233 Disclosures in relation to the remuneration committee that are required within the annual report are as follows:

■ The remuneration report should include a description where an executive director serves as a non-executive director elsewhere, whether or not the director will retain such earnings and, if so, what the remuneration is. [Code D.1.2].

■ The remuneration report should include a description of the work of the remuneration committee. Where remuneration consultants are appointed, they should be identified in the annual report and a statement made as to whether they have any other connection with the company. [Code D.2.1].

The second disclosure provision overlaps with the DTR and the guidance in DTR 7.2.8G confirms that, if a company provides the information specified by Code provision D.2.1 above, it will satisfy the relevant requirements of DTR 7.2.7R in respect of this committee as long as this information is given within the corporate governance statement itself.

The level and components of remuneration

4.234 The following detailed provisions in relation to the level and components of remuneration should be complied with, or explanations given:

■ In designing schemes of performance-related remuneration for executive directors, the remuneration committee should follow the provisions in Schedule A to the Code. Schemes should include provisions that would enable the company to recover sums paid or withhold the payment of any sum, and specify the circumstances in which it would be appropriate to do so. [Code D.1.1].

■ Levels of remuneration for non-executive directors should reflect the time commitment and responsibilities of the role. Remuneration for non-executive directors should not include share options or other performance-related elements. If, exceptionally, options are granted, shareholder approval should be sought in advance and any shares acquired by exercise of the options should be held until at least one year after the non-executive director leaves the board. Holding of share options could be relevant to determining a non-executive director's independence (as set out in provision B.1.1). [Code D.1.3].

■ The remuneration committee should carefully consider what compensation commitments (including pension contributions and all other elements) their directors' terms of appointment would entail in the event of early termination. The aim should be to avoid rewarding poor performance. They should take a robust line on reducing compensation to reflect departing directors' obligations to mitigate loss. [Code D.1.4].

■ Notice or contract periods should be set at one year or less. If it is necessary to offer longer notice or contract periods to new directors recruited from outside, such periods should reduce to one year or less after the initial period. [Code D.1.5].

Procedure

4.235 The Code includes specific provisions regarding the procedures relating to remuneration.

■ The remuneration committee should have delegated responsibility for setting remuneration for all executive directors and the chairman, including pension rights and any compensation payments. The committee should also recommend and monitor the level and structure of remuneration for senior management. The definition of 'senior management' for this purpose should be determined by the board, but should normally include the first layer of management below board level. [Code D.2.2].

■ The board itself or, where required by the Articles of Association, the shareholders should determine the remuneration of the non-executive directors within the limits set in the Articles of Association. Where permitted by the Articles, the board may however delegate this responsibility to a committee, which might include the chief executive. [Code D.2.3].

■ Shareholders should be invited specifically to approve all new long-term incentive schemes (as defined in the Listing Rules) and significant changes to existing schemes, save in the circumstances permitted by the Listing Rules. [Code D.2.4].

Good practice disclosure

4.236 The Code principles and best practice provisions concerning directors' remuneration are considered in more detail in chapter 5.

[The next paragraph is 4.238.]

Dialogue with shareholders

Principles

4.238 The main principle that should be applied by companies in relation to dialogue with institutional shareholders is as follows:

■ There should be a dialogue with shareholders based on the mutual understanding of objectives. The board as a whole has responsibility for ensuring that a satisfactory dialogue with shareholders takes place. [Code E.1].

4.239 The supporting principles relevant to this dialogue include the following:

■ Whilst recognising that most shareholder contact is with the chief executive and finance director, the chairman (and the senior independent director and other directors as appropriate) should maintain sufficient contact with major shareholders to understand their issues and concerns. [Code Supporting principle E.1].

■ The board should keep in touch with shareholder opinion in whatever ways are most practical and efficient. [Code Supporting principle E.1].

Disclosure requirements

4.240 Disclosures in relation to this dialogue that are required within the annual report are as follows:

■ Disclosure should be made of the steps that the board has taken to ensure that the members of the board, and in particular the non-executive directors, develop an understanding of the views of the major shareholders (for example through direct face-to-face contact, analysts' or brokers' briefings and surveys of shareholder opinion) about their company. [Code E.1.2].

Other related provisions

4.241 The following provisions are not disclosure provisions. However it is envisaged that compliance with these detailed provisions will mean that the main principle has been applied.

■ The chairman should ensure that the views of shareholders are communicated to the board as a whole. [Code E.1.1].

■ The chairman should discuss governance and strategy with major shareholders. Non-executive directors should be offered the opportunity to attend meetings with major shareholders and should expect to attend them if requested by major shareholders. The senior independent director should also attend sufficient meetings with a range of major shareholders to listen to their views. [Code E.1.1].

Good practice disclosure

4.242 Current good practice and transparent reporting in this area may include the following:

■ The use of an independent third party to assist the board in obtaining investor views; this demonstrates commitment and encourages openness.

■ Company-specific disclosure about two-way communication and the investor relations process.

- Recognition in practice and in the annual report of the importance of the whole investor base, including non-institutional investors, where applicable; diagrams breaking down the current investor base by size of holding, type organisation, geography and so on can be helpful to potential investors.

- Effective use of technology to enhance shareholder communications, such as reference to websites where investor relations information is held.

4.243 In the Preface to the 2014 Code, the FRC encourages companies *"to recognise the contribution made by other providers of capital and to confirm the board's interest in listening to the views of such providers insofar as these are relevant to the company's overall approach to governance"*. Some companies therefore report on their investor relations activities in respect of bondholders as well as shareholders.

Constructive use of general meetings

Principles

4.244 The main principle that should be applied in relation to constructive use of general meetings is as follows:

- The board should use general meetings to communicate with investors and to encourage their participation. [Code Main principle E.2].

Other related provisions

4.245 There are no disclosure provisions associated with constructive use of general meetings. However, the following detailed provisions should be implemented by the company:

- The chairman should arrange for the chairmen of the audit, remuneration and nomination committees to be available to answer questions at the AGM and for all directors to attend. [Code E.2.3].

- The company should propose a separate resolution on each substantially separate issue and should in particular propose a resolution at the AGM relating to the report and accounts. For each resolution, proxy appointment forms should provide shareholders with the option to direct their proxy to vote either for or against the resolution or to withhold their vote. The proxy form and any announcement of the results of a vote should make clear that a 'vote withheld' is not a vote in law and will not be counted in the calculation of the proportion of the votes for and against the resolution. [Code E.2.1].

- The company should ensure that all valid proxy appointments received for general meetings are properly recorded and counted. For each resolution, after a vote has been taken, except where taken on a poll, the company should ensure that the following information is given at the meeting and made available as soon as reasonably practicable on the company's website:

  - the number of shares in respect of which proxy appointments have been validly made; and

  - the number of votes (i) for, and (ii) against the resolution, and (iii) the number of shares in respect of which the vote was directed to be withheld.

  [Code E.2.2].

- When, in the opinion of the board, a significant proportion of votes have been cast against a resolution at any general meeting, the company should explain when announcing the results of voting what actions it intends to take to understand the reasons behind the vote result. [Code E.2.2].

- The company should arrange for the Notice of the AGM and related papers to be sent to shareholders at least 20 working days before the meeting. For other general meetings this should be at least 14 working days in advance. [Code E.2.4].

4.246 The AGM is the main formal opportunity for dialogue and communication between the company and its shareholders. From the company's point of view, the AGM provides a forum for the board to inform its shareholders about what the company does and how well it has performed during the year. For investors, it provides a forum to learn more about the business and ask questions of the directors, (particularly the chairmen of the audit, remuneration and nomination committees) and to use their votes responsibly.

4.246.1 The requirement to explain when announcing general meeting votes what actions a company intends to take to understand the reasons behind a 'significant vote against' a resolution was introduced in the

2014 Code. Companies have already started to provide these explanations in their RNS announcements. 'Significance' needs to be a matter of judgement, and no guidance on this is provided by the FRC. However, the GC100 group of FTSE 100 General Counsels has indicated a 20% threshold.

Good practice disclosure

4.247 Current good practice reporting in this area may explain that the company:

■ Ensures shareholders are aware of meeting protocol, such as by referring to a separate Notice of Meeting booklet.

■ Appoints an independent assessor to scrutinise the AGM to strengthen reporting and enhance transparency.

Other guidance

4.248 There are a number of proxy voting advisers active in the UK market; these organisations can have a significant effect on the outcome of company AGMs. In essence (among other services they may offer), proxy advisers advise their clients (who are largely institutional shareholders or asset managers) on the corporate governance matters that are voted on at companies' AGMs. As well as the (re)appointment of auditors, these matters include, for instance, the re-election of directors, variations of shareholder rights, and high-profile areas such as the approval of the remuneration report. Their recommendations and/or notes are contained in written reports that proxy advisers issue to their clients shortly before the AGM date.

4.249 Probably the three most high-profile proxy advisers in the UK market at the present time are: the Pensions and Investment Research Council ('PIRC'); the Institutional Shareholder Services ('ISS'), which in the UK uses the National Association of Pension Funds ('NAPF') corporate governance guidance; and the Institutional Voting Information Service ('IVIS'), which was previously under the auspices of the Association of British Insurers ('ABI') but has now merged with the Investment Management Association ('IMA') to become the Investment Association. Each of these has a different operating model as well as different 'policies' on the governance arrangements that they advocate for their clients' investee companies. PIRC has a largely campaigning purpose and generally takes a hard line on companies that do not comply with its policies, rarely taking into account 'comply-or-explain' explanations; it does not engage to any great extent with companies. The IVIS approach is designed to have its impact over time, consistent with the 'comply-or-explain' mechanism that underpins the UK corporate governance framework, and companies generally bring their arrangements into line with the market gradually in response to IVIS notes to shareholders (which may be familiar to readers as 'blue', 'amber' and 'red tops'). ISS takes a similar approach to IVIS, but they make specific voting recommendations. PIRC and ISS publish an annual set of guidelines or policies which companies should be aware of when preparing their governance reports.

4.250 The activities of the proxy advisers have come under some scrutiny in recent times, both in the UK and internationally, largely around a perceived lack of accountability on their part. A number of them are signatories to the FRC's Stewardship Code, however, and so there is some transparency around the activities of those organisations. There is no question that proxy advisers can play a useful role with their analyses of companies' governance arrangements, but the Stewardship Code is clear that investors should not follow their recommendations blindly.

Auditors' responsibilities for companies reporting against the UK Corporate Governance Code

Listing Rules requirement

4.251 The Listing Rules were amended with effect from 23 October 2015 to refer to the 2014 version of the Code, for periods ending on or after 30 September 2015.

4.252 The Listing Rules state that auditors should review companies' disclosures in relation to thirteen provisions of the UK Corporate Governance Code. This includes provision C.1.3, relating to going concern, and provision C.2.2, the viability statement, which are specifically required to be reported on by companies under Listing Rule 9.8.6R(3). The remaining eleven provisions covered by the auditors' review requirement are stated in Listing Rule 9.8.10R(2) and are set out below:

- The directors should explain in the annual report their responsibility for preparing the annual report and accounts, and state that they consider the annual report and accounts, taken as a whole, is fair, balanced and understandable and provides the information necessary for shareholders to assess the company's position and performance, business model and strategy. There should be a statement by the auditors about their reporting responsibilities. [Code C.1.1].

- The directors should confirm in the annual report that they have carried out a robust assessment of the principal risks facing the company, including those that would threaten its business model, future performance, solvency or liquidity. The directors should describe those risks and explain how they are being managed or mitigated. [Code C.2.1]. *New in the 2014 Code.*

- The board should monitor the company's risk management and internal control systems and, at least annually, carry out a review of their effectiveness, and report on that review in the annual report. The monitoring and review should cover all material controls, including financial, operational and compliance controls. [Code C.2.3]. *Amended in the 2014 Code.*

- The board should establish an audit committee of at least three, or in the case of smaller companies two, independent non-executive directors. In smaller companies the company chairman may be a member of, but not chair, the committee in addition to the independent non-executive directors, provided he or she was considered independent on appointment as chairman. The board should satisfy itself that at least one member of the audit committee has recent and relevant financial experience. [Code C.3.1].

- The main role and responsibilities of the audit committee should be set out in written terms of reference and should include:

  - To monitor the integrity of the company's financial statements and any formal announcements relating to the company's financial performance, reviewing significant financial reporting judgements contained in them.

  - To review the company's internal financial controls and, unless expressly addressed by a separate board risk committee composed of independent directors, or by the board itself, to review the company's internal control and risk management systems.

  - To monitor and review the effectiveness of the company's internal audit function.

  - To make recommendations to the board, for it to put to the shareholders for their approval in general meeting, in relation to the appointment, re-appointment and removal of the external auditor and to approve the remuneration and terms of engagement of the external auditor.

  - To review and monitor the external auditor's independence and objectivity and the effectiveness of the audit process, taking into consideration relevant UK professional and regulatory requirements.

  - To develop and implement policy on the engagement of the external auditor to supply non-audit services, taking into account relevant ethical guidance regarding the provision of non-audit services by the external audit firm.

  - To report to the board on how it has discharged its responsibilities.

  [Code C.3.2].

- The terms of reference of the audit committee, including its role and the authority delegated to it by the board, should be made available. A separate section of the annual report should describe the work of the committee in discharging those responsibilities. [Code C.3.3].

- Where requested by the board, the audit committee should provide advice on whether the annual report and accounts, taken as a whole, is fair, balanced and understandable and provides the information necessary for shareholders to assess the company's position and performance, business model and strategy. [Code C.3.4].

- The audit committee should review arrangements by which the company's staff may, in confidence, raise concerns about possible improprieties in matters of financial reporting or other matters. The audit committee's objective should be to ensure that arrangements are in place for the proportionate and independent investigation of such matters and for appropriate follow-up action. [Code C.3.5].

- The audit committee should monitor and review the effectiveness of the internal audit activities. Where there is no internal audit function, the audit committee should consider annually whether there is a need for an internal audit function and make a recommendation to the board, and the reasons for the absence of such a function should be explained in the relevant section of the annual report. [Code C.3.6].

- The audit committee should have primary responsibility for making a recommendation on the appointment, re-appointment and removal of the external auditors. If the board does not accept the audit committee's recommendation, it should include in the annual report, and in any papers recommending appointment or re-appointment, a statement from the audit committee explaining the recommendation and should set out reasons why the board has taken a different position. [Code C.3.7].

- A separate section of the annual report should describe the work of the committee in discharging its responsibilities. The report should include:

  - The significant issues that the committee considered in relation to the financial statements, and how these issues were addressed;

  - An explanation of how it assessed the effectiveness of the external audit process and the approach taken to the appointment or reappointment of the external auditor, and information on the length of tenure of the current audit firm and when a tender was last conducted; and

  - If the external auditor provides non-audit services, and explanation of how auditor objectivity and independence is safeguarded. [Code C.3.8].

APB guidance on auditors' review under the Listing Rules

4.253 Detailed guidance on how to perform the auditors' review in relation to companies' reporting under the Code was issued by the APB in Bulletin 2006/05, 'The Combined Code on corporate governance: requirements of auditors under the Listing Rules of the Financial Services Authority and the Irish Stock Exchange'. This sets out specific procedures to be followed in relation to each relevant provision other than the new and amended provisions of the 2014 Code and provision C.3.4. The auditors' responsibilities in respect of the directors' statement on going concern are also addressed in APB Bulletin 2009/04, 'Developments in corporate governance affecting the responsibilities of auditors of UK companies'. For the time being, audit firms will need to design their own procedures to meet the requirement to 'review' the new and amended provisions of the 2014 Code (that is, C.1.3, C.2.1, C.2.2, C.2.3 (and C.3.4)).

[The next paragraph is 4.257.]

Auditors' responsibilities under the revised ISA (UK&I) 700 in respect of companies that report against the UK Corporate Governance Code

4.257 In June 2013, the FRC revised ISA (UK&I) 700, 'The independent auditor's report on financial statements', to require auditors' reports to provide insight into key audit scope and planning judgements. The new requirements were effective for audits of financial statements for periods commencing on or after 1 October 2012 and apply for any company that reports against the UK Corporate Governance Code, whether on a mandatory or voluntary basis. This therefore includes not only companies that have a premium listing on the London Stock Exchange main market, but also AIM companies that report against the Code on a voluntary basis and, indeed, a number of other types of organisation that are required to report against the Code, or an FRC-endorsed annotated version of it such as the AIC Code (see para 4.80).

4.258 Specifically, audit reports are required to:

- describe the risks of material misstatement that had the greatest effect on the overall audit strategy; the allocation of resources in the audit; and directing the efforts of the engagement team;

- provide an explanation of how the auditor applied the concept of materiality in planning and performing the audit (including specifying the overall materiality level used by the auditor); and

- provide an overview of the scope of the audit, including an explanation of how the scope addressed the risks of material misstatement described above and was influenced by the auditor's application of materiality.

ISA (UK&I) 700 para 19A].

4.259 For the same companies, auditors now also report by exception if the fair, balanced and understandable statement made by the directors is inconsistent with their knowledge or if the audit committee's reporting of significant issues does not appropriately address matters communicated to the audit committee. [ISA (UK&I) 700 para 22A, 22B].

4.260 As a package, the requirements in paragraph 19A of ISA (UK&I) 700 represented a step-change in auditor reporting, and audit committees and auditors need to work together closely to deal with them. Audit reports were previously generic templates that contained little in the way of company-specific information other than relatively brief explanations of modifications or qualifications, or emphases of matter that referred the reader to the company's disclosures. The new requirements of ISA (UK&I) 700 move away from this model. There is therefore a risk that the new disclosures could highlight the gap that exists between some investors' expectations of the nature of an audit and the requirements of auditing standards. So, for instance, they may be surprised to see the level of materiality that has been used, or they may expect that auditors visit and carry out a full scope audit of every location every year. If this is likely to happen, companies should consider engaging with the relevant investors in advance of the first report under the new standard.

4.261 Although they add no new audit procedures, the reporting requirements of paragraphs 22A and 22B of ISA (UK&I) 700 create a very clear responsibility for auditors to consider the directors' fair, balanced and understandable statement and the audit committee's reporting of the significant issues that it considered in relation to the financial statements. Together with the formal statement by the directors, this has raised the bar on what is acceptable in terms of corporate reporting in general.

4.261.1 In September 2014 further amendments were made to ISA (UK&I) 700 to require auditors to report by exception *'whether they had anything material to add or draw attention to'* in relation to a number of the new and amended directors' disclosures under the 2014 UK Corporate Governance Code. This reporting is based only on the procedures carried out for the purposes of the audit of the financial statements and covers:

- The directors' confirmation in the annual report that they have carried out a robust assessment of the principal risks facing the entity, including those that would threaten its business model, future performance, solvency or liquidity.

- The disclosures in the annual report that describe those risks and explain how they are being managed or mitigated.

- The directors' statement in the financial statements about whether they considered it appropriate to adopt the going concern basis of accounting in preparing them, and their identification of any material uncertainties to the entity's ability to continue to do so over a period of at least twelve months from the date of approval of the financial statements.

- The director's explanation in the annual report as to how they have assessed the prospects of the entity, over what period they have done so and why they consider that period to be appropriate, and their statement as to whether they have a reasonable expectation that the entity will be able to continue in operation and meet its liabilities as they fall due over the period of their assessment, including any related disclosures drawing attention to any necessary qualifications or assumptions.

[ISA (UK&I) 700 para 22C].

Impact of DTR on the company and auditors' reporting on governance

4.262 As discussed in paragraph 4.40, the DTR require certain companies to present a corporate governance statement, which may be included as part of the directors' report. Alternatively, it can be separately issued to accompany the annual report or may be made available on the company's website, but with cross-references in the directors' report. Where the company publishes a separate corporate governance statement, there are specific requirements for the auditors under the Companies Act 2006, which were introduced by SI 2009/1581, 'The Companies Act 2006 (Accounts, Reports and Audit) Regulations 2009'. This SI amended Parts 15 and 16 of the Companies Act 2006 to deal with the approval, signing and filing of the corporate governance statement where companies choose to present such a statement separately, rather than including it in the directors' report, and includes additional duties for the auditors. The auditor is required to give an opinion on whether certain information in the corporate governance statement is consistent with the financial statements. Where the company chooses to present a separate corporate governance statement, the auditor has to give a separate opinion in the audit report.

Approval, signing and filing of separate corporate governance statement

4.263 Where the corporate governance statement is included as part of the directors' report it will be approved on behalf of the board and filed with the Registrar of Companies as part of the directors' report. For companies presenting a separate corporate governance statement, the SI is effectively putting into law the same provisions regarding approval, signing and filing that would apply if the corporate governance statement had been included within the directors' report.

4.264   Section 419A of the Companies Act 2006 (approval and signing of directors' report) requires that any separate corporate governance statement must be approved by the board of directors and signed on behalf of the board by a director or the company secretary.

4.265   Sections 446 and 447 of the Companies Act 2006 provide that the directors of a quoted or an unquoted company must deliver to the Registrar of Companies a copy of any separate corporate governance statement, in addition to the company's annual financial statements, the directors' remuneration report (for quoted companies only) and the directors' report. The separate corporate governance statement must state the name of the person who signed it on behalf of the board under section 419A and must be signed on behalf of the board by a director or the company secretary. They must also deliver a copy of the auditors' report on any separate corporate governance statement.

Auditors' report and auditors' duties on separate corporate governance statement

4.266   There are different requirements of auditors depending on which option a company exercises for the publication of its corporate governance statement, as explained below.

4.267   If the company reports under DTR 7.2.1R, so the corporate governance statement is included as part of the directors' report, the audit requirement is covered by section 496 of the Companies Act 2006. That is, the corporate governance statement is covered by the existing requirement for the auditors to state in their report on the company's annual financial statements whether, in their opinion, the information given in the directors' report for the financial year for which the financial statements are prepared is consistent with those accounts.

4.268   But, if the company reports under DTR 7.2.9R, so the corporate governance statement is not included within the directors' report, section 497A of the Companies Act 2006 provides that the auditors must state in their report whether, in their opinion, the information given in the corporate governance statement in compliance with rules 7.2.5 and 7.2.6 of the FCA's Disclosure Rules and Transparency Rules (Corporate Governance Rules) regarding internal control and risk management systems and certain disclosures on share capital structures is consistent with the annual financial statements for the year. For the other information in the corporate governance statement, auditors must check that the information has been included.

4.269   Finally, section 498A of the Companies Act 2006 (duties of auditor) provides that, where a company is required to prepare a corporate governance statement and has neither included such a statement as part of its directors' report nor prepared a separate corporate governance statement, the auditors must state that fact in their report.

4.270   The APB recommends that, prior to the release of the annual report, the auditors communicate and discuss with the directors the scope and factual findings of their review.

The UK Stewardship Code

4.271   The FRC published the first Stewardship Code for institutional investors in July 2010. The purpose of the Stewardship Code is to improve the quality of corporate governance through promoting better dialogue between shareholders and company boards, and more transparency about the way in which investors oversee the companies they own. A revised version of the Code was effective for periods beginning on or after 1 October 2012. The changes were limited in scope but included:

- Clarification of the respective responsibilities of asset managers and asset owners for stewardship, and for stewardship activities that they have chosen to outsource.

- Investors were to explain more clearly how they manage conflicts of interest, the circumstances in which they will take part in collective engagement, and the use that they make of proxy voting agencies.

- Asset managers were encouraged to have the processes that support their stewardship activities independently verified, to provide greater assurance to their clients (principle 7 of the revised Code says they 'should' do so).

The changes were designed to give companies and investors a better understanding of how signatories to the Code are exercising their stewardship responsibilities.

4.272 The Preface to the Stewardship Code has also been restructured to follow the pattern of the UK Corporate Governance Code.

[The next paragraph is 4.274.]

Who should apply the Code

4.274 The Code is addressed in the first instance to firms who manage assets on behalf of institutional shareholders such as pension funds, insurance companies, investment trusts and other collective investment vehicles. The FCA made it mandatory for all UK-authorised asset managers to produce a statement of commitment to the Stewardship Code or explain why it is not appropriate to their business model from 6 December 2010.

4.275 The responsibility for monitoring company performance does not rest with fund managers alone. The FRC, therefore, strongly encourages all institutional investors to publicly report if and how they have complied with the Code. Pension funds and other owners may not wish to become directly involved in engagement, but they can make a significant contribution by, for example, mandating their fund managers to do so on their behalf.

4.276 The guidance on Principle 6 of the Code (see para 4.279 onwards) states that institutional investors that outsource to proxy voting and other advisory services should disclose how they are used. The FRC encourages those service providers in turn to disclose how they carry out the wishes of their clients by applying the principles of the Code that are relevant to their activities.

4.277 The FRC also hopes that investors based outside the UK will commit to the Code. It is recognised that, in practice, local institutions usually take the lead in engagement.

'Comply-or-explain'

4.278 Like the UK Corporate Governance Code, the UK Stewardship Code is to be applied on a 'comply-or-explain' basis. This currently entails providing a statement on the institutional investor's website (or in another accessible form) that:

- describes how the signatory has applied each of the seven principles of the Code and discloses the specific information requested in the guidance to the principles; or

- if one or more of the principles have not been applied or the specific information requested in the guidance has not been disclosed, explains why the signatory has not complied with those elements of the Code.

Content of the UK Stewardship Code

4.279 The UK Stewardship Code is based on the Institutional Shareholders' Committee (ISC) Code and consists of the following seven principles and further guidance on each of them.

Institutional investors should:

1. Publicly disclose their policy on how they will discharge their stewardship responsibilities.

2. Have a robust policy on managing conflicts of interest in relation to stewardship and this policy should be publicly disclosed.

3. Monitor their investee companies.

4. Establish clear guidelines on when and how they will escalate their activities as a method of protecting and enhancing shareholder value.

5. Be willing to act collectively with other investors where appropriate.

6. Have a clear policy on voting and disclosure of voting activity.

7. Report periodically on their stewardship and voting activities.

4.280 The amendments made to the ISC Code to arrive at the UK Stewardship Code were intended to incorporate guidance to institutional investors previously contained in Section E of the 2008 Combined Code, and to align this Code with the guidance on engagement provided to companies in the new UK Corporate Governance Code. Specifically, the guidance on Principle 3 (on the monitoring of companies) was amended to encourage investors to:

- meet the chairman of investee companies, and other board members where appropriate, as part of their ongoing monitoring and not only when they have concerns;

- attend the General Meetings of companies in which they have a major holding, where appropriate and practicable; and

- consider carefully explanations given by investee companies for departure from the UK Corporate Governance Code, and advise the company where they do not accept its position.

Reporting to clients

4.281 Under the Stewardship Code, investment firms and other agents should report at least annually to their clients on how they have discharged their responsibilities. The Code also recommends that investors who sign up to it should obtain an independent audit opinion on their engagement and voting processes and that the existence of such assurance reports should be publicly disclosed. The most relevant existing reporting standard is the Audit and Assurance Faculty (AAF) 01/06 guidance, produced by the ICAEW.

Monitoring

4.282 The FRC maintains on its website a list of those institutions that have published a statement on their compliance or otherwise with the Stewardship Code. It is a priority for the FRC to see greater effectiveness being achieved in the implementation of the Stewardship Code. This is addressed at some length in the FRC's 'Developments in corporate governance and stewardship 2014' report, where it states that it will consider *"how we can increase our scrutiny of adherence to the Code in order to improve the quality of practice and reporting"*.

Ongoing and future corporate governance developments

Introduction

4.283 Over the past few years, the UK, and in particular the FRC, has moved first in a number of areas of 'governance' while international debates have still continued – the changes to audit committee and auditor reporting (see paras 4.148 and 4.257 onwards) and the addition of a provision on audit tendering to the UK Corporate Governance Code (see para 4.167 onwards) are examples of this, as is the focus on shareholder engagement in the UK Stewardship Code (see para 4.271 onwards). The FRC has continued to move forward on this basis, notably in the changes to going concern and risk reporting that are included in the 2014 revisions to the UK Corporate Governance Code, with the conscious aim of putting the UK at the forefront of governance and reporting.

4.284 At the end of October 2015 the FRC published its Strategy for 2016-19. This marks a change in the FRC's priorities going forward:

> *"The FRC's strategy for 2013/16 was driven by the lessons of the global financial crisis, in particular the need to improve the management and reporting of risk, encourage companies and investors to take a long-term perspective, and to enhance the quality of audit...*
>
> *The FRC believes that, those actions having been taken, there is a need for a change of emphasis. Our priority now is to help companies embed the requirements that have already been introduced to ensure that the intended benefits are secured. In doing so we will bring together companies, investors and the professions to raise the quality of reporting and governance."* [FRC Strategy 2016-19, Our mission and objectives, page 1].

4.285 However, 2015 and 2016 sit at the end of the 2013-16 strategic period, meaning that the process of responding to the *'lessons of the...financial crisis'* is still being completed, alongside initiatives that look toward the new priorities. A major part of the effort to complete the response to the financial crisis relates to the implementation of the EU Audit Regulation & Directive ('ARD') and the elements of the Competition and Markets Authority ('CMA') remedies that are within the FRC's remit. The FRC is working on these alongside the Department for Business Innovation and Skills, and a summary of the findings and requirements of the CMA and EU is set out below.

Competition Commission investigation into the FTSE 350 audit market

4.286   In October 2013 the CMA issued its final report on remedies to be applied in the FTSE 350 audit market. The CMA stipulated that:

- FTSE 350 companies must put their statutory audit engagement out to tender at least every ten years; this differs from the FRC provision on tendering, in that there is no 'comply-or-explain' option – a tender is mandatory.

- The FRC's Audit Quality Review (AQR) team should review every audit engagement in the FTSE 350 on average every five years. The audit committee should report to shareholders on the findings of any AQR report concluded on the company's audit engagement during the reporting period.

- The AQR team should review and report on the firms in its scope on an annual basis, where such firms conduct sufficient public interest entity (PIE) audits for this to be practicable.

- There will be a prohibition of 'Big-4-only' clauses in loan documentation (that is, clauses that limit a company's choice of auditor to a pre-selected list).

- A shareholders' vote will be introduced on whether the audit committee report in a company's annual report contains sufficient information.

- Measures will be put in place to strengthen the accountability of the external auditor to the audit committee and reduce the influence of management, including a stipulation that only the audit committee is permitted to negotiate and agree audit fees and the scope of audit work, initiate tender processes, make recommendations for appointment of auditors, and authorise the external audit firm to carry out non-audit services.

- The FRC should amend its articles of association, to include a secondary objective to have due regard to competition.

The CMA therefore amended its final decision to a ten-year mandatory tendering period, having originally proposed tenders every five years. It also decided against bringing in measures requiring: mandatory audit firm rotation; further constraints on audit firms providing non-audit services; joint audits; shareholder or FRC responsibility for auditor reappointment; or independently resourced risk and audit committees.

4.287   Each of the CMA's remedies is enacted into law via an Order, or structured as a Recommendation to another body. Orders are legally binding, whereas Recommendations are not. This means that the bodies to whom Recommendations have been made, including the FRC, must carefully consider the CMA's proposals, but have a degree of discretion over when, how and even whether the remedies are implemented. As an illustration of this, the FRC does not currently propose to implement the CMA's recommendation for a shareholders' vote will be introduced on the audit committee report section of the annual report.

4.288   The CMA Order confirms that FTSE 350 companies will need to go to tender at least every ten years. The CMA has amended its transitional arrangements to be, in essence, consistent with those of the EU (see para 4.292 onwards) rather than tied to engagement partner rotation in any way. So:

- For companies who have an auditor who has been in place for 20 years or more at 16 June 2014, the CMA's Order will make them tender in respect of the next auditor appointment after 17 June 2020.

- For companies who have an auditor who has been in place for 11 years or more, but fewer than 20 years at 16 June 2014, the CMA's Order will make them tender in respect of the next auditor appointment after 17 June 2023.

However, if companies have an auditor who has been place for fewer than 11 years, the Order will apply directly, with no transitional relief, for audit appointments made on or after 17 June 2016. This means that some companies in this category will be required to tender sooner than companies with a long incumbent auditor.

4.288.1 Another important distinction between the CMA and the EU requirements is that auditor tenure is counted regardless of whether the relevant company was in the FTSE 350 when the auditor was appointed. This can mean that a tender is required much sooner under the CMA transitional rules. It also means that a company entering the FTSE 350 may need to tender on an urgent basis.

4.289 The CMA Order applies for periods beginning on or after 1 January 2015 (subject to the transitional rules on the introduction of audit tendering discussed above). See paragraph 4.150 for details of the disclosure requirements that apply for the 2015 reporting season.

European Commission – audit reform

4.290 In November 2011 the Commission released proposals intended to reform the European Public Interest Entity (PIE) audit market, relationships with audit clients, and the scope of services provided by the audit firm. Debate on these stretched through to December 2013, but agreement was finally reached between the European institutions on the two main areas of contention:

- Audit firms will be required to rotate every ten years, with an extension of ten further years possible if a tender is held at the ten-year point (subject to Member State implementation, which the UK intends to adopt).

- A cap of 70% of the audit fee will be imposed on the provision of non-audit services (based on a three-year average at the group level), and there will be an extensive list of prohibited services, including tax compliance and many types of deal work (subject to local regulatory interpretation).

4.291 The final Audit Directive (2014/56/EU) and Regulation (537/2014) were published in the Official Journal of the EU in June 2014, making 16 June 2014 and 17 June 2016 the key dates for the transitional arrangements around which the EU requirements need to be implemented.

4.292 The transitional arrangements vary, depending on the length of the audit appointment at the date the new rules came into force (that is, 16 June 2014). If the auditor had been in place for 20 years or more at that date, the company cannot enter into or renew an audit engagement more than six years from that date (that is, 17 June 2020). If the auditor had been in place for between 11 and 20 years, the company cannot enter into or renew an audit engagement more than nine years from that date (that is, 17 June 2023). It should be noted that rotation does not have to have occurred by these dates in 2020 or 2023 – an audit in progress (to which the auditor was appointed prior to 17 June) can still be completed.

4.293 As with the CMA rules, if companies had an auditor who had been place for fewer than 11 years at 16 June 2014, there is no transitional relief and a tender (because the UK will take the Member State option to allow this rather than rotation) will be needed at the first ten year point. Companies with auditor tenure that exceeds 10 years between 16 June 2014 and 17 June 2016 should take further advice as to how the requirements should be applied.

4.294 It should be noted that the definition of a PIE means that the EU requirements will affect companies not affected by the FRC or CMA regime, which focused on the FTSE 350. The PIE definition applies even where a company is part of a group listed outside Europe. European subsidiaries of US groups, for example, will be caught if they have EU-listed securities or an EU banking licence, or they undertake insurance activities. This could cause complexity by forcing subsidiaries to rotate auditors even if the parent (listed outside Europe) is not required to rotate.

4.295 As noted, the Department for Business, Innovation & Skills is leading the UK implementation of the EU Regulation and Directive, working closely with the FRC. Arrangements are not expected to be finalised until well into 2016.

FRC consultation: Enhancing Confidence in Audit: proposed revisions to the Ethical Standard, Auditing Standards, UK Corporate Governance Code and Guidance on Audit Committees

4.296 The final major piece of the FRC's strategic programme for the 2013–16 period is the implementation of the EU Audit Regulation and Directive ('ARD'). The 'Enhancing Confidence in Audit' ('ECA') consultation paper taking this forward was issued in September 2015. The FRC is taking responsibility for the implementation of the ARD alongside the Department for Business, Innovation and Skills ('BIS'), which is focusing on introducing the rules on mandatory rotation of audit firms and of mandatory audit tendering (see para 4.307 for information on the latest consultation from BIS). The EU ARD needs to be implemented in the UK by 17 June 2016 and, subject to the transitional rules, will be effective for periods beginning on or after that date.

4.297 The ECA consultation includes proposals to update the Ethical Standard for auditors (including around the provision by auditors of non-audit services), as well as proposed changes to Auditing Standards to reflect recent updates to audit reports introduced by the EU ARD and the International Audit and Assurance Standards Board ('IAASB'). These proposals will largely affect auditors but there will of course be an impact on companies from the rules on the provision of non-audit services.

4.298 ECA also includes proposed changes to the UK Corporate Governance Code which would be made in the 2016 version of the Code; the FRC has indicated that there will then be no further changes to the Code for the subsequent three years. Alongside the Code changes, there are proposed revisions to the Guidance on Audit Committees to reflect the EU ARD and other latest good practice considerations.

Summary of significant proposals in ECA

Non-audit services that firms are prohibited from providing

4.299 The EU ARD requires that member states impose greater restrictions on the non-audit services ('NAS') that auditors of a 'public interest entity' ('PIE') can provide to an audited company – including a 'black list' of prohibited NAS. For this purpose, PIEs are those companies whose securities are listed on a regulated exchange, banks and insurance undertakings. The FRC is proposing that the new UK Ethical Standard for auditors will incorporate the EU's black list, and that auditors will be prohibited from providing these NAS to their PIE clients. Services on the EU black list include:

- tax services.
- playing any part in management.
- bookkeeping.
- payroll services.
- designing and implementing certain control/ risk systems (subject to a 12 month 'cooling in' period).
- valuation services.
- certain legal services.
- internal audit.
- services linked to financing, capital structure & allocation & investment strategy.
- certain human resource services.

4.300 The use of a 'blacklist' is a significant change from the 'whitelist' that had previously been proposed by the FRC in an earlier round of consultation, and should allow audit committee members more flexibility than would have been the case under such an approach. The FRC is not proposing to add additional prohibitions to the black list, but is proposing to include the Member State options in respect of certain tax and valuation services. These services are on the black list, but may be provided in the UK as long as they have no direct, or a clearly inconsequential, effect on the audited financial statements. There will no doubt be debate as to the meaning of these terms.

Non-audit services cap

4.301 The EU Regulation also requires that the non-audit fees earned by the auditor of a PIE are capped at 70% of the previous three years' statutory audit fees. The FRC is proposing to adopt this rule, with some important amendments:

- Fees earned by network firms of the auditor must be incorporated into the calculation.
- If a year passes where no non-audit fees are earned, the three year period will not restart (unlike in the basic EU calculation).

4.302 The FRC has also proposed some clarification on which NAS fees may be excluded from the cap calculation. Fees in respect of any services required by legislation, or by a rule issued by a regulator under powers granted by legislation, can be excluded. This means that fees for public reporting aspects of reporting accountants' work (required by the UK Listing Rules) and certain regulatory services (such as CASS assurance work, s166 reports) are likely to be excluded from the cap calculations.

4.303   It is also worth noting that the need to build up a three-year track record of audit fees *may* mean that the cap will not strike in practice until the fourth year that the ARD applies to a particular company, even if the auditors have been in place for three years or more. This has not yet been explicitly addressed by the FRC.

Changes for audit committees

4.304   The FRC are proposing changes both to the Code and to the associated Guidance on audit committees:

■   At least one member of the audit committee is to have competence in accounting and/or auditing – this reflects an existing requirement in the Disclosure and Transparency Rules and would replace the existing Code requirement for at least one member to have "recent and relevant financial experience".

■   The audit committee as a whole is to have 'competence relevant to the sector in which the company operates'.

■   The audit committee is to discuss with their auditors the findings of any review carried out by the FRC's Audit Quality Review team; if the findings are significant, disclosure is to be made (of the findings and actions which the committee and their auditors plan to make). Disclosure of the audit quality category (that is, the inspection grade) is not required.

■   The 10 year audit tendering regime currently incorporated in the Code for FTSE 350 companies will be removed (in 2016). This regime has now been superseded by the EU rotation requirements, and the CMA's Order mandating 10 year tendering for FTSE 350 companies.

4.305   In September 2015 the FCA consulted on updating the DTR for the first two points above. In relation to the second point, the FCA indicated that "it considered competence relevant to the sector to be broader than knowledge of the sector.

4.306   The FCA also consulted on implementing the requirement in the EU ARD for a majority of the audit committee to be independent (see also paragraph 4.39.1). This change overlaps with the provisions of the UK Corporate Governance Code, which already requires that at least two members of the audit committee should be independent (or the whole committee, for FTSE 350 companies). It could, however, be significant for standard listed companies that do not apply the Code because they would previously have been compliant with the DTR if only one member of the audit committee was independent.

BIS Consultation on the technical legislative implementation of the EU Audit Directive and Regulation

4.307   At the end of October 2015, BIS issued a further consultation on its implementation of the ARD. It is, however, clear that more draft legislation will be issued for informal consultation in due course. The headline from the BIS consultation is that the Government is committed to a minimal implementation approach, so only the mandatory changes required by the EU reforms and other changes that would result in a benefit to the UK business environment will be applied.

4.308   The consultation confirms that no additional entities will be included in the definition of a Public Interest Entity, that is PIEs will only be those entities with securities admitted to trading on a regulated market, banks, building societies, and insurers. Companies traded on AIM will not be PIEs. The 10 + 10 year regime for tendering and rotation is confirmed. PIEs that retendered before the application date (17 June 2016) will be able to take benefit from transitional recognition of that tender. Further guidance will be published on this in due course.

Chapter 5

Directors' remuneration quoted companies

Chapter 5

Directors' remuneration – quoted companies

Introduction

5.1 Directors' remuneration is one of the most sensitive and closely regulated aspects of financial reporting. In recent times, directors' pay levels have been the subject of much discussion in the media and elsewhere, prompting a change in legislation both to increase the power of quoted company shareholders in determining directors' pay and to encourage a stronger link between pay and long-term performance.

5.2 Section 420 of the Companies Act 2006 requires all quoted companies to prepare a directors' remuneration report. Schedule 8 to SI 2008/410, 'The Large and Medium-sized Companies and Groups (Accounts and Reports) Regulations' (SI 2008/410), sets out the disclosure requirements for the directors' remuneration report. Quoted companies are also required to comply with Schedule 5 to SI 2008/410, which sets out directors' remuneration disclosure requirements for the notes to the financial statements.

[The next paragraph is 5.5.]

Scope of this chapter

5.5 This chapter deals with the requirements for quoted companies in reporting on directors' remuneration in annual reports. The requirements for unquoted companies are dealt with in chapter 7, which is available online on inform.pwc.com.

5.6 Quoted companies are required to make disclosures on directors' remuneration in both the notes to the financial statements and in the directors' remuneration report. This chapter deals with definitions and principles applying to all legal disclosure requirements. It then describes the disclosures required in the notes, followed by those required in the directors' remuneration report.

5.7 Companies listed on AIM are not quoted companies for the purpose of directors' remuneration disclosure. The specific requirements relevant for AIM companies are discussed in paragraph 5.308, but AIM companies should otherwise refer to chapter 7.

Approval of the remuneration report

5.8 Section 447 of the 2006 Act requires that the directors' remuneration report is approved by the board of directors and signed on behalf of the board by a director or the secretary of the company. [CA06 Sec 447(3)]. Also, companies are required to seek shareholder approval of the annual report on remuneration (that is, the 'implementation part' of the directors' remuneration report) (an advisory vote – see para 5.258) and of the directors' remuneration policy (a binding vote – see para 5.259).

Quoted companies

Definition

5.9 A quoted company is a UK-incorporated company that is:

"... a company whose equity share capital –

(a) has been included in the official list in accordance with the provisions of Part 6 of the Financial Services and Markets Act 2000 (c 8); or

(b) is officially listed in an EEA State; or

(c) is admitted to dealing on either the New York Stock Exchange or the exchange known as Nasdaq.

In paragraph (a) 'the official list' has the meaning given by section 103(1) of the Financial Services and Markets Act 2000."

[CA06 Sec 385(2)].

5.10 So 'quoted' means having 'equity share capital' listed on the London Stock Exchange or officially listed in the European Economic Area (which includes EU Member States plus Iceland, Norway and Liechtenstein) or admitted to dealing on the New York Stock Exchange or on Nasdaq. A company whose equity share capital is not listed on any of these exchanges but has other securities so listed is not quoted. Similarly, companies listed on AIM are not quoted. The requirements for unquoted companies are dealt with in chapter 7, which is available online on inform.pwc.com. The AIM rules regarding directors' remuneration are discussed from paragraph 5.308 onwards.

Disclosure rules applying to quoted companies

5.11 Disclosure of directors' remuneration for quoted companies is governed by:

- The Companies Act 2006.

- Part 1 of Schedule 5 to 'The Large and Medium-sized Companies and Groups (Accounts and Reports) Regulations 2008' (SI 2008/410).

- Schedule 8 to 'The Large and Medium-sized Companies and Groups (Accounts and Reports) Regulations 2008' (SI 2008/410).

- The Listing Rules of the FCA.

- The UK Corporate Governance Code ('the Code').

5.12 The 2006 Act clarifies that *"a company is a quoted company in relation to a financial year if it is a quoted company immediately before the end of the accounting reference period by reference to which that financial year was determined"*. [CA06 Sec 385(1)]. The status of the company at the end of the financial year determines whether the disclosure requirements in law and accounting standards that are applicable to quoted companies are given. If the company ceases to be quoted during the financial year, such disclosure requirements do not apply. On the other hand, if a company ceases to be quoted after the year end, these disclosures are given.

5.13 The position is different for Listing Rule disclosure requirements. Here, it is the status of the company when the financial statements are authorised for issue that determines whether these disclosures are required. Where a company delists after the year end, it is not required to comply with Listing Rule disclosure requirements.

5.14 Where a UK-incorporated company's equity shares are quoted on an overseas exchange specified in paragraph 5.9, but the company has only debt or fixed income shares listed in the UK, it has to comply with the directors' remuneration disclosure requirements contained in Part 1 of Schedule 5 and in Schedule 8 to SI 2008/410. This is because the law defines such a company as quoted, so the legal disclosure requirements relevant to quoted companies apply. But the Listing Rule disclosure requirements on directors' remuneration apply only to companies that have an FSA premium listing of equity shares. [LR 9.1.1].

5.15 For companies that are preparing their financial statements in accordance with IFRS, accounting standards require disclosure of 'key management personnel compensation' in the notes to the financial statements. The requirements of IAS 24 differ from those contained in the law and are considered in chapter 29 of the Manual of accounting – IFRS for the UK.

Directors' and auditors' duties

5.16 A company's directors have a duty to give information about their remuneration (including pensions, long-term incentive schemes, compensation for loss of office and sums paid to third parties) to the company so that the information can be disclosed in the financial statements. This requirement also applies to a person who has been a director of the company within the preceding five years. Any director failing to give notice of the required information to the company is liable to a fine. [CA06 Sec 412(5)(6)].

5.17 If required information is omitted from the financial statements or the directors' remuneration report, the auditor has a duty to include the information (so far as he is reasonably able to do so) in his audit report. [CA06 Sec 498(4)].

5.18 Some, but not all, of the information included in the directors' remuneration report is subject to audit. The audit requirements are explained from paragraph 5.315 onwards.

Location of disclosures in the annual report

Notes to the financial statements

5.19 SI 2008/410 requires that the disclosures under Schedule 5 are given in the notes to the financial statements. [SI 2008/410 para 8(1)]. These are described from paragraph 5.56 onwards.

5.20 The Schedule 5 requirements are dealt with in one of two ways: either they are given in the notes to the financial statements or the disclosures are given in the directors' remuneration report with a cross reference to that report included in the notes. This cross-reference should be to the particular page or section of the directors' remuneration report where the disclosure is given; it is not sufficient to cross-reference to the directors' remuneration report as a whole.

Directors' remuneration report

5.21 Schedule 8 of SI 2008/410 sets out the disclosures required in the directors' remuneration report. The Listing Rules do not specify the location of its required disclosures; they can be given anywhere in the annual report. Typically, companies deal with the Listing Rule disclosure requirements in the directors' remuneration report. The disclosure requirements for the directors' remuneration report are described from paragraph 5.90 onwards.

Principles applying to all disclosures required by law

5.22 There are some common principles that apply in making the disclosures under Schedule 5 and Schedule 8 to SI 2008/410. These are discussed below.

Qualifying services

5.23 Most of the disclosure requirements apply to amounts or benefits received or receivable for qualifying services. Qualifying services means:

- Services as a director of the company.

- Services at any time while a director of the company:

    - as a director of any subsidiary undertaking of the company at that time;

    - as a director of any other undertaking of which he/she is a director by virtue of the company's nomination (direct or indirect); and

    - in connection with the management of the affairs of either the company or any such subsidiary undertaking or any such other undertaking.

[SI 2008/410 5 Sch 14(1)(2), 15(1); 8 Sch 44].

5.24 Whether the director receives remuneration for services as a director of the company or in connection with the management of its affairs is a question of fact. It should be presumed that all payments for services made to a director will generally fall within one of these categories, unless it can clearly be demonstrated otherwise. This is especially the case when the payments are for services provided by an executive director who works full-time for the company.

5.25 An exception could arise where payments have been made to a director in a self-employed or professional capacity.

> **Example – Director paid on a self-employed basis**
>
> A director of a company is paid for technical services supplied on a 'self-employed persons' basis. How should this be disclosed?
>
> Provided that it can be clearly established that the fees are genuinely for technical services and that they are not connected with management services (which they might be if the director were a technical director), then the amounts paid need not be disclosed as remuneration. But it is often difficult to make such a precise distinction and, in such cases, the remuneration for other services is often included with directors' remuneration.

Under IAS 24, the transaction will be disclosed as a related party transaction regardless of the type of service provided. Related party disclosures are discussed in chapter 29 of the Manual of accounting – IFRS for the UK.

5.26 When considering directors' remuneration disclosure, there is no need to distinguish between a director's service contract and a contract for services that a director has with the company. Remuneration received in either capacity is disclosed in the company's financial statements as directors' remuneration. But if a director has a service contract, he is an employee of the company and his pay is included in staff costs. On the other hand, if the director has a contract for services, he is not regarded as an employee. Amounts invoiced by him to the company are recognised as an expense, but are not classified as 'staff costs'.

5.27 If the company has nominated (either directly or indirectly) the director to be a director of another company, services by that director to the other company are qualifying services and the remuneration for those services is included in the company's directors' remuneration disclosure. Similarly, compensation for loss of office should include any such amount he receives as a director of that other company. [SI 2008/410 5 Sch 14; SI 2008/410 8 Sch 44(1)(2)].

Example – Nominated director of an associate

Company A has nominated one of its directors to the board of its associate, company B. Company B pays £20,000 per year to the director in respect of his services to that company. Does this £20,000 have to be disclosed as directors' remuneration in company A's financial statements?

The law requires disclosure of remuneration received by a company director for qualifying services which includes services as a director of the company or its subsidiaries. But qualifying services also includes services as a director of any other undertaking by virtue of the company's nomination. This is the case even if the other undertaking is not the company's subsidiary.

Because the director has been nominated by company A as a director of the associate, the associate is treated for the purposes of directors' remuneration disclosure in the same way as a subsidiary. The director is performing qualifying services for company A by being its representative on company B's board. The director discloses to company A, as remuneration, the amount (£20,000) that he receives from company B. Company A discloses, as directors' remuneration, the aggregate of the amount paid to the director in respect of his services as director of company A and the amount he receives from company B.

If, on the other hand, the amount of £20,000 is paid to company A (that is, as a sum to be accounted for to the company, see para 5.48) and not to the director personally, then this amount need not be included as directors' remuneration in company A's financial statements. But company A is a related party of company B and the transaction would be disclosable under IAS 24.

5.28 Where a director is appointed during the year, only the remuneration while he is a director of the company is disclosable as director's remuneration.

Example 1 – Employee appointed as director during year

If a person has been an employee for part of the year and is then appointed a director during the year, should the figures disclosed for him include remuneration paid to him whilst he was an employee or should it just include remuneration paid to or receivable by him whilst a director?

SI 2008/410 requires only the amounts paid to or receivable by the person in respect of 'qualifying services' to be disclosed. 'Qualifying services' (see para 5.23) are performed only whilst a director of the company. So only the remuneration while he is a director of the company is disclosable as directors' remuneration. Similarly, the amounts paid or receivable in the previous financial year (when he was an employee but not a director) would be excluded from the comparative information on directors' remuneration.

Sometimes an employee is in an annual scheme or long-term incentive plan (LTIP) and his entitlement to bonus vests after his appointment as a director.

In the case of an annual bonus, only the portion that is earned after his appointment as director is included in the remuneration disclosures because only that portion relates to qualifying services. Typically, annual performance bonuses are based on a percentage of salary. On promotion to the board, new pay arrangements are put in place, often including an increase in salary. The change in the arrangements should form the basis of the pro-rating of the annual bonus between the pre-appointment and post-appointment periods.

For LTIPs, although the performance period straddles more than one financial year, amounts receivable under such plans are disclosed in the year in which the performance conditions are met (see para 5.31). The amounts are not apportioned between the financial years of the performance period. Similarly, when the performance conditions are met after the employee becomes a director, the amount receivable should be disclosed as directors' remuneration. If the performance conditions were met before he became a director, the amount receivable would not be disclosed as directors' remuneration.

Under IFRS, additional disclosure for the whole period might be necessary. IAS 24 requires disclosure of remuneration (in total and split into five categories) for key management personnel in respect of services provided to the entity. In this context we consider that the services provided to the entity means services while the person is a member of key management personnel. If a director was a member of key management prior to appointment as a director, remuneration for the whole financial year should be given in the IAS 24 disclosure in addition to the disclosures required in respect of directors' remuneration.

Example 2 – Director leaves the board during the year

If a person has been a director but steps down from the board during the year, how should the figures for the remuneration disclosures be determined?

As described in example 1, SI 2008/410 requires only the amounts paid to or receivable by the person in respect of 'qualifying services' to be disclosed, so only the remuneration while he is a director of the company is disclosable as directors' remuneration. The amounts paid or receivable in the previous financial year (when he was a director for the full year) would be included in the comparative information on directors' remuneration.

Sometimes a director is in an annual scheme or long-term incentive plan (LTIP) and the normal bonus vesting date is after he leaves the board.

As described in example 1, where a director steps down from the board but stays on as an employee of the company, for the annual bonus, only the portion that is earned as a director is included in the remuneration disclosures, because only that portion relates to qualifying services. For LTIPs, although the performance period straddles more than one financial year, amounts receivable under such plans are disclosed in the year in which the performance measures are met (see para 5.31). The amounts are not apportioned between the financial years of the performance period. Similarly, when the performance conditions are met after the director leaves the board, the amount receivable should not be disclosed as directors' remuneration. If the performance conditions were met before he left the board, the amount receivable would be disclosed as directors' remuneration.

But often, where a director leaves the board during the year and does not stay on as an employee, 'good leaver' provisions mean that his LTIP entitlements are pro-rated. Where a director leaves the board, say, at the end of year two, and does not stay on as an employee, but the 'good leaver' provisions entitle him to, say, two-thirds of a three-year LTIP award, an estimate of that two-third award would be included as remuneration in year two. This is because his leaving has caused two-thirds of the LTIP award to vest. His termination arrangements should be disclosed, including those related to the LTIP. In year three, if the actual amount payable exceeded the estimate included in year two, the difference would be disclosable as a payment to a former director. If he remained as an employee, his LTIP would not vest whilst a director and would not be included as directors' remuneration at all. A footnote to the year two single figure table in the directors' remuneration report should explain the position. In this case, it would not be necessary to include any disclosure of the actual award in year three, because it would be attributable to employment services which are exempt from the disclosure requirements for payments to past directors.

Under IFRS, additional disclosure for the whole period might be necessary. IAS 24 requires disclosure of remuneration for key management personnel in respect of 'services rendered to the entity'. In this context, we consider that 'services rendered to the entity' means services while the person is a member of key management personnel. If a director was a member of key management after he ceased to be a director, remuneration for the whole financial year should be included in the IAS 24 disclosure in addition to the disclosures required in respect of directors' remuneration.

5.29 Schedule 8 states that a payment or other benefit received in advance of a director commencing qualifying services, but in anticipation of performing qualifying services, is to be treated as if received on the first day of performance of the qualifying services. [SI 2008/410 8 Sch 11(2)]. Although this is not specifically stated in Schedule 5, such advance payments would be treated as payments to a director for qualifying services in the notes to the financial statements. Such a treatment is consistent with the approach taken for signing-on bonuses (see para 5.55).

Apportionment of remuneration

5.30 If it is necessary to apportion remuneration between the matters in respect of which it has been paid or is receivable, the directors may apportion it in any way that they consider appropriate. [SI 2008/410 5 Sch 7(6); SI 2008/410 8 Sch 48].

Disclosure in which year?

5.31 The director's remuneration disclosed in the financial statements for a particular year is the remuneration receivable by the director in respect of that year, regardless of when it is paid to the director. [SI 2008/410 5 Sch 7(4); SI 2008/410 8 Sch 47(1)]. For example, if a bonus is receivable by a director in respect of services performed in year one, but is not paid to the director until year two, it is disclosable as that director's remuneration in year one. [SI 2008/410 8 Sch 7(1)(c)].

5.32 In the case of remuneration that is receivable by a director in respect of a period that extends beyond the financial year, for example, a long-term incentive scheme covering a period of three years, where the only condition is the achievement of a profit target for the three year period (with no bonus payable unless that three year target is reached), disclosure should be made in year three (but also see para 5.34). [SI 2008/410 5 Sch 7(4); SI 2008/410 8 Sch 47(1)]. Whilst not explicitly stated in Schedule 5 (dealing with disclosures in the notes to the financial statements), the implication of this is that where remuneration is receivable in respect of a period, be that a period of one year or more than one year, it should be disclosed in the notes to the financial statements when the entitlement vests, regardless of when it is paid. This approach is consistent with that taken in Schedule 8 dealing with the directors' remuneration report (which would also require disclosure in year three). In the directors' remuneration report, the amount to be included is:

> "*money or other assets received or receivable for periods of more than one financial year where final vesting –*
>
> *(i)   is determined as a result of the achievement of performance measures or targets relating to a period ending in the relevant financial year; and*
>
> *(ii) is not subject to the achievement of performance measures or targets in a future financial year;...*"

[SI 2008/410 8 Sch 7(1)(d)].

5.33 Where remuneration is not receivable in respect of a period, whether of a single financial year or a period of over one financial year, it should be disclosed in the financial statements of the period in which it is paid. This might apply, for instance, when a single *ex gratia* payment is made to a director that is unrelated to a financial year or other period. An example might be a payment made as compensation for a reduction in the length of a director's service contract.

5.34 Sometimes bonus and long-term incentive schemes specify a performance period, but also require that a director remains with the company for a further period before he becomes entitled to receive any amounts under the scheme.

> **Example 1 – Bonuses paid after the end of the period**
>
> A company calculates its directors' bonuses by reference to the company's profits for the year ended 31 December 20X1. Under the terms of the bonus scheme, the bonuses are paid on 28 February 20X2. If the director is not in office at 28 February 20X2, entitlement to the bonus is forfeited.
>
> How is this bonus dealt with in:
>
> (a)   The directors' remuneration report?
> (b)   The notes to the financial statements?
>
> (a)   The directors' remuneration report
>
> > In the directors' remuneration report, the classification of the bonus in the 'single figure table' (see para 5.99) is based on the timing of the achievement of 'performance measures and targets'; the bonus related to achievement of a performance measure or target relating to a single financial year is included in the column C (commonly headed 'annual bonus') in the table. Where the performance measures or targets are in respect of a longer period, the related bonus is disclosed in column D (commonly headed 'long-term incentive plan') (see para 5.131).
> >
> > But the performance measures and targets, as defined in paragraph 44 of Schedule 8 for application to the directors' remuneration report, specifically exclude *"any condition related to service"*. This means that the service condition is not relevant to the classification of the bonus in the single figure table; only the achievement of the profit target is relevant for this purpose. So, in this example, because the performance measure is satisfied in a single financial year, the bonus is disclosed in the 'annual bonus' column of the table for the year ended 31 December 20X1.

If the director were to forfeit his bonus by leaving after 31 December 20X1 but before 28 February 20X2, the bonus would still be included in the single figure table in 20X1. In the 20X2 table, a 'recovery' of the bonus would be shown as a negative number in a separate column in the table. In both years, a footnote to the table should explain the situation.

(b)   The notes to the financial statements.

Schedule 5 requires that the aggregate amount receivable by the directors under long-term incentive schemes is disclosed in the notes to the financial statements. A long-term incentive scheme is defined as *"an agreement or arrangement (a) under which money or other assets may become receivable by a director, and (b) which includes one or more qualifying conditions with respect to service or performance which cannot be fulfilled within a single financial year"*. The definition specifically excludes bonuses which are determined by reference to service or performance within a single financial year. [SI 2008/410 5 Sch 11(1)].

The amount of the bonus is not calculated by reference to service or performance conditions that can be fulfilled within a single financial year. Instead it is calculated by reference to the company's performance for the financial year ended 31 December 20X1 and the directors' service for the fourteen month period to 28 February 20X2. Even though column D of the single figure table is commonly known as the 'long-term incentive plan' column, the amounts to be included in that column do not follow the definition of a 'scheme' (in Schedule 8) (see para 5.173) or 'long-term incentive scheme' (in Schedule 5). These definitions include service as a possible condition whereas the amounts to be included in column D are not affected by any service condition.

In the 31 December 20X1 annual report, the legal disclosure requirements could be met by disclosing the bonus as 'annual bonus' in the remuneration report with no disclosure in the notes to the financial statements. Then, in the 31 December 20X2 annual report, the bonus would not be included in the single figure table but would be disclosed in the notes to the financial statements as an amount received under a long-term incentive scheme. This would mean that the notes to the financial statements and the directors' remuneration report would be inconsistent in both the classification and timing of disclosure of the bonus.

We consider that this inconsistency is undesirable because it creates confusion. We also believe that the remuneration report disclosure, being the more detailed disclosure framework and reflective of the most recent thinking, should drive disclosures in the notes to the financial statements.

Paragraph 6(2) of Schedule 5 states *"For the purposes of this Schedule, any information is treated as shown if it is capable of being readily ascertained from other information which is shown"*. In our view, in this situation, the notes disclosure requirements are best met by including in the notes a cross-reference to the directors' remuneration report. In the 31 December 20X2 annual report, the bonus will be included as a comparative in the 'annual bonus' column and notes to the table will disclose that the bonus was deferred and why. In our view, this approach means that the information required by Schedule 5 can be 'readily ascertained'.

Example 2 – Bonus based only on service condition

A listed company makes an acquisition on 1 January 20X1 and, on that date, appoints the CEO of the acquired business to the main board. To incentivise the new director to stay with the company, the company agrees to give the director a bonus of £150,000 if he is still with the company on 31 December 20X3. He will receive no bonus if he leaves before that date. The company's year end is 31 December. How should the bonus be dealt with in:

(a)   The directors' remuneration report?
(b)   The notes to the financial statements?

(a)   The directors' remuneration report?

This amount is not salary or a taxable benefit so should not be included in either column A or column B of the single figure table. Columns C and D of the table deal with amounts receivable in respect of the achievement of performance measures or targets but these exclude service conditions. So the bonus should not be disclosed as relating to such an achievement. Neither is this bonus a pension related benefit.

So the bonus does not fit into any of the columns specified in Schedule 8. But Schedule 8 requires an additional column to be inserted for any other items in the nature of remuneration. [SI 2008/410 8 Sch 6(1)(a)]. Since this bonus is clearly in the nature of remuneration, an additional column should be inserted in the table for the year ended 31 December 20X3. The notes to the table should explain the bonus. [SI 2008/410 8 Sch 12(5)].

In the year ended 31 December 20X1, the company will also disclose the arrangement as a 'scheme interest' awarded during the year (see para 5.173). [SI 2008/410 8 Sch 14].

(b)   The notes to the financial statements

As described in example 1, a long-term incentive scheme is one in which the qualifying conditions with respect to service or performance cannot be fulfilled within a single financial year. To receive the bonus, the director has to stay with the company for more than one financial year so this is a long-term incentive scheme for the purposes of the notes to the financial statements. It is disclosed as such in the year ended 31 December 20X3 as this is the year in which it becomes receivable.

5.35 Sometimes a scheme provides for a bonus payable in respect of the year, but part of the bonus may be taken in shares, which if held for a further three years are then supplemented by a further award of shares, dependent on cumulative performance over the three years. In this case, the whole of the initial bonus, whether reinvested in shares or not, is included in column C ('annual bonus') in year one because it is receivable in respect of that year, but the additional potential award is treated as a long-term incentive plan.

5.36 Under IAS 24, long-term benefits include long-service, profit-sharing, bonuses and deferred compensation not payable wholly within 12 months of the end of the period. SI 2008/410 does not divide bonuses between amounts payable within a year of the period end and amounts payable in more than one year from the period end. Instead, it divides them by reference to the period of service to which they relate.

Substantial completion of performance measures and targets

5.37 Paragraphs 7(1)(c)(d) and 8 of Schedule 8 (on directors' remuneration reports) deal with the disclosure of annual bonuses and long-term incentive plans in the single figure table (see para 5.99). Paragraph 8(1) states:

"In respect of any items in paragraph 7(1)(c) or (d) where the performance measures or targets are substantially (but not fully) completed by the end of the relevant financial year:

(a) the sum given in the table may include sums which relate to the following financial year; but

(b) where such sums are included, those sums must not be included in the corresponding column of the single total figure table prepared for that following financial year; and

(c) a note to the table must explain the basis of the calculation."

[SI 2008/410 8 Sch 8].

5.38 So Schedule 8 permits the company to include the amounts due under the scheme in the current financial year's directors' remuneration report, if the performance measures or targets are "*substantially (but not fully) completed*" by the year end. Disclosing annual bonuses or long-term incentives on the basis of substantial (as opposed to full) completion of performance measures and targets is optional; it is equally acceptable to base the timing of bonus or long-term incentive disclosure on full completion of measures and targets.

5.39 In determining the year in which the amounts due under a plan are disclosed (that is, the year the performance period ends or the next financial year, when the amounts are payable), the company should consider the substance of the arrangement. Although Schedule 5 (dealing with directors' remuneration disclosure in the notes) does not include the concept of 'substantially' complete performance, we believe that the disclosures in the notes and the directors' remuneration report should be determined on a consistent basis.

[The next paragraph is 5.41.]

5.41 Sometimes, the performance conditions are met by the end of the financial year but there is a final approval process that takes place in the following financial year. Where this approval process is essentially a 'rubber-stamping' exercise with approval generally being given, the performance conditions have, in substance, been met in the current financial year and, in such a case, disclosure would usually be made in the year in which the performance conditions are met.

5.42 Where performance measures or targets are substantially (but not fully) completed by the end of the relevant financial year, the amount disclosed in the table may include sums that relate to the following financial year. For example, where a company prepares its annual report for the year ended 31 December 20X1 but full completion of performance targets is not achieved until 31 March 20X2, the company can include the full amount payable in respect of performance to 31 March 20X2 in its 20X1 disclosures, provided those targets are substantially complete at 31 December 20X1.

5.43 Whichever method is chosen, the basis of calculation is explained in a footnote to the single figure table. [SI 2008/410 8 Sch 8(1)]. Companies should report on a consistent basis year on year.

5.44 The term 'substantially (but not fully) completed' is not defined in the legislation and will be a matter of judgement in each case. In the case of an amount to be classified as an annual bonus, where the performance measures or targets are related to the financial year in question, substantial completion could, in our view, only have occurred by the year end if full completion was achieved within a very short timescale, and at least before the financial statements are authorised for issue. A longer 'cut-off period' might be considered appropriate in the case of a long-term incentive plan.

5.45 Sometimes the period over which performance is assessed is not based on financial years but on another specified period. Whether performance is substantially complete at the year end is a matter of judgement and will depend on the proportion of the performance completed by the year end. Where performance is measured over, say, a three year period ending three months after the year end, and the performance target is met at that time, performance could be regarded as substantially complete at the financial year end.

5.46 Performance measures and targets are discussed further from paragraph 5.124.

Payments made by another party to the director

5.47 All payments should be disclosed, whether those payments are made by the company, or by a subsidiary undertaking of the company, or by any other person, unless the director has to account for the receipt of the remuneration as described in paragraph 5.48. [SI 2008/410 5 Sch 8(1); SI 2008/410 8 Sch 46(2)].

> **Example – Director paid by non-group company**
>
> Mr Smith spends part of his time as an executive director of company A and part of his time as an employee of company B, which is controlled by him. Company B pays Mr Smith's salary and it invoices company A for an amount to cover that part of the time that Mr Smith spends working for company A. Although Mr Smith is paid by company B (and not by company A of which he is a director), the amount that he receives from company B is partially in respect of his services as a director of company A.
>
> Mr Smith should disclose to company A, and company A should disclose as remuneration in its financial statements and directors' remuneration report, the proportion of his salary that relates to his services as a director of company A. This figure might not be the same as the amount that company B has invoiced company A. This will depend on whether the invoiced amount is intended to cover an amount that is different from the actual cost of the director's services to company A (that is, whether the invoiced amount reflects the amount that the director has received from company B in respect of his qualifying services to company A).

Exclusion of specified sums

5.48 The following items are excluded from directors' remuneration:

■ Amounts that the director accounts for to the company, any of its subsidiaries or any other undertaking of which any person has been a director while director of the company.

■ Amounts that the director accounts for to past or present members of the company (or any of its subsidiaries) in respect of payments for loss of office resulting from a takeover. This would occur if the payments for loss of office are not approved by members in accordance with section 219 of the Act.

[SI 2008/410 5 Sch 8(1); 8 Sch 46(2)].

5.49 Where amounts are excluded for either of these reasons, and these reasons are subsequently found not to be justified, the remuneration is disclosed in a note to the first financial statements and in the first directors' remuneration report in which it is practicable for this to be done, and the remuneration is identified separately. This also applies to compensation for loss of office. [SI 2008/410 5 Sch 7(5), 8; SI 2008/410 8 Sch 47].

Payments to persons connected to the director

5.50 Amounts paid to or receivable by a director, including amounts paid in respect of compensation for loss of office, include amounts paid to or receivable by a person connected with, or a body corporate controlled by, that director (but such amounts should not be counted twice). [Sec 412(4); SI 2008/410 5 Sch 7(3); SI 2008/410 8 Sch 46(3)]. The definitions of connected persons and body corporate controlled by a director are set out in sections 252 to 255 of the Act (see para 5.214). [SI 2008/410 5 Sch 15(2); SI 2008/410 8 Sch 44(4)].

5.51 So even where a director sets up another company specifically to receive remuneration for his qualifying services, the remuneration is deemed to be remuneration received by him if that company is controlled by him. Similarly, where the company makes a contribution to the money purchase pension scheme of a director's spouse that would otherwise be paid into his own pension scheme, such a payment is disclosed in the same way as a contribution to the director's pension scheme.

Director's tax liability paid by the company

5.52 Where a company pays a director's income tax liability on remuneration, the tax paid by the company should be included in the remuneration disclosures.

5.53 Where the company agrees to pay the tax on a cash element of remuneration, the tax should be included as aggregate remuneration in the notes to the financial statements and in the relevant column in the single figure table in the directors' remuneration report (see para 5.99). For example, where the company has agreed to pay the tax in respect of an annual bonus, the amount disclosed in aggregate remuneration in the notes to the financial statements and in column C (annual bonus) of the table should be grossed up for the tax paid; that is, the amount disclosed should reflect the gross amount payable in cash to leave the director in the same position had the company not paid the tax on his behalf. For example, if the cash received is a net amount of £100,000 and the tax rate is 40%, then the gross amount the director would receive is $100,000/(1 - 0.4) = £167,000$; £167,000 should be included in the remuneration disclosures as annual bonus. Similar principles would apply to employee national insurance paid by the company on behalf of the director. Employer national insurance is the company's own liability and is not remuneration under any circumstances.

5.54 Where the company agrees to pay the tax on a benefit in kind or other non-cash element of remuneration (for example, share options), the tax should be included as aggregate remuneration in the notes to the financial statements and in the single figure table. Paying a director's tax liability that he would otherwise have to settle himself in cash can be argued to be equivalent to an increase in salary and disclosable as such in column A (salary and fees). An alternative would be to include the tax in column B, C or D (depending on the type of non-cash reward) or to show the tax paid in a separate column (see Table 5.3.1 in para 5.120). Whichever method is chosen, the basis of calculation of the amounts in the single figure table should be disclosed and applied consistently each year.

Signing-on bonuses ('golden hellos')

5.55 Amounts paid or share options granted in respect of a person accepting office are treated as payments and options granted in respect of services as a director. [SI 2008/410 5 Sch 15(3);SI 2008/410 8 Sch 45]. So an incentive payment (often called a 'golden hello') made by a company to attract a person to join its board of directors is disclosed as remuneration. Usually these payments are conditional on a specified service period, in which case they should be disclosed as remuneration for the period in which the entitlement to the payment becomes unconditional.

Disclosures required in the notes

5.56 Schedule 5 to SI 2008/410 requires the following information to be disclosed in the notes to the financial statements:

- The aggregate amount of remuneration paid to or receivable by directors in respect of qualifying services.

- The aggregate of the amount of gains made by directors on the exercise of share options.

- The aggregate of the amount of money paid to or receivable by directors, and the net value of assets (other than money and share options) received or receivable by directors, under long-term incentive schemes in respect of qualifying services.

- The aggregate value of any company contributions paid, or treated as paid, to a pension scheme in respect of directors' qualifying services, being contributions by reference to which the rate or amount of any money purchase benefits that may become payable will be calculated.

- The number of directors (if any) to whom retirement benefits are accruing in respect of qualifying services under:

  - Money purchase schemes.

  - Defined benefit schemes.

[SI 2008/410 5 Sch 1].

5.57 A Schedule 5 disclosure requirement is regarded as met if the information can be readily ascertained from other information provided. For example, a company that gives detailed information by individual director in its directors' remuneration report (as required by Schedule 8 to SI 2008/410) could satisfy the Schedule 5 requirement for disclosure of the aggregate remuneration if the total is readily ascertainable from the directors' remuneration report. This is provided that there is a cross-reference from the notes to the financial statements (where the Schedule 5 disclosure is required to be given) to the relevant part of the directors' remuneration report. But the basis of calculation of amounts to be disclosed under Schedule 5 is not always the same as under Schedule 8, so Schedule 5 disclosures might not be 'readily ascertainable' without additional disclosure in the directors' remuneration report.

Aggregate remuneration

5.58 Aggregate remuneration includes:

- Salary, fees and bonuses.

- Any expense allowances (to the extent that they are chargeable to UK income tax) (see para 5.63).

- The estimated money value of any other benefits received otherwise than in cash (see para 5.60).

- Remuneration in respect of a person accepting office as director.

[SI 2008/410 5 Sch 9(1), 15(3)].

5.59 The term 'remuneration' does not include the value of share options granted to or exercised by directors. It does not include any company pension contributions paid on behalf of directors (although it does include contributions that directors themselves pay by way of a compulsory deduction from salary) nor any benefits to which directors are entitled under any pension scheme. Also excluded from the definition are money or other assets paid to or receivable by directors under long-term incentive schemes. [SI 2008/410 5 Sch 9(2)]. These elements are the subject of separate disclosure requirements.

Benefits in kind and expense allowances

5.60 The estimated money value of a benefit in kind included in directors' remuneration should be the market value of the facility that is provided for the director's private benefit, less any contribution the director pays.

5.61 The amount used to assess the tax payable on the benefit should be used *only* where it is an approximation of the market value of the benefit. Otherwise the tax treatment is not relevant in determining the amount to be disclosed. Where there is a tax concession such that part of a benefit is not taxable, even though it is a benefit for the director (as opposed to a valid business expense), the taxable amount is not such an approximation.

5.62 Benefits in kind might include: provision of accommodation at below market rates; provision of a car or health benefit. Gains on exercise of share options and amounts or assets receivable under long-term incentive schemes are dealt with separately (see from para 5.66 onwards).

> **Example 1 – Premium paid for director's life assurance cover**
>
> A company pays a premium to an insurance company to purchase life assurance cover for a director. This life cover is in addition to the life cover provided by the pension scheme and is an entirely separate arrangement. The beneficiary would be the next of kin of the director. How should this be disclosed for the purpose of directors' remuneration?
>
> The premium should be included as a benefit in kind in arriving at the aggregate directors' remuneration disclosed in the notes to the financial statements. The benefit would also be disclosed in taxable benefits received by the director (even though it is not taxable), which is required to be shown separately in the table of individual directors' remuneration in the directors' remuneration report, together with the nature of the benefit (see further para 5.118). [SI 2008/410 8 Sch 7(1)(b), 11(1)(b)].

Example 2 – Security cameras at director's home

A company director of a high profile company has had demonstrators protesting against the company's policies outside his private residence. As a result the company has had security cameras installed at his house at a cost of £20,000. There are no provisions for the company to retain ownership of the cameras if the director leaves office. Is this disclosable?

We consider that the provision of security cameras would usually fall within the definition of a benefit in kind and would be included in the aggregate remuneration disclosed in the notes to the financial statements. The benefit would also be disclosed as 'taxable benefits' received by the director, which are shown separately in the table of individual directors' remuneration in the directors' remuneration report (see para 5.99). The nature (and value, if significant) of the benefit would also be disclosed. [SI 2008/410 8 Sch 7(1)(b), 12(1)(b)].

IAS 24 requires disclosure of remuneration (in total and split into five categories) for key management personnel in respect of services provided to the entity. This disclosure includes non-monetary benefits for employees; the provision of security cameras would seem to fall into this category. The value of the benefit would be included in the amount of key management personnel compensation disclosed under IAS 24.

In some cases, the company and HM Revenue and Customs considers that risk caused to the director by the protesters is so severe that the security cameras are a valid business expense of the company. In such a case, the security cameras are excluded from the director's remuneration disclosures because they are not a reward for his services. But disclosure would still be required under IAS 24 because the provision of the security cameras represents a transfer of assets to a related party.

5.63 Expense allowances are included in the aggregate remuneration disclosed in the notes to the financial statements to the extent they are chargeable to UK income tax. [SI 2008/410 5 Sch 9(1)]. The intention of the legislators seems to be to exclude from remuneration amounts that are reimbursements of expenses incurred in the course of the director's performance of his duties (for example, business travel expenses). In the directors' remuneration report, expense allowances are included in remuneration to the extent they are chargeable to UK income tax (or would be if the person were an individual or would be if the person were tax resident in the UK). [SI 2008/410 8 Sch 11(a)]. This difference in definition of disclosable expense allowances creates a potential conflict between the disclosures of remuneration in the notes compared with the directors' remuneration report.

5.64 Sometimes, companies refer to items as 'allowances' that are regarded as benefits in kind for disclosure purposes. For example, relocation allowances are not incurred in the performance of the director's duties but are paid as an inducement for a director to join the company or to change his role within it. These are often regarded as benefits in kind.

5.65 Where a director receives an expense allowance that is not chargeable to UK income tax it is normally excluded from the aggregate remuneration disclosed in the notes to the financial statements. But if the allowance was not taxable in the UK just because, say, the director was not UK tax resident, this would mean that the amount included in respect of allowances in the notes to the financial statements is not consistent with the amount included in the directors' remuneration report. In such a case, in our view, the notes should disclose the amount of the expense allowance that would be taxable if the director were resident in the UK. Alternatively, it would be permissible to include the allowance in aggregate remuneration. This is permitted under the law because 'aggregate remuneration' is defined as including specified items but there is no legal prohibition on including non-taxable expense allowances. In many cases, the 'allowance' can be regarded as a benefit in kind and the inconsistency avoided.

Travel and accommodation expenses

5.65.1 Reimbursement of 'travel to work' expenses is a taxable benefit under UK tax law. 'Aggregate remuneration' includes expense allowances to the extent that they are chargeable to UK income tax (see para 5.58). Also, the single figure table in the directors' remuneration report includes a column dealing with 'taxable benefits' (see para 5.118). Although this term is not defined, the law states that it includes expense allowances that are chargeable to UK income tax (or would be chargeable if the director was a UK tax resident). It also includes any benefits (whether or not in cash) that are emoluments; the tax status of such benefits is irrelevant and so, anomalous though it might be, a non-taxable benefit could be a 'taxable benefit'. This might apply, for example, to certain relocation benefits.

5.65.2 A director's place of work might be the head office where all board meetings are held. In this case, the reimbursement of travel expenses to board meetings would be disclosable as taxable benefits. But companies might have their board meetings in a variety of locations and, in such cases, non-executive directors might be able to agree with HM Revenue & Customs (HMRC) that there is no permanent place of business and that reimbursement of travel expenses is not taxable. The tax rules can be complicated; there are a number of exemptions available, with the result that reimbursed travel and accommodation expenses are not always taxable. The tax treatment of similar expenses can vary according to the circumstances of the particular director.

5.65.3 It is debatable whether the reimbursement of travel and accommodation expenses is a benefit to a director, because he makes no profit on the arrangement and would probably prefer not to travel if it could be avoided. The counter-argument is that shareholders have a right to know how much it costs to hire a director. In particular, non-executive directors' expenses can be significant, with travel expenses sometimes exceeding their fees. But it seems reasonable to conclude that, if HMRC regard a reimbursement as taxable, at least that amount (together with the associated income tax and national insurance, if paid by the company) should be included in the single figure table and, in the notes to the financial statements, in aggregate remuneration. Also, it might be obvious that there is a benefit to the director; for example, if a UK director moves to his holiday home abroad and the company then pays his travel expenses for attendance at board meetings in the UK, the payment of his travel expenses would clearly be treated as a disclosable benefit. But often the position is not so clear-cut. Whatever disclosure treatment a company adopts for such reimbursements, the remuneration report should be transparent in stating how these amounts have been dealt with in the table and why the company has adopted that approach. A consistent treatment should be adopted in the directors' remuneration report and the notes to the financial statements.

Gains on share options

5.66 Quoted and AIM companies are required to disclose the aggregate of gains made by directors on exercising share options. [SI 2008/410 5 Sch 1(1)(b)]. (For quoted companies, this is in addition to the inclusion in the single total figure of the value of share options vesting in the financial year.)

5.67 Share options are defined as the right to acquire shares. [SI 2008/410 5 Sch 12(b)]. 'Shares' means shares (whether allotted or not) in the company, or an undertaking which is a group undertaking in relation to the company, and includes a share warrant as defined by Section 779(1) of the Act. A share warrant is a warrant that states that the bearer of the warrant is entitled to the shares specified in it. The phrase *"any undertaking which is a group undertaking in relation to the company"* includes the parent undertaking and fellow subsidiary undertakings as well as subsidiary undertakings of the company.

5.68 Although not defined in Schedule 5 to SI 2008/410 governing disclosures in the notes to the financial statements, Schedule 8, dealing with the directors' remuneration report, defines a gain on the exercise of a share option as the difference between the market price of the shares on which the option was exercised and the price actually paid for the shares. [SI 2008/410 8 Sch 44(1)].

5.69 Share options granted in respect of a person's accepting office as a director are to be treated as share options granted in respect of that person's services as a director. [SI 2008/410 5 Sch 15(3)].

[The next paragraph is 5.71.]

5.71 'Market price' is not defined in the legislation. We consider that the mid-market price is the price that should be used. The FCA Listing Rules define market value as the middle market quotation for a share as derived from the Daily Official List of the London Stock Exchange. [LR 9.5.10R (2)].

Amounts receivable under long-term incentive schemes

5.72 Companies are required to disclose the aggregate of amounts of money and the net value of other assets received or receivable under long-term incentive schemes in the notes to the financial statements.

5.73 A long-term incentive scheme is defined as *"an agreement or arrangement (a) under which money or other assets may become receivable by a director, and (b) which includes one or more qualifying conditions with respect to service or performance which cannot be fulfilled within a single financial year"*. [SI 2008/410 5 Sch 11(1)]. The definition specifically excludes:

■ Bonuses the amount of which is determined by reference to service or performance within a single financial year.

- Compensation for loss of office, payments for breach of contract and other termination payments.

- Retirement benefits.

[SI 2008/410 5 Sch 11(2)].

5.74 Amounts received or receivable means amounts that become due to directors during the financial year. For example, if a long-term incentive scheme runs for three years and amounts or other assets become due to the directors at the end of the third year, they are disclosable in that year, even if they are not actually paid over to or received by the directors until the following year. The year of disclosure in the notes to the financial statements and its interaction with the disclosure in the single figure table are considered more fully from paragraph 5.31.

5.75 Other assets received or receivable under long-term incentive schemes might include, for example, diamonds, gold, wine or works of art. Usually, 'other assets' are shares. The 'value' of the shares received or receivable is defined elsewhere in SI 2008/410 as the market price of the shares on the day the shares are received or receivable. [SI 2008/410 8 Sch 44(1)].

5.76 The net value of other assets received or receivable by a director under a long-term incentive scheme means the value after deducting any money paid or other value given by the director. [SI 2008/410 5 Sch 15(1)].

Pension contributions

5.77 Company pension contributions do not form part of aggregate remuneration described in paragraph 5.58. Instead, Schedule 5 requires separate disclosure of the aggregate value of company contributions paid, or treated as paid, to a money purchase pension scheme in respect of directors' qualifying services by a person other than the director. Contributions mean those according to which the rate or amount of any money purchase benefits that may become payable will be calculated. [SI 2008/410 5 Sch 1(1)(d)]. There is no requirement to disclose, in the notes to the financial statements, contributions to defined benefit schemes.

5.78 Companies are also required to disclose separately the number of directors to whom retirement benefits are accruing under money purchase schemes and under defined benefit schemes in respect of qualifying services. [SI 2008/410 5 Sch 1(2)].

5.79 Pension schemes are defined as meaning retirement benefit schemes under section 611 of the Income and Corporation Taxes Act 1988 (ICTA). [SI 2008/410 5 Sch 13(1)]. Section 611 of ICTA defines a retirement benefits scheme as a scheme for the provision of benefits consisting of or including relevant benefits, but not including any national scheme providing such benefits. References to a scheme include references to a deed, agreement, series of agreements or other arrangements providing for relevant benefits notwithstanding that it relates or they relate only to:

- A small number of employees, or to a single employee (including company payments to personal pension plans – see example below).

- The payments of a pension starting immediately on the making of the arrangements.

> **Example – Payments to director's personal pension plan**
>
> A company makes a payment to a personal pension plan for one if its directors. The pension plan was arranged by the director some time before joining the company. Should these payments be disclosed as company contributions to money purchase schemes?
>
> 1. Yes, if the company makes the payments to the pension scheme, the payments should be disclosed in the aggregate of company contributions to money purchase schemes in respect of directors' qualifying services. [SI 2008/410 5 Sch 1(1)(d)]. (There should also be disclosure of the contributions in respect of each individual director in the directors' remuneration report– see para 5.141.)

5.80 The definition of pension schemes above is generally interpreted as extending to unfunded pension arrangements. So where a company makes provisions in respect of unfunded pensions of a money purchase type, it discloses the amounts provided as contributions to money purchase schemes.

5.81 'Retirement benefits' has the meaning given by section 612 of ICTA 1988. [SI 2008/410 5 Sch 13(1)]. It is any pension, lump sum, gratuity or other like benefit given or to be given:

- on retirement;

- on death;

- in anticipation of retirement;

- in connection with past service, after retirement or death; or

- to be given on or in anticipation of or in connection with any change in the nature of the service of the employee in question;

except that it does not include any benefit which is to be afforded solely by reason of the disablement by accident of a person occurring during his service or of his death by accident so occurring and for no other reason.

5.82 'Money purchase benefits' for the purpose of the requirement set out in paragraph 5.77 means retirement benefits payable under a pension scheme the rate or amount of which is calculated by reference to payments made, or treated as made, by the director or by any other person in respect of the director and which are not average salary benefits. [SI 2008/410 5 Sch 13(4)].

5.83 'Company contributions' do not have to be paid by the company itself as the definition states that the term means any payments (including insurance premiums) made, or treated as made to the scheme in respect of the director by a person other than the director. [SI 2008/410 5 Sch 13(3)].

5.84 A 'money purchase scheme' for the purpose of the requirement set out in paragraph 5.78 means a pension scheme under which all of the benefits that may become payable to or in respect of the director are money purchase benefits. A 'defined benefit scheme' is a pension scheme that is not a money purchase scheme. [SI 2008/410 5 Sch 13(4)].

5.85 The disclosure for the purpose of directors' remuneration is based on the legal form of the pension scheme. This is particularly relevant where a company does not account for a pension scheme as defined benefit (where it is entitled to an exemption in the relevant accounting standard for pensions), as illustrated in the following example.

> **Example – Industry-wide pension scheme**
>
> Company A participates in an industry-wide defined benefit pension scheme. Company A is unable to identify its share of the scheme's underlying assets and liabilities and has taken the exemption available to it to account for the scheme as a defined contribution scheme, with the appropriate disclosure.
>
> In the disclosure of directors' remuneration, should the scheme be treated as a defined contribution scheme so that the disclosures are consistent?
>
> The disclosure of the directors' remuneration required by Schedule 5 to SI 2008/410 is determined by the pension scheme's legal form and not by the accounting treatment. Company A should not make disclosure of the contributions paid to the industry-wide scheme as 'company contributions to money purchase schemes'.
>
> Disclosure should be made of the number of directors to whom benefits are accruing under the defined benefit scheme. [SI 2008/410 5 Sch 1(2)(b)].
>
> It might be useful to include some disclosure in the directors' remuneration note to the financial statements to explain the apparent inconsistency.

5.86 Where a pension scheme is a hybrid scheme and provides that any benefits that become payable will be the greater of money purchase benefits as determined under the scheme and defined benefits as determined, the company may elect to treat the scheme as a money purchase scheme or as a defined benefit scheme in its entirety, whichever seems more likely at the end of the financial year. [SI 2008/410 5 Sch 13(6)]. If the scheme is classified as a money purchase arrangement, the relevant disclosures as described in paragraph 5.77 are made. If the scheme is classified as a defined benefit arrangement, the disclosure required by paragraph 5.78 is made. Alternatively, the company can elect not to take advantage of the option and treat the scheme as defined benefit whilst also making separate disclosure of information relating to the money purchase element of the scheme following the requirement in paragraph 5.77. Given that the disclosures in the directors' remuneration report would be made in respect of both the defined benefit and defined contribution elements, it would be preferable to take the same approach in the notes to the financial statements.

5.87 For the purpose of determining whether a pension scheme is a money purchase or defined benefit scheme any death in service benefits provided by the scheme are disregarded. [SI 2008/410 5 Sch 13(7)].

Comparative information in the notes to the financial statements

5.88 IAS 1 requires that entities disclose comparative information in respect of the previous period for all amounts reported in the current period's financial statements. [IAS 1 para 38]. The previous period for a financial year is the previous financial year. Financial years are not always of the same duration.

5.89 Under the Act, a company is permitted to end its financial year on the same day in the week rather than on the same date, if it wishes to. Therefore, a financial year (and, consequently, the financial statements) may cover a period slightly longer or shorter than one year. In this situation, the amounts disclosed for directors' remuneration are those in respect of the financial year, as explained in the following example.

> **Example – Remuneration for a 53-week period**
>
> A company has a 53-week financial year and its previous financial year was 52 weeks. Can the disclosure of directors' remuneration be given for a 52-week (365-day) period, rather than for 53 weeks?
>
> The amounts of remuneration to be shown for any financial year are the sums receivable in respect of that year (whenever paid). [SI 2008/410 5 Sch 7 (4)].
>
> Section 390(3) of the Companies Act 2006 states that *"subsequent financial years begin with the day immediately following the end of the company's previous financial year and end with the last day of its next accounting reference period or such other date, not more than seven days before or after the end of that period, as the directors may determine"*. The company's financial year is 53 weeks, and so the amounts to be disclosed are for the 53 weeks of the financial year.
>
> The comparative information will be for the 52-week previous financial year. The disclosures should make it clear that the comparative period is a 52-week period, while the current period is 53 weeks.
>
> Similarly, if the company prepares statutory accounts for a short period (for example, nine months), the amounts to be disclosed under the Act are the remuneration for that period (that is, nine months). Again, the comparative period will be the previous financial year and, where this is of a different duration from the current period, the financial statements should make that clear.

Directors' remuneration report

Overview

5.90 The directors' remuneration report consists of three elements:

- Annual statement by the chairman of the remuneration committee. See paragraph 5.95.

- Annual report on remuneration. This part of the directors' remuneration report is sometimes known as the 'implementation report' or 'implementation part'. It requires disclosures on the following subjects:

    - Single total figure of remuneration for each director and additional information. See paragraph 5.99 onwards.

    - Total pension entitlements. See paragraph 5.165.

    - Scheme interests awarded during the financial year. See paragraph 5.173.

    - Payments to past directors. See paragraph 5.187.

    - Payments for loss of office. See paragraph 5.190.

    - Statements of directors' shareholding and share interests. See paragraph 5.197.

    The above elements are the only parts of the directors' remuneration report that are auditable.

    - Performance graph and table of CEO remuneration. See paragraphs 5.216 and 5.228.

- Percentage change in the remuneration of the director undertaking the role of chief executive officer. See paragraph 5.232.

- Relative importance of spend on pay. See paragraph 5.237.

- Statement of implementation policy in the following year. See paragraph 5.242.

- Consideration by the directors of matters relating to directors' remuneration. See paragraph 5.248.

- Statement of voting at the last general meeting. See paragraph 5.254.

- Directors' remuneration policy.

  This part of the directors' remuneration report is sometimes known as the 'policy report' or 'policy part'. The policy report can be omitted from the directors' remuneration report if the company does not intend to ask shareholders to approve the remuneration policy at the general meeting at which the annual accounts and reports will be laid ('the accounts meeting'). The requirements for remuneration policy approval are discussed in paragraph 5.259.

  It requires disclosures on the following subjects:

  - Future policy table. See paragraph 5.269.

  - Approach to recruitment remuneration. See paragraph 5.280.

  - Service contracts. See paragraph 5.284.

  - Illustrations of application of remuneration policy. See paragraph 5.297.

  - Policy on payment for loss of office. See paragraph 5.291.

  - Statement of consideration of employment conditions elsewhere in the company. See paragraph 5.304.

  - Statement of consideration of shareholder views. See paragraph 5.305.

[The next paragraph is 5.94.]

5.94 The following general rules apply to information disclosed in the directors' remuneration report:

- Information required to be shown in respect of a particular person should be shown in a manner that links that information to that person identified by name. [SI 2008/410 8 Sch 2(1)].

- Information may be provided in greater detail than is required. [SI 2008/410 8 Sch 2(2)].

- Disclosures may be provided for executive directors separately from non-executive directors. [SI 2008/410 8 Sch 2(3)].

- Where a requirement is not applicable to a non-executive director, it may be omitted or modified provided that the particulars of, and reasons for, the omission or modification are disclosed. [SI 2008/410 8 Sch 2(4)].

Annual statement by remuneration committee chairman

5.95 The UK Corporate Governance Code recommends that the board establishes a remuneration committee of at least three or, in the case of a company outside the FTSE 350, two independent non-executive directors. [UK CGC D2.1]. Other Code provisions relating to the remuneration committee are included in the Annex to this chapter.

5.95.1 The directors' remuneration report is required to include a statement by the chair of the remuneration committee. Where there is no such person, the statement is made by the director nominated by the directors to make the statement. [SI 2008/410 8 Sch 3].

5.96 The statement is required to summarise for the financial year:

- The major decisions on directors' remuneration.

- Any substantial changes relating to directors' remuneration made during the year.

- The context in which those changes occurred and decisions have been taken.

[SI 2008/410 8 Sch 3].

5.97 Although not specified in the law, useful disclosures might include:

- How directors' remuneration policy is aligned with the business strategy.

- An explanation of the impact of the economic climate on remuneration decisions.

- A description of the effect of the business environment on those decisions.

- An explanation of how business performance (as evidenced by key metrics) is reflected in remuneration.

- An explanation of the remuneration committee's response to shareholder concerns about remuneration.

- A summary of incentive payments.

- The background to any discretion exercised by the remuneration committee.

- The remuneration committee's future plans.

5.98 Table 5.1 is an example of a remuneration committee chairman's annual statement.

Table 5.1 Remuneration committee chairman's statement

Marks and Spencer plc – Annual report and financial statements – 28 March 2015

Remuneration (extract)

On behalf of the Board, I am pleased to present our Remuneration Report for 2014/15, my first as the Chairman of the Remuneration Committee. Following the new reporting regulations adopted last year, this report is split into two distinct sections. Although we are not required to include the policy report approved by shareholders last year, the Committee has decided to continue to do so in order to maintain full, transparent reporting. For easy reference, we have included a 'summary' of the remuneration policy on pages 54 to 60. Information on the policy since its approval last year is shown on pages 60 and 61.

Our remuneration framework is designed to support and drive our strategy, and ensure our business is run by high-quality leaders with the skills and expertise necessary to deliver our long-term business priorities.

The Committee made good progress against the action plan it set itself last year. As planned, the Committee reviewed and retendered the independent external advisers to the Committee following the appointment of Deloitte as the Company's auditor. After an extensive process, PwC was appointed to advise the Committee.

REMUNERATION REVIEW AND PROPOSED AMENDMENTS

This year, and with PwC's support, we undertook a thorough review of the current executive remuneration framework and targets to ensure they remained aligned with the strategic business priorities and were balanced against the Company-wide remuneration offering. The Committee was particularly keen to ensure that the incentive arrangements remained sufficiently motivating for management to deliver while encouraging the behaviours, values and ethics which underpin Fit for the Future and the way we do business at M&S.

The timing of this review was also linked to our requirement to renew our existing share plans, as outlined last year. The Committee has reviewed the Plan rules and framework, along with changes in market practice and feedback from stakeholders. Overall, the Committee concluded that while the structure of the framework remains appropriate, it is time to refresh some elements within the Performance Share Plan in order to provide an even clearer fit with the business's current strategic priorities, following four years of intensive investment and transformation. The Plan will continue to retain the metrics of EPS and ROCE and their associated weightings of 50% and 20% respectively.

The financial strategic scorecard element will retain targets for International and M&S.com sales as before as we continue to grow these areas of the business, but will now include targets for two key business priorities of GM gross margin growth and the delivery of free cash flow, as set out in the Company's key performance indicators. While these amendments are within the parameters of the remuneration policy approved by shareholders at last year's AGM, we value the views of, and input from, our shareholders and therefore consulted with them on the proposed amendments and associated targets for the 2015/16 awards. As a result, we believe the proposed changes and targets are timely and appropriate and will ensure the awards remain stretching but motivating for the senior management team.

CLAWBACK

In updating the associated plan rules, the Committee has also taken the opportunity to introduce clawback in line with updated UK corporate governance guidance. Clawback provisions will apply to any bonus awards in 2016 and beyond and under any of the Company's executive share schemes from 2015 onwards. Details of this are provided on page 60.

KEY POINTS FOR THE YEAR

Salary review

Executive director salaries were reviewed and discussed by the Committee during the year. The Committee took into account the salary review applicable for the rest of the organisation and directors' individual performance when assessing the appropriateness of any increase. The Committee was also mindful that the executive directors had requested not to receive an increase last year, despite a 2% average pay review for the business. Further, the annual salary review date has been moved from January to July to fit better with the annual performance cycle. In line with previous years, Marc Bolland has again, at his own request, not received an increase. He has not received a salary increase since his appointment in 2010. The highest increase has been awarded to Steve Rowe in recognition of his strong performance over the period. However, while there is some variation in salary increase across the executive directors, the resulting average salary increase awarded to the executive directors as a group is in line with the rest of the organisation and the market median for the same period since the last review. Further details of the directors' salary increases are shown on page 63.

Our new Chief Finance Officer, Helen Weir joined the Board on 1 April, after our year end on 28 March, and was not eligible for this salary review. We provide full details of her recruitment arrangement and future pay on page 73.

Performance-related payments

The Committee also reviewed the performance of both the business and each director against targets set at the beginning of the year for the Annual Bonus Scheme. This year, the business met its corporate Profit Before Tax (PBT) target and a bonus was paid across the organisation.

The bonus payments outlined on page 64 reflect both the delivery against corporate or business area targets and the progress made by each director against their specific individual objectives. Underlying Group PBT at £661.2m was above the minimum threshold of £650m at which level payments against financial targets were triggered for directors. Performance against the Company's overall Plan A targets was also taken into consideration by the Committee in determining the resulting outturn for each director. The Committee undertook a rigorous review of the achievement against financial and individual objectives to ensure the level of bonus payment was appropriate and fair given the overall business performance. The highest bonus payment was made to Steve Rowe, Executive Director, Food at c.60% of maximum bonus opportunity reflecting strong performance in the Food business. The other bonus payments range from 18% to around 30% of maximum.

The Performance Share Plan awards granted in 2012 were measured for the three-year period up to 28 March 2015 against challenging Earnings per Share (EPS), Return on Capital Employed (ROCE) and Revenue targets. As a result of performance against these targets, executive directors will receive only 4.7% of the original award when it vests in 2015. This level of vesting reflects delivery against ROCE targets; all other targets were not met. Further details are shown on page 66.

SHAREHOLDER CONSULTATION

We remain committed to reporting openly the details of our executive director pay arrangements. Following constructive shareholder feedback, we are providing further disclosure around our bonus targets this year. We will continue to maintain a dialogue with investors regarding our disclosures to ensure we clearly communicate our arrangements as far as possible without it impacting our commerciality.

Together with the rest of the Board, I look forward to hearing your views on our remuneration arrangements and will be available to answer any questions you may have at the AGM.

Vindi Banga
Chairman of the Remuneration Committee

Annual report on remuneration

Single total figure of remuneration for each director

5.99 The directors' remuneration report should include a table setting out the components of remuneration for each person who served as a director at any time in the financial year. Unless otherwise indicated, the amounts to be disclosed are those that relate to qualifying services. [SI 2008/410 8 Sch 4(1)(3)].

5.100 The amounts to be disclosed under SI 2008/410 for each director are:

Column	Amount to be disclosed in column
A	The total amount of salary and fees. See paragraph 5.116.
B	All taxable benefits. See paragraph 5.118.
C	Money or other assets received or receivable for the relevant financial year as a result of the achievement of performance measures or targets relating to a period ending in that financial year other than:

- those that result from awards made in a previous financial year and where final vesting is determined as a result of the achievement of performance measures or targets relating to a period ending in the relevant financial year; or
- those receivable subject to the achievement of performance measures or targets in a future financial year.

This category is commonly referred to as 'annual bonus'. See paragraph 5.122.

D	Money or other assets received or receivable for periods of more than one financial year where final vesting is both: determined as a result of the achievement of performance measures or targets relating to a period ending in the relevant financial year; and is not subject to re achievement of performance measures or targets in a future financial year. This category is commonly known as 'long-term incentive plans'. See paragraph 5.131.
E	All pension related benefits. See paragraph 5.141.
F	The total of the items in columns (A) to (E) above.

5.101 The form of the table required is as follows:

Single figure table

	Salary and fees		Taxable benefits		Annual bonus		Long-term incentive plans		Pension related benefits		Total	
	20X1	20X0	20X1	20X0	20X1	20X0	20X1	20X0	20X1	20X0	20X1	20X0
Director 1												
Director 2												

[SI 2008/410 8 Sch 5(1)].

5.102 It is permissible to display the table using the alternative orientation below. This might be preferable when there are fewer directors than components of remuneration.

Single figure table

	Director 1		Director 2	
	20X1	20X0	20X1	20X0
Salary and fees				
Taxable benefits				
Annual bonus				
Long-term incentive plans				
Pension-related benefits				
Total				

[SI 2008/410 8 Sch 5(2)].

5.103 Paragraph 6(1) of Schedule 8 requires a company to insert additional columns to set out items that are in the nature of remuneration but that are not covered by the columns specified in the legislation (for example, salary and fees, taxable benefits). This might include retention bonuses payable on completion of a specified service period without any performance condition, and HMRC-approved SAYE options and share incentive plan awards.

5.104 Additional columns and sub-totals are permitted if the directors consider them necessary for an understanding of the table. Any additional columns in the nature of remuneration should be presented before the 'total' column. [SI 2008/410 8 Sch 6 (1)(2)]. Where an additional column is inserted, the basis of calculating the amounts in that column and any other details necessary for an understanding of those amounts is given in a note to the table. These details are to include any performance measures related to those amounts and, if there are none, an explanation of why not. [2008/410 8 Sch 12(5)].

5.105 Companies are permitted to present columns A to E in a different order to facilitate the creation of sub-totals. [SI 2008/410 8 Sch 7(2)].

5.106 Companies may present two tables: one for executive directors, the other for non-executive directors. [SI 2008/410 8 Sch 4(2)]. Table 5.2 is an example of disclosure of the single figure table, taking the two table approach.

Table 5.2 Single total figure table

Vodafone Group Plc – Annual report – 31 March 2015

Directors' remuneration (extract)

2015 remuneration (extract 1)

Total remuneration for the 2015 financial year (audited)

	Vittorio Colao		Stephen Pusey		Nick Read[1]	
	2015 £'000	2014 £'000	**2015 £'000**	2014 £'000	**2015 £'000**	2014 £'000
Salary/fees	1,140	1,110	594	575	675	–
Taxable benefits[2]	40	38	21	21	28	–
Annual bonus: GSTIP (see below for further detail)	1,287	982	671	509	755	–
Total long-term incentive:	–	5,550	–	1,858	–	–
GLTI vesting during the year[3]	–	4,716	–	1,579	–	–
Cash in lieu of GLTI dividends[4]	–	834	–	279	–	–
Cash in lieu of pension	342	333	178	173	203	–
Other[5]	1	1	–	–	1	–
Total	**2,810**	**8,014**	**1,464**	**3,136**	**1,662**	**–**

Notes:
1. Nick Read was appointed to the Board on 1 April 2014.
2. Taxable benefits include amounts in respect of:
   – Private healthcare (2015: £1,854; 2014 £1,734);
   – Cash car allowance £19,200 p.a.; and
   – Travel (2015: Vittorio Colao £18,022; Nick Read £7,164; 2014: Vittorio Colao £17,155).
3. The value shown in the 2014 column is the award which vested on 28 June 2014 and is valued using the execution share price on 30 June 2014 of 196.19 pence. Please note that the values disclosed in this table in 2014 are slightly different as the value was based on an average of the closing share price over the last quarter of the 2014 financial year of 234.23 pence.
4. Participants also receive a cash award, equivalent in value to the dividends that would have been paid during the vesting period on any shares that vest. The cash in lieu of dividend value shown in 2014 relates to the award which vested on 28 June 2014.
5. Reflects the value of the SAYE benefit which is calculated as £250 × 12 months × 20% to reflect the discount applied based on savings made during the year.

2015 remuneration (extract 2)

2015 remuneration for the Chairman and Non-Executive Directors (audited)

	Salary/fees		Benefits[1]		Total	
	2015 **£'000**	2014 £'000	**2015** **£'000**	2014 £'000	**2015** **£'000**	2014 £'000
Chairman						
Gerard Kleisterlee	625	600	66	58	691	658
Senior Independent Director						
Luc Vandevelde	160	160	6	11	166	171
Non-executive directors						
Sir Crispin Davis (appointed 28 July 2014)	78	–	26	–	104	–
Dame Clara Furse (appointed 1 September 2014)	67	–	–	–	67	–
Valerie Gooding	115	19	5	–	120	19
Renee James[2]	145	139	11	5	156	144
Samuel Jonah[2]	151	151	5	9	156	160
Nick Land	140	140	1	1	141	141
Philip Yea	115	115	–	–	115	115
Former non-executive directors						
Alan Jebson[2] (retired 31 July 2014)	56	151	32	40	88	191
Omid Kordestani[2] (retired 31 December 2014)	116	151	14	33	130	184
Anne Lauvergeon (retired 31 July 2014)	38	115	1	5	39	120
Anthony Watson (retired 31 July 2014)	38	115	4	1	42	116
Total	**1,844**	**1,856**	**171**	**163**	**2,015**	**2,019**

Notes:

1. We have been advised that for Non-Executive Directors, certain travel and accommodation expenses in relation to attending Board meetings should be treated as a taxable benefit. The table above includes these travel expenses and the corresponding tax contribution.

2 Salary/fees include an additional allowance of £6,000 per meeting for Directors based outside of Europe.

5.107 The requirements for comparative information are discussed from paragraph 5.157.

[The next paragraph is 5.114.]

Listing Rules requirements

5.114 The Listing Rules require listed companies to disclose particulars of any arrangement under which a director has either waived or agreed to waive any future or current emoluments and details of such waivers. This applies in respect of emoluments from either the company or any of its subsidiaries. [LR 9.8.4R (5)(6)].

5.115 LR 9.8.4C requires the company to include all of the information required by LR 9.8.4R (which includes the disclosure described in para 5.114) in a single identifiable section, unless the annual report includes a cross-reference table indicating where that information is set out. See chapter 2 for more details.

Salary and fees

5.116 The amount to be included in the first column of the single figure table is 'salary and fees'. [SI 2008/410 8 Sch 7(1)(a)]. This amount is the cash paid to or receivable by the director in respect of the relevant financial year. [SI 2008/410 8 Sch 10(1)(a)].

> **Example – Flexible benefits scheme**
>
> A quoted company has a flexible benefits scheme, whereby a director may apply part of his salary in purchasing additional holiday or benefits such as health cover. Assuming the director takes advantage of this and purchases, say, two weeks additional holiday and health cover, should the amounts disclosed in the single figure table required by Schedule 8 to SI 2008/410 as 'salary and fees' or as 'taxable benefits' be adjusted?
>
> The salary figures should not be adjusted (reduced) as long as the amount that the director is 'charged' for the benefits is based on the cost or value of those benefits. This is because he is entitled to the salary and it is his option to apply it in purchasing whatever he wants. The fact that the benefits are purchased from the company rather than from a third party is not relevant.
>
> But, if additional benefits and reduction in salary were imposed on the director (that is, it was not at his option), the salary disclosed would be reduced. Any non-cash benefit (such as health cover) would be included in the taxable

benefits column disclosed in the single figure table, with the nature and value (if significant) of the benefit also being disclosed. [SI 2008/410 8 Sch 12(1)(a)(b)].

If additional holiday and a reduction in salary were imposed on the director, the salary disclosed would be reduced but there would be no additional amount to be disclosed in the 'taxable benefits' column. An imposed holiday is equivalent to a reduction in working time with a consequent reduction in salary.

5.117 Sometimes, directors are paid in a currency other than the company's presentation currency. This is considered in the following example.

Example – Director paid in foreign currency

Most of a UK company's directors are UK resident and are paid by the company in sterling (which is both the company's functional and presentation currency). But one of its directors is resident in the United States and his salary is denominated in US dollars and paid in US dollars. Should his salary be disclosed in US dollars or sterling?

Schedule 8 to SI 2008/410 is silent as to the currency in which the directors' remuneration should be presented.

The company has a choice of whether to present the information in sterling or US dollars. Generally, disclosure in the company's presentation currency will be the most transparent approach. Disclosing each director's remuneration in its denominated currency can make it difficult to compare a director's remuneration with that of his peers. Also, it does not reflect the sterling cost to the UK company of employing the US resident director.

Presenting the information in sterling might mean that the amount disclosed as the director's salary would change each year, just because of movements in the exchange rate. It would be helpful if the US dollar salary and the exchange rate used for translation were disclosed as a footnote to the table.

Taxable benefits

5.118 'Taxable benefits' are calculated as the *"gross value before payment of tax"*. [SI 2008/410 8 Sch 10(b)]. Taxable benefits include (to the extent they are in respect of qualifying services):

■ Expense allowances that are chargeable to UK income tax (or would be if the person were an individual, or would be if the person were resident in the UK for tax purposes).

■ Any benefits received by the person, other than salary, (whether or not in cash) that are emoluments of the person.

[SI 2008/410 8 Sch 11(1)].

5.119 Companies are required to disclose, after the single figure table, the types of benefits that are included under the second bullet above and the value of each of them, where significant. 'Significant' is not defined but in our view, should be interpreted in terms of significance to the director rather than to the company. [SI 2008/410 8 Sch 12(1)]. Table 5.3 is an example of where the types of benefits are disclosed together with the value of significant benefits.

Table 5.3 – Taxable benefits

The Sage Group plc – Annual report – 30 September 2014

Directors' remuneration report

Single figure for total remuneration (audited information)The following table sets out the single figure for total remuneration for executive directors for the financial years ended 30 September 2013 and 2014.

	(a) Salary/fees £'000		(b) Benefits[1] £'000		(c) Bonus[2] £'000		(d) Pension[3] £'000		(e) PSP awards[4] £'000		Total £'000	
Director	2014	2013	2014	2013	2014	2013	2014	2013	2014	2013	2014	2013
Executive directors												
G S Berruyer[5]	765	719	121	120	539	651	191	180	–	–	1,616	1,670
S Hare[6]	360	–	15	–	256	–	89	–	–	–	720	–
Non–executive directors[7]												
D H Brydon	360	360	46	–	–	–	–	–	–	–	406	360
R Markland	88	87	–	–	–	–	–	–	–	–	88	87
N Berkett	60	15	–	–	–	–	–	–	–	–	60	15
D Hall	45	–	–	–	–	–	–	–	–	–	45	–
J Howell	74	23	–	–	–	–	–	–	–	–	74	23
I Kuznetsova	34	–	–	–	–	–	–	–	–	–	34	–
I Mason	10	59	–	–	–	–	–	–	–	–	10	59
M Rolfe	13	76	–	–	–	–	–	–	–	–	13	76

Extract from footnotes

[1] Benefits provided to the executive directors included: car benefits or cash equivalent, private medical insurance, permanent health insurance, life assurance and financial advice. A housing allowance of £100,000 per annum was provided to Guy Berruyer. Donald Brydon receives a company car benefit.

5.120 So, 'taxable benefits' include both taxable expense allowances and benefits in kind (whether taxable or not). The term *"gross value before payment of tax"* is not defined but, in our view, for the purposes of determining benefits in kind, it is equivalent to the *"estimated money value"* that forms the basis of the disclosure requirements in Schedule 5 (see para 5.60). Table 5.3.1 is an example showing each type of benefit with separate disclosure of the tax paid by the company.

Table 5.3.1 – Taxable benefits

Thomas Cook Group plc – Annual report – 30 September 2014

Governance: Report on Directors' Remuneration (extract)

Benefits
The following table sets out the benefits received and the tax paid by the Company in respect of certain benefits:

Name	Car allowance	Private medical	Life assurance	Income protection	Accommodation costs	Tax on accommodation costs	Travel costs	Tax on travel costs	FY14 Total	FY13 Total
	£	£	£	£	£	£	£	£	£	£
Harriet Green[1]	15,000	1,887	1,416	9,906	41,894	34,277	26,736	21,875	152,991	185,767
Michael Healy	20,000	1,887	943	–	–	–	812	664	24,306	22,489
Frank Meysman[2]	–	–	–	–	14,893	12,185	14,038	–	41,116	37,794

[1] Harriet Green received provision of accommodation in London and travel costs reimbursed by the Company and includes the income tax assessed by HMRC as payable on accommodation and travel elements. Of the benefits disclosed for Harriet Green circa £69,000 net relate to accommodation and travel costs, which are considered necessary due to late and early meetings necessitated by the scale and pace of our ambitious Transformation. The overall benefits figure for Harriet Green for FY14 has reduced by 17.6% from FY13, which includes a reduction in hotel costs (31% year-on-year reduction), and removal of the £20,000 car allowance for Harriet Green from 1 July 2014 onwards.

[2] The figure disclosed for Frank Meysman is in respect of accommodation in London and travel costs reimbursed by the Company and the income tax assessed by HMRC as payable on the London accommodation element. Frank Meysman's travel expenses between Belgium and the UK are not taxable, as he is domiciled in Belgium and is entitled to a specific deduction under HMRC rules.

Other than noted above, income tax and employees NI is not paid by the Company on any other elements of the benefits received by Harriet Green, Michael Healy and Frank Meysman.

[The next paragraph is 5.122.]

Annual bonus

5.122 This category (column C of the single figure table) deals with bonuses payable in respect of performance in a single financial year. Where a bonus is granted for performance over, say, a two year period and that period ends in the current financial year, that bonus would be included in column D (long-term incentive plans) of the single figure table (see para 5.99). The year in which bonuses are disclosed in discussed further from paragraph 5.31.

5.123 The amount to be disclosed in column C of the single figure table is:

"Money or other assets received or receivable for the relevant financial year as a result of the achievement of performance measures or targets relating to a period ending in that financial year other than:

- *those which result from awards made in a previous financial year and where final vesting is determined as a result of the achievement of performance measures or targets relating to a period ending in the relevant financial year; or*

- *those receivable subject to the achievement of performance measures or targets in a future financial year."*

[SI 2008/410 8 Sch 7(1)(c)].

5.124 Where amounts are included in column C or D (see para 5.99), Schedule 8 requires additional information to be set out after the table as follows:

"(2) For every component the value of which is included in the sums required to be set out in the columns headed "c" and "d" of the table by paragraphs 7(1)(c) and (d), there must be set out after the table the relevant details.

(3) In sub-paragraph (2) "the relevant details" means—

(a) details of any performance measures and the relative weighting of each;

(b) within each performance measure, the performance targets set at the beginning of the performance period and corresponding value of the award achievable;

(c) for each performance measure, details of actual performance relative to the targets set and measured over the relevant reporting period, and the resulting level of award; and

(d) where any discretion has been exercised in respect of the award, particulars must be given of how the discretion was exercised and how the resulting level of award was determined."

[SI 2008/410 8 Sch 12(2)(3)].

5.125 When the directors consider that information about performance measures or targets is commercially sensitive, this information need not be disclosed. But if this information is omitted, particulars of, and the reasons for, the omission are disclosed. An indication is also given as to when (if at all) the information is to be reported to members of the company. [SI 2008/410 8 Sch 1(5)(6)].

5.126 The amount to be included in the single figure table as 'annual bonus' is the total cash equivalent including any amount deferred, other than where the deferral is subject to the achievement of further performance measures or targets in a future financial year. [SI 2008/410 8 Sch 10(c)].

5.126.1 Sometimes, where the deferred annual bonus is payable in shares, the director will receive on vesting, in addition to the shares, a cash amount equivalent to dividends notionally attributable to those shares over the deferral period. This additional cash payment is not included in the single figure table, because the amount included in the table on achievement of the performance measures in respect of the shares is the value of the shares at that date. This value represents the present value of future dividends; to also include the additional cash payment over the deferral period would be to double count. The position is different for long-term incentives (see para 5.135.1).

5.127 Where a deferred bonus is included in this category in the single figure table, the directors' remuneration report discloses the percentage deferred, whether it was deferred in cash or shares and whether the deferral was subject to conditions other than performance measures. [SI 2008/410 8 Sch 12(4)]. Table 5.3.2 is an example that gives the additional information required in respect of columns C and D.

Table 5.3.2 – Additional information on bonuses and LTIPs

easyJet plc – Annual report – 30 September 2013

Directors' remuneration report (extract)

What did the Directors earn in relation to the 2013 financial year? (extract)
We have set out the amount earned by the Directors in the table below (£000) (Audited):

£'000	Fees and Salary	Benefits[3]	Bonus[4]	LTIP[5]	Pension[6]	Total	Fees and Salary	Benefits	Bonus	LTIP	Pension	Total
						2013						**2012**
Executive												
Carolyn McCall OBE	**665**	**5**	**1,153**	**4,565**	**47**	**6,435**	665	5	1,274	1,703	47	3,694
Chris Kennedy	**410**	**5**	**533**	**2,746**	**30**	**3,724**	400	5	373	1,024	29	1,831
Non-Executive												
John Barton[1]	**125**	–	–	–	–	**125**	–	–	–	–	–	–
Sir Michael Rake[2]	**175**	–	–	–	–	**175**	300	–	–	–	–	300
Charles Gurassa	**90**	–	–	–	–	**90**	85	–	–	–	–	85
David Bennett	**75**	–	–	–	–	**75**	65	–	–	–	–	65
Rigas Doganis	**63**	–	–	–	–	**63**	55	–	–	–	–	55
John Browett	**55**	–	–	–	–	**55**	55	–	–	–	–	55
Keith Hamill OBE	**55**	–	–	–	–	**55**	60	–	–	–	–	60
Adèle Anderson	**55**	–	–	–	–	**55**	55	–	–	–	–	55
Andy Martin	**55**	–	–	–	–	**55**	55	–	–	–	–	55
Total	**1,823**	**10**	**1,686**	**7,311**	**77**	**10,907**	1,795	10	1,647	2,727	76	6,255

[4] One third of the bonus will be compulsorily deferred in shares for three years and subject to forfeiture. Carolyn McCall chose to defer the maximum 50% of her bonus and Chris Kennedy chose to defer the maximum one third of his bonus.

How was pay linked to performance in 2013?

Measure	As a percentage of maximum bonus opportunity CEO	CFO	Threshold	On-Target	Maximum	Actual	Payout
				Performance required			
Profit before tax (£m)	70%	60%	283	315	362	478	100%
On-time performance	10%	10%	80%	83%	88%	87%	94%
Customer satisfaction targets[1]	10%	10%	77%	82%	85%	83%	62%
Cost per seat (ex. fuel)[2]	10%	10%	£36.82	£36.59	£36.24	£36.81	11.7%
Departmental objectives	–	10%	Successful	Exceeding	Outstanding	Outstanding	100%

[1] easyJet changed survey provider during the year and future targets will be set on the basis of a different survey provided by Milward Brown. For future reference, the correlated customer satisfaction scores for achievement and targets above, on the basis of the new provider, would be: 80.4% achieved versus targets of 74.8% threshold, 79.7% on target and 82.6% stretch.
[2] Cost per seat (excluding fuel) targets are at constant (plan) currency.

Annual bonus

The following chart shows the performance against bonus targets for 2013:

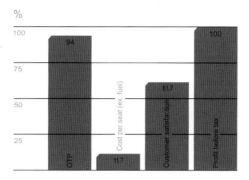

A sliding scale of targets for each objective was set at the start of the financial year. 10% of each element is payable for achieving the threshold target, increasing to 50% for on-target performance and 100% for achieving maximum performance.

The safety of our customers and people underpins all of the operational activities of the Group and the bonus plan includes an underpin that enables the Committee to scale back the bonus earned in the event that there is a safety event that occurs that it considers warrants the use of such discretion. No such event occurred in 2012/13.

Performance highlights during the year were:

■ profit before tax – Achievement was up by 50.9% to £478 million and pre-tax profit margins grew by 3 percentage points to 11.2%, considerably exceeding market consensus at the time the targets were set;

■ on-time performance – Strong sustained on-time performance of 87.4% of arrivals within 15 minutes;

■ customer satisfaction targets – 82.7% of customers satisfied with the service;

■ total costs per seat excluding fuel at constant currency – 3.9% increase, reflecting increases at regulated airports and increased use of de-icing fluid following one of the longest periods of adverse weather experienced across the network in recent years; and

■ CFO's departmental objectives – These were met in full.

86.7% of the maximum bonus was awarded to the CEO and CFO in respect of performance for the year ended 30 September 2013. This resulted in a bonus payment of £1,153,110 to the CEO and £533,205 to the CFO. One-third of the bonus is compulsorily deferred into shares for three years and subject to continued employment. In addition, Executive Directors can voluntarily defer a portion of their bonus which may be eligible for Matching Share Awards.

The Committee is satisfied with the overall payments in light of the level of performance achieved.

LTIP

The awards made to Executive Directors in 2011 were subject to ROCE (excluding operating lease adjustments) performance in the financial year ended 30 September 2013. The percentage which could be earned was determined using the following vesting schedule:

	Threshold	Target	Maximum
ROCE y/e 30	(25% vesting)	(50% vesting)	(100% vesting)
September 2013			
Award One (up to 100% of salary)	7.0%	8.5%	12.0%
Award Two (over 100% of salary)	10.0%	12.0%	13.0%

There were no Matching Awards made in 2011.

ROCE (excluding operating lease adjustments) in the year ended 30 September 2013 was 23%; correspondingly 100% of awards are due to vest in March 2014, subject to continued service.

[The next paragraph is 5.129.]

5.129 Performance measures are defined as *"the measure by which performance is to be assessed, but does not include any condition relating to service"*. A 'performance target' is *"the specific level of performance to be attained in respect of a performance measure"*. [SI 2008/410 8 Sch 44.]

5.130 Performance measures are often financial measures (such as profit or earnings per share) but could be non-financial measures (such as employee retention rates or customer satisfaction ratings). They do not include service conditions. This means that where a bonus is payable based on achievement of a performance measure in the year, it is disclosed in the directors' remuneration report of that year, even if the director has to stay with the company for a further period before he becomes entitled to the bonus (see para 5.34). Such a bonus would be a deferred bonus and subject to additional disclosure as described above.

Long-term incentive plans

5.131   This category deals with awards for performance over more than one financial year. The amount to be disclosed is:

> *"Money or other assets received or receivable for periods of more than one financial year where final vesting is both*

> ■   *determined as a result of the achievement of performance measures or targets relating to a period ending in the relevant financial year; and*

> ■   *is not subject to the achievement of performance measures or targets in a future financial year."*

[SI 2008/410 8 Sch 7(1)(d)].

5.132   As described in paragraph 5.124, additional information is disclosed if any amount is disclosed in this category.

5.133   Performance measures and targets are defined as described in paragraph 5.129 and exclude service conditions. So, where a director achieves a target set for a three year period in the financial year but is not entitled to receive the related award unless he/she remains with the company for a further year, the long-term incentive is disclosed in the single figure table in the financial year in which the performance target is met (as opposed to year four when both the target and the service condition are met). The year in which long-term incentives are disclosed is discussed further from paragraph 5.31.

5.134   The details of scheme interests awarded during the year are disclosed in the directors' remuneration report (see from para 5.173). These scheme interests will include the long-term incentive plans dealt with in column D of the single figure table but could also include other schemes. Amounts receivable in respect of a scheme in which the only vesting condition is a service condition (for example, that the director remains with the company for a specified period) are not included in 'column D' but will be included in column C or in a separate additional column. But such schemes are within the scope of the scheme interest awards disclosures.

5.135   The amounts included in column D (long-term incentive plans) comprise:

■   The cash value of any monetary award.

■   The value of any shares or share options awarded, calculated by:

   ■   multiplying the original number of shares granted by the proportion that vest (or an estimate);

   ■   multiplying the total arrived at above by the market price of shares at the date on which the shares vest (see para 5.136); and

   ■   deducting the amount paid or payable by the director for the shares or to exercise the share options.

■   The value of any additional cash or shares receivable in respect of dividends accrued (actually or notionally).

[SI 2008/410 8 Sch 10(1)(d),(3)(b)].

5.136   Where the market price of the shares at vesting date is not ascertainable, an estimate of the market price is used and is calculated on the basis of an average market value over the last quarter of the financial year. [SI 2008/410 8 Sch 10(3)(a)].

5.136.1   Unlike the dividend equivalent payments in respect of a deferred annual bonus (see para 5.126.1), additional cash payable in respect of notional or actual dividends on shares awarded under long-term incentive schemes is included in the single figure table (in column D). This is because the column D amount for share awards is based on the share price at vesting rather than the earlier date on which the performance measures are met; that is, the dividend accrues before the measurement date for single figure table purposes. In the case of a deferred annual bonus, the value of the shares at the date the performance measures are met is included in the single figure table; dividends that accrue between that date and vesting date are not included. This is illustrated in the following example.

Example – Dividend equivalents

Company A has a long-term incentive scheme for Mr X, a director. Under the scheme, Mr X is entitled to receive 100,000 of company A's ordinary shares if specified profit targets for the three years to 31 December 20X3 are met, provided that he completes a further year of service as a director. Mr X becomes unconditionally entitled to the shares on 31 December 20X4. At 31 December 20X4, Mr X is also entitled to receive cash equivalent to the dividend paid on 100,000 shares in the year ended 31 December 20X4.

The market values of company A's ordinary shares are as follows:

At 31 December 20X3	£2.00
At 31 December 20X4	£2.10
Average for the 3 months ended 31 December 20X3	£1.95

A dividend of 10p per share was paid in 20X4.

a) What should be included in the single figure table for the years ended 31 December 20X3 and 31 December 20X4?

31 December 20X3

The amounts to be included in the single figure table for long-term incentive schemes (LTIPs) are based on the market price of the shares at vesting. The entitlement to shares vests on 31 December 20X4, but amounts receivable under LTIPs are included in the single figure table when the performance measures are met; any additional service condition is disregarded for this purpose. At 31 December 20X3, the price at vesting is not known and must be estimated as the average market price over the last quarter of the year. So the amount included in column D of the single figure table for the year ended 31 December 20X3 is £195,000 (100,000 × £1.95).

31 December 20X4

At 31 December 20X4, the award vests and the amount for single figure purposes can be finalised as the market value of the award at vesting date plus the cash payment equivalent to the dividend. This is calculated as:

(100,000 × £2.10) + (100,000 × 10p) = £220,000

As described in paragraph 5.160, where an actual amount is different from an estimate included in the prior year, the comparative is restated. So, in the directors' remuneration report for the year ended 31 December 20X4, the current year amount included in column D is nil and the comparative is restated as £220,000. A note to the single figure table is included to explain the restatement.

b) What would be disclosed in respect of the same entitlement under an annual bonus scheme where the performance measures are met in the year ended 31 December 20X3?

Assume that Mr X is entitled to receive 100,000 of company A's ordinary shares if a specified profit target for the year to 31 December 20X3 is met, provided that he completes a further year of service as a director. Mr X becomes unconditionally entitled to the shares on 31 December 20X4. At 31 December 20X4, Mr X is also entitled to receive cash equivalent to the dividend paid on 100,000 shares in the year ended 31 December 20X4.

The amount included in column C in respect of non-cash awards is based on the 'cash equivalent' of the award (see para 5.126) when the performance measures are met; any additional service condition is disregarded for this purpose. The value of the award at final vesting date is not relevant for the measurement of the amount to be included in the single figure table; instead, the annual bonus figure is measured as the value at the date the performance measures are met. So the amount included in column D of the single figure table for the year ended 31 December 20X3 is £200,000 (100,000 × £2).

In the year ended 31 December 20X4, the comparative figure is £200,000. The cash payment made in lieu of dividends is not included in the current year figures; neither is the comparative restated.

For LTIPs, the law requires inclusion of dividend equivalents in the amounts reported for single figure purposes; no such provision exists for annual bonus arrangements. But the measurement basis of the share award is different for LTIPs, being based on the price at vesting and not, as applies for annual bonuses, at the price when the performance measures are met.

The treatment of annual bonus share awards is consistent with that which would apply if the shares vested at performance date (31 December 20X3); where shares are awarded without further service conditions, subsequent dividend payments are not included in reporting remuneration, because the dividends are a reward for investment and not a reward for services. Since the measurement of the award at performance date is the same as would apply if the shares were awarded at that time, it is appropriate to extend the consistency of treatment to subsequent dividends.

> The value of the share when performance measures are met is a reflection of the expected income stream from that share, including the next year's expected dividend.

5.137 Like annual bonuses, the amounts to be disclosed may be based on substantial (but not full) completion by the year end (see para 5.37). [SI 2008/410 8 Sch 8(1)].

5.138 Although there is a requirement to disclose details of amounts included in column C (annual bonus) that are deferred (see para 5.128), there is no equivalent disclosure requirement in respect of amounts included in column D (long-term incentives). But we consider it desirable for companies to disclose details of any amounts deferred until further service conditions are met.

Clawback and malus provisions

5.139 Under the UK Corporate Governance Code, an executive director's remuneration contract should include 'clawback' or 'malus' provisions. [UK CGC D1.1]. (See the Annex to this chapter). Under a 'clawback' provision, a director is required, in specified circumstances, to pay back an amount already received in cash or shares. Under a 'malus' provision, the company withholds payment of a deferred award. Such provisions might state that an award is to be repaid by the director or withheld from him if the performance measure on which the award was based is subsequently found to be overstated. Or it might be that the award is to be repaid or withheld if the director is discovered to have been, at the time the award was made, in serious breach of his employment contract.

5.140 Where money or other assets reported in the single figure table in a prior year is to be recovered or withheld from a director, this amount is shown in a separate column in the single figure table. It is shown as a negative value and is deducted in arriving at the total in the total column. An explanation and the basis of calculation are given in a note to the table. [SI 2008/410 8 Sch 8(2)(a)(b)].

Pension related benefits

5.141 The 'pension related benefits' column (column E) includes:

(a) The cash value of payments (whether in cash or otherwise) in lieu of retirement benefits.

(b) All benefits in the year from participating in pension schemes.

[SI 2008/410 8 Sch 7(e), 10(1)(e)(i)].

5.142 The amount to be included in the single figure table as the benefit of participating in a pension scheme is the 'pension input amount' for the 'pension input period' using definitions that are based on, but not exactly the same as, those contained in section 229 of the Finance Act 2004.

5.142.1 Pension contributions paid by the director are deducted from the pension input amount. [SI 2008/410 8 Sch 10 (e)(ii)(cc)]. (See para 5.156.) Where a director's contributions exceed the pension input amount, the amount included in column E is nil; it is not permissible to include a negative value in column E. [SI 2008/410 8 Sch 8(3)].

5.143 Contributions that directors themselves pay by way of a deduction from salary are disclosed as part of salary and fees, rather than pension-related benefits. Sometimes a director has a choice as to whether to receive cash or pension benefits, as illustrated in the examples below.

> **Example 1 – Cash in lieu of pension contributions**
>
> Some of the directors have contributions paid by the company into its defined contribution scheme. Other directors have elected instead to receive a direct payment through payroll, in lieu of the contributions that would have been made by the company to the defined contribution scheme. Although it is expected that they will use the cash in a personal pension scheme, they are under no obligation to do so. How should the payments be presented in the single figure table?
>
> These payments should be classified as pension-related benefits. Although the cash is paid directly to the directors, the payments are *"in lieu of retirement benefits"*.

Example 2 – Waiver of bonus in favour of pension contributions

A director of a quoted company is entitled to an annual salary and other benefits, including an annual bonus. After the end of the year, the value of his bonus is determined and he is given three options:

(a)   He receives the bonus in cash.

(b)   He waives the bonus and the company pays the same amount into his defined contribution pension arrangement.

(c)   He waives the bonus and the company pays the same amount into his final salary-based pension to buy additional years' service in the scheme.

What would be disclosed in the single figure table under each of these options?

(a)   If the bonus is received in cash, it is included in column C ('annual bonus').

(b)   If the bonus is paid into either a defined contribution or defined benefit pension scheme, it will not be included in column C ('annual bonus'). Instead, the calculation of the pension input amount to be included in column E will reflect the additional pension related benefits (see para 5.147).

Types of pension scheme

5.144   A 'pension scheme' means a retirement benefits scheme within the meaning given by section 150(1) of the Finance Act 2004 which is

■   one in which the company participates; or

■   one to which the company paid a contribution during the financial year.

[SI 2008/410 8 Sch 44(1)].

5.145   A 'pension scheme' is as defined in section 150(1) of the Finance Act 2004 as:

"... a scheme or other arrangements, comprised in one or more instruments or agreements, having or capable of having effect so as to provide benefits to or in respect of persons —

(a)   on retirement,

(b)   on death,

(c)   on having reached a particular age,

(d)   on the onset of serious ill-health or incapacity, or

(e)   in similar circumstances."

[Finance Act 2004 Sec 150(1)].

5.146   Different types of arrangement are outlined in the Finance Act 2004. These are:

■   Money purchase arrangements. Under these arrangements, the member builds up an entitlement to benefits that is based on the amount available to purchase those benefits; that is, the benefits are based on the value of the 'pension pot'. Under the Finance Act 2004, these can be one of two types:

   ■   Cash balance arrangements. In a cash balance arrangement the pot is not calculated wholly by reference to such payments made by or on behalf of the member. Instead, all or part of the member's pot is promised or guaranteed, and so the pot cannot be said to be calculated wholly by reference to payments under the scheme.

   ■   Other money purchase arrangements. In these arrangements the pot is calculated wholly by reference to payments made under the pension scheme by or on behalf of the member. This means amounts going into the pension scheme under the individual's arrangement will include individual and employer contributions, minimum payments under Pensions Schemes Act 1993, a transfer into the scheme of the member's rights under another pension scheme, and a credit received following a pension sharing order. So the member's pot is solely derived (whether directly or indirectly) from payments made under the arrangement.

■   Defined benefit arrangements. Under these arrangements, the member's benefits are not based on a pension pot but are calculated based on other factors, typically earnings and service period.

- Hybrid arrangements. A hybrid arrangement is one where the member will receives two or more of the following types of benefits: cash balance benefits, other money purchase benefits and defined benefits.

Calculation of pension input amounts

5.147 The amount included in the table for the 'pension input amount' is that amount for the 'pension input period'. This period is the financial year except where the director is appointed during the year in which case it is from the date of appointment to the end of the year. [SI 2008/410 8 Sch 10(e)(ii)(aa)].

5.148 Schedule 8 states that amounts to be included in the table are those in respect of qualifying services *"unless otherwise indicated"*. [SI 2008/410 8 Sch 4(3)]. There are specific rules for calculating the pension input period so these overrule the normal rule that only amounts relating to qualifying services are included. Where a director leaves office during the financial year, the pension input period is not adjusted; that is, the pension input period for that director is the full financial year (assuming he was appointed in a prior year). The amount of pension related benefits in the single figure is reduced by pensions or lump sums paid after retirement because they either reduce the size of the pension pot (for money purchase arrangements) or settle part of the liability for future pensions (for defined benefit arrangements). But, in the financial year of retirement, amounts paid in pension or lump sums between retirement and the end of the year would be disclosed as payments to past directors (see para 5.187).

5.149 For cash balance arrangements, the 'pension input amount' is the amount of any increase in the value of the individual's rights under the arrangement during the pension input period. The increase is measured as the difference between the value at the beginning of the period, as adjusted for inflation, and the value at the end of the period. If there is no such increase, the pension input amount is measured as nil. [Finance Act 2004 Secs 230(1), (5B), 231].

5.150 For this purpose, 'value' is assessed using the following assumptions:

"(a)   if the person has not left the employment to which the arrangement relates on or before the date, that the person left that employment on the date with a prospective right to benefits under the arrangement,

(b)   if the person has not reached such age (if any) as must have been reached to avoid any reduction in the benefits on account of age, that on the date the person is entitled to receive the benefits without any reduction on account of age, and

(c)   that the person's right to receive the benefits had not been occasioned by physical or mental impairment."

[SI 2008/410 8 Sch 10(e)(ii)(ff)].

5.151 For other money purchase arrangements, the pension input amount is the total pension contributions paid by or on behalf of the individual and pension contributions paid in respect of the arrangement by the employer. [Finance Act 2004 Sec 233(1)]. (The director's own pension contributions are deducted from the pension input amount for inclusion in the single figure table). Where a company contribution has not been made but has been notionally allocated to the scheme in respect of a director, the contribution is treated as if it had been paid for the purposes of calculating the pension input amount. [SI 2008/410 8 Sch 10(2)].

5.152 For defined benefit arrangements, the pension input amount is the increase in value of the director's rights under the arrangement. If there is no such increase, the pension input amount is measured as nil. Again, value is assessed on the basis set out in paragraph 5.150. This increase is calculated as:

$$((20 \times PE) + LSE) - ((20 \times PB) + LSB)$$

where:

PE is the annual rate of pension that would be payable to the director if he became entitled to it at the end of the period.

PB is the annual rate of pension, adjusted for inflation, that would be payable to the director if he became entitled to it at the beginning of the period.

LSE is the amount of lump sum that would be payable to the director if he became entitled to it at the end of the period.

LSB is the amount of lump sum, adjusted for inflation, that would be payable to the director if he became entitled to it at the beginning of the period.

[SI 2008/410 8 Sch 10(1)(e); Finance Act 2004 Sec 234(1)].

5.153 This calculation can result in a negative number. This will occur when the inflationary uplift in the opening value exceeds the combined effect of any increase in pay and the additional year of service. Because the Finance Act 2004 describes the pension input amount as the amount of any *increase* in value, any decrease is not a pension input amount. So, where the calculation results in a negative number, the pension input amount is nil. It might be that the pension input amount is less that the director's own pension contributions, so that the net amount is negative. As described in paragraph 5.142.1, the amount included in column E (assuming the director participates in only one pension scheme) would be nil.

5.154 For hybrid arrangements, the pension input amount is the higher of the following:

■ The pension input amount that would apply if the benefits were cash balance benefits (if cash benefits might be provided under the arrangement).

■ The pension input amount that would apply if the benefits were other money purchase benefits (if money purchase benefits might be provided under the arrangement).

■ The pension input amount that would apply if the benefits were defined benefits (if defined benefits might be provided under the arrangement).

5.155 Where a director is a deferred member of a scheme throughout the year (or since his appointment), no pension related benefit is disclosed in the single figure table.

5.156 In summary, the amounts to be included as pension related benefits are:

■ For cash balance arrangements, the 'real' increase in value of the 'pension pot' over the financial year (or since date of appointment, if later) less the director's own contributions to that pot.

■ For money purchase arrangements, the amount of company contributions paid or payable in respect of the director over the financial year (or since date of appointment, if later).

■ For a defined benefit arrangements, the 'real' growth in the capital value (calculated as prescribed) of the director's entitlement to pension less the director's own contributions.

■ For hybrid arrangements, the highest of the possible benefits, calculated under the previous three bullets.

Comparatives for the single figure table

5.157 Each column in the single figure table is required to show the amount for the current year and the amount for the previous year. [SI 2008/410 8 Sch 9(1)]. In cases where a director's remuneration package includes all five of the elements that are to be shown separately in the single figure table, this will mean that 12 figures (five elements plus a total for each of the two years) are reported in respect of each director.

5.158 The comparative amounts should be reported in *"such a manner as to permit comparison"* with the current year amounts. [SI 2008/410 8 Sch 9(1)]. Comparison is easiest when the prior year amount is shown next to the current year amount. Where there are several elements in a director's remuneration package, it might not be sensible to present all 12 amounts in a single line as to do so could be confusing. Instead, the company could present the comparative information as follows, distinguishing the current year amounts by, for example, emboldening the text, using a different font, or italicising the comparative amount:

Single figure table

	Salary and fees	Taxable benefits	Annual bonus	Long-term incentive plans	Pension related benefits	Total
20X1: Director 1	x	x	X	x	X	x
20X0: Director 1	*x*	*x*	*X*	*x*	*X*	*x*
20X1: Director 2	x	x	x	x	X	x
20X0: Director 2	*x*	*x*	*x*	*x*	*X*	*x*

5.159 It is not acceptable to present the comparative information in a separate table as this would not comply with the requirement that the comparative is shown in the same column as the current year amount. Presenting all the comparative information as additional lines at the bottom of the table will not usually meet the requirement that the information is presented in a manner to permit comparison.

5.160 Sometimes an amount that was included in the table in the prior year was an estimate. In the current year, the actual amount might be determined to be different from that estimate. If this is so, the comparative amount reported in the current year is restated to the actual amount; that is, the revision of the estimate is dealt with by restating the comparative rather than by adjusting the current year. In other words, the revision of the estimate is a prior year adjustment; this is despite the fact that, in accordance with IAS 8, the prior year income statement is not restated for a revision of an estimate of remuneration expense. Where such a restatement of the comparative in the single figure table occurs, details of the calculation of the revised amount is given in a note to the table. [SI 2008/410 8 Sch 9(2)].

5.161 The single figure table includes information in respect of each person who has served as a director of the company at any time during the *relevant financial year*. The relevant financial year means the financial year in respect of which the report is prepared. [SI 2008/410 8 Sch 1(1)]. SI 2008/410 does not require disclosure of the comparatives in respect of individual directors who retired in the previous financial year. But it is common practice for such disclosure to be made as it provides useful additional information for readers.

5.162 As described above (see para 5.37), the amounts included in the table may be based on substantial (not full) completion of performance measures or targets. Where this was done in the prior year, the amounts reported in the prior year are shown as comparative amounts in the current year. Even though full completion occurs in the current year, the amounts are dealt with as being related to the prior year. [SI 2008/410 8 Sch 8(1)(b)].

[The next paragraph is 5.164.]

5.164 In the first year of application of the directors' remuneration report requirements, some of the comparative amounts might not be readily ascertainable from the previous report because it was prepared under different disclosure rules. Where this is so, the company estimates the relevant comparative amounts and discloses that it has done so and on what basis. [SI 2008/410 8 Sch 1(7)].

Total pension entitlements

5.165 The directors' remuneration report is required to disclose pension benefits for each director of the company who has served as such at any time during the financial year. The Department for Business Innovation & Skills (BIS) has suggested that where there are no such entitlements, it would be useful to state that fact.

5.165.1 Where such a director has a prospective entitlement to defined benefits or cash balance benefits (or benefits under a hybrid arrangement that includes such benefits) in respect of qualifying services, the following information is disclosed:

■ Details of those rights as at the end of the year, including the director's normal retirement date.

■ A description of any additional benefit that will become receivable by the director if he retires early.

■ Where a director has rights under different types of scheme identified in column E (pension related benefits) of the single figure table, separate details of each type of pension benefit. This would seem to mean that where a director is a member of both a defined benefit scheme and a money purchase scheme that is not a cash balance benefit scheme, details of both schemes are disclosed. If the director was a member of only a money purchase scheme (not a cash balance benefit scheme), no disclosure would be made other than the inclusion of the company's contributions in column E.

[SI 2008/410 8 Sch 13(1)(2)].

5.166   The normal retirement date is the earliest age at which, while the director continues to accrue benefits under the pension scheme, entitlement to a benefit arises:

■   without consent (whether of an employer, the trustees or managers of the scheme or otherwise); and

■   without an actuarial reduction;

but disregarding any special provision as to early repayment on grounds of ill health, redundancy or dismissal.

[SI 2008/410 8 Sch 13(3)].

5.167   An example of disclosure of pension benefits is Table 5.4. Only one director's pension entitlements are shown below, for illustration purposes.

Table 5.4 – Pension benefits

GlaxoSmithKline plc – Annual report – 31 December 2014

Annual report on remuneration (extract)

Total remuneration for 2014 (audited) (extract)

	Sir Andrew Witty, CEO				Simon Dingemans, CFO				Dr Moncef Slaoui, Chairman, Global Vaccines			
	2014 £000	% of total	2013 £000	% of total	2014 £000	% of total	2013 £000	% of total	2014 $000	% of total	2013 $000	% of total
A. Fixed pay												
Salary	1,087		1,059		718		699		1,212		1,180	
Benefits (1)	70		67		79		65		571		747	
Total fixed pay	1,157	30%	1,126	16%	797	43%	764	23%	1,783	41%	1,927	23%
B. Pay for performance												
Annual bonus – including the amount deferred	917		1,875		446		886		1,108		1,973	
Value earned from LTI awards (2):												
Matching awards under Deferred Annual Bonus Plan	111		249		65		n/a		138		485	
Performance Share Plan	1,035		3,250		398		1,502		939		3,763	
Total value earned from LTI awards	1,146		3,499		463		1,502		1,077		4,248	
Total pay for performance	2,063	53%	5,374	74%	909	49%	2,388	73%	2,185	51%	6,221	74%
C. Pension (3)	671	17%	707	10%	144	8%	140	4%	365	8%	266	3%
Total remuneration (4)	3,891		7,207		1,850		3,292		4,333		8,414	

Notes:

(1) Certain expenses incurred in the normal course of business are considered to be taxable benefits by UK HM Revenue & Customs and as such the table above includes these figures for 2013 and 2014. Further details are provided on page 98.

(2) An analysis of the value of LTIs earned by Sir Andrew Witty, Simon Dingemans and Dr Moncef Slaoui is set out on pages 113 to 116.

(3) Full details of the pension contributions and pensions accrued to date for the Executive Directors are given on page 106.

(4) The Committee may in specific circumstances, and in line with stated principles, apply clawback/malus, as it determines appropriate. Following due consideration by the Committee, there has been no reduction of outstanding awards or vesting levels (malus) applied during 2014 in respect of any of the Executive Directors.

Pension (audited) (extract)

The arrangements for the current Executive Directors are set out in the table below.

Pension arrangements (extract)

Sir Andrew Witty   Sir Andrew Witty is a member of the Glaxo Wellcome defined benefit pension plan with an accrual rate of 1/30th of final pensionable salary. This plan has been closed to new entrants since 2001. The section of the plan that Sir Andrew is a member of provides for a normal retirement age of 60 and a maximum pension value of 2/3rds of pensionable salary. Since 1 April 2013, pensionable earnings increases are limited to 2% per annum for all members, including Sir Andrew.

The following table shows the breakdown of the pension values set out on page 97.

| | Sir Andrew Witty | |
| | 2014 | 2013 |
Pension remuneration values	£000	£000
UK defined benefit	703	739
US defined benefit	–	–
Belgian defined benefit	–	–
Employer cash contributions	–	–
Member contributions to defined benefit plans	(32)	(32)
Total pension remuneration value	671	707

(a) The pension remuneration figures have been calculated in accordance with the methodology set out in the Remuneration Regulations. In calculating the defined benefit pension values for 2014, the difference between the accrued pension as at 31 December 2014 and the accrued pension as at 31 December 2013 increased by inflation (2.7% for UK defined benefit, 1.3% for US defined benefit, 1.3% for Belgium defined benefit) has been multiplied by 20. Where this results in a negative value, this has been deemed to be zero. In calculating total values, amounts have been translated from Euros into US dollars using an exchange rate of 1.33 for 2014 and 1.38 for 2013.

(b) For Sir Andrew, further details regarding the 2014 pension values are set out in the table below.

Sir Andrew Witty	Accrued pension as at 31 December 2014 (£ p.a.)	Accrued pension as at 31 December 2013 (£ p.a.)	Pension remuneration value for 2014 (£000)
UK – Funded	70,810	68,913	1
UK – Unfunded	613,521	563,193	702
Total	684,331	632,106	703

Sir Andrew joined GSK predecessor companies in 1991 and progressed through roles of increasing seniority within GSK until he was appointed CEO in May 2008. During this time, he built up pensionable service through the different tiers of the Glaxo Wellcome Pension Plan. His current pension entitlement is a product of his service and progression within GSK. Please note that the 2013 figures have had a small adjustment made to them, following a change to the inflationary measure used to value the Funded pension; the Total Pension number is unchanged.

[The next paragraph is 5.172.]

5.172   The examples below consider the implications for disclosure in respect of pension entitlements in various situations, including when the director is appointed or retires in the year. The examples cover the following situations:

■   A director (who was previously an employee) is appointed during the year (example 1).

■   Serving director receives pension (example 2).

■   Director retires during year, but remains an employee (example 3).

■   Director retires and commutes pension (example 4).

Example 1 – Director (previously an employee) appointed during the year

A quoted company is preparing its directors' remuneration report. One of the directors has been an employee of the company and a member of its final salary pension scheme for a number of years, but was appointed as a director of the company during this year.

Under Schedule 8 to SI 2008/410, should the disclosures in respect of the pension entitlements accruing to that director under the defined benefits scheme include all entitlements accruing or just those that have accrued to him in respect of qualifying services?

Paragraph 13 of Schedule 8 to SI 2008/410 requires disclosure of specified information (see para 5.165) in respect of a person who has served as a director at any time during the year and who *"... has a prospective entitlement to defined benefits scheme ... in respect of qualifying services..."*. It requires disclosure of *"... details of those rights as at the end of the year..."*. As the director was appointed in the year, only some of the rights accrued at the year-end are in respect of the qualifying services.

But it might be impracticable to distinguish between the entitlements that are in respect of qualifying services and those that are not. Pension entitlement is based on the final salary and the number of years of service. The final salary in the qualifying service period might be different from the salary at the date of appointment as director. The years of service used to determine the pension are only partly qualifying service. It could be argued that any uplift in pension entitlement that arises from an increase in salary after his appointment is entirely in respect of qualifying service because the pay increase arose entirely in a qualifying service period. On the other hand, it could be argued that this uplift is attributable to non-qualifying service for the proportion of service that was prior to his appointment as director.

Disclosure of the entitlements arising just from qualifying services might not be useful to readers and could be misleading. In our view, a sensible approach would be to disclose the director's total pension entitlement (for qualifying and non-qualifying services) but to also disclose that the director's entitlement is based on his total years of service to the company, of which (insert number) years were prior to his appointment as director on (insert date).

The single figure table includes pension benefits accrued by the director during the year (as opposed to the cumulative entitlements dealt with in the total pension entitlements disclosures). The pension input amount, calculated as specified (see para 5.153) is included in column E in the single figure table. As described from paragraph 5.147, the pension input period for a person who becomes a director during the year, is the date of appointment to the year end so the pension input amount relates only to qualifying services. The pension input amount calculation is based on his accrued pension immediately before his appointment as director and his accrued pension at the end of the year. This means that, if a director is a member of a final salary scheme and receives a pay rise on his appointment to the board, the pension input amount will reflect the 'capital value' of the increase in accrued pension attributable to the pay rise.

Example 2 – Serving director receives pension

The chairman of a quoted company is past retirement age and has been receiving a pension from the company for the whole of the current year, in addition to his salary (which is not pensionable). Does the disclosure of total pension entitlements have to include details of the chairman's pension entitlements?

The disclosure requirements for the chairman's defined benefit pension entitlements apply only to those prospective entitlements that arise from qualifying services. But the law does not limit this disclosure requirement to cases where some of the entitlements are in respect of qualifying services provided in the year. Instead, the disclosure of the information specified in paragraph 13 of Schedule 8 to SI 2008/410 is given in respect of each person's defined benefit pension entitlements where those entitlements are in respect of qualifying services (which the chairman's are) regardless of the period in which those services were provided. So, even though the chairman received no pensionable salary during the year (so no further benefits accrued to him during the year), full disclosure is required.

The single figure table includes the 'pension input amount' (see para 5.147) for the year (as opposed to the cumulative entitlements dealt with in the total pension entitlements disclosures). If the chairman's entitlements have not been enhanced since his retirement (apart from inflationary increases), the pension input amount will be nil.

Example 3 – Director retires during year, but remains an employee

A quoted company is preparing its directors' remuneration report. One of the directors, a member of its final salary pension scheme, resigned as a director of the company during this year, but remains an employee of the company, accruing further pensionable service.

(a) Should the disclosures in respect of the entitlements accruing to that person under the defined benefits scheme include all benefits accruing or just those that have accrued to him in respect of his services as a director?

Schedule 8 to SI 2008/410 requires disclosure of specified information in respect of any person who has served as a director at any time during the year and has defined benefit pension entitlements; these requirements apply only in respect of entitlements arising from qualifying services. As he resigned as a director in the year, not all of the entitlements accrued at the year-end are in respect of qualifying services.

As in example 1 above, it might be impracticable to distinguish between those entitlements that are in respect of qualifying services (that is, services as a director) and those that are not (that is, services as an employee). This will particularly be the case if there has been a change in salary since the date of resignation as director.

Disclosure of the entitlements arising just from qualifying services might not be useful to readers and could be misleading. As in example 1, in our view, a sensible approach would be to disclose the director's total pension entitlement (for qualifying and non-qualifying services) but to also disclose that the director's entitlement is based on his total years of service to the company.

The amounts included for pension related benefits in the single figure table are based on the pension input period. As described from paragraph 5.147 onwards, the pension input period is the financial year; the only exception is where the person was appointed as director during the year. So the single figure table will include pension related benefits for the full year even though some of these did not accrue from qualifying services. It would be sensible to include a footnote to the table to explain the position.

Example 4 – Director retires and commutes pension

A quoted company is preparing its directors' remuneration report for the year ended 31 December 20X1. One of its directors reached normal retirement age in the previous year. She retired in the current year and, as permitted by the rules of the defined benefit pension scheme, commuted part of her pension entitlement into a tax-free lump sum. In the 20X0 remuneration report, her disclosed accrued benefit was £100,000. By the time she retired, this had risen to £102,000 as a result of inflation. When she retired, she elected to forfeit £25,500 of her annual pension entitlement in consideration for a cash receipt of £235,000. At retirement date her accrued pension was £76,500. At 31 December 20X1 her accrued pension is £77,000 (the further £500 increase being inflationary). She made no personal contributions during the year.

What should be disclosed as pension entitlements in this year's remuneration report?

Schedule 8 to SI 2008/410 requires disclosure of pension entitlements in respect of any person who has served as a director at any time during the year, which were accrued in respect of qualifying services. So full disclosure in accordance with paragraph 13 of Schedule 8 to SI 2008/410 is required of information about the director's pension entitlement even though she retired during the year.

Disclosure is required of details of rights as at the year end. In this case, the director has an entitlement to a pension of £77,000 at the year-end and this should be disclosed. In the previous year, her entitlement to a pension of £100,000 would also have been disclosed. In our view, 'details of rights' in respect of pensions would include information about the commutation rights. So her right to commute part of this pension into a lump sum would also have been disclosable. If payment of this lump sum was made when she was no longer a director, it could be argued to be a payment to a past director that is disclosable because it is not a regular pension benefit commenced in a previous year (see para 5.187). Even if this were not the case, in our view, the report should disclose the fact that 25% of the pension was commuted and a lump sum of £235,000 paid. Without this information, the reader would not be able to interpret the disclosures of the current year compared with those made in the previous year.

Scheme interests awarded

5.173 A scheme is defined under SI 2008/410 as *"… any agreement or arrangement under which money or other assets may become receivable by a person and which includes one or more qualifying conditions with respect to service or performance that cannot be fulfilled within a single financial year"*. A scheme does not include bonuses the amount of which fall to be determined by reference to service or performance within a single financial year. [SI 2008/410 8 Sch 44(1)]. A 'scheme' is the same as a 'long-term incentive scheme' in Schedule 5 of SI 2008/410, which deals with disclosures in the notes to the financial statements. [SI 2008/410 5 Sch 11(1)].

5.174 The definitions take service conditions into account in determining whether an arrangement is a scheme (and long-term incentive scheme). But, as described in paragraph 5.34, the disclosures in the single figure table are based on amounts payable on achievement of performance measures and targets; these measures and targets do not include service conditions. A feature of many bonus arrangements is that a bonus is payable after the end of the financial year based on financial performance of that year, but only if the director is in service at the payment date. Such amounts are reported in column C (usually described as 'annual bonus'); even so, the bonus might fall within the definition of a scheme. This means that such an arrangement could be regarded as 'annual' for single figure purposes but a long-term scheme for the purposes of scheme interest disclosures.

5.175 A scheme does not include compensation for loss of office, payments for breach of contract and other termination payments. Nor does it include retirement benefits. [SI 2008/410 8 Sch 44(1)].

5.176 The difference between a scheme interest and a deferred bonus can be difficult to determine. For example, if a three-year performance-based scheme is introduced whereby a director is entitled to an award if the performance of the company over the three years satisfies certain conditions, it is a 'scheme'. This is because the award relates to a three-year period and the conditions cannot be fulfilled within a single financial year. But, as described in the example below, if a bonus is payable in respect of separate targets for each of three years, this could be a deferred bonus arrangement.

5.177 The example below considers the disclosure requirements for a scheme where the performance conditions have been met, but the final award of shares is still subject to approval.

> **Example – Share awards subject to approval**
>
> A quoted company with a premium listing operates a long-term incentive scheme for directors based on performance targets over a three-year period. At the end of the current reporting period, the performance targets have been met, but the final award of shares will not be approved until after the date of approval of the financial statements. What should be disclosed for directors' remuneration?
>
> *Notes to the financial statements*
>
> Paragraph 1(1)(c) of Schedule 5 requires separate disclosure in the notes to the financial statements of the aggregate of (i) the amount of money paid to or receivable by directors under long-term incentive schemes in respect of qualifying services and (ii) the net value of assets (other than money and share options) received or receivable by directors under such schemes in respect of such services.
>
> This disclosure will depend upon when the amounts were receivable (and can be quantified). The relevant amount would be measured as at the date the shares were receivable by the directors, that is, the award is no longer contingent. If the award is subject to approval after the date of approval of the financial statements, the amounts would be contingent at that date and would not be disclosed in the notes to the financial statements as finally awarded until the following year.
>
> *Directors' remuneration report*
>
> The award is included in the single figure table of the current year (year three). Inclusion in that table is based on the timing of achievement of performance measures and targets. Since the performance targets were met in the current year, the award is included in the current year even though approval had not been granted by the year end.
>
> The Schedule 8 disclosure requirements on scheme interests are only in respect of those awarded during the year (see para 5.179).

5.178 Where a scheme lasts three years, but a director has an entitlement in each of those three years dependent on the performance of that year, this is an annual bonus arrangement. If the aggregate three years of bonus is only payable after the end of the third year, it is a deferred bonus, but not a long-term incentive, because the conditions were satisfied by reference to performance in each of the three years, considered separately. But if the total bonus, although earned by reference to each of the individual years, is only payable if the director stays for the full three year term, this may fall within the definition of a long-term incentive scheme as there is then an additional service condition that cannot be satisfied within one year.

5.179 The directors' remuneration report is required to include information about directors' scheme interests. A scheme is as defined in paragraph 5.173. The following information for each person who was a director during the year should be presented in a table:

- Details of scheme interests awarded to each director during the financial year. [SI 2008/410 8 Sch 14(1)].

- For each scheme interest:
    - A description of the type of interest awarded.
    - A description of the basis on which the award is made.
    - The face value of the award (see para 5.180).
    - The percentage of scheme interests that would be receivable if the minimum performance was achieved.
    - For a scheme interest that is a share option, an explanation of any difference between the exercise price and the price specified under paragraph 14(3) of SI 2008/410 (see para 5.181).
    - The end of the period over which the performance measures and targets for that interest have to be achieved (or if there are different periods for different performance measures and targets, the end of whichever of those periods ends last).
    - A summary of the performance measures and targets if not set out elsewhere in the report.

[SI 2008/410 8 Sch 14(1)(b)].

5.180 For scheme interest that relates to shares or share options, 'face value' means the maximum number of shares that would vest if all performance measures and targets are met multiplied by either:

■ the share price at the grant date; or

■ the average share price used to determine the number of shares awarded.

[SI 2008/410 8 Sch 14(2)].

5.181 Where the face value of an award in respect of shares or share options is disclosed, the following information is disclosed:

■ Whether the face value has been calculated using the share price at the grant date or the average share price.

■ Where the share price at grant date is used, that share price and the date of grant.

■ Where the average share price is used, that share price and the period used to calculate it.

[SI 2008/410 8 Sch 14(3)].

[The next paragraph is 5.184.]

Long-term incentive scheme for an individual

5.184 Where the only participant in a long-term incentive scheme is a director (or a prospective director) and the arrangement is established specifically to facilitate, in unusual circumstances, the recruitment or retention of the relevant individual, disclosure of the following details are required to be given in the first annual report and accounts published by the company following the date on which the individual becomes eligible to participate in the arrangement:

■ The full text of the scheme or a description of its principal terms.

■ Details of trusteeship in the scheme or interest in the trustees, if any, of directors of the company.

■ A statement that the principal provisions of the scheme (set out in detail in rule 13.8.11R(3) of the Listing Rules) cannot be altered to the advantage of the participant without shareholders' approval.

■ A statement as to whether benefits under the scheme will be pensionable and if so the reasons for this.

■ The name of the sole participant.

■ The date on which he or she first became eligible to participate in the arrangement.

■ An explanation as to why the circumstances in which the arrangement was established were unusual.

■ The conditions to be satisfied under the arrangement's terms.

■ The maximum award(s) under the arrangement's terms, or, if there is no maximum, the basis on which the awards will be determined.

[LR 9.4.3R, LR 9.8.4R, LR 13.8.11R].

5.185 LR 9.8.4R requires specified disclosures in annual reports. Although most of the Listing Rules disclosure requirements on directors' remuneration have been deleted, the disclosures set out in paragraph 5.184 are still required. For financial years ending on or after 31 August 2014, LR 9.8.4C requires the company to include all of the information required by LR 9.8.4R in a single identifiable section, unless the annual report includes a cross-reference table indicating where that information is set out.

[The next paragraph is 5.187.]

Payments to past directors

5.187 Quoted companies' remuneration reports are required to disclose details of any payments of money or assets to any person who was not a director at the time the payment was made, but who had been a director previously. BIS has suggested that if there have been no such payments, it would be useful to state that fact.

5.187.1   This category excludes:

- Compensation for loss of office (see para 5.190).

- Amounts disclosed in the single figure table in the current year.

- Any payments disclosed in a previous directors' remuneration report.

- Payments of regular pension benefits started in a prior year.

- Dividend payments in respect of scheme interests retained on leaving office.

- Payments in respect of employment with or other contractual service performed for the company other than as a director.

- Payments below a de minimis threshold set by the company and stated in the report.

[SI 2008/410 8 Sch 15].

5.188   As stated under the final bullet above, where the company has set a de minimis threshold for disclosure, that threshold is stated in the report. No guidance is provided on how to set the de minimis threshold under the law. In our view, amounts that are 'significant' to either the company or any former director should be disclosed and the de minimis threshold set accordingly. In most cases, the de minimis threshold will be the same each year; if it is changed, an explanation should be included.

5.189   A director might remain an employee or be contracted on some other basis immediately after his resignation from the board. Or a former director might be appointed to a paid position at the company's pension fund (or another organisation connected with the company). If either of these apply, the company should consider disclosing the situation in its own directors' remuneration report. The requirement to disclose payments to former directors also covers payments that are over and above *"regular pension benefits commenced in a previous year"*. Where a former director receives a pension based on his accrued entitlements at the date of retirement (including any additional entitlements given in connection with his retirement and reported as payments for loss of office (see para 5.190)), such a pension does not require disclosure after the year in which he leaves office. But in the year in which he leaves office, the amounts paid after retirement are disclosed as payments to past directors.

> **Example 1 – Awards to former directors**
>
> (i) How should the directors' remuneration report deal with amounts paid in the current period to a director who retires in the period?
>
> *Single figure table*
>
> The table includes information in respect of each person who has served as a director of the company at any time during the year. [SI 2008/410 8 Sch 4(1)]. So if a director retires in the period his remuneration should be included in the table. For salary, benefits in kind and annual bonuses the amounts to be included are the amounts earned in respect of qualifying services. See example 2 in paragraph 5.28 for more details.
>
> For pension related benefits, the amount included in the table is the pension input amount and this is based on the pension input period. The pension input period is the full financial year even though the director retired in the year (see para 5.148). But the pension input amount related to the post retirement period will be nil if the director's pension entitlements are not increased after retirement (except for inflationary increases).
>
> *Payments to past director*
>
> Any pensions (or lump sums) or any other benefits he receives from the date of retirement to the end of the financial year is disclosed (unless below the de minimis threshold) as payments to a former director because they are not regular pension benefits commenced in a previous year.
>
> *Payments for loss of office*
>
> Payments for loss of office (that are above any de minimis set by the company) are disclosed in the report.
>
> *Total pension entitlements*
>
> The director's total pension entitlements as at the year end are disclosed. These disclosures apply to each person who was a director at any time during the financial year (see para 5.165).

(ii) Are payments to a director who retired in a previous year disclosed by individual director or can they be disclosed in aggregate?

The requirement is to disclose details of any payments 'to any person' who is a former director (not 'any persons' who were former directors). The company should disclose the payments by individual director.

Example 2 – Consultancy contract with former director

During the year a quoted company entered into a consultancy contract with a former director of the company who had resigned as a director three years previously. The rate being paid to the former director is in excess of the market rate for the services he is contracted to provide.

(a) Does the company have to disclose payments made under this contract in the directors' remuneration report?
(b) Would it make any difference if the payment for services was at an arm's length rate?

(a) Where the former director receives reward for the services he provides to the company at a value in excess of arm's length, the excess over the arm's length amount would be a disclosable payment. This is because this payment is not, in substance, for the service provided but for some other purpose. The 'excess' paid should be disclosed and an explanation given.

(b) Where the former director receives payment at a value that is arm's length, the award of the contract to the former director would not require disclosure as it is a payment for contractual service other than as a director. But it would be good practice to disclose the award of the contract to a former director who resigned in recent years.

Payments for loss of office

5.190   The directors' remuneration report is required to disclose for each director and former director:

- The total amount of any payment for loss of office paid to, or receivable by, the person in respect of that financial year, broken down into each component comprised in that payment and the value of each component.

- An explanation of how each component was calculated.

- Any other payments paid to or receivable by the person in connection with the termination of qualifying services, whether by way of compensation for loss of office or otherwise, including the treatment of outstanding incentive awards that vest on or following termination.

- Where any discretion was exercised in respect of the payment, an explanation of how it was exercised.

[SI 2008/410 8 Sch 16].

BIS has suggested that if there have been no such payments, it would be useful to state that fact.

5.191   As with payments to former directors, companies can set a de minimis threshold for reporting such amounts, provided that they state the threshold in the report.

5.192   There is a requirement to make disclosures about the exercise of discretion in making loss of office payments. Although there is no specific requirement for a company to disclose how it distinguishes between different types of leaver or to disclose the circumstances in which a director left, there is a requirement to disclose how the components of loss of office payments were calculated. To explain this calculation, it is likely that the circumstances of a director's loss of office would need to be disclosed. In any event, such payments are often of particular interest to shareholders so companies might voluntarily provide the information. Information about the timing of payments might be another useful disclosure.

5.193   'Compensation in respect of loss of office' includes compensation for:

- Loss of office as director of the company.

- Loss, while director of the company or on or in connection with his ceasing to be a director of it, of:

  - Any other office in connection with the management of the company's affairs.

  - Any office as director or otherwise in connection with the management of company's affairs (or the affairs of its subsidiary undertaking or an undertaking of which he is a director by virtue of the company's nomination (direct or indirect)).

- Compensation in consideration for, or in connection with, a person's retirement from office.

- Where such a retirement is caused by a breach of the person's contract with the company (or its subsidiary undertaking or an undertaking of which he is a director by virtue of the company's nomination):

    - Payments made by way of damages for the breach.

    - Payments made by way of settlement or compromise of any claim in respect of the breach.

[SI 2008/410 8 Sch 44(2)].

5.194 Payments for loss of office include benefits otherwise than in cash. The value of the benefit should be determined according to its estimated money value. [SI 2008/410 8 Sch 44(3)]. For example, the compensation might include, as well as a cash payment, the gift to the director of a car that he had previously used, but that was owned by the company. The car is a separate component of the compensation and is disclosed separately.

5.195 Where a director receives an enhancement to his existing pension rights as a part of his compensation package, the value of the 'pension top up' is taken into account in calculating the pension input amount that is included as pension-related benefits in the single figure table (see para 5.148).

[The next paragraph is 5.197.]

Statement of directors' shareholding and share interests

5.197 The directors' remuneration report includes, for each person who has served as a director of the company at any time during the year, a statement of any requirements or guidelines for the director to own shares in the company and confirmation of whether those requirements or guidelines have been met. [SI 2008/ 410 8 Sch 17(a)].

5.198 Schedule 8 is not specific about the details that should be disclosed if there are director shareholding requirements. Companies might disclose:

- The amount a director is required to hold in shares (for example, the percentage of salary).

- Whether the provision is a requirement or guideline and the approach that the company would take if the requirement or guideline is not met in the specified period.

- The period within which the company expects or requires the provisions to be met.

- Details of any requirements in relation to vested awards (for example a requirement that a specified percentage of them needs to be held until the provision is met).

- Details of any requirements for directors to hold shares once they have left the company.

- Details of which shares can be included to meet the provision (for example, whether it includes any deferred or unvested shares or shares subject to vested but unexercised options).

- The date at which the holding is to be measured.

5.199 In Table 5.5, Pearson plc discloses the shares held outright and subject to service conditions against the shareholding guideline.

Table 5.5 – Shareholding guideline

Pearson plc – Annual report and accounts – 31 December 2013

Report on directors' remuneration (extract)

Interests of directors and value of shareholdings
Directors' interests

	Ordinary shares at 31 Dec 13	Conditional shares at 31 Dec 13	Total number of ordinary and conditional shares at 31 Dec 13	Value (x salary)	Guideline (x salary)	Guideline met
Chairman						
Glen Moreno	150,000	–	–	–	–	–
Executive directors						
John Fallon	262,569	43,639	306,208	4.5	2.0	✓
Robin Freestone	478,507	37,077	515,584	10.5	1.25	✓
Will Ethridge	397,017	43,639	440,656	7.2	1.25	✓
Non-executive directors						
David Arculus	16,301	–	–	–	–	–
Vivienne Cox	1,351	–	–	–	–	–
Ken Hydon	17,818	–	–	–	–	–
Josh Lewis	5,681	–	–	–	–	–
Linda Lorimar (appointed 1 July 2013)	637	–	–	–	–	–
Harish Manwani (appointed 1 October 2013)	180	–	–	–	–	–

Note 1 Conditional shares means shares which have vested but remain held subject to continuing employment for a pre-defined holding period.

Note 2 The current value of the executive directors' holdings of ordinary and conditional shares is based on the middle market value of Pearson shares of 1,113.0p on 21 February 2014 against base salaries in 2013. All executive directors comfortably exceeded the shareholding guidelines. The shareholding guidelines do not apply to the chairman and non-executive directors.

Note 3 Ordinary shares include both ordinary shares listed on the London Stock Exchange and American Depositary Receipts (ADRs) listed on the New York Stock Exchange. The figures include both shares and ADRs acquired by individuals investing part of their own after-tax annual bonus in Pearson shares under the annual bonus and annual bonus share matching plan.

Note 4 From 2004, Marjorie Scardino is also deemed to be interested in a further number of shares under her unfunded pension arrangement described in this report, which provides the opportunity to convert a proportion of her notional cash account into a notional share account reflecting the value of a number of Pearson shares

Note 5 The register of directors' interests (which is open to inspection during normal office hours) contains full details of directors' shareholdings and options to subscribe for shares. The market price on 31 December 2013 was 1,341.0p per share and the range during the year was 1,119.0p to 1,365.0p.

Note 6 There were no movements in ordinary shares between 1 January 2014 and a month prior to the sign-off of this report.

Note 7 Ordinary shares do not include any shares vested but held pending release under a restricted share plan.

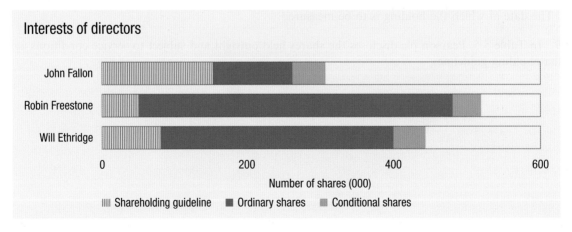

Shareholding guidelines for executive directors

Executive directors are expected to build up a substantial shareholding in the company in line with the policy of encouraging widespread employee ownership and to align further the interests of executives and shareholders. With effect from 2014, target holding is 300% of salary for the chief executive and 200% of salary for the other executive directors.

Shares that count towards these guidelines include any shares held unencumbered by the executive, their spouse and/or dependent children plus any shares vested but held pending release under a restricted share plan. Executive directors have five years from the date of appointment to reach the guideline.

There are currently no mandatory share ownership guidelines below executive director level, although employees are encouraged to become shareholders in the company by retaining shares acquired through the company's discretionary and all-employee stock programmes. The shareholding guidelines do not apply to the chairman and non-executive directors.

5.200 The following directors' share interests are disclosed in tabular form for each director:

■ The total number of interests in shares in the company, including interests of connected persons (as defined for the purposes of section 96B(2) of the Financial Services and Markets Act 2000). (For definition of connected persons, see para 5.209.)

■ The total number of scheme interests differentiating between:

■ shares and share options; and

■ those with or without performance measures.

■ Details of those scheme interests (unless included elsewhere in the report).

■ Details of share options that are:

■ vested but unexercised; and

■ exercised in the relevant financial year.

[SI 2008/410 8 Sch 17].

5.201 Schedule 8 does not specify the date at which the above interests are to be disclosed. But the disclosures are required for each person who was a director during the year and for share options exercised during the year. So it is implied that the disclosures should be given as at the year end.

5.202 Other useful disclosures might include:

■ Prior year comparative information.

■ The intrinsic value of shares and long-term incentive interests at the year end.

■ The weighted average exercise price for vested and unvested share options.

■ The weighted average vesting period outstanding.

■ The number of shares outstanding for each scheme interest awarded.

5.203 The Listing Rules require a listed company's annual report to include a statement setting out all the interests, as at the year end, of each person who is a director of the company as at the end of the period under review including:

■ all changes in the interests of each director that have occurred between the end of the period under review and a date not more than one month prior to the date of the notice of the annual general meeting; or

■ if there have been no changes in the interests of each director in the period described above, a statement that there have been no changes.

[LR 9.8.6R(1)].

5.204 The interests required to be disclosed are those in respect of transactions that are notifiable to the company under DTR 3.1.2R. Under that rule, persons discharging managerial responsibilities ('managers') and their connected persons, must notify the issuer in writing of the occurrence of all transactions conducted on their own account in the shares of the issuer, or derivatives or any other financial instruments relating to those shares within four business days of the day on which the transaction occurred. Although this notification requirement applies to 'managers' (which includes but is not restricted to, directors), the Listing Rules annual report disclosure requirement applies only in respect of directors and their connected persons. Connected persons are considered further from paragraph 5.209.

5.205   Under the Listing Rules, persons who are directors during, but not at the end of, the year need not be included. [LR 9.8.6A G(1)]. But the legal disclosure requirements are required in respect of each person who was a director during the year. This means that, although the share interests as at the year end are disclosable for each person who was a director during the year, the disclosure of changes in interests since the year end is not required in respect of former directors.

5.206   The Listing Rules note that a listed company unable to compile the statement in LR 9.8.6R(1) from information already available to it might need to seek the relevant information, or confirmation, from the director, including that in relation to connected persons, but would not be expected to obtain information directly from connected persons. [LR 9.8.6A G(2)].

[The next paragraph is 5.209.]

Connected persons

Share interests

5.209   Under the Listing Rules, 'connected persons' are as defined in section 96B of the Financial Services and Markets Act 2000. This definition also applies to the legal disclosure requirement in respect of directors' share interests in the directors' remuneration report.

5.210   The requirements in the Financial Services and Markets Act are written in the context of a 'manager' (see para 5.204) and the following are 'connected persons' of a 'manager':

- Members of the manager's family, including:
    - The manager's spouse or civil partner.
    - Any relative of the manager who, on the date of the transaction in question, has shared the same household as the manager for at least 12 months.
    - The manager's children or step-children under the age of 18.
- A body corporate with which the manager is 'associated'.
- A trustee of a trust of which the beneficiary is (or can be, at the discretion of the trustee) the manager (or a family member or associated body corporate as defined above) other than a trust for the purposes of an employee share scheme or pension scheme.
- A person acting in capacity as partner of the manager (or any person connected with him).
- A partnership that is a legal person in which the manager (or any person connected with him) is a partner.
- A partnership that is a legal person with a partner that is, itself, a partnership, where the director (or a connected person of his) is a partner.

[FSMA 2000 11B Sch 2].

5.211   The following are 'associated' bodies corporate:

- A body corporate in which the manager (or a person connected to him) is a director or a senior executive who has the power to make management decisions affecting the future development and business prospects of that body corporate.
- A body corporate in which the manager and his connected persons are interested in at least 20% of the body corporate's equity share capital (excluding treasury shares), or are entitled to exercise or control at least 20% of the voting power at any general meeting (excluding votes attached to treasury shares).

[FSMA 2000 11B Sch 4].

5.212   For the above purpose, an 'interest' in shares is defined in Schedule 11B to the Financial Services and Markets Act 2000 and is taken to mean any interest whatsoever and includes any right to acquire shares or control of the voting rights attached to the shares.

Other disclosures

5.213 For the purposes of the directors' remuneration report, amounts paid to or receivable by a director include amounts paid to or receivable by a person connected to him. In this context, 'connected persons' are as defined in sections 252 to 255 of the Companies Act 2006. This definition is not the same as the definition in the Financial Services and Management Act 2000 that forms the basis of share interests disclosures (see para 5.209). For example, a director's parent is a connected person under sections 253 of the Companies Act 2006 but is not under the Financial Services and Management Act 2000, unless that parent has shared the same household as the manager for at least 12 months.

5.214 Under the definition in sections 252 to 255 of the Companies Act 2006 , 'connected persons' are:

■ Members of the director's family, including:

■ The director's spouse, civil partner or any other person with whom the director lives as a partner in an enduring family relationship.

■ The director's children or step-children.

■ Any children or step-children (under the age of 18) of the director's enduring life partner who live with the director.

■ The director's parents.

■ A body corporate with which the director is connected (see para 5.215).

■ A trustee of a trust of which the beneficiary is (or can be, at the discretion of the trustee) the director (or a family member or connected body corporate as defined above) other than a trust for the purposes of an employee share scheme or pension scheme.

■ A person acting in capacity as a partner of the director (or any person connected with him).

■ A partnership that is a legal person in which the director (or any person connected with him) is a partner.

■ A partnership that is a legal person with a partner that is, itself, a partnership, where the director (or a connected person of his) is a partner.

[CA06 Secs 252, 253].

5.215 A body corporate is a connected person of a director if the director and his connected persons are interested in at least 20% of the nominal value of the body corporate's equity share capital (excluding treasury shares), or are entitled to control at least 20% of the voting power at any general meeting (excluding votes attached to treasury shares). [CA06 Sec 254]. For this purpose, an 'interest' in shares is defined in Schedule 1 to the Companies Act 2006 and is taken to mean any interest whatsoever and includes any right to acquire shares or control of the voting rights attached to the shares.

Performance graph

5.216 The directors' remuneration report is required to include a performance graph showing the total shareholder return for each financial year in the 'relevant period' for the company against the total shareholder return for each financial year for an index.

5.217 In the first year that the company prepares its remuneration report in accordance with SI 2008/410, the graph should cover five financial years of which the last is the current financial year (that is, the year for which financial statements are being presented). [SI 2008/410 8 Sch(4)(a)]. The graph is drawn by joining up points plotted to represent each of the financial years.

5.218 In the second year, the graph should cover six years; that is, the five years presented in the previous financial year plus the current financial year. In the third year, the graph covers seven years and so on in subsequent years until, in the sixth year, the graph covers a ten-year period. The graph for the seventh and all subsequent periods should cover ten years. [SI 2008/410 8 Sch(4)(b)(c)].

5.219 A graph is presented to show the total shareholder return for each of:

■   A holding of shares of the company's equity share capital whose listing or admission to dealing has led to the company being defined as a quoted company (see para 5.9).

■   A hypothetical holding of shares made up of shares of the same kind and number as those by reference to which a broad based equity market index is calculated.

[SI 2008/410 8 Sch 18(1)(a)].

5.220 The name of the index selected for the purpose of the graph and the reason for selecting that index should be disclosed. [SI 2008/410 8 Sch 18(1)(b)].

5.221 Total shareholder return is calculated using a fair method that:

■   Starts with the percentage change in the market price of the holding over the period.

■   Makes the following assumptions as to reinvestment of income:

(a)   Any benefit in the form of shares of the same kind as those in the holding is added to the holding when that benefit becomes receivable.

(b)   Any benefit in cash, and the value of any benefit not in cash and not falling into (a) above, is used when the benefit becomes receivable to purchase shares of the same kind as the existing holding at market price and that the notional shares so purchased are added to the existing holding at that time.

(c)   'Benefit' means any benefit (including dividends) receivable in respect of the holding from the company of whose share capital the holding forms part.

■   Makes the following assumptions as to the funding of liabilities:

(a)   Where the holder has a liability to the company of whose share capital the holding forms part, shares are sold from the holding:

(i)   immediately before the time by which the liability is due to be settled; and

(ii)   they are sold in such numbers that, at the time of sale, the market price of the shares sold equals the amount of the liability in respect of the shares in the holding that are not sold.

(b)   In paragraph (a) 'liability' means a liability in respect of any shares in the holding or from the exercise of a right attached to any of those shares.

■   Makes provision for any replacement of shares in the holding by shares of a different description.

[SI 2008/410 8 Sch 18(6)-(10)].

5.222 The same method must be used for each of the holdings mentioned in paragraph 5.219.

5.223 A number of indices are widely available and show total returns. For example the UK Series of the FTSE Actuaries Share indices include Total Return indices. SI 2008/410 requires disclosure of the name of the index; so it is not acceptable to use an index created by the company alone, although it might be acceptable to give some disclosure as additional information. This is considered in the example below.

> **Example – Selection of index for total shareholder return graph**
>
> A quoted company is preparing its directors' remuneration report and is selecting the index to use in the total shareholder return graph. Can the company 'create' an index of companies of a similar size and nature? If not, which index should it use?
>
> Given the requirement to disclose of the name of the index (see para 5.220), using an index created by the company alone is not acceptable.
>
> A number of published indices for total shareholder return are publicly available. These include industry-based indices, such as the TechMark index, and size-based indices, such as the FTSE 100.
>
> When selecting an index, the directors should generally use an index in which the company is included. It should be one that they use internally to measure the company's performance against its peers. The remuneration committee

should consider a range of appropriate indices and, based on the relative merits of each, select the index that is, in their opinion, most appropriate.

But, if a company has also devised a more specific index for a peer group of companies and it uses this index to set performance targets, a total return graph, plotting the company's performance against the performance of the peer group, could be given as additional information. The composition of the peer group, the basis of preparation of the graph and reasons for producing it, should be given.

5.224 An example of disclosure is given in Table 5.6.

Table 5.6 – Performance graph

Rolls-Royce Holdings plc – Annual Report – 31 December 2014

Directors' remuneration report (extract)

TSR performance

The Company's TSR performance over the previous six years compared to a broad equity market index is shown in the graph below. The FTSE 100 has been chosen as the comparator because it contains a broad range of other UK listed companies.

The graph shows the growth in value of a hypothetical £100 holding in the Company's ordinary shares over six years, relative to the FTSE 100 index. The values of the hypothetical £100 holdings at the end of the six-year period were £302.23 and £184.40 respectively.

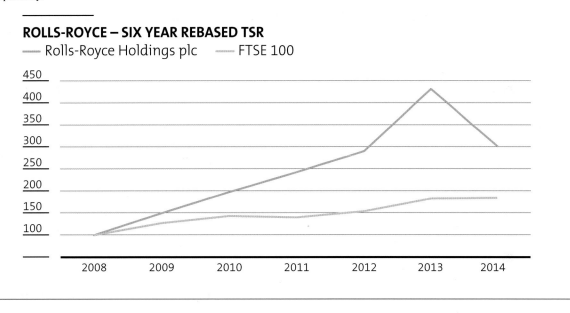

ROLLS-ROYCE – SIX YEAR REBASED TSR

5.225 The company might have been in existence for less than the relevant period as defined above. Or the company could have existed for longer, but have been listed for less than the relevant period. Paragraph 18(6) of Schedule 8 to SI 2008/410 states that TSR is calculated taking as the starting point the percentage change in the market price over the relevant period. Where the company was listed within the relevant period (either because it was incorporated in that period or otherwise), it only has a listed market price since the date of its listing. So, the company's TSR should be calculated taking the change in the period from the listing date to the end of the financial year in which the listing occurred as the starting point.

5.226 A company's total shareholder return might sometimes not be available for the relevant period, such as where there has been a demerger. An example of a company's total shareholder return compared with a relevant index, in this instance showing the period since demerger, is provided in Table 5.7.

Table 5.7 – Performance graph

Carphone Warehouse Group plc – Annual report – 31 March 2013

Remuneration report (extract)

Performance graph

The graph below shows the Group's performance measured through TSR, compared with the FTSE 250 Index, since 29 March 2010 when the Company was first admitted to the London Stock Exchange following the Demerger. The FTSE 250 Index was selected as it is a broad market which includes competitors of the Company.

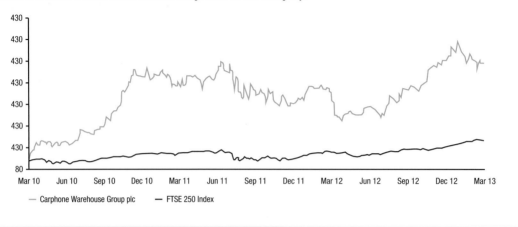

5.227 Sometimes, the index being used has existed for less than five years. This is considered in the following example.

> **Example – New index used for total shareholder return graph**
>
> A quoted company is preparing its directors' remuneration report for the year ended 31 December 20X1 and is selecting the index to use in the total shareholder return graph. The remuneration committee consider that the most appropriate index to use would be a new index, but this has only existed since 20X0. The remuneration committee consider that the second most appropriate index would be the FTSE All Share index. The remuneration committee do not want to use the FTSE All Share index until 20X5 and then change to the new index and explain the change. What should it do?
>
> As the information for the new index is not available for the entire relevant period, selecting this index would not comply with the legal disclosure requirements.
>
> Schedule 8 does not preclude the presentation of two performance graphs: one showing a comparison against the FTSE All Share index and the other showing a comparison with the new index. When a full history for the new index is available, the graph based on the FTSE All Share index can be omitted from the remuneration report.

CEO remuneration

5.228 The remuneration report is required to include information, provided in a table, about the remuneration of the company's chief executive officer. The table is required to show, for the 'relevant period' (see para 5.216), the following information in respect of the director(s) who acted as chief executive officer in each year:

- Total remuneration as set out in the single figure table.

- The amount shown in column C (annual bonus, see para 5.100) as a percentage of the maximum that could have been paid out in the financial year.

- The amount shown in column D (long-term incentive plans, see para 5.100) restated as:

  - if in shares, a percentage of the number of shares vesting against the maximum number of shares that could have been achieved; or

  - if in money or other assets, a percentage of the maximum that could have been paid.

[SI 2008/410 8 Sch 18(2)].

5.229 Consistent with the performance graph, the CEO remuneration table will ultimately include ten years of information, including the current financial year. But there are transition reliefs as set out in paragraph 5.217. So in the first year a company discloses the CEO remuneration table, it will include information for five financial years, including the current year. The information disclosed in the CEO remuneration table is based on the single figure table, a disclosure that, in most cases, will not have been made in the prior years. Where this is the case, the figures are estimated and a note of explanation given. [SI 2008/410 8 Sch 1(7)].

5.230 Table 5.8 is an example of CEO remuneration disclosure. This example contains some information in addition to the legal disclosure requirements.

Table 5.8 – CEO remuneration

WPP plc – Annual report and accounts – 31 December 2013

Aligning pay and performance

As set out in the Executive Remuneration Policy, the committee seeks to align the variable remuneration with the key strategic priorities of WPP, therefore seeking to maximise the dynamic between pay and performance.

This dynamic is contingent upon the committee setting challenging targets each year. The following graph and table demonstrate the relationship between pay and performance over the last five years for the Group's chief executive.

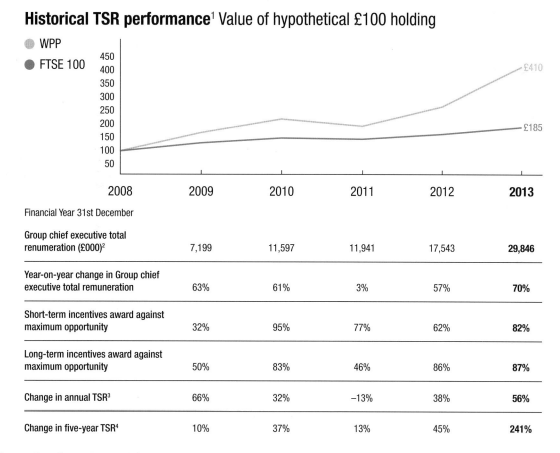

Historical TSR performance[1] Value of hypothetical £100 holding

Financial Year 31st December

	2008	2009	2010	2011	2012	2013
Group chief executive total renumeration (£000)[2]		7,199	11,597	11,941	17,543	**29,846**
Year-on-year change in Group chief executive total remuneration		63%	61%	3%	57%	**70%**
Short-term incentives award against maximum opportunity		32%	95%	77%	62%	**82%**
Long-term incentives award against maximum opportunity		50%	83%	46%	86%	**87%**
Change in annual TSR[3]		66%	32%	–13%	38%	**56%**
Change in five-year TSR[4]		10%	37%	13%	45%	**241%**

Source: DataStream Return Index

[1] Growth in the value of a hypothetical £100 holding in WPP ordinary shares over five years against an equivalent holding in the FTSE 100 (the broad market equity index of which WPP is a constituent) – comparison based on one-month average of trading day values.

[2] Calculated using the single figure methodology.

[3] TSR calculated using a one-month trading day average, consistent with the data shown in the graph.

[4] TSR calculated using a six-month averaging period, consistent with the calculation methodology under LEAP/EPSP.

5.231 There might have been more than one CEO in the period covered by the table. In such cases, the table should include the pay of both individuals but only for the period in which they were CEO. This can be done by presenting the pay of each person separately, as illustrated in the table below. Or a company could present the aggregate of the pay of both CEOs, as illustrated in Table 5.8.1. Whichever approach is taken, a note explaining the change would be a useful disclosure, as illustrated in the example below and in Table 5.8.1.

CEO pay		CEO Single figure of total remuneration £000	Annual variable element award rates against maximum opportunity	Long-term incentive vesting rates against maximum opportunity
20X3	CEO2	X	X%	X%
20X2	CEO2	X	X%	X%
20X1 (see note)	CEO2	X	X%	X%
	CEO1	X	X%	X%
20X1	CEO1	X	X%	X%
20X0	CEO1	X	X%	X%

Note: CEO1 retired at the AGM on 21 May, and CEO2 became CEO on that date, having previously been the COO.

Table 5.8.1 – CEO remuneration

Bellway p.l.c. – Annual report – 31 July 2013

Chief Executive total remuneration

The table below sets out the total remuneration for the Chief Executive over the same five year period as for the chart above, together with the annual bonus paid and the vesting percentage of long-term incentives, as a percentage of the maximum (relating to the performance periods ending in that year).

	2009	2010	2011	2012	**2013**
Total remuneration (£000)	1,312	1,532	1,899	1,396	**1,243**[1]
Annual bonus paid (as % of maximum)	20.3%	76.9%	100.0%	99.3%	**100.0%**
PSP vesting (as % of maximum)	100.0%	48.3%	99.6%	0.0%	**0.0%**

Notes:
1. John Watson held the role of Chief Executive up to 31 January 2013 and Ted Ayres was Chief Executive for the remainder of the financial year from 1 February 2013 to 31 July 2013. The total remuneration for the period as Chief Executive was £714,053 for John Watson and £528,500 for Ted Ayres.

5.231.1 Where a director becomes a CEO during the year, it will be necessary to determine how much of his pay for the year is attributable to service whilst a CEO. The apportionment method should be the same as applies when an employee becomes a director, as illustrated in example 2 in paragraph 5.28.

Percentage change in CEO and employee pay

5.232 Schedule 8 also requires disclosure of the percentage change in both CEO and employee pay from the previous financial year to the current financial year. These two percentages should be presented *"in a manner which permits comparison"*; that is, in close proximity to each other, not in different parts of the report. [SI 2008/410 8 Sch 19(1)]. This disclosure requirement has been introduced in response to concerns that increases in executive pay have not, in many cases, been matched by increases in employee pay.

5.233 Where the company is a parent company, the disclosures are in respect of CEO of the parent company and the employees of the group. [SI 2008/410 8 Sch 19(3)].

5.234 The CEO percentage change is in respect of *"the director undertaking the role of chief executive officer"*. The law is silent on how the calculation should be performed if the company has more than one CEO in either the current or prior year. It would be sensible to aggregate the pay of the CEOs for this purpose and to disclose the basis of calculation.

5.235 The components of CEO pay to be compared are those set out in columns A, B and C of the single figure table (see para 5.100); that is, each of salary/fees, taxable benefits and annual bonus. There is no requirement to disclose a comparison of amounts vested under long-term incentive plans or pension related benefits. For employees, equivalent types of remuneration are included. [SI 2008/410 8 Sch 19(1)].

5.236 The calculation of the percentage change in employee pay is based on the employees of the company (or group) as a whole. Where the employees of the company as a whole are considered an inappropriate comparator group, the company may use another group of employees as a comparator group but, if it does so, it is required to explain why that group was chosen. [SI 2008/410 8 Sch 19(2)]. This might be the case when the group has foreign operations and local pay levels are substantially different from those in the UK. It is, of course, open to companies to disclose additional percentage changes for additional groups of employees, provided that these do not obscure the legally required disclosures. Although companies have a free choice as to which employee group is used as the comparator, companies should not choose a narrow comparator group as this would frustrate the purpose of the disclosure requirement. Usually the same comparator group should be used each year; if a change is made, it should be explained. Table 5.8.1.1 is an example of disclosure where there has been more than one CEO in the financial year.

Table 5.8.1.1 – Percentage increase in CEO and employee pay

BT Group plc – Annual report – 31 March 2014

Report on Directors' remuneration (extract)

Percentage change in Chief Executive remuneration (comparing 2012/13 to 2013/14)

The table below illustrates the increase in salary, benefits and annual bonus for the Chief Executive and that of a representative group of the company's employees.

For these purposes, we have used the UK management and technical employee population representing around 23,000 people because they also participate in performance related pay arrangements on a similar basis as executive directors.

	Salary	Benefits[b]	Bonus[c]
% Change in Chief Executive remuneration[a]	0%	31%	–9%
% Change in comparator group[d]	3.1%	0%	29.7%

[a] Represents the change for the role of Chief Executive during the period. Ian Livingston was Chief Executive until 10 September 2013 when he stepped down and Gavin Patterson was appointed. The Chief Executive package at on target remuneration was reduced by around 20% on change of incumbent representing around £0.8m.

[b] The increase in benefits for the Chief Executive was £8,704.

[c] The bonus comparator is based on cash bonus only to give a better like for like comparison. A combination of cash and deferred bonus would indicate a reduction of 43%.

[d] Comparator group is the UK management and technical employee population representing around 23,000 individuals.

Relative importance of spend on pay

5.237 The directors' remuneration report is required to include either a graph or table that shows, for the relevant financial year and the immediately preceding financial year, the actual expenditure and difference in spend between the years in respect of:

- Employees' remuneration.

- Dividend distributions and share buybacks.

- Any other significant distributions and payments or other uses of profit or cash flow helpful to an understanding of the relative importance of spend on pay.

[SI 2008/410 8 Sch 20(1)].

5.238 In respect of matters disclosed under the third bullet above, the company should explain why it selected those particular items for disclosure. Where the company changes the matters it reports from those reported in the prior year, it should give an explanation of the change. [SI 2008/410 8 Sch 20(2)(3)].

5.239 Although this disclosure is made in the directors' remuneration report, it need not include any information about directors' pay. Neither is there any requirement to show the total group profit.

5.240 For this disclosure, the employees to be included are the employees of the group; it is not permissible to select a particular group of employees, as would be permitted for the disclosure on the percentage change in CEO and employee pay.

5.241 Typically, companies pay an interim dividend during the year but also propose a dividend for the year that will be paid after the year end. The legislation refers to 'actual expenditure' and to 'spend' which might suggest that, for the purposes of disclosure of the relative importance of spend on pay, the amounts reported as dividends should be the cash paid during the year (that is, the dividend proposed for the prior year plus the interim dividend paid during the year). But the legislation also states that the amounts reported should be 'in respect of the financial year' which might suggest that the amounts reported should be the dividends declared in the year (that is, the interim dividend paid plus the final dividend proposed for the current year). In our view, either approach is acceptable, provided that the method of calculation is clear. In Table 5.9, the company bases the tabular disclosure on the amounts paid in the year (which aligns with the accounting treatment) but also discloses the dividends declared for the year.

Table 5.9 – Relative importance of spend on pay

GlaxoSmithKline plc – Annual report – 31 December 2014

Remuneration Report (extract)

Relative importance of pay

The following table sets out the percentage changes in the Group's dividends paid to shareholders, share buy-back and total employee pay.

	2014 £m	2013 £m	% change
Total employee pay	**7,520**	7,591	(2)%
Dividends	**3,843**	3,680	4.4%
Share buy-back	**238**	1,504	(85)%

The figures in the table above are as set out on pages 139 and 153. Dividends declared in respect of 2014 were £3,865 million (2013: £3,754 million), i.e. an increase of 2.95%. In determining specific share repurchase levels, the company considers the development of free cash flow during the year. Given the impact of the sustained strength of Sterling on free cash flow, the company suspended its share repurchase programme during 2014. Following the completion of the three-part Novartis transaction, GSK intends to return to shareholders £4 billion of the net proceeds. The company does not expect to make any ordinary share repurchases in 2015.

Total employee pay is for all Group employees globally.

Statement of implementation of policy in the following financial year

5.242   The company's directors' remuneration policy is subject to binding shareholder approval. Once approved, companies can only make payments that are consistent with that policy. Should a company wish to amend the policy, any changes must be approved by the shareholders. Companies can seek shareholder approval of the changes at any general meeting. The remuneration policy must be approved by shareholders at least every three years. See paragraph 5.259 for more details on the approval process.

5.243   The directors' remuneration report is required to state how the company intends to implement the most recently approved remuneration policy (whether that is the one approved at the last AGM or at a later general meeting) in the forthcoming financial year. The company must disclose:

- The performance measures and relative weightings for each.
- The performance targets determined for the performance measures (unless the directors consider them to be commercially sensitive) and how awards will be calculated.

[SI 2008/410 8 Sch 21(1)(2)].

5.244   Performance measures and targets are as defined in paragraph 5.129.

5.245   Where this is not the first year of the approved remuneration policy, the company should disclose any 'significant changes' to the way the policy will be implemented in the next year compared with how it was implemented in the current year. [SI 2008/410 8 Sch 21(3)].

5.246   'Significant changes' are not defined in Schedule 8. Companies might disclose:

- Any change in basic salary or fees.
- Any change in the weighting of performance measures or any change in performance targets.
- Any change to scheme interests to be awarded compared with the current year (as set out in the statement on scheme interests awarded (see para 5.173)).
- Any other changes in the way that the approved remuneration policy will be implemented even if it is in accordance with the approved future policy table.

5.247   If there are no changes to the implementation of the remuneration policy then the company could state that fact. The statement can be given anywhere in the directors' remuneration report, including the directors' remuneration policy part. Because inclusion of the directors' remuneration policy in the directors' remuneration report is required every three years (that is, only when it is to be approved at the next general meeting, normally the AGM), a company may sometimes give the statement on policy implementation without including the policy itself in the directors' remuneration report. It might be, if policy changes were approved at a general meeting, that the current policy has never been included in any previous year's directors' remuneration report. In many cases, even when not required to do so, companies are likely to include the policy in each year's directors' remuneration report. This would enable shareholders to interpret the statement on policy implementation in the light of the policy described in the same document.

Consideration by the directors of matters relating to directors' remuneration

5.248   Schedule 8 requires that if a committee of the company's directors has considered matters relating to directors' remuneration for the year, specified disclosures are made. These disclosures also apply in respect of a committee that considers remuneration issues during consideration of an individual's nomination as director. [SI 2008/410 8 Sch 22(1)(4)].

5.249   The names of each of the directors on the committee should be disclosed in the directors' remuneration report. [SI 2008/410 8 Sch 22(1)(a)].

5.250   The company also discloses the name of any other person who provided advice or services to the committee that materially assisted it in its consideration of any matter related to directors' remuneration. If that person was not a director or employee of the company or a person who provided legal advice on compliance with any relevant legislation, the following are also disclosed:

- The nature of any other services that that person has provided to the company during the year. (Companies are not required to disclose the fees charged for those services.)

- Who appointed the person, whether or not by the remuneration committee, and how they were selected.

- Whether and how the remuneration committee has satisfied itself that the advice received was objective and independent.

- The fees (or other charge) paid for the advice or services and the basis on which it was charged.

[SI 2008/410 8 Sch 22(b)(c)].

5.250.1   The UK Corporate Governance Code also requires that, where remuneration consultants are appointed, they should be identified in the annual report and a statement made as to whether they have any connections with the company. [UK CGC D2.1].

5.251   The disclosures are illustrated in the following examples.

> **Example 1 – Report benchmarking remuneration**
>
> The remuneration committee of a quoted company engaged an HR consultant to prepare a report benchmarking the remuneration of the company's directors against the remuneration of directors of comparable companies. Does this constitute material assistance for the purpose of disclosure under Schedule 8 of SI 2008/410?
>
> This would be material assistance. The HR consultant prepared a report with the purpose of assisting the remuneration committee in their consideration of directors' remuneration by benchmarking against similar companies.

> **Example 2 – Independent benchmarking survey**
>
> A different HR consultant has prepared and published widely an independent benchmarking survey that the remuneration committee has used when considering whether the relative importance of performance-related and non-performance-related remuneration is appropriate. Would this constitute material assistance?
>
> This would not be material assistance. The HR consultant prepared a report for the purposes of general publication, which the remuneration committee used to assist itself in its consideration of directors' remuneration. No assistance was given by the HR consultant specifically to this remuneration committee.

> **Example 3 – Preparation of performance graph**
>
> A third HR consultant was engaged by the same remuneration committee to prepare the total shareholder return graph for inclusion in the directors' remuneration report. Would this constitute material assistance?

This would not be material assistance. The HR consultant is putting together a graph of factual information, all of which is publicly available, for the purposes of disclosure and not to assist the remuneration committee in its consideration of directors' remuneration.

Example 4 – Auditors' review of remuneration report

During the course of an audit, the auditors reviewed the directors' remuneration report and made some comments to the directors on the presentation and content of the remuneration report. Would this constitute material assistance?

This would not be material assistance. The review of the directors' remuneration report is undertaken by the auditor as part of the audit and does not assist the remuneration committee in its consideration of directors' remuneration.

5.252 An example of disclosure of details of those who provided advice or services to the remuneration committee is given in Table 5.10.

Table 5.10 – External advisers

AstraZeneca PLC – Annual Report – 31 December 2014

DIRECTORS' REMUNERATION REPORT (extract)

Independent Adviser to the Remuneration Committee

The Remuneration Committee re-appointed Deloitte as its independent adviser following a tender process undertaken in 2013, which involved interviews with both the Company's management and the Chairman of the Remuneration Committee. Deloitte's service to the Remuneration Committee was provided on a time-spent basis at a cost to the Company of £71,300 (excluding VAT). During the year, Deloitte also provided taxation advice and other specific non-audit advisory services to the Group. The Remuneration Committee reviewed the potential for conflicts of interest and judged that there were no conflicts. Deloitte is a member of the Remuneration Consultants' Group, which is responsible for the stewardship and development of the voluntary code of conduct in relation to executive remuneration consulting in the UK. The principles on which the code is based are transparency, integrity, objectivity, competence, due care and confidentiality. Deloitte adheres to the code.

[The next paragraph is 5.254.]

Statement of voting at general meeting

5.254 The directors' remuneration report must state, in respect of the relevant resolution at the last general meeting:

- Resolution to approve the directors' remuneration report: the percentage of votes cast for and against and the number of votes withheld. This is an annual advisory vote.

- Resolution to approve the directors' remuneration policy: the percentage of votes cast for and against and the number of votes withheld. This is a binding vote. Approval of the policy is sought at least every three years (see para 5.259).

- Where there was a significant percentage of votes against either resolution, a summary of the reasons for those votes, as far as known to the directors, and any actions taken by the directors in response to those concerns. No guidance is provided on how to determine whether the percentage of votes against the resolution is 'significant'.

[SI 2008/410 8 Sch 23].

5.254.1 The UK Corporate Governance Code also contains a provision that, when, in the opinion of the board, a significant proportion of votes have been cast against a resolution (not only resolutions relating to directors' remuneration) at any general meeting, the company should explain, when announcing the results of voting, what actions it intends to take to understand the reasons behind the vote result. [UK CGC E.2.2].

5.255 In Table 5.11, the company sets out the result of the advisory vote (see para 5.258) on the remuneration report. In Table 5.12, the company describes the actions taken following the loss of the advisory vote.

Table 5.11 – Statement of shareholder voting

Marshalls plc – Annual report – 31 December 2012

Directors' Remuneration Report (extract)

Statement of Shareholder Voting

The table below shows the voting outcome at the May 2012 AGM for the approval of the 2011 Remuneration Report.

	For	For as a % of votes cast	Against	Against as a % of votes cast	Abstain
Voters	138,951,048	98.24%	2,488,811	1.76%	2,758,646

The Committee believes the 98.24 per cent votes in favour of the Remuneration Report shows very strong Shareholder support for the Group's remuneration arrangements.

Table 5.12 – Actions following loss of advisory vote

Aviva plc – Annual report – 31 December 2013

Directors' Remuneration Report (extract)

Statement of voting at AGM

The result of the shareholder vote at the Company's 2013 AGM in respect of the 2012 directors' remuneration report is set out in table 24 below.

Table 24: Result of the vote on the directors' remuneration report at 2013 AGM

	Votes cast	For	Against	Votes withheld
2013 vote	1,605,225,273	88.29%	11.71%	19,812,203

The Remuneration Committee consulted extensively with institutional shareholders in the course of 2012/13 following the loss of the directors' remuneration vote in 2012 and implemented a number of changes to approach and policy as set out in our 2012 DRR. Following the result of the 2013 vote, the committee has continued its active engagement to understand and address any remaining concerns. In particular, the committee has discussed with shareholders terms for the departure arrangements of Mr Trevor Matthews and discussed our policies to gain comment and insight when reviewing and drafting our policy report. That active engagement will continue.

Directors' remuneration policy

Introduction

5.256 Shareholders have a binding vote on the remuneration policy (see para 5.259). Generally, shareholders expect that their approval of any remuneration policy would have immediate effect; that is, the remuneration policy would come into force from the date of the AGM at which it is approved. The requirement for approval of the remuneration policy is in addition to the requirement for an advisory vote on the implementation part of the report.

[The next paragraph is 5.258.]

Approval of the directors' remuneration report (advisory vote)

5.258 A quoted company is required by section 439 of the 2006 Act to give notice to members, prior to the general meeting at which accounts are laid (the 'accounts meeting'), of its intention to move an ordinary resolution approving the directors' remuneration report, excluding the policy part. No entitlement of a director to remuneration is made conditional on this resolution being passed; that is, the vote is an advisory vote. [CA06 Sec 439(2)]. But, if this resolution is not passed, the company is required to seek approval of the remuneration policy the following year (see para 5.259). So, where a company prepares a remuneration report for the year ended 31 December 20X0, has its AGM in early 20X1 and the advisory vote is not passed, it is required to seek approval for the remuneration policy (which will have to be included in its 31 December 20X1 annual report) at its next AGM in early 20X2.

Approval of the directors' remuneration policy (binding vote)

5.259 A quoted company is required by section 439A of the Act to give notice to members of its intention to move an ordinary resolution to approve the directors' remuneration policy at the relevant meeting. A quoted company is required to seek shareholder approval of the company's remuneration policy:

■ At the accounts meeting held in the first financial year which begins on or after the date on which the company becomes a quoted company.

■ At an accounts or other general meeting held no later than the end of the three financial year period that starts at the beginning of the financial year that commences after the general meeting at which the last remuneration policy was put to a shareholder resolution. The company must put the remuneration policy back to shareholders by the end of the third full financial year.

■ At the next accounts meeting following one where the advisory vote on the remuneration report was not passed (see para 5.262).

[CA06 Sec 439A(1)(2)].

[The next paragraph is 5.261.]

5.261 Quoted companies are prohibited from making remuneration payments or payments for loss of office that have not been approved by shareholders. If a proposed payment is not consistent with the approved remuneration policy, separate approval is sought. [CA06 Secs 226B, 226C].

5.262 If shareholders do not approve the remuneration policy, the company does one of the following:

■ Continues to operate according to the last remuneration policy to have been approved by a shareholder resolution.

■ Continues to operate according to the last remuneration policy to have been approved by a shareholder resolution and seek separate shareholder approval for any specific remuneration or loss of office payments which are not consistent with the policy.

■ Calls a general meeting and puts a remuneration policy to shareholders for approval. This could, but need not be, an amended version of the policy last put to shareholders for approval.

Revised directors' remuneration policy

5.263 Companies are required to comply with the remuneration policy approved by the shareholders. If they wish to change that policy, they are required to obtain shareholder approval of the new policy before it can be implemented.

5.264 The new policy can be approved at any general meeting; companies do not have to wait until the next accounts meeting. Whether the new remuneration policy is to be approved earlier in another general meeting, the policy part of the report for which approval is sought is required to contain all the information and be set out in the manner as in Part 4 of Schedule 8; that is, the policy report is to be the same as would be included in the annual report if it were to be approved at the AGM. [SI 2008/410 8 Sch 42, 43].

[The next paragraph is 5.266.]

Inclusion of the policy in the directors' remuneration report

5.266 Companies are not legally required to include the policy part in the remuneration report if the company does not intend to seek approval of the policy at the accounts meeting at which that report will be laid. Where the advisory vote described in paragraph 5.258 is passed each year, this will mean that the policy part of the remuneration report has to be included in that report at least once every three years. [SI 2008/410 8 Sch 1(2)].

5.267 Where the remuneration policy is excluded from the remuneration report, the following information is disclosed in the report:

■ The date of the last general meeting at which the policy was approved.

■ Where, on the company's web site or elsewhere, the remuneration policy can be inspected by members.

[SI 2008/410 8 Sch 3].

5.268 Companies usually take the view that the implementation report is hard to understand in the absence of an explanation of the policy that is being implemented. Most companies include some policy information in the remuneration report even if that information is not required by the law. Some include the full policy, as approved by shareholders; others set out a summary of the key elements of the policy, usually including the future policy table (see para 5.269). Where the full policy is not included in the remuneration report, the information set out in paragraph 5.267 is given.

General rules applying to the policy part of the report

5.268.1 Where the remuneration policy in the report is the first to be subject to a binding shareholder vote, the report is required to state the date from which the policy will take effect. [SI 2008/410 8 Sch 24(5)].

5.268.2 Where the remuneration policy is to be approved by shareholders and some or all of the provisions of the previously approved policy are to continue to apply after the approval is granted (even though they are inconsistent with the new policy), that fact is stated in the policy report. Those provisions should be clearly identified and the period of time for which it is intended they will apply should be stated in the policy report. [SI 2008/410 8 Sch 24(2)].

5.268.3 Where any aspect of the remuneration policy provides for the exercise of discretion by the directors, the policy must clearly set out the extent of that discretion in respect of any such variation, change or amendment. [SI 2008/410 8 Sch 24(4)]. The directors' remuneration policy must be approved by shareholders at least every three years. Some discretion is likely to be appropriate so that directors have sufficient flexibility to adapt to particular circumstances as they arise over that period. This is important because payments cannot be made if they are inconsistent with the approved policy. So companies need to strike a balance between being prescriptive enough to satisfy shareholders whilst being sufficiently flexible for the policy to be operable for three years without change. Shareholders have pushed back on some companies that have included open-ended discretion (particularly in the context of recruitment policy), resulting in companies having to include clarifying statements about how they will implement their remuneration policies on their websites.

Future policy table

5.269 The policy part must include a table setting out a description of each of the components of the remuneration package for the directors of the company. [SI 2008/410 8 Sch 25(1)]. 'Components' includes, but is not restricted to, the items that are presented in each of the columns in the single figure table. [SI 2008/410 8 Sch 25(3)]. The table should identify which provisions apply to all directors and include any particular arrangements that are specific to any director individually. [SI 2008/410 8 Sch 25(2)].

5.270 In respect of each of the components, the following information is given in the table:

■ How that component supports the short and long-term strategic objectives of the company (or, where the company is a parent company, the group).

■ An explanation of how that component of the remuneration package operates.

■ The maximum that may be paid in respect of that component (which may be expressed in monetary terms, or otherwise).

■ Where applicable, a description of the framework used to assess performance including:

  ■ A description of any performance measures which apply and, where more than one performance measure applies, an indication of the weighting of the performance measure or group of performance measures.

  ■ Details of any performance period.

  ■ The amount (which may be expressed in monetary terms or otherwise) that may be paid in respect of:

    (a) the minimum level of performance that results in any payment under the policy; and

    (b) any further levels of performance set in accordance with the policy.

■   An explanation as to whether there are any provisions for the recovery of sums paid or the withholding of the payment of any sum (that is, clawback or malus provisions).

[SI 2008/410 8 Sch 26].

5.271   BIS has observed that there has been a significant level of non-compliance with the requirement to specify clearly, in monetary terms or otherwise, the maximum future salary that might be paid under the remuneration policy. This requirement is not met by describing the process or principles that would be used to set salary (for example, that the rate of pay increase is typically linked to that of the wider workforce). Although it is not a requirement to disclose an absolute monetary amount, BIS considers that sufficient information should be disclosed to enable the reader to calculate such a figure (for example, the maximum percentage increase).

5.271.1   To the extent that they could result in future payments by the company to directors, the future policy should include details of the following items:

■   Commitments made to directors before 27 June 2012.

■   Commitments made to directors before the new policy came into effect (see para 5.268.2).

■   Commitments made to directors before the company became quoted.

■   Commitments made to a director before he was appointed to the board.

5.272   Often, companies include a general 'grandfathering provision' to cover such commitments. But, even if they do, they should disclose the terms of the arrangements in the future policy table, unless they were granted prior to the director's appointment to the board and are not predicated on service as a director. Typically, these commitments are in respect of unvested share options given as long-term incentives.

5.272.1   The maximum amount of each component should be disclosed. For salaries, this maximum might be expressed as a salary amount or as a maximum percentage of increase in salary. For benefits, it can be difficult to determine a maximum amount, and the policy will need to be sufficiently flexible to deal with reasonable but unforeseen changes. Benefits costs can vary considerably; for example, healthcare costs can vary according to the director's location or personal circumstances. Relocation costs can be high, because they often cover not just removal and accommodation costs but also items such as school fees, tax equalisation and family travel costs. A specific director's relocation is often not envisaged at the time the policy is set, so the policy should allow for this possibility.

5.272.2   Frequently, performance-related pay, particularly in the form of annual bonuses, is subject to a period of deferral. If so, in explaining how this remuneration component operates, disclosures would include: the deferral period; any other conditions to be met; whether the deferred pay is payable in cash or shares; and any matching awards payable at the end of the deferral period, together with any right or discretionary right to dividend equivalents.

5.273   Notes to the table are required to set out:

■   An explanation of why the performance measures were chosen and how any performance targets are set. (Performance targets need not be disclosed.)

■   For any component (other than salary, fees, benefits and pension) that is not subject to performance measures, an explanation of why there are no such measures.

■   Any changes to components in the last approved remuneration policy, and the reasons for the change.

■   An explanation of the differences (if any) in the company's policy on the remuneration of directors from the policy on the remuneration of employees generally (within the company, or where the company is a parent company, the group).

[SI 2008/410 8 Sch 27].

5.273.1   In Table 5.13.1, the company provides its statement of consideration of employment conditions elsewhere in the company (see para 5.304) and sets out the differences from the Executive Director Policy.

Table 5.13.1 – General employment conditions and differences from directors' pay policy

Smith & Nephew plc – Annual report – 31 December 2013

Directors' remuneration report (extract)

Statement of consideration of employment conditions elsewhere in the Company and differences to the Executive Director Policy

All employees across the Group including the Executive Directors are incentivised in a similar manner. Although the salary levels and maximum opportunities under bonus and share plans differ, generally speaking the same targets and performance conditions relating to the Company's strategy apply throughout the organisation.

Executive Director base salaries will generally increase at a rate in line with the average salary increases awarded across the Company. Given the diverse geographic markets within which the Company operates, the Committee will generally be informed by the average salary increase in both the market local to the Executive and the UK, recognising the Company's place of listing, and will also consider market data periodically.

A range of different pension arrangements operate across the Group depending on location and/or length of service. Executive Directors and Executive Officers either participate in the legacy pension arrangements relevant to their local market or receive a cash payment of 30% of salary in lieu of a pension. Senior Executives who do not participate in a local Company pension plan receive a cash payment of 20% of salary in lieu of pension. Differing amounts apply for lower levels within the Company.

The Company has established a benefits framework under which the nature of benefits varies by geography. Executive Directors participate in benefit arrangements similar to those applied for employees within the applicable location.

All employees are set objectives at the beginning of each year, which link through to the objectives set for the Executive Directors. Annual cash incentives payable to employees across the Company depend on the satisfactory completion of these objectives as well as performance against relevant Group and divisional financial targets relating to revenue, trading profit and trading cash, similar to the financial targets set for the Executive Directors.

Executive Officers and Senior Executives (currently 72) participate in the annual Equity Incentive Programme and the Performance Share Programme. The maximum amounts payable are lower, but the performance conditions are the same as those that apply to the Executive Directors.

No specific consultation with employees has been undertaken relating to Director remuneration. However, regular employee surveys are conducted across the Group, which cover a wide range of issues relating to local employment conditions and an understanding of Group-wide strategic matters. Currently over 4,500 employees in 32 countries participate in one or more of our global share plans.

5.274 Information in respect of non-executive directors can be set out in a separate table. This table is required to set out the company approach determining:

■ The fee payable to such directors.

■ Any additional fees payable for any other duties to the company.

■ Any other items in the nature of remuneration.

[SI 2008/410 8 Sch 28].

5.275 A director's pay might be denominated in a foreign currency. In such cases, the policy disclosures might be translated into the company's functional currency. Changes in exchange rates could distort these amounts year on year and, if this is so, an explanation should be provided.

[The next paragraph is 5.279.]

5.279 The principles of the Code that relate to directors' remuneration are described the Annex to this chapter. Whilst the law sets out disclosure requirements, the Code contains best practice provisions for setting the level and components of remuneration and the procedure to be followed in developing remuneration policy. The Code's main principles on remuneration recommend that the executive directors' remuneration is designed to promote the long-term success of the company and that performance-related elements are transparent, stretching and rigorously applied. The company should have a transparent procedure for developing remuneration policy. The Code includes provisions dealing with levels of pay, awarding options, long-term incentive schemes and service contract periods.

Approach to recruitment remuneration

5.280 Schedule 8 requires that the policy contains a statement of the principles to be applied by the company in agreeing the components of a remuneration package for new directors. The statement should include the various components that would be considered for inclusion in the remuneration package and the approach to be taken in respect of each of those components. [SI 2008/410 8 Sch 29(1)(2)].

5.281 Also, the statement should state the maximum level of variable remuneration that may be granted. This can be expressed in monetary terms or otherwise (for example, as a percentage). It is often the policy that new directors will have the same annual bonus and long-term incentive entitlements as existing directors and, if so, that fact should be stated. This 'maximum level' disclosure does not include 'buy out awards' to compensate a director for the forfeit of an award from a previous employer. But such awards are to be dealt with in the more general disclosure of principles to be applied to agreeing remuneration components and the approach to be taken in respect of them. [SI 2008/410 8 Sch 29(3)(4)].

5.282 When describing the approach to compensatory payments for forfeited awards, the principles applying could include:

■ Paying what is necessary to attract individuals of appropriate calibre.

■ Paying fair value equivalence with amounts forfeited.

■ Matching vesting periods with those awards foregone.

■ Attaching performance conditions to awards replacing performance-related awards.

■ Including a requirement for continued employment with clawback for a period before vesting.

5.283 A company will not be permitted to make a 'sign-on' payment unless the remuneration policy specifically covers such payments. The policy should set out the types of awards that can be made (for example, cash or shares), any performance criteria or holding periods and any recovery or withholding policies.

5.283.1 New directors, particularly those relocating from overseas, are sometimes reimbursed for relocation and other costs. As described in paragraph 5.272.3, the company's policy on these items should be disclosed.

5.283.2 As described in paragraph 5.272.1, where employees might be promoted to the board, the company should disclose its policy on honouring pre-appointment commitments on bonuses and incentive awards.

Service contracts

5.284 Schedule 8 states:

> *"The directors' remuneration policy must contain a description of any obligation on the company which:*
> ■ *is contained in all directors' service contracts;*
> ■ *is contained in the service contracts of any one or more existing directors (not being covered by the previous bullet); or*
> ■ *it is proposed would be contained in directors' service contracts to be entered into by the company*
>
> *and which could give rise to, or impact on, remuneration payments or payments for loss of office but which is not disclosed elsewhere in this report."*

[SI 2008/410 8 Sch 30].

5.285 Where the service contracts are not available for inspection at the company's registered office, the remuneration report is required to disclose details of where the contracts are kept, and if the contracts are available on a web site, a link to that web site. [SI 2008/410 8 Sch 31].

5.286 These disclosures apply in respect of both executive and non-executive directors. The requirements apply also to directors' letters of appointment. [SI 2008/410 8 Sch 32]. They encompass all written agreements between a director and the company under which the director agrees to perform services for the company, regardless of the legal form that those agreements may take. So, they apply whether the 'service contract' is a contract of service (an employment contract) or a contract for services.

[The next paragraph is 5.289.]

5.289 A company that has securities carrying voting rights admitted to trading on a regulated market at the end of its financial year is required to disclose, in its directors' report, details of any agreement with employees (including directors) of the company providing for compensation for loss of office on the takeover of the company. [SI 2008/410 7 Sch 13(2)(k)]. Disclosures in respect of contracts relating to takeovers are dealt with in chapter 2.

5.290 An example of disclosure in respect service contracts is given in Table 5.14.

Table 5.14 – Details of service contracts

BG Group plc – Annual Report – 31 December 2013

Remuneration report (extracts)

EXECUTIVE DIRECTORS' SERVICE CONTRACTS

The Executive Directors' service contracts, including arrangements for early termination, are carefully considered by the Committee and are designed to recruit, retain and motivate Executive Directors of the quality required to manage the Company. The Committee considers that a notice period of one year is normally appropriate.

The Committee has discretion, in order to attract and retain suitable candidates, to offer contracts that contain an initial notice period in excess of one year, reducing to a one-year notice period after the expiry of this initial period.

Executive Directors' service contracts as at 31 December 2013

Details of the service contracts of the Executive Directors who served during the year are set out below:

Executive Directors	Contract date	Notice period
Chris Finlayson	14 Mar 12	1 year
Simon Lowth[a]	3 July 13	1 year

[a] Simon Lowth was appointed as Executive Director and Chief Financial Officer on 2 December 2013. He is subject to election as a Director by shareholders at the 2014 AGM.

SUMMARY OF KEY ELEMENTS OF SERVICE CONTRACTS OF THE EXECUTIVE DIRECTORS

Provision	Summary of key terms
Notice period	12 months.
Retirement date	There is no default retirement age. Requests for retirement are considered on a case by case basis. At the Executive Director level, it is expected that at least 12 months' notice will be provided in accordance with the contractual notice period.
Remuneration	Base salary. Pension or cash alternative. Company car or cash in lieu. Eligibility to participate in annual and long-term incentive arrangements operated from time to time.
Termination payment	Contractual provisions exist in the event of termination following a change of control. A payment in lieu of notice may also be made comprising base salary and cash in lieu of pension. The rules of the AIS and LTIP also include certain provisions on termination of employment. These provisions are discussed further in the Exit payments policy section.

NON-EXECUTIVE DIRECTORS' LETTERS OF APPOINTMENT

The Board aims to recruit Non-Executive Directors of a high calibre, with broad commercial, international and/or other relevant experience. Non-Executive Directors are appointed by the Board on the recommendation of the Nominations Committee. Their appointment is for an initial term of three years, subject to election by shareholders at the first AGM following their appointment and annual re-election thereafter. The terms of engagement of the Non-Executive Directors are set out in a letter of appointment. Other than the Chairman, the Non-Executive Directors' letters of appointment do not contain any notice period or provision for compensation in the event of early termination of their appointment.

Chairman

Andrew Gould was appointed Chairman with effect from the conclusion of the AGM on 16 May 2012 for a three-year term. His fee is reviewed annually. His appointment is subject to annual re-election by shareholders at the AGM. He has a six-month notice period, which the Company considers is appropriate.

The Company is entitled to terminate the Chairman's appointment without notice by making a payment in lieu of notice equal to the chairman's fee for six months. Other than payment in lieu of notice, there is no provision for payment in the event of early termination.

Chairman and Non-Executive Directors' letters of appointment	Initial appointment	Date of appointment or re-appointment	Expiry of term
Andrew Gould	1 Jun 11	16 May 12	May 15
Peter Backhouse	19 Jul 00	12 May 11	May 14
Vivienne Cox	8 Feb 12	8 Feb 12	Feb 15
Pam Daley[a]	1Jan 14	1 Jan 14	Dec 16
Martin Ferguson[a]	1Jan 14	1 Jan 14	Dec 16
Baroness Hogg	27 Jan 05	12 May 11	May 14
Dr John Hood	26 Apr 07	12 May 11	May 14
Caio Koch-Weser	1 Nov 10	31 Oct 13	Oct 16
Lim Haw-Kuang	4 Mar 13	4 Mar 13	Mar 16
Sir David Manning	1 Jul 08	12 May 11	May 14
Mark Seligman	3 Dec 09	3 Dec 12	Dec 15
Patrick Thomas	15 Dec 10	14 Dec 13	Dec 16

[a] Pam Daley and Martin Ferguson were appointed as Non-Executive Directors on 1 January 2014, subject to confirmation by election by shareholders as the 2014 AGM.

Exit payments policy

The Company's policy is to include change of control provisions in the Executive Directors' service contracts. The Committee considers that these provisions assist with recruitment and retention and that their inclusion is therefore in the best interests of shareholders. Should an Executive Director's employment be terminated within 12 months of a change of control, they are entitled to liquidated damages equal to one year's gross salary plus 30% of base salary (as a pension contribution or as cash in lieu of pension) less any deductions the employer is required to make. The Committee considers this to be a genuine pre-estimate of loss.

The Company is entitled to terminate an Executive Director's employment without notice by making a payment in lieu of notice in accordance with their contract, which will not exceed an amount equal to annual base salary and cash in lieu of pension. As an alternative to making a payment in lieu of notice, the Company may terminate an Executive Director's service contract in breach of contract and make a payment of damages in respect of that breach, taking into account a variety of factors, including individual and Company performance, the obligation for the Executive Director to mitigate his or her own loss (for example, by gaining new employment) and the Executive Director's length of service. It is expected that any such payments would not exceed one year's base salary and benefits (including pension) consistent with their notice period of 12 months. In connection with the termination of an Executive Director's contract, the Company may make a payment on account of accrued but untaken leave and may pay outplacement fees and legal fees for support provided to the individual. Other than change of control or payment in lieu of notice, the Executive Directors' service contracts do not contain provisions for compensation in the event of early termination.

The rules of the AIS provide that in the event of: (i) a change in control where the AIS is not carried forward under new ownership; or (ii) an employee ceasing employment for a specified reason (such as ill health, agreed retirement, redundancy or in such other circumstances as the Committee considers appropriate taking account of the individual's performance and the circumstances of their departure), then, to the extent the performance measures have been satisfied at the date of the change in control or cessation of employment (as appropriate), AIS amounts may be paid on a time-apportioned basis.

DBP awards do not normally vest for three years and are subject to forfeiture in the event of leaving employment (other than for reasons such as ill health, agreed retirement, redundancy or in such other circumstances as the Committee considers appropriate taking account of the individual's performance and the circumstances of their departure, where share awards would vest when employment ceases). Share awards under the VBDP do not normally vest for three months and are subject to forfeiture in the event of leaving employment for misconduct.

LTIP awards do not normally vest and are subject to forfeiture in the event of leaving employment. For LTIP awards granted before 1 September 2013, if an employee ceases employment prior to the vesting of an award for a specified reason (such as ill health, agreed retirement, redundancy or in such other circumstances as the Committee considers appropriate taking account of the individual's performance and the circumstances of their departure), the awards will normally vest on the last day of employment, to the extent the performance measures are forecast at that time to be met, on a time-apportioned basis. For LTIP awards granted on or after 1 September 2013, the awards will normally vest on schedule, to the extent any performance measures have been met, on a time-apportioned basis.

Additionally, all the Company's share plans contain provisions relating to a change of control. In general, outstanding awards and options would normally vest and become exercisable on a change of control, to the extent that any performance conditions have been satisfied at that time. If the Committee considers it appropriate, given the circumstances of the change of control, time apportionment may also apply. The Committee has discretion to vary the treatment of awards for leavers under the Company's plans, including the AIS, DBP, VBDP and LTIP. Awards under the SIP and Sharesave may vest or become exercisable on or following termination, in accordance with the rules of the plan.

The Committee retains discretion to make payments to mitigate against statutory and other legal claims where it considers it prudent to do so.

Policy on payment for loss of office

5.291 The policy should set out the company's policy on setting notice periods for directors' service contracts. [SI 2008/410 8 Sch 36]. The UK Corporate Governance Code recommends that notice or contract periods should be set at one year or less. [UK CGC D1.5]. See the Annex to this chapter.

5.292 It should also set out the principles on which payments for loss of office will be determined, including:

- An indication of how each component of the payment will be calculated.

- Whether, and if so how, the circumstances of the director's loss of office are relevant to the exercise of discretion.

- Any contractual provision agreed before 27 June 2012 that could affect the payment amount (see below).

[SI 2008/410 8 Sch 37].

5.293 The following disclosures would be useful:

- A clear description of the circumstances in which a leaver would fall into a particular category that would affect any exit payment (that is, 'good leaver/bad leaver' provisions).

- An explanation of how each category of leaver is treated including:

  - when awards vest;

  - whether they are pro-rated; and

  - the extent to which performance is taken into account.

- The extent of any directors' discretion over exit payments.

- Tabular disclosure of each element of remuneration and its treatment on loss of office.

- Payment policy applying in the event of a change in control.

- Whether there is a policy on mitigation and, if so, how it is to be applied.

5.294 Table 5.14 includes many of these disclosures. Table 5.15 is an example of tabular presentation of service contracts and termination payments.

Table 5.15 – Tabular presentation of termination payments

Johnson Matthey Plc – Annual report and accounts – 31 March 2014

Remuneration report (extract)

Service Contracts and Policy on Payment for Loss of Office

The table below summarises relevant key provisions of executive directors' service contracts and the treatment of payments on termination of employment. The full contracts of service of the executive directors (as well as the terms and conditions of appointment of the non-executive directors) are available for inspection at the registered office of the company during normal business hours as well as prior to and during the forthcoming AGM of the company. In exceptional circumstances, the MDRC may authorise, where it considers it to be in the best interests of the company and shareholders, entering into contractual arrangements with a departing executive director, for example a settlement, confidentiality, restrictive covenant or other arrangement, pursuant to which sums not set out in the following table may become payable. In these exceptional circumstances, full disclosure of the payments will be made in accordance with the new remuneration reporting requirements.

The following table describes the contractual conditions pertaining to the contracts for Robert MacLeod, Larry Pentz and John Walker and for any executive director joining after the 1st April 2014. Neil Carson was appointed as an executive director on 1st August 1999 under a service agreement of the same date. Mr Carson will be retiring on 30th September 2014 and his termination arrangements are described on page 114.

Directors' remuneration – quoted companies

	Robert MacLeod	Larry Pentz[1]	John Walker[1]
Date of service agreement	31st January 2014	31st January 2014	31st January 2014
Date of appointment as director	22nd June 2009	1st August 2003	9th October 2013
Employing company	Johnson Matthey Plc	Johnson Matthey Plc	Johnson Matthey Plc
Contract duration	No fixed term.		
Notice period	Not less than 12 months' notice of termination by the company. Not less than six months' notice of termination by the director.		
Post-termination restrictions	The contracts of employment contain the following restrictions on the director for the following periods from the date of termination of employment: – non-compete – six months; – non-dealing and non-solicitation of client / customers – 12 months; – non-solicitation of suppliers and non-interference with supply chain – 12 months; and – non-solicitation of employees – 12 months.		
Summary termination – payment in lieu of notice (PILON)	The company may, in its absolute discretion, terminate the employment of the director with immediate effect by giving written notice together with payment of a sum equivalent to the director's base salary and the value of his contractual benefits as at the date such notice is given, in respect of the director's notice period, less any period of notice actually worked. The company may elect to pay the PILON in equal monthly instalments. The director is under a duty to seek alternative employment and to keep the company informed about whether he has been successful. If the director commences alternative employment, the monthly instalments shall be reduced (if appropriate to nil) by the amount of the director's gross earnings from the alternative employment. A PILON paid to a director who is a US taxpayer (currently Larry Pentz and John Walker) would be in equal monthly instalments.		
Termination payment – change of control	If, within one year after a change of control, the director's service agreement is terminated by the company (other than in accordance with the summary termination provisions), the company shall pay, as liquidated damages, one year's base salary, together with a sum equivalent to the value of the director's contractual benefits, as at the date of termination, less the period of any notice given by the company to the director.		
Termination – treatment of annual bonus	Annual bonus awards are made at the discretion of the MDRC. Employees leaving the company's employment will receive a bonus, pro-rata to service, unless the reason for leaving is resignation or misconduct. Any bonus awarded would continue to be subject to deferral as set out in the Remuneration Policy. In relation to deferred bonus awards which have already been made, shares will be released on the normal vesting date unless one of the following circumstances applies, and subject to the discretion of the MDRC: ● the participant leaves as a result of misconduct; or ● the participant, prior to vesting, breaches one of the post-termination restrictions or covenants provided for in his employment contract, termination agreement or similar agreement.		
Termination – treatment of LTIP awards	Employees leaving the company's employment will normally lose their LTIP awards unless they leave for a specified 'good leaver' reason, in which case their shares will be released on the normal release dates, subject to the performance condition. The MDRC has discretion to accelerate vesting, in which case the performance condition would be assessed to the end of the financial year preceding the accelerated vesting date. In either case, unless the MDRC determines otherwise, the level of vesting shall be pro-rated to reflect the proportion of the performance period which has elapsed due to the date of leaving. In the post-vesting deferral period, only those who leave due to misconduct will lose their shares.		
Redundancy scheme	The director is not entitled to any benefit under any redundancy payments scheme operated by the company.		
Holiday	Upon termination for any reason, directors will be entitled to payment in lieu of accrued but untaken holiday entitlement.		

[1] Larry Pentz and John Walker are eligible for continuing post-retirement medical benefits provided they satisfy the conditions of this plan and retire directly from Johnson Matthey.

Retirement arrangements for Neil Carson

The following sets out the remuneration arrangements which are in place for Neil Carson, who will be retiring from the board on 30th September 2014.

Folllowing his retirement, Mr Carson will receive no remuneration or loss of office payments. The remuneration receivable by Mr Carson following his retirement will be as follows:

Annual bonus	Subject to the performance conditions of the annual bonus plan being met, Mr Carson will receive a bonus for the year ended 31st March 2015 on the normal bonus award date in 2015, such bonus will be pro-rated for service up to his retirement date. The maximum level of bonus possible will therefore be 90% of base salary. In accordance with the Remuneration Policy, a proportion of the bonus will be awarded as shares which will be deferred for a period of three years. Mr Carson was awarded 12,902 shares under the deferred bonus plan in 2012. These will be released to him on the normal release date in 2015. No bonus was paid in 2013 and so there is no deferred bonus award in respect of that year.
LTIP	Shares allocated to Mr Carson in July 2012 and August 2013 under the LTIP will be released to him on the normal vesting dates in 2015 and 2016 respectively. The number of shares under these awards will be pro-rated on leaving to 52,252 and 28,178 shares based on his completed service since the start of the performance period and final vesting will be determined by reference to the achievement of performance conditions. No LTIP award will be made to Mr Carson in 2014.
Post-retirement medical insurance	Under the terms of his contract, Mr Carson is entitled to continuing private medical insurance for himself and his spouse / dependents.

5.295 Under transition provisions in the Enterprise and Regulatory Reform Act 2013, the requirements of Sections 226A to 226 F of the Companies Act 2006 do not apply to agreements entered into on or before 27 June 2012 (see para 5.271). Sections 226A to 226F require quoted companies to make remuneration or loss of office payments only in accordance with an approved policy or after approval of the payment by the passing of a members' resolution at a general meeting. Payments for loss of office made in respect of an agreement made before 27 June 2012 would be subject to the approval requirements that are contained in Sections 215 to 222 of the Companies Act 2006; these requirements continue to apply to unquoted companies (regardless of the date of the agreement to make the payment).

Non-executive appointments at other companies

5.296 For listed companies, the Code recommends that where a company releases an executive director to serve as a non-executive director elsewhere, the remuneration report should include a statement as to whether or not the director will retain such earnings and, if so, what the remuneration is. [UK CGC D.1.2]. An example disclosure is provided in Table 5.16.

Table 5.16 – Executive directors retain fees for services provided as non-executive directors elsewhere

Pearson plc – Annual report and accounts – 31 December 2013

Report on directors' remuneration (extract)

Directors' remuneration policy report (extract)

Executive directors' non-executive directorships

The committee's policy is that executive directors may, by agreement with the board, serve as non-executives of other companies and retain any fees payable for their services.

Annual remuneration report (extract)

Executive directors' non-executive directorships

In accordance with policy, the following executive directors served as non-executive directors elsewhere and retained fees or other benefits for the period covered by this report as follows:

	Company	**Fees/benefits**
Rona Fairhead	HSBC Holdings plc	£83,333

Other executive directors served as non-executive directors elsewhere but either waived or did not receive fees.

Illustrations of remuneration policy application

5.297   The policy should include, in the form of a bar chart, an indication of the level of remuneration that would be received for each executive director in accordance with the remuneration policy in the first year to which the policy applies. [SI 2008/410 8 Sch 33].

5.298   The bar chart should contain separate bars representing:

■   Minimum remuneration (including salary, fees, benefits and pension). (This is typically described as 'fixed' pay).

■   Remuneration for on-target or on-plan performance (that is, where the performance measures and targets achieved are in line with the company's expectations).

■   Maximum remuneration (not allowing for any share price appreciation).

[SI 2008/410 8 Sch 34(1)].

5.299   Each of the three bars should be analysed in percentage terms between the following parts:

■   Minimum remuneration.

■   Remuneration in respect of performance measures or targets relating to one financial year.

■   Remuneration in respect of performance measures or targets relating to more than one financial year.

[SI 2008/410 8 Sch 34(2)(3)(a)].

5.299.1   Although not specified in the law, it seems sensible that salary, for this purpose, will be the most recently confirmed salary (which might be different from that shown in the single figure table). Benefits will usually be the amount shown in the single figure table, unless the company has specific information that the future benefits will be different; for example, if the current year single figure table included a relocation benefit that will not recur, the relevant amount would be excluded from the amount included in the bar chart for benefits. For pension arrangements, the pension amount to be included in the bar chart will be the pension input amount that will be shown in the single figure table, based on the most recently confirmed salary.

5.299.2   Annual bonuses are usually based on a percentage of salary, so the bar chart amount for the annual bonus should, like the salary element, be based on the most recently confirmed salary. If the bonus arrangement allows the director to receive matching shares if he invests some of his bonus entitlement in shares, those matching shares should be included as part of the annual bonus for bar chart purposes.

5.299.3   Similarly, the calculation of the amounts for long-term incentive awards is not specified in the law but, where the amounts are based on a percentage of salary, the most recently confirmed salary would be used for bar chart purposes. Where they are based on a fixed number of shares, the bar chart amounts will be based on the face value of those shares. In our view, this face value could be based on a spot price at a suitable date (for example, the year end price or the price at a date close to the remuneration report finalisation date) or on an average share price. Whichever valuation method is chosen, it should be disclosed.

5.299.4   Where awards are made in share options worth a percentage of salary, the most recently confirmed salary should be used. Where awards are made as a fixed number of options, the bar chart amount would be based on the number and value of share options receivable. To value the share options, the Financial Reporting Lab's report, 'Reporting of pay and performance', suggests the use of a rule of thumb established by common practice; its initial suggestion is that the share options' value should be calculated as one third of the market value of the shares under option. Again, the method of calculation should be disclosed.

5.300   The total value of remuneration under each of the three scenarios (minimum, on-target and maximum) should also be disclosed. [SI 2008/410 8 Sch 34(3)(b)].

5.301   A description of the basis of calculation and the assumptions used to compile the bar chart should be presented to enable an understanding of the charts presented. [SI 2008/410 8 Sch 35(1)]. It is not necessary to repeat any of the disclosures already made in the future policy table. [SI 2008/410 8 Sch 35(2)].

5.302   Table 5.17 is an example of the required disclosures. As illustrated in this example, judgement might be required in determining what is meant by 'on-plan' performance, depending on the company's performance measure. In this case, Vodafone explains how it has interpreted TSR performance for the purposes of the scenario disclosure.

Table 5.17 – Scenarios disclosure

Vodafone Group Plc – Annual report for the year end 31 March 2014

Directors' remuneration (extract)

Estimates of total future potential remuneration from 2015 pay packages

The tables below provide estimates of the potential future remuneration for each of the executive directors based on the remuneration opportunity granted in the 2015 financial year. Potential outcomes based on different performance scenarios are provided for each executive director.

The assumptions underlying each scenario are described below.

		Base (£'000)	Benefits (£'000)	Pension (£'000)	Total fixed (£'000)
Fixed	Consists of base salary, benefits and pension.				
	Base salary is at 1 July 2014.				
	Benefits are valued using the figures in the total remuneration for the 2014 financial year on page 78 (of the 2014 report) and on a similar basis for Nick Read (promoted to the Board on 1 April 2014).				
	Pensions are valued by applying cash allowance rate of 30% of base salary at 1 July 2014.				
	Chief Executive	1,150	38	345	1,533
	Chief Financial Officer	675	23	203	901
	Chief Technology Officer	600	21	180	801
On target	Based on what a director would receive if performance was in line with plan.				
	The target award opportunity for the annual bonus ('GSTIP') is 100% of base salary.				
	The target award opportunity for the long-term incentive ('GLTI') is 237.5% of base salary for the Chief Executive and 210% for others. We assumed that TSR performance was at median				
Maximum	Two times the target award opportunity is payable under the annual bonus ('GSTIP').				
	The maximum levels of performance for the long-term incentive ('GLTI') are 250% of target award opportunity. We assumed that TSR performance was at or above the 80th percentile equivalent.				
All scenarios	Each executive is assumed to co-invest the maximum allowed under the GLTI, 100% of salary, and the GLTI award reflects this.				
	Long-term incentives consist of share awards only which are measured at face value i.e. no assumption for increase in share price or cash dividend equivalents payable.				

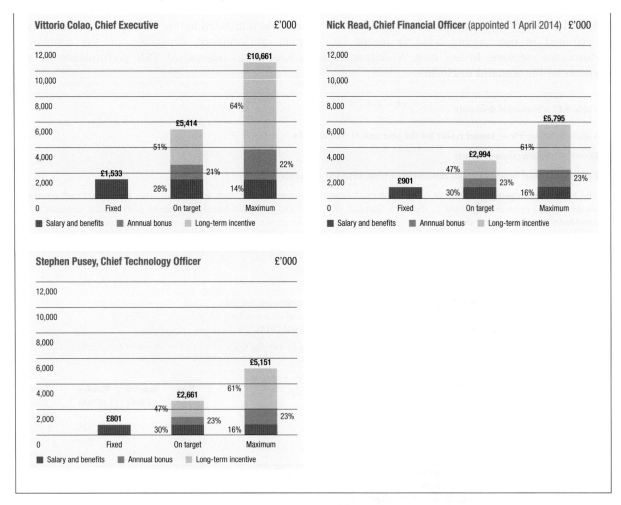

5.303 In Table 5.18, Centrica plc presents actual pay for the current and comparative periods against the total pay under the policy in each of the performance scenarios. (This disclosure is made voluntarily.)

Table 5.18 – Actual pay against scenarios

Centrica plc – Annual report and accounts – 31 December 2013

Remuneration report (extract)

Maximum total remuneration opportunity and total remuneration received in 2013

The chart below sets out the total remuneration received for the year for each Executive Director, prepared on the same basis as the single figure for remuneration table set out on page 76. In addition, for comparison purposes, the chart provides an indication of minimum, on-target and maximum total remuneration, prepared on the same basis.

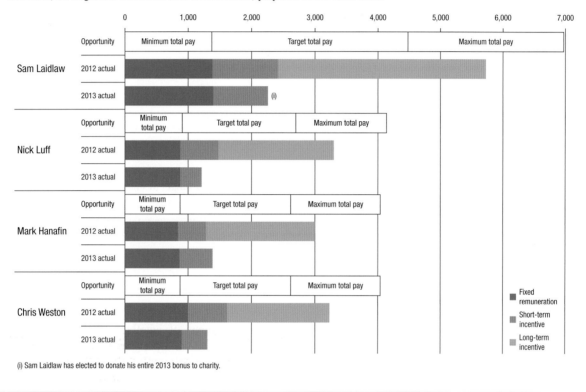

(i) Sam Laidlaw has elected to donate his entire 2013 bonus to charity.

Statement of consideration of employment conditions elsewhere in the company

5.304   Under Schedule 8, there is a requirement to state in the directors' remuneration report how the pay and employment conditions of the company's (and group's) employees (other than directors) were taken into account when setting the directors' remuneration policy. [SI 2008/410 8 Sch 38]. BIS has observed that many companies, whilst disclosing that they have considered the pay and employment conditions of employees, have failed to disclose how such consideration operated in practice.

5.304.1   Also, the report should state whether, and if so how, the company consulted with its employees in drawing up that policy. It should state whether any remuneration comparison measurements were used and, if so, what they were and how they were taken into account. [SI 2008/410 8 Sch 39]. Table 5.19 is an example of disclosure of pay conditions throughout the group. In Table 5.13.1, the company combines this disclosure with the disclosure required in respect of differences between the pay policy for directors and that for employees.

Table 5.19 – Consideration of pay conditions throughout the group

Marshalls plc – Annual report – 31 December 2012

Directors' Remuneration Report (extract)

Remuneration Policy for other Employees

There are other job related incentives that may be awarded at the levels below senior management.

There will be no increase in the basic salaries of senior management for 2013, except in the case of promotions, the assumption of significant additional responsibilities or where necessary to attract a new recruit for a particular position.

The general workforce has been asked to consider a pay offer involving no increase in basic pay for 2013. There were increases in 2012 to take account of inflation.

Consideration of conditions elsewhere in the Group

In applying its policy, the Committee takes into account the wider economic conditions and the pay and reward packages elsewhere in the Sector and the business.

With the exception of a single inflation-related pay increase of 3 per cent awarded in January 2012, Executive Directors' salaries have not increased in the last five years. This has been at their own request, to recognise the need for restraint in the context of pay in the wider workforce and the prevailing economic conditions in the UK that have affected the business. Further, with effect from 1 January 2013, Graham Holden's remuneration will fall by 20 per cent through deduction from anticipated PIP and LTIP earnings.

By comparison, the pay awards for Marshalls' weekly-paid employees were 2 per cent in 2011, and 3 per cent in 2012 under a two year agreement, while pay awards for monthly paid employees were 1.5 per cent in 2011 subject to a minimum and maximum total value, and 3 per cent in 2012.

The Committee has not specifically canvassed the views of the Company's employees on its remuneration policy, although the views of employees on matters that include pay and conditions generally are canvassed by means of the Company's periodic "Pulse" surveys, the results of which are regularly and openly communicated to the Board.

Statement of consideration of shareholder views

5.305 The directors' remuneration report should contain a statement of whether, and if so how, any shareholder views on directors' remuneration, whether expressed to the company at a general meeting or otherwise, have been taken into account in setting the directors' remuneration policy. [SI 2008/410 8 Sch 40]. In Table 5.20, the company describes its actions following consideration of shareholder views.

Table 5.20 – Consideration of shareholder views

Booker Group plc – Annual report – 29 March 2013

REMUNERATION REPORT (extract)

Chairman's Introduction to the Remuneration Report (extract)

The work of the Remuneration Committee in 2013 was influenced by the shareholder vote in respect of the Remuneration Report at the 2012 AGM where 76.2% of votes cast were in favour of the resolution to approve the Report. Following the AGM, the Committee sought feedback from the Company's major shareholders. This feedback indicated that the votes against the Report were largely as a result of an objection to the single performance condition required under the Performance Share Plan ("PSP"), which was based on the share price exceeding certain pre-determined targets for at least sixty consecutive days at any time during the three year vesting period. The Committee considered the points raised by shareholders and decided to change the performance conditions for future PSP awards so that they are more similar to those in other FTSE companies' equivalent plans.

PSP options (extract)

PSP options granted in 2012

In November 2012, the Company made awards under the PSP in relation to a total of 6.3m new Ordinary Shares. As a result of concerns expressed by shareholders during 2012, the Committee decided to review the structure of the PSP performance conditions so that they were more in line with equivalent plans used by other FTSE companies. As a result new performance conditions relating to the 2012 PSP awards were adopted and will apply as follows:

- 50% of each award would be linked to an Absolute TSR performance target with 25% of this element vesting at 8% growth per annum and rising on a straight line basis with full vesting for 15% growth per annum, when measured over the 3 years from the award date.

- 50% of each award would be linked to an Absolute EPS performance target with 25% of this element vesting for achieving Absolute EPS growth of 6% per annum and rising on a straight line basis with full vesting requiring 12% growth per annum, as measured between March 2012 and March 2015.

The options granted will vest and become exercisable three years from the date of award, subject to continued employment and the performance conditions outlined above being satisfied and will lapse if not exercised within 10 years of the date of award.

Further guidance

5.306 Further guidance is available from the GC100 and Investor Group's publication, 'Directors' Remuneration Reporting Guidance'. This provides practical good practice guidance on how to comply with the disclosure requirements to meet the needs of investors.

5.307 Examples of good practice can be found at www.pwc.com/corporatereporting.

AIM companies

5.308 AIM companies are unquoted companies under the definitions in the Act. So, unlike quoted companies, they are not required to produce a directors' remuneration report in the form set out in Schedule 8 to SI 2008/410. The requirements relating to unquoted companies are explained in chapter 7, which is available online on inform.pwc.com.

5.309 But AIM companies have to give certain information that other unquoted companies not listed on AIM do not have to give. The additional requirements are set out in the law and the AIM Rules as follows.

Legal disclosure requirements

5.310 Schedule 5 to SI 2008/410 requires AIM companies to provide disclosures of aggregate gains made by directors on the exercise of share options and the aggregate net value of shares received or receivable under long-term incentive schemes. [SI 2008/410 5 Sch 1(b)(c)].

5.311 Also, in their disclosure of highest paid director's emoluments, AIM companies have to include amounts in respect of gains on the exercise of share options and the net value of shares received or receivable under long-term incentive schemes. [SI 2008/410 5 Sch 2(1)(a)].

AIM Rules disclosure requirements

5.312 AIM Rule 19 requires the following to be disclosed for each director:

- Emoluments and compensation (this will include both cash and non-cash benefits).
- Details of share options and other long-term incentive schemes (this will include information on all outstanding options and awards).
- The value of any company contribution made to a pension scheme.

5.313 There is limited detailed guidance on these requirements; for example, there is little clarity on the extent of the detail to be provided in relation to share options and long-term incentive schemes. So AIM-listed companies could look to the current requirements in Schedule 5 (requirements for all companies) and Schedule 8 (requirements for quoted companies) to SI 2008/410 for further guidance.

5.314 AIM Rule 19 refers to the requirement to disclose remuneration earned *"by each director of the AIM company acting in such capacity during the financial year"*. The definition in Schedule 5 to SI 2008/410 is more specific, requiring all companies to disclose aggregate remuneration paid to or receivable by directors in respect of qualifying services. Qualifying services are defined in paragraph 5.23. We believe that, consistent with SI 2008/410's definition, disclosures should be in respect of remuneration of directors for their work for the whole group, not just work for the parent company.

Audit requirements

5.315 Schedule 8 requires part of the remuneration report ('the auditable part') to be audited. This requirement, and the general provisions of the Act in relation to auditors' duties in respect of directors' remuneration information given in financial statements or accompanying them, are discussed below.

5.316 The Act requires that the auditor determines whether the accounts (including the notes) and the auditable part of the company's directors' remuneration report (in the case of quoted companies) are in accordance with the accounting records and returns and the auditor should include a statement in its report if they are not in agreement. [CA06 Sec 498(1)(2)].

5.317 The auditor is required to report on the auditable part of the directors' remuneration report and to state in its report whether, in its opinion, that part of the directors' remuneration report has been properly prepared in accordance with the Act. [CA06 Sec 497(1)].

5.318 If the requirements of Schedule 5 and, where a remuneration report is required to be prepared (that is, for quoted companies), Schedule 8 in respect of the auditable part of that report, are not complied with, the auditor includes, so far as it is reasonably able to do so, the required information in its report. [CA06 Sec 498(4)].

5.319 The auditable part of the directors' remuneration report is the part containing the information required by paragraphs 4 to 17 (inclusive) of Schedule 8. [SI 2008/410 8 Sch 41]. These paragraphs deal with the following:

- Single figure of remuneration for each director and additional information (see from para 5.99).

- Total pension entitlements (see from para 5.165).

- Scheme interests awarded during the financial year (see from para 5.173).

- Payments to past directors (see from para 5.187).

- Payments for loss of office (see from para 5.190).

- Statement of directors' shareholding and share interests (see from para 5.197).

5.320 A key matter for auditors is to be satisfied that there is clear identification of the information that has been audited.

Example – Identification of auditable and non-auditable information

A quoted company is preparing its directors' remuneration report. The company is proposing to mix the auditable information and the non-auditable information within the remuneration report, rather than keeping them as separate parts. Is this acceptable under Schedule 8 to SI 2008/410?

There is no requirement in SI 2008/410 to separate the auditable and the non-auditable information within the remuneration report, or even to state in that report which information has been audited and which has not. But there are practical difficulties in describing, in the audit opinion, the audit's scope when only part of a section in the annual report has been audited. Directors and the company's auditor cannot assume that the annual report's users will know which information has and which has not been audited.

So the auditor should discuss the directors' remuneration report format with management before the year end and should agree, possibly by including terms in the letter of engagement, that the auditable and the non-auditable parts of the remuneration report will be clearly distinguished. Where this is the case, a cross-reference in the audit opinion to the identifiable audited part will satisfy the need to make clear the scope of the opinion.

But where the remuneration report does not clearly distinguish the auditable and non-auditable information, the audit report should identify specifically, by page and paragraph number or heading if necessary, each directors' remuneration report section that has been audited. This will need to be sufficient to enable the user to identify the information that has and has not been audited.

[The next paragraph is 5.322.]

5.322 Although the policy part of the directors' remuneration report is not audited, the auditor is required to read it, as well as all of the other unaudited information, to check that it is consistent with the financial statements and with knowledge acquired during the audit. As described from paragraph 5.265, companies do not have to include the policy part in the remuneration report every year. Where the policy is omitted from the annual report, a cross-reference to where it can be found on the company's website is included in the directors' remuneration report. Whether the policy description is within the annual report or incorporated by cross-reference to the company's website, the auditor has a 'read responsibility' towards it.

Annex – UK Corporate Governance Code ('the Code')

The Code is dealt with in detail in chapter 4. The main principles, supporting principles and related good practice provisions concerning directors' remuneration are set out below.

Section D of the Code contains two main principles relating to directors' remuneration. The Listing Rules require all companies with a Premium Listing of equity shares to provide a statement on how they have applied the principles of the Code and to give a statement confirming whether they have complied with its provisions (providing an explanation where they have not complied). The main principles, supporting principles and related best practice provisions are described below.

The level and components of remuneration

The first main principle concerning directors' remuneration states that levels of remuneration should be designed to promote the long-term success of the company. Performance-related elements should be transparent, stretching and rigorously applied. [UK CGC D.1].

This is supplemented by a supporting principle, which states that the remuneration committee should judge where to position their company relative to other companies. But they should use comparisons with caution in view of the risk of an upward ratchet of remuneration levels with no corresponding improvement in corporate and individual performance, and should avoid paying more than is necessary. They should also be sensitive to pay and employment conditions elsewhere in the group, especially when determining annual salary increases. [UK CGC D.1].

The Code provisions relevant to the application of these principles are as follows:

■ The remuneration committee should follow Schedule A (see below) in designing schemes for performance-related remuneration. Schemes should include provisions that would enable the company to recover sums paid or withhold the payment of any sum, and specify the circumstances in which it would be appropriate to do so ('clawback' or 'malus' provisions). [UK CGC D.1.1].

■ Where a company releases an executive director to serve as a non-executive director elsewhere, the remuneration report should include a statement as to whether or not the director will retain such earnings and, if so, what the remuneration is. [UK CGC D.1.2].

■ Levels of remuneration for non-executive directors should reflect the time commitment and responsibilities of the role. Non-executive directors' remuneration should not include share options or other performance-related elements. But if options are granted, shareholder approval should be sought in advance and any shares acquired by exercise of the options should be held until at least one year after the non-executive director leaves the board. Holding of share options could be relevant to the determination of a non-executive director's independence (as set out in Code provision B.1.1). [UK CGC D.1.3].

■ The remuneration committee should carefully consider what compensation commitments (including pension contributions and all other elements) their directors' terms of appointment would entail in the event of early termination. The aim should be to avoid rewarding poor performance. They should take a robust line on reducing compensation to reflect departing directors' obligations to mitigate loss. [UK CGC D.1.4].

■ Notice or contract periods should be set at one year or less. If it is necessary to offer longer notice or contract periods to new directors recruited from outside, such periods should reduce to one year or less after the initial period. [UK CGC D.1.5].

Procedure

The main principle in this area is that there should be a formal and transparent procedure for developing policy on executive remuneration and for fixing the remuneration packages of individual directors. No director should be involved in deciding his or her own remuneration. [UK CGC D.2].

In support of this main principle are the following supporting principles:

■ The remuneration committee should take care to recognise and manage conflicts of interest when receiving views from executive directors or senior management, or consulting the chief executive about its proposals. The remuneration committee should also be responsible for appointing any consultants in respect of executive director remuneration.

- The chairman of the board should ensure that the company maintains contact as required with its principal shareholders about remuneration.

[UK CGC D.2].

The Code provisions relevant to the application of these principles are as follows:

- The board should establish a remuneration committee of at least three, or in the case of smaller companies (that is, those falling outside the FTSE 350 throughout the year immediately prior to the reporting year), two independent non-executive directors. In addition the company chairman may also be a member of, but not chair, the committee if he or she was considered independent on appointment as chairman. The remuneration committee should make available its terms of reference, explaining its role and the authority delegated to it by the board. Where remuneration consultants are appointed, they should be identified in the annual report and a statement made as to whether they have any other connection with the company. [UK CGC D.2.1].

- The remuneration committee should have delegated responsibility for setting remuneration for all executive directors and the chairman, including pension rights and any compensation payments. The committee should also recommend and monitor the level and structure of senior managements' remuneration. The definition of 'senior management' for this purpose should be determined by the board, but should normally include the first layer of management below board level. (Note that disclosure of the remuneration committee's activities throughout the year is considered to be good practice.) [UK CGC D.2.2].

- The board itself or, where required by the articles of association, the shareholders should determine the non-executive directors' remuneration within the limits set in the articles of association. Where permitted by the articles, the board may, however, delegate this responsibility to a committee, which might include the chief executive. [UK CGC D.2.3].

- Shareholders should be invited specifically to approve all new long-term incentive schemes (as defined in the Listing Rules) and significant changes to existing schemes, save in the circumstances permitted by the Listing Rules. [UK CGC D.2.4].

Schedule A – The design of performance-related remuneration for executive directors

Schedule A of the Code, which is referred to above, deals with the design of performance-related remuneration and includes the following:

- The remuneration committee should determine an appropriate balance between fixed and performance-related, immediate and deferred remuneration. Performance conditions, including non-financial metrics where appropriate, should be relevant, stretching and designed to promote the long-term success of the company. Remuneration incentives should be compatible with risk policies and systems. Upper limits should be set and disclosed.

- The remuneration committee needs to consider whether the directors should be eligible for annual bonuses and/or benefits under long-term incentive schemes.

- Traditional share option schemes should be weighed against other kinds of long-term incentive scheme. Executive share option schemes should not be offered at a discount, except as permitted by the relevant provisions of the Listing Rules.

- For share-based remuneration the remuneration committee should consider requiring directors to hold a minimum number of shares for a further period after vesting or exercise, including a period after leaving the company, subject to the need to finance any costs of acquisition and associated tax liabilities.

- Generally, shares granted or other forms of deferred remuneration should not vest or be paid, and options should not be exercisable, in less than three years. Longer periods might be appropriate.

- Any new long-term incentive schemes that are proposed should be approved by shareholders and should preferably replace any existing schemes or at least form part of a well-considered overall plan, incorporating existing schemes. Also, the total rewards potentially available should not be excessive.

- Normally, grants under executive share option and other long-term incentive schemes should be phased rather than awarded in one large block.

- Generally, only basic salary should be pensionable. Remuneration committees need to consider the pension consequences and associated costs to the company of basic salary increases and any other changes in pensionable remuneration, especially for directors close to retirement.

[UK CGC Sch A].

Index

Locators are:

  paragraph numbers: 11.149, for Chapter 11, paragraph 149

Entries are in word-by-word alphabetical order, where a group of letters followed by a space is filed before the same group of letters followed by a letter, eg 'capital structure and treasury policy' will appear before 'capitalisation'. In determining alphabetical arrangement, initial articles, conjunctions and small prepositions are ignored.

Index

Index

Index

Index

'seriously prejudicial' information, 2.42
  social matters, 2.35–2.37
  strategy of company, 2.24–2.27
definitions, 3.23–3.25
detailed guidance within disclosure framework
  business model, 3.86–3.95
  principal objectives and strategies, 3.71–3.85.2
development and performance of the business
  accounting policies, 3.187–3.190
  acquisitions and disposals, 3.181–3.186
  capital structure, 3.149–3.154
  cash flows, 3.145–3.148
  current year, in the, 3.175–3.180
  generally, 3.138–3.144
  liquidity, 3.155–3.170
  tax disclosure, 3.191–3.205
  treasury policies, 3.149–3.154
diversity, 3.230–3.239
entity-principle, 3.53–3.57
environmental matters, 3.125–3.137.4
factors affecting the business, 3.96–3.107
fair, balanced and understandable, 3.30–3.36
future development, performance and position of business, 3.96–3.107
forward-looking, 3.45–3.52
FRC guidance
  approach, 3.26
  content elements, 3.66–3.70
  definitions, 3.23–3.25
  development and performance of the business, 3.138–3.205
  detailed guidance within disclosure framework, 3.71–3.95
  diversity, 3.230–3.239
  environmental matters, 3.125–3.137.4
  key performance indicators, 3.206–3.229
  objective, 3.27–3.28.4
  principal risks and uncertainties, 3.108–3.124
  principles, 3.29–3.65.2
  scope, 3.23–3.25
  social matters, 3.125–3.137.4
  trends, 3.96–3.107
good practice reporting, 3.8–3.11
highlight linkages, 3.58–3.63.1
IFRS, and, 2.7
integrated reporting, and, 3.12–3.22
introduction, 3.1–3.7
key performance indicators
  generally, 3.206–3.220
  reporting, 3.221–3.229
liquidity, 3.155–3.170
matters of strategic importance, 3.240–3.242
objective, 3.27–3.28.4
other content elements, 3.240–3.242
placement within annual report, 2.13–2.15.2
presentation, 3.64–3.65
principal objectives and strategies, 3.71–3.85.2
principal risks and uncertainties, 3.108–3.124
principles
  annual review, 3.64–3.65.2
  concise, 3.37–3.43
  entity-principle, 3.53–3.57
  fair, balanced and understandable, 3.30–3.36
  forward-looking, 3.45–3.52
  highlight linkages, 3.58–3.63.1
  introduction, 3.29
purpose, 2.16

quoted company, and, 2.12
risks and uncertainties, 3.108–3.124
scope, 3.23–3.25
social matters, 3.125–3.137.4
strategically important matters, 3.240–3.242
strategies, 3.71–3.85.2
structure, 3.64–3.65
tax disclosure, 3.191–3.205
treasury policies, 3.149–3.154
trends affecting the business, 3.96–3.107
Strategy
  strategic report, and, 2.24–2.27, 3.71–3.85.2

Tax disclosure
  strategic report, and, 3.191–3.205
Taxable benefits
  directors' remuneration, and, 5.118–5.120
Third party indemnity provisions
  directors' report, and, 2.83–2.86
Total pension entitlements
  directors' remuneration, and, 5.165–5.172
Training
  Combined Code, and
    good practice disclosure, 4.142
    introduction, 4.139
    principles, 4.140–4.141
Transactions with controlling shareholder
  directors' report, and
    contracts with controlling shareholder, 2.128–2.129
    generally, 2.127–2.127.1
    independence of controlling shareholder, 2.129.1–2.129.3
Transparency Rules
  corporate governance, and
    generally, 4.30–4.32
    interaction with Combined Code, 4.49–4.50
Travel expenses
  directors' remuneration, and, 5.65.1–5.65.3
Treasury policy
  strategic report, and, 3.149–3.154
Treasury shares
  sale
    directors' report, 2.64–2.65
    listed companies, 2.66
Trends affecting the business
  strategic report, and, 3.96–3.107

UK corporate governance code
  directors' reports, and, 2.97–2.100
UK Stewardship Code
  application, 4.274–4.277
  background, 4.19.1
  'comply or explain', 4.278
  content, 4.279–4.280
  introduction, 4.271–4.272
  monitoring, 4.282
  reporting to clients, 4.281

Viability statement
  narrative reporting, and, 4.206–4.218
Voting at general meeting
  directors' remuneration, and, 5.254–5.255

Walker Report
  generally, 4.12